Assessing the Marketing Environment 2008–2009

Assessing the Marketing Environment 2008–2009

Dr Diana Luck

AMSTERDAM • BOSTON • HEIDELBERG • LONDON • NEW YORK • OXFORD
PARIS • SAN DIEGO • SAN FRANCISCO • SINGAPORE • SYDNEY • TOKYO

Butterworth-Heinemann is an imprint of Elsevier

Butterworth-Heinemann is an imprint of Elsevier
Linacre House, Jordan Hill, Oxford OX2 8DP, UK
30 Corporate Drive, Suite 400, Burlington, MA 01803, USA

First edition 2008

Notice

British Library Cataloguing in Publication Data
A catalogue record for this book is available from the British Library

Library of Congress Cataloguing in Publication Data
A catalogue record for this book is available from the Library of Congress

ISBN: 978 0 7506 8965 6

For information on all Butterworth-Heinemann publications
visit our website at http://www.elsevierdirect.com

Designed by P.K. McBride

Typeset by Butford Technical Publishing Ltd, Birlingham, Worcs.

Printed and bound in Italy
08 09 10 11 12   10 9 8 7 6 5 4 3 2 1

Contents

Contents

Unit 1

The nature of the organization and the impact of its environment

Study guide

Table 1.1 on the following page maps the syllabus learning outcomes and the units where these are covered. As depicted, this first unit will provide a framework and organizational setting to explore the dynamic interrelationships between businesses and the various environments in which they can operate. Although the content of this unit is relatively straightforward, it is critical to the understanding of the subsequent units explored within this textbook since it provides a foundation upon which the other units are built.

The marketing environment is not only a very broad entity, but perhaps even more importantly, it keeps changing. This said, it is essential that you understand that you, as a student, need to ensure that you relate the course material to current developments; even though the latter may be changing too. Accordingly, you need to acquire the habit of 'scanning' the general press, business publications and of course marketing trade and professional publications and information sources for up-to-date articles, reviews and surveys. This will help you to relate business to its environment in line with any change. You should ideally also supplement this knowledge and research with regular exposure to news analysis programmes on TV, radio or indeed the Internet. The Internet can be used to access various websites with databases relating to the environment. As you will see under 'Exam hints' throughout this unit, you will need to be prepared for broad questions which test your grasp and general appreciation of the evolving marketing environment. The appreciation of the evolving nature of the marketing environment is the pivot of this module.

This first unit will also help you to familiarize yourself with the approach and style of our coursebooks. It will also help you acquire the knowledge necessary for examination success.

Table 1.1 Mapping of learning outcomes according to the units where these are explored

Learning outcomes	Study units/ syllabus reference
Distinguish between the types of organization within the public, private and voluntary sectors. Understand their objectives and appreciate the factors that influence them	Unit 1
Explain the main elements of an organization's marketing environment. Evaluate the significance of current and future environmental challenges on organizations.	Units 2, 9
Describe the interactions between the main elements of the marketing environment	Units 2, 4, 9
Assess how key trends in the social, technical, economic, environmental, political, legal and ethical environments can potentially impact organizations.	Units 4–8
Demonstrate an understanding of an organization's micro-environment	Units 2–3
Explain the process of collecting information about the marketing environment from relevant primary and secondary sources	Units 3, 4, 9
Compare and contrast various techniques for collecting information about the marketing environment	Unit 9

It will help you acquire and refine the skills you need to be able to apply the academic knowledge in the examination as well as in your work as a professional marketer. You will find the boxed panels clearly signposted to help you practise your skills, evaluate your understanding and even extend your knowledge. These boxed panels will be used throughout this coursebook so that you can manage your own learning in terms of both pace and depth. You of course need to ensure that your level of understanding of the module is in line with what is expected at this level of study.

Study tip

Start as you mean to go on in the organization of your study materials:

◆ Use a PC, laptop or file dividers to index broad topic area notes.

◆ Add relevant materials, activity output, articles and clippings as you acquire them.

◆ Summarize articles to provide you with current examples for exam answers.

◆ Cross-reference to other sections of the file since the marketing environment is interrelated and questions may involve more than one part of the syllabus.

◆ Produce and collate implications for the marketer and for every aspect of the syllabus. CIM questions generally require you to apply your knowledge in a stated context.

◆ Incorporate past questions, examiner reports, specimen answers and revision notes in your answers. This will help you frame your personal study. However, please note that in September 2008 a new syllabus and assessment will be introduced. Referring to past papers is fine as the core syllabus content has not changed significantly but you should also refer to the specimen paper to understand the new exam format.

◆ Key points to remember are:

  ◆ The new assessment is exam only (there is no assignment option).

  ◆ The exam will consist of five short questions and three long questions. All will be based on a mini-case. Overall weighting within questions is: 40 per cent for theory and 60 per cent for evaluation, application and format.

  ◆ The mini-case will be issued in advance.

  ◆ Students can take four sides A4 SWOT and PEST analysis into the exam.

  ◆ All questions are compulsory.

◆ Edit and summarize your notes into bullet points for easy memorizing. This will also come in very handy when revising for your examinations. Remember marketing is interrelated. Hence these may help you with the revision for your CIM examinations too.

By following this structured approach to this module, your understanding and appreciation and contemporary grasp of the marketing environment will be systematic. This approach is also bound to help you greatly in your revision prior to the examination.

The importance of the marketing environment

The CIM defines marketing as:

The management process which identifies, anticipates and supplies customer requirements efficiently and profitably.

This definition emphasizes the importance of the marketing environment. Indeed, the identification and anticipation of customer requirements would be impossible to achieve unless the organization not only reviews its situation, but also looks outward. As a matter of fact, the understanding of its external environment and the implications of changes taking place in that external environment directly affects an organization's current as well as its future profitability. Quintessentially, few businesses can afford to adopt any given business orientation, not even the production orientation, without taking into consideration the evolving opportunities and threats in its market-place.

Question 1.1

List the aspects of the environment that you consider to be most important to a marketer's understanding of:

1   Its potential customers

2   Its potential profitability

Provide four different examples of external factors where you feel 'change' seems

Activity 1.1

Key skills – Interpreting information

Interpretation of the CIM definition formed part of a past examination paper. Candidates who scored high marks demonstrated their understanding of each aspect of the quotation.

The marketer must be aware of not only the dynamics of the marketing environment within which his or her organization operates but also the pressures from a range of interested groups. For instance, not only should the shareholders be considered, but so too should the stakeholders (i.e. the employees, the customers). The actual or potential main competitors also need to be considered.

Large firms, particularly multinationals, may be able to exert greater influence over their business situation due to their financial clout, but SME (small and medium enterprises) may have the advantage of being able to respond to the need for change more aptly and quickly due to the simpler and flatter organizational structures that they possess.

Question 1.2

Make a list of the dimensions which you think an organization must take into consideration with regards to operating in a given market environment.

How do you think this list and its subsequent analysis will vary in line with the size and nature of an organization?

Study tip

Acquire the habit of using the glossary in www.marketingonline.co.uk for definitions of all key terms.

Defining organizations

Before exploring the nature of an environment and assessing a marketer's approach to it, a study of the different forms of business organizations involved in the economy is called for.

The purpose of organizations is to bring together people with common interests in a systematic effort to produce goods and services that they could not readily have produced as individuals. Organizations enable the specialization and division of labour. This saves time and raises productivity. Organizations are also social in nature as they provide mutual support and opportunity for development.

Multinationals are enterprises that are engaged in simultaneous manufacturing or operations in a number of countries. Thus, they have to take decisions from a global perspective. The financial and business capacity of some multinationals is so powerful that the world-wide annual turnover of some such as Exxon (Esso) and Toyota is said to exceed the gross domestic product of many of the smaller Western European countries.

We routinely come into contact with organizations when we purchase products or services. Whatever the type, size, structure or purpose of an organization, it is bound to have some common characteristics. These are:

◆ A framework of written or tacit rules (e.g. articles of association)

◆ A decision-making hierarchy (e.g. Board of Directors)

◆ A record of proceedings (e.g. minutes of meetings)

◆ A means of co-ordinating efforts and resources to determine what and how to produce, in what quantities, using what channels of distribution (e.g. Chief Executive).

Business classifications

It is important for marketers to appreciate how organizations and businesses are diverse both nationally and internationally. Although there are countless ways in which an organization can be different, the following are some of the main areas around which diversification can revolve:

◆ Based on its individual objectives, strengths and even weaknesses, an organization would target potential customers in different ways. Its objectives, strengths and weaknesses will also have a direct effect on the way in which an organization deals with its existing customers.

◆ Businesses operate as buyers as well as sellers. They may operate as business to business enterprises or business to customer enterprises. However, while multinationals tend to purchase in bulk and hence be able to benefit strongly from economies of scale, smaller companies tend to purchase and sell on a much more limited scale.

◆ The implications of competition, growth and innovation vary not only in terms of the size of the business but also with regards to the market environment within which an organization operates.

◆ The growth in self-employment, the reduction of the size of the public sector and the rising importance of entrepreneurial non-profit makers such as charities and social enterprises, have all had a direct impact on the market environment. In the UK, there are currently more than 20,000 registered non-profit organizations. Although they by all means vary in size and power, these organizations nonetheless follow business structures. However in contrast to regular businesses, their profits are used for charitable purposes rather than to pay dividends to private owners or shareholders. Oxfam is one of the most well-known charities and has been actively contributing to the alleviation of poverty worldwide.

In order to understand the diversity of business, the various types of businesses must first be classified. Only then can a framework for understanding their characteristics be formed.

There are a number of ways in which organizations may be classified. For example, these can be in terms of the following:

◆ **Ownership** – Is the business private, public, owned by a co-operative?

◆ **Legal form** – Is the business a limited company? Is it owned by a sole proprietor? Is there a partnership (more than one owner)?

◆ **Control** – Who is in charge of decisions? Are there directors? Are the shareholders the main decision takers? Are the trustees or the council members the main decision makers (this tends to be the case with charities)?

◆ **Sector** – Is the business operating in the public sector, the private sector, or even in the voluntary sector?

◆ **Objectives** – What is the main objective of the organization? Is the organization in business for profit? Is the public welfare the main objective?

◆ **Accountability** – To whom is the organization accountable? To its shareholders, to the ministers, to its customers, or even to its employees?

◆ **Activity** – What type of activity is the organization involved with? Is it agriculture, manufacturing, services, utilities, construction, tourism etc.?

◆ **Size** – How big is the organization? Is it an SME? Is it a large corporation? Does it operate only nationally or globally?

Activity 1.2

Suggest three examples of each classification and differentiation based on the following dimensions:

◆ Sector

◆ Activity

◆ Size

The formal and informal economy

An economy is made up of three parts: the public sector, the private sector and the informal economy.

The public sector

This includes activities that revolve around the provision of goods and services by the state or government. Several means of revenue such as taxes imposed on wages and salaries (income tax), sales (VAT), sales of properties, properties (council tax) and profits of businesses help finance these activities. Television licences help raise finance for use by channels run by the state. Governments also borrow money from either international sources, thereby implying foreign debt, or national sources. These resources are allocated to the various departments of the government or of the state. These departments historically plan their expenditure according to government objectives rather than market forces. Objectives may be socially desirable and involve embracing civil rights. For instance, in the UK there are incapacity benefits, housing benefits and old age pensions. These all have monetary value.

The state can also take responsibility in some areas where provision by the private sector is not seen as adequate or even appropriate. Public goods such as defence, law, order and emergency services comprise one major category. Merit goods such as health, education and other social services provide the other. A number of other industries might come into the domain of the state for various reasons including strategic considerations, health and safety, natural monopolies and national security. In the UK even though the private health sector is growing, the NHS (the National Health Service) is still state owned and largely run by the state. However, increasingly private consultants and sundry services are being called upon to assist in operational activities previously led by the state. Governments in West Europe tend to spend on average about 40 percent of their gross domestic product (GDP) on the provision of social welfare. However, Scandinavian countries have a history of more generous social benefit provision. Accordingly, Scandinavian countries spend closer to 50 per cent of their GDP. In contrast, more free enterprise economies in East Asia for instance tend to opt for lower taxes and private provision.

Direct government spending on goods and services has recently been falling in many countries due to the widespread trend towards privatization and deregulation of industries. In contrast, payments to fund pensions and health services for ageing populations have been steadily increasing, particularly in some developed economies such as Japan and Italy. Many developing economies such as Mauritius continue to rely on government spending to provide educational and physical infrastructures.

Activity 1.3

Match the terms with the correct definition: (1) Contracting out, (2) Natural monopoly, (3) Privatization, (4) Merit goods, (5) Public goods, (6) Quango:

a   Can also be provided by the private sector but concern for equity and doubt regarding sufficient goods and services lead to public provision.

b   A good or service which cannot be priced accurately and therefore cannot be efficiently supplied by the private sector. Consumption by one person does not reduce supply for others (e.g. TV signals/street lighting). No consumer can be excluded even if they refuse to pay (e.g. public health) and no one may abstain from consumption (e.g. defence). All people may consume equally. However they have no incentive to pay for what must be provided in any case.

c   A quasi-autonomous non-government organization, which is neither an elected nor a private business organization. However this type of organization has executive or administrative authority to implement or advance government policy. The marketer is likely to encounter a large number of such bodies (e.g. regulators, standards authorities).

d   A firm that can satisfy all the market demands, but still has unexploited cost savings. Competition would duplicate expensive resources.

e   This is practiced by governments and by businesses. Instead of doing so themselves, governments or businesses employ an outside agent to perform some specific task, project or part of a project.

f   The transfer of ownership of 51 per cent or more shares from a nationalized organization or state to private hands or ownership.

Market disciplines

Many governments have been introducing market disciplines into what remains of their public sector. For instance, management and compulsory competitive tendering for central and local government services have been increasingly deployed in recent years. This has in turn led to a degree of marketing orientation in a wide cross-section of public services, which were previously much more producer-orientated. Indeed, government and government agencies as well as businesses have realized that it is only when they can relate their offerings to their existing and even potential client needs that the necessary contract, budget or funding will be forthcoming. Although international aid agencies appear to favour more structured markets, the rapid introduction of market structures in many countries in the former Eastern bloc and Russia has, however, had mixed results.

Insight: The French 'Social model' versus the Anglo-Saxon 'Market model'

France has traditionally invested heavily in its public sector, intervenes to protect its industry from foreign competition and supports its small shopkeepers, farmers and rural communities. It has national champions in most product sectors. This is turn has reflected a well educated managerial and administrative elite renowned world-wide for developing a culture of excellence. Although competition is often encouraged between private and public sectors, producing global players as in the water industry, there has however been a lack of innovation in newer hi-tech industries and the service sector. Consequently, France has gradually stagnated. A statutory 35-hour working week implies that employees in France work only 70 per cent of the amount of time that employees in England work. This has led to employers in France investing heavily in labour-saving equipment. Subsequently, in spite of the difference in the amount of time employees spend at work, productivity has not been impaired. However, while British wages have risen on average by 20 per cent in less than a decade, salaries in France have not undergone such increases. Unemployment has also risen to almost double the British level at around an estimated 10 per cent. Unemployment in France is much higher among the young and among immigrant populations. Despite the 'No' vote for the EU Constitution, increasing public borrowing and rising discontent amongst disadvantaged groups, there is nonetheless still a strong reluctance to adopt free-market remedies. On the other hand British-owned businesses such as stock exchanges, airports, banks, ports, gas and water utilities in spite of traditionally being hailed as state owned and run services, have all more or less been sold off to private enterprises. The sale of these services to foreign companies has helped the UK fund a record £56 billion trade deficit. Although the transition from state ownership to private ownership has brought forth many positive as well as negative after-effects, in the UK such services are now largely privatized. Meanwhile even though such assets and brands have arguably become the building blocks of some of the country's corporate ambitions, employees have had no say in their own destinies.

Facilitators versus direct providers

Public organizations of all types are becoming facilitators or commissioners of services instead of merely remaining providers of such services. Rather than using directly employed labour to provide building, maintenance and waste disposal/refuse services as was the norm in the past, these services are now increasingly being contracted out to companies from the private sector. Accordingly, the role of the public sector managers has changed from overseeing the operations to awarding the contracts to external companies. Additionally, public sector managers also have to ensure that quality is being monitored and quality standards are met. They also need to ensure that cost targets and performance targets are met. They also in brief need to secure value for money for the taxpayer and the state. In the past few years, a large percentage of state schools have followed prisons and contracted out their catering services. Subsequently, public agencies have concentrated on core services that no other sector can sensibly or willingly supply. Powers have also been devolved, through a large number of executive agencies, also known as quangos, to supervise a wide variety of activities. Quangos are publicly appointed bodies with considerable powers over the disposal of resources and important regulatory activities. Their non-elected nature and lack of direct accountability, however, has raised many concerns in relation to their responsiveness and efficiency.

Exam hint

A key skill for marketers is to show companies how to improve their learning and performance. This involves identifying targets, planning how these will be reached and reviewing progress. Your target is to pass your exam. To achieve this, you need to plan your work in line with the timescale associated with the exams and of course your work and personal commitments and responsibilities. Ideally, you should have some intermediate targets or milestones. These will help you work towards reaching your ultimate goal and the completion of this module. Your plan must be realistic, achievable within the time-frame but also controllable through regular reviews of your progress against the targets you have set. Deviations or falling behind due to work pressures or social commitments must be corrected if progress is to be maintained and desired goals reached. Approach this course like you would do with a marketing plan.

Public and private partnerships

This hybrid or combined type of partnerships seeks to combine the strengths of private sector management with the social concerns and community benefits of the public sector. For example, local government agencies may sponsor a joint construction scheme that combines the use of government-owned land to develop an integrated dwelling and shopping development, incorporating private businesses, sheltered housing and social amenities. Since most successful economies exemplify a blend of public and private entities, this idea takes the concept of the best of both worlds to a realistic integration.

The public sector owns or controls a complex variety of organizations. However the distinction between these public agencies or organizations and private organizations or organizations in other sectors is becoming increasingly blurred as more and more competition is introduced into the market environment.

The private sector

This sector normally accounts for the majority of domestic output, investment goods and exports. Resources are privately owned and businesses compete to satisfy consumers' wants and needs. The majority of companies operating in that sector are profit motivated. On the one hand, decisions are made about what products and services to create, and how to create them, by identifying and anticipating market demands. On the other hand, resources and capabilities need to be assessed in line with these demands.

Although they are not part of the public sector, non-profit-making organizations such as trade unions and employer associations would normally be classified as voluntary organizations.

Activity 1.4

Spend a few minutes to reflect upon the identified strengths and weaknesses of the public sector and those of the private sector. Then, attempt to think of more strengths and weaknesses that could be associated with these two sectors.

Table 1.2 Strengths and weaknesses of the public sector and the private sector

	Public sector	**Private sector**
Strengths (there are of course many more)	Provide essential but non-profit-making services	Private ownership can lead to enhanced initiative
	Avoid wasteful duplication of expensive resources	Strong motivation to use resources well
	Funds are easily raised through taxation	Funds are efficiently and effectively used and monitored
	Can overcome failings in the market	Companies tend to respond quickly to market signals
	Employees are motivated by public service	Employees are paid by results
Weaknesses (again there are many more)	Tendency towards political interference	May mean ruthless exploitation
	Monopolies don't serve public	Competition may end in monopoly (mergers and acquisitions)
	Over-accountability may limit entrepreneurship	Competitive over-investment may ultimately be wasteful
	Unions tend to be powerful and taxpayers may have less power	Ignore costs that damage society
	Public expectations of 'free' services	Everything has a price!

The informal economy

The activities of the public sector and the private sector constitute the formal economic activities of a country. The combined output of both the public sector and the private sector is referred to and measured by the GDP (Gross Domestic Product). However, three other sectors should be recognized and understood by the marketer. The summation of these is referred to as the informal economy.

The household economy includes the unpaid domestic services of homemakers, mothers and house-husbands. Such services include childcare, cooking and cleaning for instance. Although it cannot be numerically measured, this part of the economy has undergone significant changes in recent years. The increasing number of women who have taken paid employment away from the home has been a major influence on the state of the informal economy.

Do-it-yourself activities are also part of the informal economy. Such activities include gardening, improvements made on existing properties, regular maintenance and even repair. Subsistence agriculture which is primordially conducted to provide food for personal use is significant not only in many developing economies, but is still practised in many developed countries too. For example in the UK, allotments have traditionally been an excellent source of fruits and vegetables. Yet, because of the fact that no market transaction is usually conducted for such activities, none of these activities are included in the GDP of a country. Consequently, they are considered to be part of the informal economy. Notwithstanding, marketers are increasingly interested in the shifting demand patterns which the informal economy can engender. Indeed, the informal economy can lead to serious implications for the lifestyles and tastes of the various household members. For instance, the increase in interest in home improvements in the UK which started in mid-1990s with the influx of television programmes such as *Changing Rooms* has led to a significant effect on the success and indeed profits of the DIY (do-it-yourself) industry. This in turn has had a significant impact on the GDP of the country. Interestingly this avid interest was still persisting in 2007.

The voluntary economy includes services that are undertaken by individuals and/or organizations, for which no money payment is normally involved. There is a non-commercial understanding between the two parties. This economy includes the activities of various unions, clubs and associations that act to promote the common interests of their members. Many of these organizations have a special status. As such, services are performed out of friendship or simply as acts of charity. For instance, activities conducted by the Salvation Army or the Samaritans focus on offering support to those in need within the general society. Some charities focus on specific segments of the population. While Oxfam focuses on alleviating poverty worldwide, Help the Aged focuses on helping meet the needs of old age pensioners. The organization Médecins Sans Frontières instead seeks to protect and assist communities and individuals affected by natural calamity. Although these organizations satisfy important needs and generate considerable social welfare, they are however not counted in the statistics about national output. Thus the output of these companies is not included in the GDP of the country. It should be noted that many of the organizations within the voluntary economy such as the Red Cross and CARE operate internationally while many only operate nationally.

Although they are registered and controlled, these types of organizations also generally also attract generous tax concessions. As a matter of fact, these associations and charities operate on principles that are very different to those to which companies in the private or public sector have to adhere to. These organizations function with dedicated employees, who often work for little monetary reward. In fact, more often than not, as is the case with the volunteers working in charity shops in the UK, no money is paid. Although making money is often not the primary objective of many of these organizations, their performance has generally become increasingly more professional and marketing informed. The competition for funding has arguably contributed to these organizations having needed to become more professional and marketing savvy. In the UK and USA, their trading activities have been reflected in the increasing presence of 'charity shops' or 'thrifts' within retail environments. As such, in contemporary terms they constitute an added element of choice for consumers and are even regarded as competition to established retailers

Ironically, much of their funding comes from successful private sector entrepreneurs and private companies. While the founder of Microsoft, Bill Gates, gave £900 million to the Stop Tuberculosis campaign, the late Dame Anita Roddick gave away half her shares in the Body Shop chain to charity. This donation was estimated at about £51 million. In recent times, there appears to have been a growing trend of private companies sponsoring charity organizations and campaigns.

Although the contributions and achievements of organizations operating within the voluntary economy are not measured in terms of a country's GDP, the effectiveness of their efforts and operations may however be measured in terms of the gross value of the contributions they raise, the degree of suffering they are able to alleviate and perhaps even their success in raising the public profile of the cause that they represent. Indeed, their skills in marketing communications are key determinants of their success with regards to the raising of their profile and the precise communication of their mission.

Activity 1.5

Think of three companies based in the UK private sector who have sponsored charity campaigns. Attempt to assess the connection between the companies and their choice of campaigns. Why do you think these companies chose those specific campaigns? Try to think along the lines of trends and concerns in contemporary terms.

Insight

The Fairtrade Foundation is a global charity founded in 1988 to get fair prices for developing world producers. Today the foundation promotes a network of about 1600 products. Recently, amid much negative press, it was contended that less than a quarter of the £200 million spent on such goods in the UK returns to the primary producers of the products. The remainder was said to be swallowed up by the supply chain. In fact it was even stated that retailers are charging much more for Fairtrade products than for their own brands because they have found out that consumers do not tend to question ethical product pricing. Thus while consumers have been altruistically paying a price premium thinking that the producers will be benefiting from the surcharge, it is in fact the supermarkets that have been reaped the financial benefits. But supermarkets such as Sainsbury's and Tesco appear to have gained consumer credibility. Consequently, in 2007, the sales for the Tesco group jumped 10.9 per cent to £46.6bn and profit for 2007 rose from 20.3 per cent to £2.5bn. Sales for Sainsbury's rose to £18.5bn in 2007 while pre-tax profit for 2007 rose 358.7 per cent to £477m. Meanwhile sales for the ASDA group were £42.6bn in 2007. Accordingly, it seems that the associations of these main supermarket chains with Fairtrade products have added to their financial success.

The hidden or shadow economy involves transactions and activities that are 'undeclared' for tax purposes. Moonlighting workers perform services outside their normal work for cash in hand and no questions asked! Although such types of employment are all too often not legally bound and are often illicit, marketers cannot afford to ignore this economy. Indeed, although not above board, these also involve purchasing power. Further they may even be in competition with above board companies. Small and medium businesses in the formal economy paying tax and insurance, charging sales tax and conforming with legislation, may indeed be at a considerable disadvantage compared to the so-called 'cowboy operators'.

Estimated to account for as much as 10–25 per cent of GDP a year, this economy tends to grow with self-employment, high taxation, illegal immigration and unemployment. Other elements of this hidden sector include pilferage, fiddles and outright illegal activities such as drug dealing, smuggling and stolen goods. For example, the huge gap between the minimal factory cost and the 'formal economy' selling price of cigarettes may provide the basis of a massive black marketing racket. Prostitution in Britain is estimated to generate at least £1.2 billion in annual revenues according to figures quoted by Marketing Week. Although governments regularly announce crackdowns on tax avoidance and evasion targeted on this shadow economy, there is nonetheless limited success associated with the objective to eradicate such activities.

Activity 1.6

Key skills – Interpreting information

Evaluate the effects that the trend of women increasingly working away from home has had on: (1) Retailers, (2) Food suppliers and (3) Household appliance manufacturers.

Has DIY increased much in recent years?

Which businesses do you think have been most affected by the 'self-service' trend?

Can you think of the business opportunities that may have arisen from this?

As discussed previously in this unit, another important way of classifying businesses is according to the sector within which a business operates. Governments normally develop a comprehensive framework that places businesses into classes, groups and activities as part of its annual measurement of national output. These are classified in four distinct sectors: primary, secondary, tertiary and quaternary sectors.

The primary sector includes agriculture, fisheries and forestry. Industrialization has brought about a dramatic decline in its share of employment. By the start of the twentieth century, the majority of workers were employed in industries such as manufacturing, energy and construction. However as the services industries (namely the secondary and tertiary sectors) grew, the primary sector has been shrinking. In fact, it has even been said that in 2005, manufacturing provided a mere 10 per cent of the labour force, with less than 3.5 million employees.

The quaternary sector involves personal rather than business services. The latter include health, education, leisure and other personal services. These services represent areas where human beings have a comparative employment advantage over computer-based technology. However, such areas of employment are assuming increasing significance as e-business-to-business (B2B) developments automate many basic business functions. Furthermore there has been a migration of jobs to developing countries. For instance, BT, HSBC and most recently Barclays have all transferred their call centre facilities to India at the expense of jobs being available in the UK.

Insight

James Dyson, the inventor and entrepreneur who took on the giants of the vacuum cleaner market and won, shifted production from Wiltshire in England to Malaysia in 2002. This resulted in a loss of 800 jobs in the UK. Despite criticism, this move however slashed the costs of the company, trebled its output and even doubled its profits. This relocation ultimately allowed Dyson not only to penetrate the US market, but even more impressively to succeed in replacing Hoover as the market leader within two years of joining the market as a new entry. This example quintessentially demonstrates how an economy like the UK's may evolve and thrive without a manufacturing base. By outsourcing, Dyson now employs more British employees. However, instead of being involved in production factories, they are in more rewarding and technically advanced jobs such as product development and research. The consequent rise in profits has led to the company now paying five times more in tax. In brief, the company has become a role model for the post-industrial economy.

The legal form of trading organizations

There are several types of organizations and businesses that operate within the private sector. In brief, these can be classified into distinct categories such as sole traders, partnerships, registered companies, co-operatives and franchised businesses. The public sector includes organizations that can be categorized as public corporations and local authorities for instance. The following sections of this unit will focus on identifying the characteristics of each of these types of organizations. Furthermore, the merits and drawbacks of each type of organizations will also be highlighted in an attempt to enable an objective assessment of their real status and contribution to the market environment.

Sole traders

While there were 2.5 million enterprises in the UK in 1979, currently there are around 3.75 million enterprises. This said, it should be pointed out that an exact number is very difficult to pin down as every day new businesses are created while many are closed down. Notwithstanding, these statistics provide clear evidence that the trend for private enterprises has been rising in the UK.

Although 97 per cent of these enterprises are said to employ fewer than 20 employees, these enterprises are however extremely significant as they in fact employ an equivalent to one-third of the total number of people employed outside government or by the private sector. Furthermore, an estimated 80 per cent of these small enterprises are said to be operated by sole traders. Although the number of small firms and sole traders operating in the private sector is by all means significant, their contribution to the total output is however not as significant in terms of the percentage of contribution to the economy. Notwithstanding, the number of private firms employing fewer than 100 people now account for over 50 per cent of turnover of the private sector in the UK. When compared with the 40 per cent that they contributed to the turnover in 1979, it is evident that the economic impact of these small firms and sole traders has been gaining in significance. The pattern observed in the UK is reproduced in other economies, such as Sri Lanka or Nigeria, where small firms dominate. Meanwhile, across the world, large firms, particularly multinationals, appear to prevail in key export and industrialized sectors.

The characteristics below emphasize the distinction of sole traders when compared to other organizations within the private sector:

◆ Sole trading is arguably the oldest type and also the most straightforward form of trading. It is also the simplest form of self-employment.

◆ Sole trading involves business usually being carried out in its own name. In essence sole trading implies that a business is not incorporated with any other type of business or people.

◆ The type of business is usually owned by a single person.

◆ Business is usually controlled by that same person. Thus he/she assumes all the rights and is ultimately responsible for all the duties associated with the business.

◆ There is a sole owner of the business, thus there is no separation of legal existence between business and individual. The owner is legally responsible for the business.

◆ Information is not needed to be disclosed to any other party. However the sole trader and owner must disclose information about the operations and profits to the tax authorities.

◆ There is no limit on the number of people that the sole trader can employ. In effect, there can be up to 100 employees.

◆ Sole trading is popular within farming, personal services, building and even the retail industry.

◆ Sole trading may originate in the hidden economy. This part of the economy was explored earlier in this unit.

Activity 1.7

In order to offer a truthful portrayal of the status of sole trading, a range of merits and drawbacks associated with sole traders have been identified below.

As you examine the table below, stop and evaluate each merit and drawback in depth.

Think about the environment within which the sole traders may operate. Think about trends. Think about the demands of business. Think about why an aspect is being hailed as a merit and why another aspect is being criticized as a drawback.

Table 1.3 The merits and drawbacks of sole traders

Merits	Drawbacks
Minimum formalities but also minimal privacy.	Unlimited liability for any debts. There is no demarcation between the owner and the business.
Complete control. No consultation is necessary if not wished for by the owner.	Raising capital can be difficult and may only be possible from personal sources and from putting profits back into the business.
Favourable tax treatment.	Specialized and risky to financial and other services. It could be difficult to get insurance.
The sole trader can be highly motivated and single-minded.	The owner may in fact have a too narrow outlook for the ultimate benefit of the business.
The least costly type of business to create.	The status of the business depends on staying healthy. Thus, there may be a lack of continuity.
The simple organization implies that the owner can remain close to his or her customers and to the employees.	The owner as well as the employees may have to work long hours and thus inadvertently lead to exploitation.
Can be a very flexible type of structure. When need be, detail can be attended to promptly.	Competition from large corporations and other small traders cannot be overruled and ignored.
Can be a niche business within the market.	Lack of management skills.
Has exemption from certain legislation.	No one to share burden.

Sole traders tend to operate in sectors where entry barriers are low and where capital requirements are limited. Although sole traders are often considered to be entrepreneurs, in fact arguably only about 10 per cent of the total number of sole traders operating in the UK market may fall into the entrepreneurial category. Even then, their inventiveness is not always sufficient to produce innovation. Sole traders tend to be financially weak compared to well-resourced companies. Consequently, even if new product developments make it to the market they often face fierce competition and alternative offerings. They are often under pressure from larger businesses; in the UK for example specialist food retailers have experienced significant repercussions from the geographical and economic expansion of supermarket chains. Limited capital restricts their growth while excessive competition often requires hard work and long working and opening hours just to survive. Their social and economic lives tend to merge. Although sole traders may indeed be motivated by self-interest, they also bear all the risks. This said, may sole traders are self-employed in name only and actually work exclusively under contract to other organizations.

Partnerships

This type of business involves two or more owners or associates. Partnerships are more attractive to the professions where capital requirements are limited.

The characteristics below emphasize the distinction of partnerships when compared to other types of businesses and organizations within the private sector:

◆ This is an unincorporated type of enterprise.

◆ There are two or more partners. However, they all should have a common view to how to achieve profit and conduct business.

◆ There is usually a limit to the number of partners that can be included in a partnership. For instance there could be a legally specified maximum number of 20 partners. This limit however does not apply to some professions.

◆ Legal formalities are few and the privacy of the partners tends to be high.

◆ The partners usually form an agreement or are bound by legislation. Codes of conduct may strongly limit the risk of financial malpractice.

◆ The partnership itself has no legal personality. It is in fact the partners who have unlimited liability and are jointly liable for what happens within their business.

◆ Partners share management decisions as well as any profit or loss that is made.

Table 1.4 The merits and drawbacks of partnerships

Merits	Drawbacks
Partners are able to raise more capital than sole trader.	Partners have unlimited liability unless the company becomes 'limited'. Even then, at least one partner must be fully liable for the business decisions.
Partners can pool together their expertise and personal funds.	There is a lack of legal identity associated with the business. It may dissolve in case of death or even disagreement.
Partners have more possibilities of specialization.	Any potential disagreement may lead to heightened expenses and even much unrest within the business.
There is no company tax on the business.	A partnership can be referred to a frozen investment.

Activity 1.8

In order to offer a comprehensive review of the status of partnerships, a range of merits and drawbacks have been identified in the previous table.

Re-examine the table and evaluate each merit and drawback in depth.

Registered companies

The characteristics below emphasize the distinction of registered companies when compared to other types of businesses and organizations:

◆ As opposed to partnerships, registered companies are incorporated. As such, they have a separate legal entity. Consequently, a registered company can enter into contracts.

◆ They are formed under specific legislation (e.g. the 1985 Companies Act).

◆ A registered company can confer various rights and duties.

◆ Members of a registered company contribute capital and own shares.

◆ This type of organization is dominant nowadays.

◆ Liability is limited to the amount of finance invested or guaranteed.

A registered company has a number of duties. These must be submitted to the Registrar of Companies. These are:

◆ Memorandum of association – This regulates the external affairs of the company and protects its investors and suppliers. This document includes the registered name of the company, its objectives and scope of business as well as its liability structures.

◆ Articles of association – This regulates the internal administration of the company. Accordingly, it should include the issuing and transfer of shares, shareholder rights, directors' powers and accounting procedures.

◆ Statutory declaration of compliance – This must be related to the relevant Act.

◆ Independently audited annual accounts and directors' report – Companies that employ less than 50 employees only need to provide a summary of their independently audited annual accounts and directors' report. 'Unlimited liability' companies are exempt from filing accounting data.

The table below illustrates some of the main differences between a public company and a private company or a limited company.

Table 1.5 Main characteristics of public and private companies

Public company (plc)	Private company (Ltd)
Two or more members.	Minimum of two members.
£50,000 and two directors.	One director + Secretary. Typical family business.
Shares are offered to the public.	Cannot offer shares to public but can do so to friends and other family members.
A business certificate must be issued before any trading or borrowing can take place.	Trading can only take place when an incorporation certificate is received.
Similar legislation is followed globally. However a different terminology may be used (e.g. in the United States 'inc.' is used to refer to a public company; in Malaysia the term 'Sdn Bhd' is used to refer to a public company).	The raising of additional bank funds is easier. However, personal guarantees may be needed to do so.

Public companies

Public companies have traditionally been popular and hence constitute a significant percentage of the number of companies operating within any market environment. In order to offer a synoptic yet comprehensive overview of public companies, a range of merits and drawbacks have been identified in the table below.

Table 1.6 The merits and drawbacks of public companies

Merits	Drawbacks
The public company represents a separate legal entity.	The company is bound by special and double taxation.
The owners have limited liability.	The structure of the company is complex and hence it is costly to form such companies.
The public company benefits from greater financial capability.	The company is bound by disclosure requirements.
It is easy to transfer the ownership of such companies.	Special government regulations apply to public companies. They must also hold an AGM and comply with Stock Exchange regulations.
The company can fund innovation as well as new product development.	Public companies can be inflexibility in terms of size.
Customers tend to trust public companies.	Public companies can become impersonal.

Not only are they bound by a wide range of regulations, the duties of care imposed on public companies can also be very restrictive. For instance in Norway, the reviewed diversity law has led to public companies being required to have at least 40 per cent of female representatives on their board by 2007. In order to ensure that public companies respect the amended law, the new minister for equality has even threatened to shut down companies for non-compliance.

At this point it should noted that business is not only operated by public or private companies. Many companies in fact hold shares in other enterprises which they may have formed or acquired. However, if any one company exceeds more than 50 per cent of the voting rights within another company, that company is then referred to as a *holding company*. Such holdings may sometimes form a pyramid, with the *ultimate holding company* having overall control. Such structures are common in Japan. In the UK, BSkyB purchased 18 per cent of ITV shares in late 2006. The intention of BSkyB was not to achieve control of ITV but to attempt to prevent the take-over of ITV by NTL, a company of which Branson was the major shareholder.

Activity 1.9

Re-examine the table depicting the main merits and drawbacks of public companies.

Select one public company and evaluate each merit and drawback relating to that that company.

Exam hint

The new assessment is exam only (there is no longer an assignment option).

The exam will consist of eight compulsory questions, five short questions (each worth 8 marks) and three long questions (each worth 20 marks). All will be based to some extent on the mini-case, which will be issued in advance. Overall weighting within questions is: 40 per cent for theory and 60 per cent for evaluation, application and format.

Please note that students can take four sides A4 SWOT and PEST analysis into the exam.

Activity 1.10

Key skills – Collecting and using information

Review the Financial Times for details about a company that is seeking plc status and offering shares for sale to the public. Read the offer carefully. Evaluate the possible advantages of this course of action for that company. What are the potential drawbacks?

Seek someone who own shares. Ask them about the dynamics of an AGM and whether they attend these. Try to assess the person's response. Draw conclusions about who you think exercises the real control in this situation.

Insight

'Blue chip' companies are large organizations that usually achieve high levels of profits. Although significant bargaining power is generally associated with such companies, the increasingly turbulent market environment within which they operate has had serious repercussions on their profit margins. Indeed, companies like Shell, Northern Foods and Sainsbury's no longer enjoy the safe and stable position that they used to. At the end of 2001, Enron, America's then seventh largest company and one of the country's most powerful companies, collapsed with an estimated $40 billion of debts. Twenty-five thousand jobs were lost, investors lost billions and the founder and his CEO were both found guilty of fraud and conspiracy. Across the Atlantic in Europe, Italy was plagued with its worst financial scandal for a decade when Parmalat, a massive agricultural processing enterprise, was found guilty of false accounting when billions were found missing from the company's balance sheet.

The dynamism and even turbulence of market environments has been having tremendous impact on even blue chip companies. As such companies are finding themselves operating under much more uncertain market conditions. For instance, the once mighty car manufacturer Ford has been recording massive losses and has consequently been planning to reduce capacity by about a quarter. Meanwhile though, one of its main rivals Toyota is about to become the world's largest carmaker by volume. Hence it can be seen how some companies have indeed been able to benefit from the increasingly competitive and volatile market environments. Vodafone posted the world's largest corporate loss of £14.9 billion in 2005. However, since then Vodafone has been able to redress the success of its operations worldwide through succinct global as well as local strategies and tactics. Consequently, the company is still one of the major players in the mobile phone market.

Many blue chip companies have failed because they have not been sensitive enough to the needs of their existing customers and potential customers. Some have been riddled by too bureaucratic structures at the expense of being able to retaliate to and even imitate their rivals.

The increasing growth of the use of technology and technological innovation within companies has had a direct effect on how companies have been able to compete within market environments. As a matter of fact, many small companies have successfully overtaken blue chip companies. For example, Hornby Group, a small model railway maker, has seen its profits consistently continue to rise sharply on sales of train sets and model locomotives. This success is partly attributable to demographics. Middle-aged men with the income to satisfy their childhood dreams are loyal customers of such products. However, the company has partly also benefited from the inclusion of newer and contemporary models. For instance one of the company's newer models, the Hogwarts Castle loco, was inspired by Harry Potter. Even though it is a small company, due to its consistent financial success, the company has recently taken over the heavily indebted company Airfix. It is anticipated the Hornby Group will seek similar success by promoting their model kits. Nonetheless, in contrast to the $100 billion revenues of Enron at its height, the Hornby Group could manage only $20–30 million.

Activity 1.11

Select a blue chip company based in the UK and attempt to evaluate what it is doing in order to compete in the current market environment.

Co-operatives

Co-operatives represent a significant but declining force in most sectors. Co-operation has contracted in the face of competition from the better-managed and more focused multiples, and has been forced to merge and specialize in other niches. Worker co-operatives among farmers and craft workers were generally established in times of recession or rapid structural decline in the industries concerned. Producer co-operatives doubled in Britain in the 1980s but currently suffer from being unable to attract managers of the right calibre. These co-operatives have also encountered much difficulty in raising capital for large-scale ventures. The Scott Bader Commonwealth, a chemical concern, is the most-quoted industrial example with an interesting constitution, which includes among other things, a limit of 350 employees per unit, a maximum remuneration spread of 1:7 and no dismissals.

The characteristics below emphasize the distinction of co-operatives when compared to other types of businesses and organizations within the public and private sectors:

◆ Co-operatives were pioneered in mid-nineteenth century.

◆ Traditionally, and nowadays, co-operatives are still most prevalent in agriculture and retailing.

◆ They are governed by relevant legislation.

◆ Although workers usually retain the ownership and control of co-operatives, in recent times closures and mergers have resulted in the number of co-operatives dwindling.

◆ Co-operatives benefit from limited liability.

◆ Each member of a co-operative is allocated a vote.

◆ Co-operatives favour self-help rather than profit maximization.

◆   Co-operatives usually operate through a management committee.

◆   Co-operatives favour the equitable distribution of dividends if and when a surplus is achieved.

Activity 1.12

Attempt to identify a co-operative. Try to find out how your selected co-operative operates differently to a private company of your choice.

Franchising

With the wide range of benefits that it offers, franchising has gained much popularity during the past few decades.

The characteristics below emphasize the distinction of franchises when compared to other types of businesses and organizations within the public and private sectors:

◆   The franchisor sells the right to market a product under its name to a franchisee.

◆   Although the various outlets within a specific franchise are in fact financially separate entities, they are all interdependent businesses.

◆   Franchising has been benefiting from rapid growth especially within the retail sector. The most well-known franchising internationally are probably McDonald's and the Body Shop.

◆   Franchising offers a ready-made opportunity for any entrepreneur who has the capital required for purchasing the franchise. By providing the franchisee with structures offering to help them run their business, risks to the franchisee are minimized. Given that the rhetoric goes that only 90 per cent of start-ups actually survive beyond 3 years, franchising provide new entrants many risk reductions.

In order for a franchise to be agreed upon, the two parties, namely the franchisor and the franchisee, need to meet a range of terms and conditions. These are outlined in the table below.

Table 1.7 The terms that franchisors and franchisees must agree to

A franchisor must agree to:	A franchisee must agree to:
Provide the business format and initial training	Pay an initial sum and pay a percentage of the profit to the franchisor
Supply product and quality control	Buy supplies of product from franchisor
Provide promotional support (e.g. advertising)	Maintain the standards stipulated by the franchisor

Activity 1.13

Key skills – Using information

Identify two franchised outlets of a national or an international company. The two outlets need to be for the same company. Observe the quality of service in the two outlets. Attempt to assess the relative strengths and weaknesses of the two outlets. Attempt to identify the differences and the similarities between the two outlets.

Reflect upon why franchising has become such an important form of business organization. What do you think makes franchising so customer orientated?

Question 1.3

McDonald's and the fast food industry

McDonald's is probably the most famous name in global franchising. Until 2002, the company appeared to have enjoyed uninterrupted growth. With 30,000 mainly franchised outlets in over 100 countries, it has been said that 1 in every 200 people across the globe visits an outlet daily. Yet, in 2002, its shares slumped by over a third and the company made the first loss in its history as plans were announced to cut back operations in ten countries.

Was the problem some fundamental flaw in the franchise concept or perhaps an environmental explanation?

Study tip

The above questions and criteria underpin the study and understanding of Marketing in the Environment. You may wish to build a portfolio of the case studies of the organizations that this coursebook reviews or that you identify as you work through the units in order to relate theory to practice.

Insight

The study of Marketing in the Environment not only considers the dynamics pertaining to companies and organizations operating within the public or private domain, but also revolves around what happens in the external environment. Thus, in your reflection about companies, you may also consider some of the external factors:

◆ The changing attitudes of consumers towards health.

◆ The current governmental concerns in the UK about obesity and the latter's link with fat, sugar and salt consumption; all of which are notoriously associated with fast food.

◆ The globalization of the popularity of fast food.

The public services

In the UK, the public services may be divided into two categories, namely: public corporations and regulated public companies (plcs). The characteristics listed below highlight the distinctions between public corporations and regulated public companies.

Public corporations

◆ These are publicly owned, controlled and accountable via specific ministers to Parliament.

◆ These are separate legal entities created by Statute or Royal Charter (e.g. Royal Mint).

◆ They are controlled by boards of management, which are appointed formally and by ministers.

◆ These organizations are financed from the revenue raised by the government or by central government funding.

◆ Although they are designed to be commercially independent, they are however subject to ministerial control.

◆ Their aim is to secure long-term strategic objectives as well as to control the economy.

◆ A shortcoming associated with these organizations is that the lack of competition and conflicting objectives may unfortunately lead to inefficiency.

◆ As they are governmental, they are susceptible to pressure group activity, such as trade unions in particular.

Regulated public companies (regulated plcs)

◆ The bulk of the nationalized industries were privatized in the 1980s and 1990s. In fact the government at the time was accused of a policy of creeping privatization in most of the social services. The bulk of these services were sold directly to the public (e.g. BT) or to management/employee buyouts (e.g. National Freight Corporation) or to other companies (e.g. Rover, British Aerospace) or even in parts (e.g. British Rail).

◆ The services that have remained regulated public companies are usually either unprofitable, unsuitable for sale (e.g. nuclear waste disposal) or ideologically difficult (e.g. the Royal Mail even though the organization lost its letter post monopoly in 2006).

◆   The transfer of ownership to private shareholders was justified under a range of political and economic factors. These are outlined in the table below.

Table 1.8 Factors that influenced the sale of some public services to private shareholders

Political factors	Economic factors
The reduced role of the state	The achievement of efficiency improvements
The deregulation of the economy and some industries	The increase of competition and choice
The intention to enable worker share ownership	The pressure on management to become marketing orientated
The encouragement of shareholding democracy among customers	The improvement of industrial relations
To cut the running costs of public services	The exploitation of new opportunities
To cut borrowing (PSBR) and taxes	To improve supply and productivity levels

The privatization of some public services has been associated with a range of successes as well as some challenges in recent times on not only a national level but also internationally. For instance, the creation of private monopolies in water, electricity, gas and telecoms in the UK was counterbalanced by new regulators with considerable powers to enforce efficiency gains and improvements in the service offered to consumers. Recent public concerns that some regulators have become increasingly influenced by the regulated (e.g. OFWAT, OFLOT) have, however, resulted in an enquiry by the Greenbury Committee into public standards and much stricter regulations being applied.

Insight

In Japan in 2005, the Osaka rail crash, which resulted in 90 deaths, was thought to have been caused by the driver speeding to make up one minute of time on the schedule. Fierce competition among Japan's privatized rail companies had increased standards of operations but also created huge pressure to run trains on time.

When small-and-medium-sized enterprises (SMEs) and large-global-sized organizations are compared, both types of organizations appear to exist as well as thrive within varied market environments. However, the success and even more survival of any organization may be dependent on whether the necessary local or global conditions are favourable.

It is generally acknowledged that both small-and medium-sized enterprises and global and large organizations benefit from a range of advantages. For instance, SMEs are reputed to be able to focus more on customer orientation at local level and remain close to its local stakeholders. In contrast, large organizations tend to benefit from centralized strategy and hence be more adept to confronting world-wide competition. Notwithstanding, it has also been noted that some global firms have also been seeking to think globally in strategic marketing terms while attempting to think locally in operational marketing terms.

Insight

Microsoft amended its Windows and Word software to suit local markets. On the fast food front, companies like McDonald's may also be said to have adopted a globalization strategy in terms of their menu choices. In some countries items containing pork are not offered. Although a global presence can by all means be very successful and effective on many levels, as depicted in the following table, going global also carries significant risks. Such implicit risk is demonstrated by the £20 million loss that Prêt-À-Manger, the sandwich chain, faced when it extended its presence internationally. Consequently, instead of benefiting straightforwardly from a stronger positioning and presence on the market-place, the company was forced to cut back on the number of its outlets.

The strengths of global organizations and the strengths of SMEs are displayed side by side in the following table in an attempt to display how a relative strength of one type of organization tends to be the weakness of the other and vice versa.

Table 1.9 A comparison of the strengths of global organizations and SMEs

The strengths of global organizations	The strengths of SMEs
Economies of scale may be exploited (e.g. discounts for volume) with regard to both supply and purchase. Thus bargaining power can be used with suppliers or even government to secure subsidies for instance.	Attracts people unwilling to work in the confines of large organizations.
The similarities between markets can be exploited. Risks may be spread across markets and similarities exploited.	Tends to cater to local consumers.
The homogeneity of product, image and advertising messages can be maximized. Thus, skills and other resources can be fully utilized. Best practice, ideas and even technological development can be exploited across the organization.	May cater to local tastes and purchasing habits.
Global brand leadership can lead to sustainable marketing advantages.	Attention to detail and to customers.
Ability to centralize strategy and confront world-wide competition.	Organization can be more flexible and adaptable. Thus may adapt or respond more quickly and easily when change is required.
Because of its size and presence, such organizations can be more attractive to suppliers and other key resources.	Can remain close to the business partners and its various stakeholders.

Local authorities

Services provided by local government include fire and police, road maintenance, consumer protection, recreation, environmental health, education and even airports. They are managed by elected councillors through full-time professional officers. As in the rest of the public sector, they have been subject to radical structural and operational changes over the past decade. Central government control has increased, but authorities have been encouraged to forge mutually beneficial links with local business communities.

Over the years, the role of local authorities has changed tremendously. As a matter of fact, exposure to market forces through compulsory competitive tendering has transformed the council officer's role into that of a facilitator rather than a direct provider of local services. For instance, nowadays competitive tendering for refuse collection involves not only the submission of a tender meeting or exceeding stated service specifications, but assurance on standards and competitive pricing must also be provided. Finance is also another area that local authorities still consistently appear to be challenged with. For example in England, plans to revalue 22 million homes for council tax were shelved until after the potential next election in 2009. Meanwhile, when in Wales properties were revalued, a third of the revalued properties were moved up the categories of properties by at least one band. This resulted in significant increases in council tax for the residents. Thousands of the appeals made due to the increase in council tax rates are still pending.

The vision and mission of organizations

Most economies are made up of a variety of organizations. Suffice to say that each of these organizations aim to achieve their objectives within a challenging environment. Consequently, the marketer needs to have a comprehensive understanding of not only what these organizations are trying to achieve but just as importantly marketers need to also appreciate what is driving the behaviour of these organizations both internally and externally.

Vision

Every organization, whether operating with a sole trader or as a multinational company, requires vision. Business vision may be defined as the ability to imagine or foresee the future prospects and potential of the organization. Effective vision is closely linked to the marketing environment since it requires the ability to discern future conditions in the industry or market concerned. It is a critical requirement at the strategic level and is normally the responsibility of the board of directors. Thus, vision may be said to involve understanding the future, anticipating how markets, tastes and technologies may evolve as well as the mobilization of resources to translate the vision into reality. This is the key to business success and competitive advantage and indeed explains why the marketing environment is so central to the marketer's role and importance.

Every organization should have a vision, which sets out its intention for itself. The vision of Coca-Cola was outlined in 1927 by its chairman who contended that the product should always be within an arm's length of desire. By maintaining focus on its vision, Coca-Cola is now in the global top ten by market capitalization and is repeatedly quoted as being amongst the most well-known global brands. In 2007 Coca-Cola was first in the Interbrand ranking of global brands with a brand value of $65,324 million. Another more recent but just as well-known vision is Bill Gates' idea of a PC with Windows software on every desk. In 1999, it became the largest company in the world. In 2007 Microsoft was second in the Interbrand ranking of global brands with a brand value of $58,709 million.

The most critical vision currently revolves around the future direction of e-commerce. This applies to organizations throughout the supply chain. Retailers, for example, have already started assessing whether the future of broadband electronic commerce rests with the currently dominant desktop PC or the digital television allowing armchair shopping.

Activity 1.14

Reflection

What is your vision for the year 2010? Will you be using your third-generation (3G) mobile phone to activate your regular delivery of shopping goods? Will you instead still be regularly visiting retail outlets?

It is anticipated that in 2010, profitable organizations will be those who today have most actively thought through their own vision of the future and made necessary investments in technology and marketing to bring it about as well as embrace the trends.

From vision to mission

Converting a vision into a mission statement produces a strong sense of overall purpose and direction. It seeks to clearly establish what the business does and what it should be doing. It thus highlights the fundamental reason for an organization's existence. It encompasses the scope of its core activities and aims to distinguish that organization from other organizations of its type by clearly defining its uniqueness. Finally, it may provide a set of corporate values intended to unify the various stakeholders in the organization and generate a strong sense of common endeavour.

The Coca-Cola vision was translated into a business mission to make the drink an integral part of consumers' lives. Accordingly, management set clear objectives that the brand must be available everywhere the consumer seeks liquid refreshment. The company then set out to deliver on its vision.

A business mission statement essentially expands on an identified vision. Accordingly, a mission statement would normally refer to a number of the following key elements:

◆ What are the organization's philosophy, values, priorities and aspirations?

◆ What are the organization's key strengths, competencies and competitive edge?

◆ What business is the organization in? Why is the organization in this type of business?

◆ Which markets does the organization compete in?

◆ Who are the organization's main customers?

◆ What are the main products and services that the organization offers?

◆ What core technology does the organization use?

◆ What are the organization's responsibilities towards society?

◆ What is the organization's position regarding key stakeholders?

It is important to make a clear distinction between a vision, a mission and a promotional statement. 'We keep your promise' is the promotional slogan of DHL, the third-party carrier. Nestlé's mission is to become the largest food supplier and to eradicate malnutrition from the world. The Sri Lankan National Bank seeks to promote a 'safe and secure future', while the vision of British Airways is to become 'the world's favourite airline'. The stated mission of Google, the popular Internet search tool, is 'to organize the world's information'.

There are some fundamental criteria that mission statements should respect. The following list, although not exhaustive, provides an outline of the most important dimensions of a mission statement:

◆ A mission statement should be brief, achievable and clear.

◆ It should have a clear statement of purpose as it is meant to enable specific, relevant and realistic objectives.

◆ A mission statement defines a common purpose. Consequently, it could mobilize the loyalty and commitment of staff/management.

◆ It provides a clear statement for stakeholders about the values and future direction of the business and should motivate their commitment. Accordingly, it needs to excite and inspire, encouraging participation through a shared vision.

◆ It acts as a control or benchmark for comparison by senior managers in evaluating the success of the business in realizing its purpose.

◆ It can motivate employees where stated organizational values coincide with their own.

◆ The mission statement is part of the corporate culture and this is the glue that unifies contributions.

◆ Unless a mission statement changes organizational behaviour, it has little value, yet its absence is like being a traveller without a destination, with no way of determining progress.

◆ A mission statement should differentiate the organization from others and establish its individuality, if not its uniqueness. It defines what the organization wishes to be and provides a unifying concept that both enlarges its view of itself and brings it into focus. In brief, it states the intentions of the organization.

◆ The mission statement must not, however, be allowed to submerge the arrival of contradictory environmental information which demands immediate decisions in order to amend its purpose. (For example, IBM's mainframe dominance in the 1980s blinded it to the emerging reality of distributed computing power.)

Objectives are the ends to be achieved in order to fulfil the business mission of an organization. Organizations pursue objectives. Objectives are the specific and more concrete guideposts by which an organization defines standards to be accomplished in key result areas such as profitability and customer service. Objectives can be classified into distinct categories, namely: strategic, tactical and operational. Each type of objective is linked into a planning process that seeks to identify and implement effective strategies and tactics to achieve them.

Strategic objectives are broad long-term goals set by senior management. Examples include:

◆ To achieve and maintain a position of leadership (be number 1 or 2 in a market).

◆ To automate business to business (B2B) transactions with supply chain partners.

◆ To maintain a product portfolio where those introduced less than 3 years ago account for 25 per cent of sales.

◆ To earn an average rate of return on capital of 20 per cent and earnings growth of 10 per cent per annum.

Tactical objectives are set by middle managers and relate to functional areas like marketing. They tend to be more measurable. Examples could include:

◆ To develop an informational website for the company

◆ To reduce operating costs by 5 per cent per annum

◆ To achieve preferred supplier status with designated customers

Operational objectives are usually set by first-line management. These tend to be more short-term. Examples could include:

◆ Daily production targets

◆ To reduce customer complaints by 5 per cent per month

General organizational objectives

Given the diversity of organizations across the business, public and voluntary sectors it is not surprising that their orientation and objectives vary. The table below offers an overview of the contrasting orientations of a range of different types of organizations.

Table 1.10 The primary and secondary orientation of organizations

Organization	Primary orientation	Secondary orientation
Private business	Profit	Growth and increase in market share
Co-operative	Members' returns	Democratic processes of business
Public corporation	Public service and profit making	Efficiency
Social services	Public service	Equity
Interest group	Members' self-interest	Raise organization's profile
Charitable	Alleviating suffering of the less fortunate	Raise contributions to help operations and mission

Primary and secondary orientations are decided by organizations. However, actual objectives can be diverse, complex and subject to considerable influence from market environments.

Insight – mini case study: Dasani

Coca-Cola's decision to recall the entire UK supply of its bottled water Dasani was a big setback to its mission to become an established player in this expanding market. The Food Standards Agency investigated when samples of the product were found to contain bromate, a by-product of the purification process, at higher levels than legally permitted for either bottled or tap water. It also emerged that the source for Dasani was mains water supplied to its factory in south London. Both issues clearly impacted the brand prestige of Coca-Cola and the perceived 'purity' of its products. But, because Dasani was introduced to the market as a separate brand, Coca-Cola brand did not suffer much.

Exam hint

Key skills – Improving your learning and performance

Because of the syllabus' emphasis on Marketing Practice and Key Skills, questions in the examination will normally be set in context. For example, you may be asked to discuss mission statements or organizational objectives in the context of a fast food company or a public sector business school. In other words, you will be required to actively apply your learning to a given situation.

Similarly, with the 'presenting information' key skill, you will be expected to read and synthesize information in the mini-case study in order to answer the questions set.

Study tip

It is always effective in examinations to refer directly to academic writers to support the points you wish to make. The famous management consultant P.F. Drucker argued that there are at least eight key result areas in which a business organization should be judged:

◆ **Market standing** – The desired share in present or new markets plus service goals to build loyalty

◆ **Innovation** – In products/services and the skills/processes required to deliver them

◆ **Human resources** – The supply, skill, development, attitude and performance of staff

- **Financial resources** – Sources of capital and effective utilization
- **Management performance**
- **Productivity** – Efficient use of resources relative to outcomes
- **Social responsibility** – Maintenance of ethical behaviour
- **Profitability** – The indicators of financial well-being

Activity 1.15

Select an organization of your choice in the private sector and attempt to asses how the above dimensions relate to that organization.

Activity 1.16

Key skills – Improving your learning and performance

- List the main objectives that you consider a competitive business could pursue.
- How do these objectives relate to the stated objectives of the business? Do they conflict? Or are they complementary?
- What do you think could be the objectives of the sales or marketing department of that business?
- Do they conflict with those of the business as a whole?

Study tip

Don't just accept at face value what you read in a text or a newspaper. Critically think about what is said, carefully and logically. Do not be afraid to have your own opinion, but be prepared to justify it to others. Critical awareness of the subject matter is something that is welcomed by the examiner but usually only evident among excellent candidates. Make the investment this needs in 'thinking' and 'discussion' time. It will repay handsome dividends.

The key is a combination of critical thinking and reflection.

Survival of businesses

This is a basic drive in all businesses and relates to the needs we have as individuals for security and the satisfaction of our economic wants. The jobs of management and workers depend on it, and this can lead to considerable sacrifices being made in times of economic hardship. The Japanese, in particular, are renowned for their willingness to accept cuts in salary and redouble efforts to restore corporate fortunes.

Many sole proprietors would continue in business even at the cost of exploiting themselves and family workers. The directors of public limited companies will also be aware of the need to avoid the possibility of a hostile takeover bid. These usually lead to the removal of top management, especially where the bid arose due to their underperformance in the eyes of shareholders. The press frequently reports examples, such as the successful £8.5 billion bid by Santander Central Hispano, Spain's largest bank, for Abbey or Air France's takeover of Dutch KLM to create Europe's largest airline.

Society is faced with the reality of scarce resources relative to its needs and wants. It requires these be managed effectively and is prepared to see businesses fail so their resources can be released for use by the more competent managers. Businesses must justify their use of resources over and over again, if they are to survive and avoid possible takeover or liquidation. This means that they must make a profit! Tesco, the United Kingdom's largest grocery retailer, has certainly done that and has seen its profit rise 20.3 per cent to £2.5bn in 2006/07. Buoyed by strong international growth and a rapidly growing non-grocery business, the company saw its group sales for 2007 jump 10.9 per cent to £46.6bn. Not satisfied with its £250 million plan to open 150 supermarkets in Wal-Mart's US backyard, it has also gone into software with a range of packages substantially undercutting Microsoft Office. Amazon, the online bookseller, is also now making profits after six years of losses and $3 billion of investment, suggesting that it might survive to become a viable long-term Internet business.

Exam hint

The need to survive is a fact of life for all candidates enrolled on professional courses like CIM. Viewed at the outset, combining the demands of work with the requirements of the syllabus and the coursebook may feel very challenging. Therefore from the beginning of your course, learn to work systematically. Remember the Chinese proverb: Many small steps make a giant stride.

Profit and profit maximization

This is the most-quoted business objective, although, strictly, it can be considered to be more of a motivation than an end in itself. It does, however, provide a *measurement system* for assessing business performance. Profit maximization implies that businesses seek to make not only a profit but also the maximum possible profit through time. Malcolm Glazer who bought-out Manchester United, for example, plans to raise ticket prices by more than 50 per cent over the period to 2010. He requires the extra profit to meet the interest payments on the money he borrowed to buy the club. Profit is the difference between revenue and cost.

Businesses are viewed as rational and self-centred in their decisions. As a matter of fact, businesses tend to seek to allocate resources so as to maximize profit. For instance, in order to maximize its potential for profit, a business may choose to adopt the following course of actions:

◆ **Supplying goods that consumers most wish to buy** – Through careful research of customer needs, an understanding and anticipation of their changing preferences can be acquired. For instance, as increasing numbers of electronic consumers indicated that they prefer the ease and convenience of obtaining their staple groceries, travel, entertainment and increasingly clothes over the Internet; existing retailers and new *e-tailers* have been responding by developing customer-friendly websites to satisfy these needs and enable sales.

◆ **Combining resource inputs to produce planned output at minimum possible cost** – Businesses will not satisfy consumer wants, irrespective of cost, just to make sales. Consequently they will cease to supply further units when additional cost exceeds the price received. At this output they will ensure that factor inputs are combined so that goods (products or services) may be produced at the lowest possible cost. For example, e-tailers will compare the relative costs and benefits of the alternative delivery systems for home shopping, such as own transport, third-party carrier, local services, post or mail-order delivery systems and then select what they consider to be the most efficient one now and into the future. More proactive companies tend to periodically re-assess their partners and their parties.

◆ **Responding quickly to changes in supply and demand conditions** – If consumer tastes change or input prices alter then it will be in the interest of the firm to adjust the marketing mix or production methods accordingly. For example, will TV, desktop PC or WAP mobile phone prevail as the best order channel or will fibre optics, satellite, aerial, enhanced phone lines or cable prevail as broadband speed increases? In either case, businesses will respond by reallocating resources and marketing effort accordingly.

The pursuit of maximum profit therefore answers two of the basic economic problems arising from scarcity:

1   What to produce and in what quantities?

2   How to produce them efficiently?

It also provides a dynamic growth incentive for the business system to:

◆ Innovate new and improved products that enhance value for money for consumers and revenue for the firm.

◆ Invest in research and development of more efficient methods of production to reduce costs.

Maximizing profit would appear to promise an ideal allocation of resources by rewarding those businesses that produce and market the right goods, in the right quantities, using the most efficient methods and ploughing back resources into producing economic growth through new products and better methods. What if businesses were content with just modest profits or decided to pursue other objectives? What if they are run by salaried managers, who stand to gain nothing from extra profit, rather than the shareholders? What if they are production-orientated and are not concerned with the consumers' real needs? These possibilities can only arise in the absence of *full and free competition*.

When competition is very strong, firms must market what consumers demand otherwise their competitors will, thereby reducing their market share and threatening their survival. Firms must be efficient, otherwise they will be undercut by lower-cost rivals. They must provide excellent service because the power lies with the consumer in such situations.

Study tip

Key skills – Learning and performance

Performing to the best of your ability and potential is a principle to apply to your CIM studies and examinations. Aim for thorough understanding from your available study time and then maximize your marks by answering all the components of the questions set in a planned and focused way. Use your coursebook to assist your learning.

Insight: Marketing environment in practice – DVD wars

Competition can also confound this process as seen in Sony's bid to dictate the future DVD standard. Microsoft and Intel have rejected its Blue-ray standard in favour of Toshiba's rival HD DVD. Most of the movie studios, electronic giants and IT companies involved are motivated by corporate loyalties, but some like Paramount are offering both formats, thus putting the outcome in the hands of the consumer.

No firm, no matter how profitable, can afford to stand still. Much of the profit earned has to be ploughed back into new product development and improved methods if the firm is to retain its competitive edge. Customers will not think twice about a badly managed business. Thus, it will go bankrupt or be taken over by firms better fitted to manage the resources. Marks & Spencer (M&S) narrowly avoided this fate in 2004 but has bounced back to a record share price in late 2006 by concentrating on retail basics.

Business therefore appears to be very much a treadmill when competition is strong. Even if an innovative business succeeds in making extra profits, this will merely attract new competitors into the market to erode away the rewards. The scope for pursuing other objectives will only exist where market imperfections exist or large firms dominate.

Question 1.4

Key skills – Problem-solving

If managers are rational and they have the choice between making either 'maximum possible profits' in the short term or just modest profits, can you think of any sound business reasons why it might be sensible to choose the latter?

Market share

Observation suggests that many businesses seek to maximize sales *subject to a profit constraint*. There may indeed be a positive correlation between profit and market share, but beyond a certain point, extra share may only be 'bought' at the expense of profit. Prices and margins will be trimmed or extra promotional expense incurred. So long as sufficient profit is made to keep shareholders content, management may see an advantage in the stability and security of a dominant position. This objective was until recently at the forefront of mobile telephone companies such as Orange, O2 and Vodafone as they vied to expand 'pay as you go' sales. A similar picture can be seen in Internet connections and digital TV. Many dot-com business-to-consumer (B2C) companies have invested massively in website advertising and promotion with little short-term prospect of profit. Companies like Amazon.com preferred to expand their customer base and market share rather than earn short-run profits until heavy losses forced a shift of emphasis. On the other hand, Boo.com, which budgeted $16 million in advertising and only generated $2.7 million in sales revenue, no longer exists.

Japanese exporters have been accused of pursuing market share in the short run in order to drive out domestic competitors prior to raising prices and profits in the longer term. *Long-run* versus *short-run profits* is an important consideration. It is suggested that most American and British companies are under considerable pressure to deliver buoyant short-run profits even at the expense of longer-term investment. This appears to be particularly the case where shareholders are involved. Japanese and German companies, by contrast, are able to give greater emphasis to the long run due to the support of shareholding banks.

Business growth

Growth and profits may be positively related but not continuously. The rapid growth in out-of-town grocery superstores appears to be a case in point. Alternatively, growth may require takeovers and acquisitions, and these may prove unsuccessful, especially if they represent diversification into unfamiliar areas. Such strategies put pressure on the management of resources.

Growth may, however, be attractive for a number of reasons. For instance:

◆　It may help resolve conflicts between stakeholders.

◆　It may provide opportunities for promotion and job satisfaction.

◆　It tends to increase market power and thus management status.

◆　It can raise morale in general.

Management objectives

If management is not under severe competitive pressure, it may decide to *satisfice*. That is, it will produce satisfactory performance and profits. Where there is a *separation of ownership from management* there is no automatic incentive for professional managers to maximize profits for shareholders.

The organization may operate with what is termed *organizational slack*. This is the difference between the cost level that would maximize profits and actual costs. These excessive costs would finance a number of 'unnecessary expenditures' such as management perks and pet projects.

The existence of *slack* enables management to maximize their security, income, status, power and job interest. They can also take in the slack without threatening core activities and programmes in times of adversity. Similarly a lack of competition, the absence of a profit incentive and powerful stakeholder groups led to an accumulation of *slack* in health, education, local authorities, state-controlled industries and government bureaucracy. This resulted in efforts by the government to improve productivity across a range of public services through various means such as:

◆　Deregulating markets or introducing internal markets

◆　Making services client-driven (through the introduction of service charters in addition to set service standards)

◆　Insisting on compulsory competitive tendering

◆　Attracting better-calibre managers while curbing the power of the trade unions

◆　Appointing powerful regulators to set price/performance standards

As the objectives have become more customer-orientated in the public sector, the nature of these organizations has also been transformed. Subsequently, the skills of the marketer have also come to the fore in the quest for more focused customer benefits.

Exam hint

Have you given any consideration to the examiner's objectives? Is it to pass only a certain proportion, for example?

The examiners objective is to their utmost to pass as many students as possible but only if students meet the CIM professional standard. Employers must have faith in what a CIM qualification stands for, and it is in your long-term career interests to see that this is maintained. So be well prepared.

How are goals established?

To understand how business goals change, we must understand how they are formed. The board of directors are responsible for deciding objectives and formulating plans and policies to secure their effective achievement. The managing director is appointed to implement policy while non-executive directors are often invited onto the board of public companies to provide an external dimension to formulating objectives.

The key influences may be summarized as internal and external influences.

Internal influences

◆ Memorandum of association:

  ◆ The *memorandum of association* or its equivalent sets limits in the objects clause to the powers of a company.

  ◆ Pursuit of purposes outside these limits will be deemed *ultra vires* and therefore legally void.

  ◆ In practice, this clause will be broadly defined to allow the directors to diversify outside their traditional business.

◆ Personal values and objectives of senior management:

  ◆ The personal values and objectives of senior management will exert significant influence on an organization, in particularly when represented to the board, for example by the marketing director.

◆ The expectations of the internal decision-makers and their degree of aversion to risk:

  ◆ This will strongly impact the risk avoidance or risk taking dimensions of tactics and even strategies.

◆ The limits set by resource availability:

  ◆ A minimum return on capital may be required in order to attract the necessary internal and external funds to finance other objectives.

◆ Key individual and institutional shareholders:

  ◆ Their expectations will greatly influence receptivity of ideas and change in particular.

◆ The force of inertia and past successes may prevent serious internal review of objectives:

  ◆ For example, Microsoft, a 30-year-old company, still relies on a 10-year-old suite of desktop applications for 80 per cent of sales, while newer products like the Xbox video game made significant early losses. The much younger Google attracts the software talent and releases a much faster stream of products directly onto the Internet.

External influences

◆ Successful businesses recognize the importance of matching the capabilities of the organization to its environment. Internal strengths and weaknesses must be set against external threats and opportunities.

◆ There is a variety of connected and external stakeholders whose interests and attitudes must be considered before objectives are set. Their contribution will often be crucial to the effective implementation of the objectives.

◆ Conflict between the interests of shareholders and various stakeholders may require compromise to retain their contribution to the achievement of set objectives.

◆ The competitive environment may constrain what are achievable objectives in terms of time.

◆ A change in government will alter previously set objectives, while changes in legislation will define what is, and is not, achievable for private businesses.

◆ External interests may be represented, for example worker or consumer directors.

Study tip

You can enhance your recall of academic ideas by relating the material to your own situation.

Consider for a moment your own goals. How frequently do you review them? How have they changed? What are the influences that have brought about the changes? Are these influences internally or externally driven? Do you review your objectives frequently enough?

What causes the goals to change?

Virtually every organization must periodically review its objectives if it is to survive and succeed. There are compelling reasons to consider changes to goals regularly:

◆ Most organizations operate in a dynamic and constantly changing environment.

◆ As these environmental forces threaten to throw the business off course, management must respond proactively by setting a new direction and a renewed focus to unify the organization's efforts.

◆ Changes in consumer wants must be anticipated and responded to with matching goals.

◆ Changes in production possibilities transform resource availability and technological options.

◆ Opportunities and threats from the various environments represent new realities and require new responses.

◆ Objectives are intended to be achieved and so require renewal as this occurs.

◆ If control processes show that objectives are not being realized, then a change to more realistic goals will provide more effective motivation for management and staff. For example, significant net debts and company pension deficits has forced Northern Foods to sell the division that makes Marks and Spencer's Melting Middle Chocolate Pudding, hailed as one of the most successful food launches of all time, in order to avoid the break-up of the company as a whole.

◆ A change in the chief executive or perhaps a merger or acquisition will tend to change the strategic goals.

◆ Larger organizations may adopt corporate planning to formalize the above process.

Corporate planning is akin to a continuing process during which the long-term objectives of an organization may be formulated and achieved by means of short-term as well as long-term strategic actions. In brief, strategic objectives are the outcome of the above internal and external influences and considerations. However, they tend to revolve around a five to ten year time frame. As such, ongoing rigorous reviews and corrections are implied. Thus, corporate strategy attempts to determine what an organization should optimally do.

Exam hint

Key skills – Improving performance

An examiner-friendly script is always recommended so that the examiner can understand your points. Your answers should therefore be legible, clear, well set out and expressed in an easy-to-understand semi-report style format. Bullet points, headings and justification are usually used. Care should also be taken with regards to spacing and size of the writing.

The organization as an open system

It is now clear that organizational objectives must be regularly reviewed and set with reference to internal and external considerations. Understanding this interplay between internal context and the wider environment has led to the organization being viewed as an open system. This approach focuses on the interrelated activities that enable inputs to be converted into outputs and provides a very useful framework for gaining insight into the relationships that prevail between the organization and its marketing environment.

There are many different systems we could identify: ourselves, the marketing department, our organization, the corporate system, the marketing environment, wider society, the global economy, the ecosystem, our galaxy and the solar system. Each has a boundary that represents its interface with the others. We will be particularly concerned with the interface between the organization and its environment. This interface is represented in and possesses the following common characteristics:

◆ Productive inputs and energy are received/obtained from the marketing environment.

◆ The organization adds value by converting these inputs into desired outputs.

◆ They discharge their outputs into their environment – both positive and negative.

◆ They apply control by monitoring the feedback on achievement of objectives.

Open systems are interdependent with their marketing environment and must adapt to change if they are to survive and develop. Open systems are vital where the environment is unstable or uncertain. Closed systems do not respond to change and only function well in stable conditions.

Open systems will also scan the external environment for opportunities and threats. When the organization adapts to this external environment it will impact on its effectiveness, whereas when it adapts its internal structure and organization it will impact on its efficiency.

Activity 1.17

Key skills – Using information

Spend a few moments applying systems thinking to your own self. Think along the lines of inputs/conversion and output.

How adaptive are you to your environment?

How effective is your interface with your marketing manager?

The interface between marketing and other functions

Most systems divide into subsystems. In some organizations, for example, purchasing or sales may be a separate function from marketing while in others they are integrated. Successful adaptation requires that relationships are co-ordinated since individual departments that seek to maximize their own outcomes inevitably detract from an optimum outcome for the system as a whole. Marketing not only operates over the external boundary with the wider environment but must also establish and maintain effective relationships across the internal boundaries with key departments such as finance, research and development, and production. We can identify four fundamental cases of business focus related to the environment. These are:

1   Production orientation
2   Product orientation
3   Selling orientation
4   Marketing orientation

Each one has implications for organizational effectiveness and the degree to which it is outward looking. Some business may evolve from an inward-looking focus on production efficiency and product quality or even selling quality to a comprehensive operational emphasis on anticipating and satisfying changing consumer requirements through greater sales awareness.

Production orientation

Where *production orientation* prevails, the emphasis is on design and operations management. Technical or finance specialists will tend to dominate the hierarchy while the sales function will be minor with no representation on the board. Examples are found in niche markets where demand far exceeds supply (e.g. TVR or Morgan cars) or in the public services like education and health before the recent efforts to break their monopoly. The latter tended to be bureaucratic, dominated by professionals with little incentive to inquire into or respond to the real needs of their captive consumers.

Companies adopting a production orientation not only focus their efforts on improving the production process, but also the efficiency of distribution channels and processes. For companies to achieve competitive advantage through the adoption of the Production Management Concept, much more than focus on the actual production process of goods is required. Accordingly, although in line with the fundamental principles of the business philosophy, businesses adopting the production orientation are likely to favour continual emphasis on production efficiency; such companies may by all means also aim to focus their operations on the reduction of operational costs or even economies of scale.

Within production orientation, primacy is given by companies to their products rather than to their customers. There are two distinct variants to the production philosophy. While companies may on the one hand believe that the development of technologically superior products is the route to success, on the other hand companies may be led by the belief that success instead lies in producing their products more efficiently than their competitors. Notwithstanding the relevance and merit of both variants, companies adopting this orientation tend to adopt ventures with little or no effort having been put into finding out whether their customers will in fact want the new features being developed, whether they would find the new or altered products attractive or whether they would eventually be willing to pay for the altered products.

Product orientation

In contrast to the production orientation where focus on the efficient production and distribution of products prevails, *product orientation* instead focuses on quality and performance. Accordingly, companies adopting this business philosophy are expected to believe that customers choose products for their quality rather than their price. Suffice to say then that the aim of businesses adopting the product orientation is to produce the best products or offer the best services on the market. Such a philosophy could indeed be deemed to be the very epitome of five-star hotels within the hotel industry.

In line with the aim to offer the best products or services, companies therefore tend to devote their energies to making continuous product improvements. It is indeed anticipated that companies would only be able to maintain their offerings of the best products and services through continuous improvements. Within the car industry, this may be achieved through the addition of new features and added value such as engine efficiency.

Although exquisite products and services, which are continually being improved, may hardly be frowned upon, adoption of the product orientation may however also create some shortcomings. In fact, some negative outcomes of regimental adherence to the business concept may be two-fold. On the one hand, a company may need to reflect its continual investments in the improvement of quality in the costs of its products and services. Consequently, it may end up pricing itself out of its market. If however, that company is not be able to pass the costs of improvements onto its customers due to it being forced by the dynamics of competition to match its competitors' prices, in this case its profitability is undoubtedly going to be damaged if not eroded. On the other hand, it is possible that the extra features that the companies have been avidly investing in may not be appreciated nor even wanted by either existing or potential customers. For instance the provision of car washing services by a five-star hotel in the centre of London, albeit being seen as a luxurious added service, may hardly be needed by its guests. On the opposite end of the spectrum of hotel types, the provision of laundry services within a budget hotel may not be considered an improvement on service offerings by its patrons.

Selling orientation

The *selling orientation* is characteristically adopted when the main aim of a company is to sell products due to over-capacity and excess supply or when customers need to be persuaded about the products. In such scenarios, having produced an excess of products companies tend to believe that they can only sell these by means of aggressive sales and promotion of their products and services. Alternatively, having produced products that are eventually not appealing to customers, companies may indeed consider aggressive selling tactics to be the only way in which they are able to penetrate the market. Within this type of orientation, companies can also aim to increase customer share. Yet, it is anticipated that even though companies adopting a selling orientation aim to increase the amount of purchases of their customers, the focus of these businesses tend to remain to sell what they have rather than to provide what their customers want. Therefore, while selling focuses on the needs of the organization, marketing focuses on the needs of the customers.

Selling orientation is not only often found in markets where supply exceeds demand, but this type of orientation also tends to be favoured by companies that have a heavy investment in fixed capital equipment such as building and technology. Here it is in fact the product, rather than the customers, which is of more importance. Subsequently, rates may be lowered in an attempt to attract a wider audience. Profitability may also be achieved through volume.

Marketing orientation

Rather than ignore the dimensions advocated for by the three other approaches to business, the *marketing orientation* appears to incorporate some aspects of each of the other business philosophies. Thus, companies following a marketing orientation believe in improving product quality just like those that are product-oriented. However, marketing-oriented businesses primarily differ from their product-oriented counterparts in the sense that the former will only invest in improvements if these have been identified as being beneficial to the customers. In essence, while improvements within product-oriented companies may be internally driven, improvements within marketing-oriented companies are invariably driven by customers. In terms of commonality with the production orientation, companies adopting a marketing orientation are also likely to identify the reduction of costs and efficient processes as primary aims. With reference to the selling orientation, businesses following a marketing orientation also tend to have recourse to promotion and price discounting. However, while such techniques are quintessentially the driving force of sales-oriented companies, marketing-oriented companies traditionally only use such tactics as short-term solutions or temporary incentives. In essence, these tactics are used merely to enhance the real driving forces of these businesses.

In spite of its similarities with the other three business philosophies, it has been argued that marketing orientation nonetheless offers a fundamentally different approach to business. marketing orientation is the only business philosophy that adopts an *outside-in perspective* as opposed to the *inside-out perspective* favoured by the other business philosophies. Instead of starting off with the organization and its products as the core of a business, marketing orientation, in contrast to the production, product and sales orientations, instead emphatically and consistently starts off with the customer at the core of the business. In fact, within companies adopting this orientation, customer focus and value are the paths to sales and profits. Consequently, companies adopting the marketing orientation in essence are said to focus on the genuine needs and wants of their target audiences. Hence, it could indeed be contended that the main difference between marketing orientation and the other business philosophies lies in the attitude of companies towards the customer and to the market in which they operate. Simply put: marketing orientation prescribes that the customer is of most importance.

Additionally, not only does the marketing orientation emphasize that the customer is key to business growth and survival, but more importantly a business adopting a marketing orientation is said to seek to provide the goods and services that its customers want to buy. For example, within the retail industry, while many high street brands are still intent on offering their personalized service in their stores, others have responded to the demonstrated preference of their customers for online shopping and offer many of their fares on their websites. Therefore, it can be clearly seen that the strength of the marketing orientation lies in the focus on the buyer as the key component in the marketing process.

Exam hint

Key skills – Improving performance

What orientation are you going to adopt in the examination?

1   A technical orientation, where all your attention goes into offering as much information as you feel is appropriate?

2   A selling orientation with a lot of terminology to try to convince examiners that you know what you are talking about?

3   A marketing orientation where you focus on what the examiner, here your customer, is actually asking for? Therefore, in this case, you would aim to provide in-depth answers to the actual questions set.

Activity 1.18

Key skills – Problem-solving

A marketing orientation places the customer at the centre of the whole organization's attention. With this in mind, make a list of desirable organizational characteristics that would achieve this.

The main difficulty confronting a business wishing to achieve a marketing orientation is the change required in organizational culture. Functional divisions within the business create potential barriers, preventing a cohesive response to customer needs. Unless there is a drive and strong leadership from the top to establish the philosophy throughout the organization, they will fail to pull together, reverting instead to narrow departmental interests. If the organization is unable to get its own internal act together, it is unlikely to respond successfully to environmental change.

Managing the marketing environment: a contingency approach

This approach to managing organizations renounces the idea of a universal formula and relies instead on tailoring the response to the specific situation encountered. Research by academics and practitioners alike have repeatedly concluded that there is no one best means of managing organizations to meet their current objectives in an uncertain environment. Marketers must therefore identify and then adapt continuously to the conditions that are found to prevail in the present and the future.

E-commerce has had serious implications for retailers and manufacturers for the past decade. This trend is set to continue. Thus, greater flexibility in view of accelerating changes is clearly needed. A comparison of the characteristics of the old economy based solely in the market-place and the new economy organizations based in the market-place too could include:

Old economy organization	New economy organization
Stable bureaucratic structures	Flexible dynamic structures
Mechanistic and hierarchical	Organic and fluid
Formalized relationships	Lateral, informal, networked relationships
Job and position focused	Task, skills and relationship focused
Permanent 9–5 jobs	Flexitime, as task completion demands
Production orientated	Market and customer orientated
Centralized decision-making	Employee involvement and participation
Salaried	Shared benefits and shared ownership

E-commerce is a challenge that affects the whole organization and will of necessity demand a 'systems' driven response. It involves radical restructuring for many organizations combined with fundamental shifts in business culture. It comes alongside a competitive environment that is already fast changing, becoming more global, consolidating, deregulating and demanding, with customers searching aggressively for greater innovation, more comprehensive service solutions and better value. Many large organizations are therefore under increasing global competitive pressure to become leaner, meaner and generally more innovative and responsive in the face of multifaceted environmental change.

Study tip

At the end of each unit, you will find a summary of some of the main learning points. If you do not fully understand a learning point, then return to the relevant part of the unit and re-read it. Be sure to undertake the various activities and questions in the unit and compare your answers with the summary answers provided at the end of each unit. Not every activity has plausible answers since, as you will have realized, some of the questions are intended to get you thinking about the subject matter in the sections that followed.

Influential trends

A number of key trends and changes are transforming the structure of organizations. The main ones will be discussed in the following sections.

Digitalization

Ever more powerful microprocessors, sophisticated software, broadband delivery and the Internet are working towards the seamless adoption and integration of information technology into our lives. As text, video, sound and vision are digitalized, compressed and transmitted at ever increasing speeds, so the potential for fully automated business transactions increases. The mobile phone is fast becoming a critical instrument in marketing at the individual level. M-advertising is set to grow rapidly. Intranet systems, allowing the mutual interrogation of customer and supplier computers, provide automatic purchasing and stock control and dramatically reduce transactions costs, unfortunately at the expense of middle managers and clerical staff. Downsizing is the process by which organizations have stripped middle managers out of the workforce leaving those who remain to take over their duties assisted by the more effective information systems.

Virtual organizations

Digitalization and the Internet make location and physical presence unnecessary. Members of the virtual organization need not necessarily come face to face, since they can communicate from any point on the globe by WAP mobile text message, e-mail or video conference. The emphasis is increasingly on flexibility, teamwork and sharing rather than authority and chains of command. Empowerment is undoubtedly part of this process as decision-making power is delegated to subordinates and task groups, with day-to-day tactical matters determined without reference to higher authority, bringing all organization members much closer to the customer.

Knowledge workers

The management guru Peter Drucker first coined the term *knowledge worker* to describe the processes of employment change in the information society. Knowledge was to become the critical factor of production facilitated through networks of information and contacts. Information is captured, processed, stored and then made available in the right form to the appropriate decision-makers and at the right time to achieve maximum competitive advantage. Organizations reinforce this decision quality by de-layering. This involves compressing the hierarchy by reducing the number of reporting levels. This speeds up the flow of information to the decision-maker, and the decisions to those who implement them at the customer interface.

Networks and relationships

In an increasingly complex world, it is argued that organizations should focus on the core capabilities where they possess competitive advantage. Other functions should be outsourced to those organizations that are best at what they specialize in. Organizations then become part of a cluster that form a value chain. This focus on core competencies while contracting third-party operations to undertake peripheral activities puts a premium on relationships, accountability and co-operation with business partners. This theme will be further developed in the next unit.

Marketing and information communication technologies

We have already seen that the marketer is at the critical interface with the customer. Marketing orientation will become even more organizationally important in future. To facilitate this role the marketer must actively develop information technology capability so that their marketing skills can be applied to maximum effect in the world of electronic commerce. Unless and until the marketer fully appreciates the potential of the e-commerce revolution and its associated technologies, they will never achieve full effectiveness. A shortcoming of the reliance on associated technologies is the speed at which technological advancements are moving. Data is a valuable commodity, and all records (e.g. shopping habits, bank details, mobile phone patterns) can be exploited by businesses.

Organizational adaptability

The future will belong to organizations that are both focused and able to deploy the resources of the large organization but with the flexibility of the small. Despite multi-billion dollar mergers and amalgamations that bring together the likes of Viacom (cables), Paramount (film/cable), Blockbuster (video) and CBS (TV), the future may lie with organizations on a smaller scale that can attract talented people and unleash their capabilities. The global accessibility provided by the Internet may also serve to break down the formality and remoteness of the big corporation. Transparency, empowerment and informality are more likely to be the style of the new economy dot-coms.

Large organizations that do not adapt quickly enough to counter threats or exploit opportunities have most to lose due to their large fixed investments. Smaller concerns, freed from the barriers of scale and location, may develop rapidly via the Internet. Marketers must participate in and respond to the challenge posed. Marketing fundamentals and associated skills will still be required, but they will be increasingly information-driven in the open systems of global electronic commerce.

Activity 1.19

Key skills – Improving learning and performance

Information and communication technologies and the development of e-commerce are important 'key skills' and themes running throughout this coursebook.

Since mini-cases will be based on this aspect of the syllabus from time to time, you should:

◆ Ensure you understand and can define all the key information and communication terms.

◆ Consolidate information on e-commerce as you work through the units in this coursebook.

◆ Summarize the impacts and implications of e-commerce.

Summary

In this unit, we have seen that:

◆ A diversity of organizations exists within a mixed economy.

◆ The strengths of one form of organization are often the weaknesses of the other.

◆ An informal economy operates alongside the formally reported one.

◆ Organizational objectives are stepping stones along the road to achieving the corporate mission.

◆ Business objectives are varied and reflect different motivations.

◆ Objectives pursued reflect internal values as well as external influences and constraints.

◆ There is an important distinction between satisfying and maximizing behaviour.

◆ Businesses are open systems which rely on interaction with their environment for survival/growth.

◆ A major part of the work of the marketer is to manage the internal and external boundaries.

◆ The marketer should respond flexibly to the realities of the changing situation.

◆ A marketing-oriented structure is the key to effective achievement of objectives.

Further study and examination preparation

The material in this wide-ranging unit covers 15 per cent of the syllabus. It should enable you to attempt any question posed on the organization. There is no guarantee of a question in any particular examination, but a full or a part/linked question is normally to be expected.

In December 2004 and 2005, two questions that related students' understanding of organizations to other aspects of the syllabus were set. In December 2005, the case was based on Microsoft. For that exam, two questions related specifically to the themes addressed in Unit 1. One related to open and closed systems while the other focused on objectives. As such organizationally-based cases occur from time to time, you must be prepared for them.

The marking scheme of a CIM examination is flexible enough to accommodate a variety of teaching approaches and national contexts. Approach each end-of-unit question in a focused manner. Therefore, consider what the question is asking for, use your understanding of the unit to plan out and answer it within the 30–35 minutes available and then compare the result with the specimen answer provided. Even if you did not get it 'right first time' do not worry but go back and find out why. The key to success is to immediately put your learning into practice, so always apply the three key words that lead to this: practise, practise and practise.

It is important that time and effort is allocated in proportion to the 'mark' allocated per question.

Extending knowledge

To supplement your reading on organizations, you may refer to the core text on the Marketing Environment Syllabus. This is the latest edition of Palmer and Hartley (2006):

Palmer A. and Hartley B. (2006) *The Business and Marketing Environment*, McGraw-Hill. Recommended chapters for this unit: Chapter 3 considers the classification of business organizations while Chapter 4 relates to organizational objectives and growth.

Other suggested reading

Palmer A. (2002) *The Business Environment*, McGraw-Hill. Chapter 2 considers types of business organizations; Chapter 3 relates to organizational growth.

Cartwright R. (2001) *Mastering the Business Environment*, Palgrave. Recommended reading: case studies in the final chapter.

These three texts are recommended throughout the units that follow.

Websites

A number of websites will also be suggested at the end of each unit. You may wish to visit these for supplementary information support.

Websites that provide material on marketing environment practice tend to be newspaper-based so they are up to date. These include:

www.ft.com – Provides extensive research materials across all industry sectors with links to specialist reports.

www.thetimes.co.uk and www.thetimes100.co.uk – Ideal for news coverage and the top 100 UK companies.

www.theeconomist.com – Holds readily researched archives of articles from back issues.

www.corporateinformation.com – Includes worldwide sources listed by country.

www.vlib.org.uk/BusinessEconomics.html – This is a virtual library for business and economics. Also holds a catalogue of high quality websites.

Practicising past exam questions

Please see Question 2, June 2004 on the CIM website www.cim.co.uk/learningzone.

Please see Question 3, June 2004 on the CIM website www.cim.co.uk/learningzone.

Please see Question 2, December 2004. Go to www.cim.co.uk/learningzone for specimen answers.

Please see Question 3a, December 2004 on the CIM website www.cim.co.uk/learningzone.

Please see Question 2, June 2005. Go to www.cim.co.uk/learningzone to obtain specimen answers.

Please see Question 1c, 1d and Question 2, December 2005.

Please see Question 2a and 2b, June 2006. Go to www.cim.co.uk/learning zone for specimen answers.

Although past paper questions remain very relevant, students must understand that the format has changed. Therefore you should also refer to the specimen paper to ensure that you are clear about the new exam format.

Unit 2 The micro-environment

Learning objectives

By the end of this unit you will:

◆ Appreciate the scope and complexity of the marketing environment (1.1/1.4/2.1).

◆ Become aware of the important stakeholder interrelationships within the micro-environment (2.1).

◆ Be able to classify the various external elements and influences (2.1/3.1).

◆ Recognize the significance of future environmental challenges and their importance for developing marketing strategy and planning (1.3/1.8/1.9/3.7).

◆ Assess the marketer's potential for influence in the micro-environment (1.3/2.2/2.3/2.5).

◆ Understand the impacts of pressure groups such as consumerists and environmentalists (2.3).

Study tip

This unit introduces the marketing environment, considers the nature and importance of environmental change and identifies some implications for marketing strategy and planning. The micro-environment may be defined as including the groups and organizations that have a two-way operational relationship with the business, and which are controlled and influenced by it to some degree. This environment is the work-a-day operational context for the organization. We saw in Unit 1 that the organization is an open system with boundaries to its immediate environment. Relationships must be established across these boundaries if supplies or credit, for example, are to be obtained. Similarly, the organization must have effective linkages, through intermediaries, to the market-place, or directly to the final customers themselves. Competitors also inhabit this environment and the marketer must understand the significance of relationships that prevail within the industry setting. This will be discussed in depth in Unit 3.

Information is critical to understanding and the marketer must draw on a network of intelligence sources, if successful change is to be made. The organization must be proactive if it is to control or at least influence the behaviour of the various stakeholders and pressure groups to be found in the micro-environment.

This syllabus area relates directly to your own experience. You are a consumer within the market environment. You supply labour services to your employer; therefore you are aware of the competitors operating in your industry. You may also deal directly with distributors or consumers as part of your job description. Your employment focuses on marketing. This specialist discipline promotes profitable relationships across the system boundaries. Therefore you are in an ideal position to appreciate the micro-environment as both a consumer and as part of a provider mechanism.

The business as a resource converter

All organizations seek, as Peter Drucker observed, to make resources productive. Every organization, irrespective of its specific objectives, has this as their common goal because resources are scarce, must be competed for, and utilized efficiently and effectively. As illustrated in Figure 1.3, various inputs are drawn (e.g. paid/volunteer) from the environment and converted in time, place or form to create utility, value and satisfaction for the ultimate consumer.

In the business environment, productive inputs are diverse and often complex entities in themselves. They can be obtained from an interrelated global economy. The traditional economic classification of land, labour and capital is simplistic since the human resource, for example, may embody numerous skills, enterprise, creativity and an ability to adapt to changing circumstances.

Capital resources are often of high technology and very specialized. They include buildings, equipment and transportation, as well as financial inputs to lubricate the process of resource conversion in advance of actual sales. Business services are important inputs as increasingly more firms outsource IT services, transport, catering and market research for instance to focus their resources and attention on their core conversion activities.

Activity 2.1

Think about a marketing resource such as marketing research or the information that can be generated from loyalty cards.

Explain the process of making this marketing resource productive.

The resource providers may also be viewed as stakeholders in the business. Organizations are, in effect, coalitions of stakeholders and it is the role of management to achieve a workable balance between the claims and interests of these groups. Shareholders, as the owners of the business, would seem to qualify as stakeholders, but strictly speaking, this term is reserved for the other providers of inputs or recipients of outputs, namely:

◆ Employees and management

◆ Suppliers and distributors

◆ Customers and creditors

◆ Local community and local government

The environmental context of the organization

The environment of business has never been so complex and challenging as it is today. Marketers, more than ever before, are confronted by increasing pressures and demands that they must seek to understand and respond to. At any given point in time, organizations will be confronted by a confusion of environmental factors that may or may not constitute threats to, or opportunities for the marketer (see Figure 2.1).

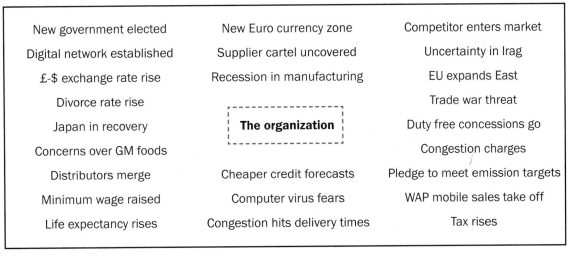

Figure 2.1 Environmental factors

To understand these, a classification is required of the persons, groups, trends and even events that affect an organization. External events can also affect an organization. Therefore a grasp of the big picture, the role of your organization and yourself within it is required.

Systems theory makes clear that every organization operates within an industry setting that in turn interacts with a societal environment that is itself influenced by a global marketplace. The global environment appears very distant to marketers operating on a regional or even a national scale, but with information technologies shrinking geographical dispersion and distances, these multinational operations are extending into every corner of the market-place. These influences may initially seep, but then cascade through into a business.

Insight

Ryanair, the low-cost airline, nearly had its business jeopardized in 2004 when the European Commission unexpectedly demanded repayment of 'illegal subsidies' arising from the cheaper fees it had negotiated with regional airports.

Dixons, the UK electrical giant, has phased out 35-mm cameras due to devastating competition from digital varieties.

To contextualize the micro-environment factors, which are relevant to the societal or macro-environment should also be classified. Within any society, all businesses face a common political, economic, social and technological environment, although any one element will often impact organizations differently depending on the size and situation of the latter. The key characteristic, however, is the inclusion of forces that impact on the business, creating opportunities and threats, but over which organizations have no real influence or control.

The macro-environment

The wider environment (Figure 2.2) over which the organization can exert little influence is often referred to by the acronym PEST (political, economic, socio-cultural, technological). The inclusion of a regulatory framework of laws, standards and customs converts the acronym to SLEPT (socio-cultural, legal, economic, political, technological) while the addition of ethics and environment (natural) converts it to STEEPLE. Several other acronyms such as DRETS (demographic, regulatory, economic, technological, socio-cultural) and PESTEL (political, economic, socio-cultural, technological, environmental, legal) are also used. Simply put, the various trends, events, threats and opportunities that occur in the environment can be classified in these categories.

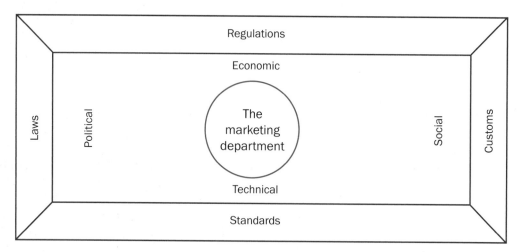

Figure 2.2 PEST factors and the regulatory framework

Although Units 4–8 will consider each of the macro-environments illustrated in Figure 2.2 in more detail, a brief overview is offered in the following sections.

Political factors

The role and impact of the government on businesses extends far beyond the setting of laws. The size of the public sector ensures a sizeable effect on business whether as supplier, customer, policy maker or regulator. The position of the government in power sets the climate for business. Thus, a change of party in office can significantly alter the thrust and direction of all aspects of their policies.

Political strife and uncertainty will also impact on business opportunities.

Terrorist attacks in Indonesia may deter direct investment while the Intifada against Israel involving the Holy Places disrupts tourism revenues. Outright war or tribal confrontation, as in parts of Africa, destroys economic resources and infrastructure. On the other hand, reconstruction, as in Iraq, creates significant, if risky, opportunities in the short term. However, business normally needs political stability to thrive so that commercial links may be developed and direct investments made.

Insight: International Charity Organization

For a marketer working in an international charity, the famine threatening southern Africa must be one of the biggest practical challenges ever faced. With an estimated 13 million people facing starvation, it is a product of turbulent and interacting macro-environmental forces. To address the problem the marketer needs to collect information in order to prioritize and focus responses. Malawi, Zambia, Mozambique, Angola, Niger and particularly Zimbabwe are badly affected in a situation where serious harvest shortfalls caused by flood and drought are compounded by the social ravages of HIV/AIDS. Political factors aggravate conditions particularly where grain reserves are corruptly disposed of, land seizure policies destroy the incentive to farm commercially and 700,000 are driven out in shanty town evictions (Operation Murambatsvina or Drive out Rubbish!). Maize production has fallen by over three-quarters over 2 years in Zimbabwe helping the inflation rate to rise to over 1600 per cent, the world's highest rate. A $100,000 note has just been introduced only four months after the $50,000 note was first printed but won't even buy a loaf of bread. This is also a disaster for neighbouring countries that used to import from this former 'breadbasket' of southern Africa.

The marketer, in raising awareness of the massive need for food aid, is confronted by donor countries that appear to be suffering from donor fatigue. This might reflect a growing belief that food crises are brought on primarily by corrupt governments and that any charity aid provided will only prop up repressive regimes. Central government control over distribution often means food aid is either denied to opposition party supporters or directly appropriated. On the other hand, China, in a bid to exert influence over resource-rich nations in Africa has pledged over $8 billion in 'no strings' loans to sub-Saharan Africa. This undermines attempts by Western banks to ensure that lending is ethical, sustainable and in accord with environmental and human rights principles. The international charity is largely powerless to control these macro-forces but it must still seek to fulfil its mission of helping the vulnerable.

Question 2.1

Can you contribute any ideas to help the marketer in this complex strategy process?

Economic factors

This is closely linked to the political environment and policies required to achieve government objectives. These impact on the costs, prices, competitiveness and profitability of businesses. The business pages of the quality press and/or the electronic pages of a news website are therefore required reading for the serious marketer since an understanding of the key economic indicators provides the necessary information for anticipating developments in the market-place.

Economic uncertainties also impact negatively on business and consumer confidence. The high but fluctuating level of oil price, for example, represents an advance indicator of future inflation and possible economic downturn.

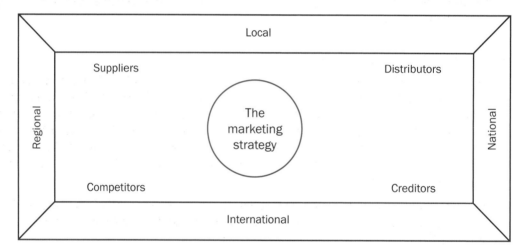

Figure 2.3 The four horizons

The economic horizons of businesses will vary greatly, as seen in Figure 2.3. Many sole traders compete in local convenience markets, but the conditions experienced here will often have cascaded down from conditions in the global economy. These in turn influence national economies and regions within them. The importance of international factors has increased in recent years with the development of e-commerce, the coming down of trading blocks, single markets and the formation of the World Trade Organization (WTO). Businesses that are reluctant to search out the opportunities presented by these developments may soon find their profitable niche markets exposed to new and often globally distant competitors.

Social or socio-cultural factors

This is perhaps the most difficult environment for the marketer to identify, evaluate and respond to. It includes changes in population characteristics, educational standards, culture, lifestyles, attitudes and beliefs. The way we think, live and behave is the outcome of complex cultural conditioning by family, friends, school, church, work and the various media. The former are referred to as reference groups. It conditions what we buy, where we buy, when we buy it, how we buy. Do we tend to use credit cards or cash for example?

Forty-five per cent of British consumers agreed that they give in to temptation and buy things because they like them and not because they need them. This was up from 30 per cent 20 years ago. Increasing growths in personal disposable income (an economic factor) has had much impact on spending patterns.

Social and demographic change may appear to change slowly, yet their impacts are likely to far outweigh any consequences of political decisions over the longer term. The trends towards lower and later births and the corresponding ageing of the population, for example, will generate massive changes over time in patterns of work and spending. Similarly, human migration, whether between continents or within an expanded economic block like the European Union, has brought social exposure to different values and outlooks as well as potential conflicts.

Technical or technological factors

These factors refer to the means, methods and knowledge that could be embraced and utilized by organizations. It is the primary means by which the production possibilities of society and the productivity of scarce resources can be expanded, enabling more wants to be satisfied. It also constitutes threats to those organizations that fail to innovate new and better products and processes. On the other hand, Bic has sold more than 100 billion Biros since 1950, enough to stretch to the moon and back 40 times, while Coca-Cola sells more than 300 billion bottles a year.

The lead time between invention, innovation and market introduction has shrunk significantly with the application of computer technology, while the development of telecommunications has combined to make the global economy a reality.

Factors affecting the speed of the diffusion process are dealt with in Unit 8. However, you will personally be experiencing the shortening lead times to critical mass of important innovations such as the fax (20–25 years), the VCR (10–15 years), the Internet (5–8 years), the WAP connected mobile (3–5 years?) and e-commerce (3–5 years?). All businesses face the challenges implied but only the more alert, flexible and proactive will translate them into opportunities and profit. Indeed Coca-Cola has launched more than 1000 new drinks or variations of existing brands world-wide this year with Coke Zero, a sugar-free version for men, leading the way. The marketing and strategy director, Mary Minnick, is also shifting the corporate image away from sugar-laden junk drinks by experimenting with 'nutraceutical' products designed to help women with skin care, weight management and detoxification.

Environmental factors

These factors can be positive (e.g. transform an arid land into productive land) or can also be negative (e.g. pollution or encroachment on rainforests). Customers are increasingly conscious of the quality and sustainability of their living environment and any marketer that fails to take these concerns fully into account will pay a heavy price. Fuller consideration of this important element in the marketing environment will be developed later in this unit as well as in Unit 4.

Activity 2.2

Key skills – Collecting and presenting information

Prepare a regular business environment brief. Produce a summary of the main events and developments affecting a business of your choice over the past week. Use the elements in your micro- and macro-environment as your headings.

Exam hint

Key skills for marketers

Activity 2.2 is an ideal means of developing the key skill of 'presenting information'. Preparing a brief involves reading and synthesizing information. Giving a brief involves making a presentation, while group participation involves contribution to discussions. All of these elements together with writing different types of documents constitute the CIM definition of this skill.

Activity 2.3

Key skills – Collecting and interpreting information

Take a typical workday of a marketing executive and log occasions and actions that link your organization to its environment.

Hint: This should include items on news bulletins and in the local papers.

Activity 2.4

Key skill – Reflection

A recurring theme in this coursebook is that various environments are in a continuous state of often-turbulent change.

What do you think this means?

What evidence do you have from the marketing environment to support your arguments?

The marketing environment is often described as being turbulent. Although this term is frequently used, it can however imply a range of very different characteristics. These can be as follows:

◆ The term 'turbulent' may suggest an environment in a degree of turmoil, buffeted by uncontrollable forces that continuously disturb any tendency towards stability.

Virtually no organization operates in static conditions, and interest centres on the degree of turbulence that may vary from industry to industry.

◆ Turbulence may suggest confusion and a state of flux.

The increasingly competitive nature of many markets fits such conditions, as could the current outlook for world stock markets, the future price of oil or the value of the once mighty dollar.

◆ Turbulence also implies uncertainty and discontinuity, but is not as strong a term as chaos or revolution.

One could argue that genetic engineering is potentially transforming the agricultural landscape or that a gender revolution is currently under way. However the timescale seems sufficiently long to remove much of the uncertainty.

On the other hand, the process of invention and innovation is inherently unpredictable along with the extremes of weather and natural disasters (acts of God) that have seemingly increased in frequency over recent years:

1 Witness the 100,000 death toll of the earthquake that devastated Kashmir in Autumn 2005 (the $5.4 billion pledged by international donors prompted President Musharraf to respond that this world is truly a global village) or the Caribbean suffering its worst hurricane season in 100 years as Ivan, Frances, Katrina, Rita and Wilma claimed hundreds of lives and caused tens of billions of dollars' worth of damage.

2 In 2004, the worst draught in 500 years sparked wildfires across the Western United States, engulfing four million acres, and this was repeated in 2006 when a heatwave caused massive power cuts as consumers put air conditioning on full.

3 The level of the Mekong river fell so low as to threaten the livelihoods of up to 100 million in Southeast Asia.

4 Low rainfall has contributed to this, but the major cause is the completion of massive dam projects in China.

5 All of these sources of natural turbulence were dwarfed by the 26 December 2004 earthquake off the coast of Indonesia registering 8.9 on the Richter scale. The dreadful consequences of the resulting tsunami on the surrounding coastlines are common knowledge but the marketing consequences for tourism, and the local economies that depend on it, will be enduring.

6 It was unsurprising that Lloyds of London declared a significant insurance loss for 2005 but more worryingly officials were still unprepared for the 5-metre wave that hit Southern Java in 2006. Despite seismic warnings these were not acted on and 500 died.

Clearly there is an array of variable environmental forces that are operating to produce a degree of ambiguity for the marketer regarding probable patterns of the future. Apart from technological forces there are other trends including globalization, religious fundamentalism and variable economic growth rates to drive the turbulence. The uncertain state of Russia, China, East Asia and many emerging countries, together with the still unfolding consequences of a post-September 11 America (and post-7/7 Britain) provides a basis for current and future volatility.

Turbulent conditions do not necessarily imply adversity for organizations. Opportunities as well as threats are created and businesses vary in their ability to 'ride' the market rapids. Swiss pharmaceutical multinational Roche is set to make millions from its anti-bird-flu vaccine, for example, despite early worries over demand and potential profitability. Recent concerns about intense farming have made organic produce very attractive. Equally, much of the associated cost may be shared with, or transferred onto, the consumer (in higher prices), the workforce (redundancies), competitors (lower sales), suppliers (lower prices), the government (subsidies/bail outs) and other stakeholder groups.

Dynamic and complex conditions

These are the two critical dimensions by which marketing environments may be judged, the dynamic and the complex. There is a spectrum of market possibilities ranging from completely static to extremely dynamic conditions in a given environment. Similarly, there is a degree of environmental complexity from the very simple (i.e. a single clear cause and effect) to the extremely complex (with many and varied interdependent causes).

Activity 2.5

Key skills – Problem-solving

Locate on a matrix of increasing environmental complexity and dynamism the following organizations: a funeral director; a computer software manufacturer; a university; a biscuit manufacturer; a pop group; an advertising agency; your own organization.

Dynamic conditions

◆ These are associated with high-energy driving forces within a wider environment with relatively few frictions.

◆ They suggest markets where significant and potentially powerful environmental forces are in motion, often producing rapid growth, change and development, and these drive the situation in which the organization finds itself.

◆ Emerging markets, driven by invention, accelerating innovation and an explosion in information technology, are clear examples of such change.

◆ Globalization with its flows of direct investment responding to changing exchange rates, labour market conditions and economic performance is another source of creative energy in the world economy.

◆ Dynamic conditions can be unleashed by a catalyst such as the deregulation of an industry (i.e. the airline industry in the USA), new channels of communication (Internet and mobile phone), new entry into a market or the changing demands of a stakeholder group.

◆ Government policy can also release dynamic conditions when red tape is curtailed and incentives for work and enterprise are enhanced.

◆ Competition policy may also be sharpened to encourage the process of creative destruction.

Activity 2.6

Key skills – Critical thinking and reflection

Think of a situation where competition policy has had a positive effect on the marketing environment.

Think of a situation where competition policy has had an adverse effect on the marketing environment.

Complex conditions

◆ Complex conditions are said to occur when diverse influences are exerted upon a market. Subsequently analysis becomes complicated.

◆ When many variables are involved, these can be interdependent or can react with one another through both positive and negative feedback loops.

◆ An example of a sustained feedback loop is shown in Figure 2.4. Negative feedback would occur if the process is reversed.

◆ Systems theory discussed in Unit 1 has demonstrated the intricate complexity of economic and social systems. These are however extremely difficult to model. For instance, weather forecasts, despite sophisticated computer analysis and simulation, are frequently criticized for their imperfections. Indeed we are quite far away from convincingly modelling societal change:

1 Complexity is very much like a 'black box'; we observe flows in and out, we apply trial and error and make predictions but we do not yet fully know how it works!

2 This is arguably why organizations are still spending so much money and energy to assess the marketing environment.

We will see later that most markets are not simple and that analysis requires consideration of at least five forces. Alternative outcomes are likely due to the interdependence of rivals. They may seek to manage the complexity through agreements and understandings but the tension created by pursuit of competitive advantage and the potential for a zero-sum game (I win/you lose) creates many options and complex uncertainties.

Figure 2.4 Sustained feedback loop

◆ Complexity means that marketers are faced by a succession of non-routine problems and situations demanding action.

◆ A few will be simple or repetitive and therefore likely to be addressed adequately and systematically through standard policy responses.

◆ Predictability is likely to be low, the environment dynamic and any action will cause reaction through a highly interconnected system. The fall in retail sales that brought M&S to crisis resulted in positive corporate actions which not only reverberated within internal departments and along the supply chain, but also to downmarket competitors (as prices have been cut) and upmarket designers:

   ◆ While more downmarket competitors in the UK such as Primark and Peacocks have extended their range and quality of products, upmarket designers have become more accessible through their selective lines in such stores as House of Fraser, Debenhams, John Lewis.

   ◆ However as Marks and Spencer also attempted to refine its offerings, a record share price and profits were up a third by late 2006. This appears set to reinforce the positive loop despite a relatively adverse trading climate.

Question 2.1

Have you heard of the 'butterfly effect'? A butterfly beating its wings in Outer Mongolia is said to affect the weather sometime later in northern England.

Can seemingly insignificant events have a transforming impact?

Can you think of an example within the marketing environment?

Is this a good case for joining a pressure group and starting some ripples?

Adaptability – the proactive response

It has been said that people's ability to change is the critical limiting factor in exploiting the full potential of information and other new technologies.

Resistance to change can arise anywhere in the marketing environment. As Henry Ford observed, 'If I had asked people what they wanted they would have said faster horses.' Management can be the countervailing force in reducing resistance or driving change, but may equally form a constraint. What is it that makes for an adaptable organization in the face of dynamic and complex change? Points to consider would include the following:

◆ Management must actively confront a difficult environment, not passively accept it.

◆ Reliance on accumulated experience and perceptions only permits reaction.

◆ Management must forecast change if it is to act proactively.

◆ One approach is to assess the environment and adapt by making business and marketing changes that resonate with it and its anticipated trends and changes. This continuous adaptation achieves a dynamic equilibrium between internal strengths and capabilities as well as external opportunities.

◆ Organic organizations, which favour decentralization of decision-making power and rapid communication up and down the chain of command, are best as bureaucratic methods tend to only be workable in relatively static conditions.

◆ Contingency plans are a means of dealing with future uncertainty. This approach could be informed by risk analysis to assess the probability and likely impact of possible environmental changes:

  ◆ Executives could be trained in crisis management.

  ◆ In 2007 when salmonella was found in one of Cadburys' main chocolate product, the company was swift in recalling entire batches of this product. Although the brand did suffer, the prompt crisis management achieved much damage control.

◆ Adaptability demands flexibility to meet new threats and opportunities.

◆ Organizations must embrace change and innovation and not wait until the maturity stage of the life cycle. The success of current product lines can create powerful resistance and even inhibit necessary development of the products of the future:

◆ Companies like 3M formalize continuous innovation in their policies as the mobile phone industry is particularly dynamic and competitive.

Even the most sophisticated environmental scanning and forecasting techniques will only be able to consider cost-effectively a limited proportion of the total of potentially useful information available. Unfortunately due to the strain on resources, many organizations decide that the change is too difficult to manage proactively and choose instead to shadow the actions of competitors as a strategy against being isolated and caught out. An alternative approach is to plan to create your own environment based on your own view or vision of the future. Action is taken to share this vision with stakeholders and build relationships that allow a flexible response to turbulence throughout its micro-environment. The organization sets the market agenda and competitors are left to follow. This said, such a course of action not only requires the right level of knowledge but also resources (i.e. money, men and measures).

The micro-environment

The micro-environment includes key stakeholders with a close, two-way operational relationship with the business. The micro-environment is controllable to some degree. As illustrated in Figure 2.5 below, the micro-environment consists of several factors. If an organization wishes to do more than just optimize its own performance, it must optimize the performance of its whole value chain.

Question 2.2

Key skills – Problem-solving

Can you allocate the elements in Figure 2.5 to the appropriate global/macro-/micro-environment?

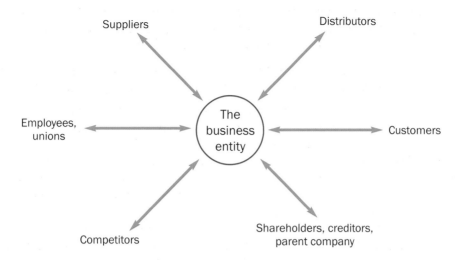

Figure 2.5 The micro-firm environment

Suppliers

No firm can supply all of its own needs. Materials, components, fuel and a host of business services are necessary inputs. Suppliers are a critical link with the environment, a source of cost but also of possible partnership. Car manufacturers for example may have hundreds of suppliers involving a two-way dependence. The suppliers need the manufacturers as business-to-business customers to sell their offerings whereas the car manufacturers (the producers) need the parts offered by suppliers to build their products (the vehicles). They are now streamlining in favour of 'preferred suppliers' in key areas, but demanding in return long-term contracts, total quality, just-in-time delivery, research and design support. Dependence on one or two suppliers, however, has considerable risks, just as it is risky for the smaller business with only one or two customers. Any action or decision may have critical consequences.

Significance of suppliers within the marketing process:

◆ Availability, delivery times and quality of the product are the key determinants.

◆ Costs of materials are an important factor in the total cost of many products.

◆ The supply chain may have many links and be susceptible to disruption.

◆ The relative power of suppliers is often critical and depends on size, substitutes and degree of actual competition between them.

◆ The quality of the supplier relationship is a crucial parameter in marketing effectiveness.

◆ Suppliers can assume the stockholding function, allowing maximum space for selling.

◆ If partnership fails to deliver marketing benefits, backward integration may be considered.

Exam hint

It is essential that you achieve a sound grasp of these basic environmental concepts. As you saw in the examples of exam questions at the end of Unit 1, they occur frequently as part of different questions referring to the environment.

Competitors

These are the exceptions in the micro-environment in that normally they continuously threaten rather than contribute to the survival of the business. As we will explore in Unit 3, the reality of competition may be in the form of hundreds of similar rivals, as in catering, or a handful of powerful multinationals, as in pharmaceuticals, or increasingly more likely a number of small, technically sophisticated and marketing-focused dot-com competitors.

Competition can also result in take-over, as in the case of the French giant L'Oreal's acquisition of Body Shop for £652 million. As a top target for animal rights campaigners because of its engagement in vivisection for research and development purposes, L'Oreal is getting a strong, ethically sound brand. Body Shop has traditionally been associated with ethical trading and sources. However, the real difficulty for L'Oreal may lie in convincing Tesco and other wholesale stakeholders that acquiring Body Shop stores in 53 countries is not going to represent a competitive threat.

The relationship is again two-way in that while competitors can constrain the achievements of the business, the marketing department can also shape and influence the competitive environment. Business has the discretion to adjust its marketing mix as conditions change. Therefore, a truly marketing-orientated company will ensure that its strategies, plans, tactics and responses will be decided not based on its internal factors (i.e. its strengths and weaknesses) but also and perhaps even more importantly with careful reference to changing threats and opportunities from the external environment.

Significance of competitors within the marketing process:

◆ No business can make decisions without reference to its competitive environment.

◆ Even a monopoly must be concerned about potential entrants or effective substitutes. (This situation tends to be rather rare nowadays.)

◆ Pricing must account for what the market will bear and the reactions of competitors.

◆ The more competitors there are and the closer their product/service offerings are (i.e. relatively undifferentiated), the more sensitively sales tend to respond to a relative change in price. (What for instance could be the likely response if the price of a loaf of Hovis Wholemeal bread increases by 50 per cent?)

◆ Price wars may erupt from time to time but non-price competition using branding and other product and promotional tactics are the norm. This is because competitive edge based on price can be relatively easy to mimic.

Customers

All businesses have customers as the final link in the input/output chain, whether these customers are organizations (business-to-business trade – B2B) or individuals (business-to-customer trade – B2C). The idea that they are stakeholders is less familiar, although the choice of withdrawing their stake or not will determine the success or failure of the enterprise. The marketer is therefore crucially concerned with all the influences affecting them.

Significance of customers within the marketing process:

◆ Customers are the only source of revenue for most organizations.

◆ If they withdraw or transfer their custom to a competitor then profit, growth and even sometimes survival are threatened.

◆ An unsatisfied customer tells many more of the experience than does a satisfied one. (Consider the effect of word of mouth.)

◆ Customer retention is normally more cost-effective than recruiting new ones due to the lifetime revenue stream that is often involved. It also costs more to attract a new customer than it does to retain an existing customer or to re-awaken a dormant or lapsed customer. Think of all the advertising costs incurred to create brand/product/service awareness and to attract new customers.

◆ Customers are looking at value for money. This is a combination of the broadly defined satisfaction deriving from consumption of the product and its relative price. However, value for money is subjective. A sticky toffee pudding from Marks and Spencer costing £4.99 may be considered value for money by one customer and be regarded as expensive by another customer.

◆ Customer preferences can change very quickly but can be influenced by the marketer. Microsoft believes in leading the market but by following the customer.

◆ Customer knowledge and scope for comparison is expanding through use of the Internet.

Intermediaries and distributors

These must also be considered as an organization does not always sell directly to the consumer. For example, Black and Decker's products are not sold to customers in Black and Deckers retail outlets but at Woolworths and Robert Dyas.

Intermediaries and distributors are important elements of the marketing channel that makes the product available to the user. They may include wholesalers, retailers, dealers, agents and franchisees.

Marketing services such as market research, advertising, media and consultancies are also in this category. Here, creativity and quality must be balanced against service and price. Their power may be significant not least in respect of retailer brands that may be promoted aggressively at the expense of manufacturer offerings. Tying in distributors may provide a competitive edge over rivals.

Significance of intermediaries and distributors within the marketing process:

◆ Distributors who are ineffective in delivering the product to the customer as, where and when they want it will negatively impact on the business. There is a need to balance cost, delivery, speed and safety.

◆ Effective partners deliver advantage in the form of transport, stock management, market knowledge, merchandising and display, together with after-sales service. They have a critical impact on availability, timing, quality and price.

◆ The marketer must be able communicate with both the final customer and the distributor(s) delivering the product to the latter (the end-user/the customer).

◆ Distributors have economic leverage arising from their strategic position that is becoming fewer in number but more powerful.

◆ They have mutual interests that form the basis of joint ventures and partnerships.

◆ E-commerce may lead to dis-intermediation in the value chain as manufacturers consider direct marketing to consumers.

Exam hint

Remember the course you are studying is first and foremost about the environment. Do not be tempted to answer questions in marketing terms alone.

Shareholders and creditors

Shareholders provide the longer-term capital while creditors such as banks and other financial institutions provide short- and medium-term funds. They can affect the business through the sale of shares or withdrawal of credit. Small businesses are particularly vulnerable to the creditor in times of recession while institutional shareholders, such as pension funds, are becoming more active in their scrutiny of public company management and remuneration.

Significance of shareholders and creditors within the marketing process:

◆ These are important to the organization. Therefore clear and timely communication with them based on an understanding of the needs of both parties is required.

◆ Adverse shareholder perceptions may lead to selling, which drives down the market valuation of the company relative to its net asset value, thereby risking unwelcome bids.

◆ Trade and bank credit are critical to a healthy cash flow, so relationships should be nurtured.

◆ The public image of the business is largely the responsibility of marketing and of public relations.

Employees and unions

Most businesses, except sole traders as discussed in Unit 1, have employees who contribute their time and skills for monetary and other rewards. They form part of a wider society and reflect its values and beliefs. They are directly affected by company activities, including harmful ones, but again the effects are two ways. They can unionize, adversely affect productivity, leave or have equally positive effects on company fortunes. The decline in trade unions has affected the freedom of many organizations and industries. Increased legislation on health, safety, employment and pollution has also added many parameters.

Significance of employees and unions within the marketing process:

- As with customers, retention of skilled staff is normally more cost-effective than the uncertainties of recruitment. Experienced employees also tend to be better at their jobs, hence have higher levels of productivity.

- The image of the organization is an important determinant in the quality of applicant attracted – it will attract the calibre of employees it deserves.

- Internal marketing in critical departments is central to the achievement of goals.

- The evolution of virtual companies will make staff much more mobile, forcing organizations to rethink remuneration and training packages.

- Increasingly employees are being regarded as internal customers.

- The effect of employees on customers is also generally appreciated nowadays. Consequently, training of employees is being conducted more than ever before.

Activity 2.7

Key skills – Interpreting information

Taking a business with which you are familiar, identify and rank its five most important suppliers, distributors, competitors, customers and creditors.

What marketing mix does it employ to:

- Retain and motivate its distributors?
- Secure a competitive edge over its rivals?

The micro-environment is of general importance to the marketing process, for the following reasons:

- The marketer can utilize the marketing mix to influence and impact on all the stakeholders.

- The same stakeholders can both damage or advantage the business.

- The micro-environment includes not only actual customers, suppliers, intermediaries and competitors but also potential ones.

◆ The marketing mix can also be deployed to convert potential customers into actual ones or to discourage potential competitors from entering the market.

◆ Successful businesses are often those that are part of larger 'clusters' of collective activity. The Dutch bulb industry is a world-beater because of the concentration of suppliers, research organizations, producers, competitors and intermediaries that complement, strengthen and support one another.

◆ Such clusters of networked organizations are preferred in e-commerce value chains.

◆ It generates a tension between competition and co-operation. Businesses compete for customers and sometimes compete for shelf space with distributors, but equally they may co-operate with suppliers over new product development or with interme- diaries for joint promotions. The marketer must assess the pay-off associated with both approaches.

◆ It forms the immediate or operational environment for the marketer and drives tac- tical responses on a daily basis. Macro-environment changes tend to drive strategic responses.

◆ The marketer is the critical interface between key stakeholders and the organization.

Stakeholder pressures

Stakeholders are defined as any group or individual who can affect or are affected by the achievement of the organization's objectives. Since they have a stake, a legitimate interest in the business, they can influence objectives. Management cannot hope to operate in iso- lation but must seek to satisfy their stakeholders' legitimate expectations if they are to con- tribute value in return (Figure 2.6).

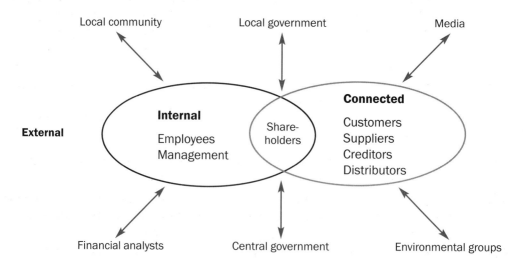

Figure 2.6 Internal, connected and external stakeholders

Direct or connected stakeholders are closely related to the core economic functions of the business. Together with the pressure exerted by competitors, they can change the goals and nature of the organization unless managed effectively.

There is a considerable potential for conflict of interest between the primary stakeholder groups. Higher wages for employees may conflict with shareholder profits or result in higher prices that upset customers. Local community concerns for health and safety may increase costs, reduce competitiveness and jeopardize jobs.

If any stakeholder considers they are not receiving sufficient return, they may withdraw their contribution to the organization. If customers no longer feel a product is value for money they will buy elsewhere. Some airlines with options on the delayed A380 super-jumbo, for example, re-considered the attractions of Boeing. If workers consider their remuneration too low, they will change jobs and their contribution, expertise and experience will be lost.

Balancing these partly conflicting stakeholder expectations while achieving objectives of growth, market share and profitability is not easily achieved, not least in times of rapid change. Internal marketing is now widely recognized as an essential part of any manager's role. Implementation and fulfilment of business strategies requires that managers identify groups of internal as well as external stakeholders and market their plans to them.

Stakeholder	Pressure exerted	Expectations
Shareholders	Delegate decision power to board but recent increase in activism over remuneration and appointments. Selling shares is the real threat as a falling share price attracts takeover predators	Above average return on equity, improving return on assets, share value rising and growth in market valuation
Employees	Absenteeism, turnover, low morale, whistle-blowing (media leaks), unionization, poor-quality work, weak productivity, lack of co-operation, unwillingness to change	Above average remuneration, training and skill development, company growth/promotion, employment security/job satisfaction, improving conditions and wages
Customers	Reduce purchases, buy from competitors, organize boycott, complain to other potential customers, press for legislation	Value for money, convenience, product safety/quality assurance, innovation/improved design, better service
Creditors	Limit credit, withdraw credit, cut credit rating, charge higher rates	Regular/timely repayment, earlynotification of problems
Distributors	Stock and promote competing brands/own label, integrate backwards, delay payment	Reliable supplies, support in promotion, progressive product development, good communications
Suppliers	Supply competitors, reduce priority, limit trade credit, poor-quality service, integrate forward	Reliable payment, regular supply schedules, development support, ability to interrogate stock/production systems

Indirect or external stakeholder groups are not directly engaged in the business operations but can exert influence on and are seriously affected by their activities. A few of these are listed below for each group.

General public

◆ This group collectively represents the nation's householders, consumers, workers, pensioners and many other sub-categories of wider society.

◆ Their attitudes and expectations are important and reflected in opinion polls.

◆ They matter to organizations because public concerns and beliefs impact on their economic decisions. Companies recognize this and the need to market themselves effectively through public relations expenditure:

  ◆ Large companies like IBM and Disney invest considerable time and resources in building and maintaining a positive public image.

  ◆ For example, Walkers Crisps, owned by PepsiCo, is currently sponsoring a 'walking' campaign to encourage healthier lifestyles.

  ◆ The company now accounts for 45 per cent of the £1.4 billion market following a decade-long series of celebrity advertisements (celebrity endorsements) featuring Gary Lineker. This move is said to have eventually forced rival Golden Wonder into administration.

Local government

◆ Interested not only in the investment, jobs, prosperity, tax revenue and prestige the organization generates locally but also in its compliance with relevant legislation, planning requirements, health and safety regulations and so on. One example of this stakeholder power is the anti-smoking laws, which now have to be applied to all workplaces, bars and restaurants.

Communities

◆ Concerned with property values, quality of life, jobs and prosperity, congestion, links with local schools and charitable activities.

◆ Can protest, mobilize the media and obstruct planning applications.

◆ While it is clearly sensible for a potentially hazardous plant in an urban location, with all its attendant risks, to take account of residents and neighbourhood organizations, the same logic applies to service organizations, like banks.

◆ Sponsorship and openness will be two of the means deployed to maintain good relations.

Financial analysts

◆ Assess past/future performance in financial and broader terms.

◆ They downgrade where suspicious of unethical behaviour and highlight undervalued assets/possible takeover.

◆ Shareholders usually tend to listen to them.

◆ Public companies, in particular, need to be aware of the information needs of these stakeholders and their influence on the company's ability to raise funds. Therefore the organization must market itself effectively to such groups to ensure that their sentiment remains positive.

Media

◆ These include news, articles, features and editorials carried by television, newspapers, radio, journals, magazines and the Internet (e.g. bloggers, online communities, social networks such as Facebook and Bebo).

◆ They can seriously enhance or damage the public image of the business.

◆ They publicize issues and corporate achievements and form a line of communication from the organization to the local/national community. The marketer must therefore seek to develop good relationships with media representatives to ensure that the organization's point of view is heard.

Central government

◆ Governments often hold a controlling influence over many public sector organizations and so are direct stakeholders.

◆ They make, interpret and enforce laws, monitor compliance, levy taxes and implement economic policies.

◆ They also provide infrastructure, spend, protect, subsidize, rescue and restructure.

◆ There is a clear need to establish effective two-way dialogue between relevant central and local agencies, and the marketing function.

◆ The organization may seek influence through trade associations, lobbying, provision of information, joint projects and even political donations. In the UK more transparency is increasingly being sought with regards to party funding.

Environment pressure groups

◆ Business decisions may be challenged by a variety of action groups concerned over specific causes or interests.

◆ They can protest, resist development and generate considerable media attention.

◆ By means for instance of interlinkages between the stakeholders, communities may exert pressure on government to get their case heard or use the media to make their point.

◆ One cause that has recently marched into prominence is ethical trading as represented by the Rough Guides and Lonely Planet books coming together to encourage travellers to fly less, stay longer and donate to carbon offset schemes.

◆ The dramatic expansion of the Fair Trade symbol, which has been mentioned in Unit 1, increased from 150 to 1500 products since 2003:

  1 To sell under this logo companies must pay proper wages plus a premium to be invested in the community.

  2 Environmental standards must be met and the charity applies a 1.8 per cent levy on wholesale prices to fund inspection.

  3 A virtuous circle of scrutiny is thereby established between all stakeholders that drives up standards.

Of course, not all stakeholders have the same degree of influence and power. Thus, environmental stakeholders need to be assessed according to their level of interest in the organization's activities on the one hand, and their real power to influence outcomes on the other.

Figure 2.7 shows an application of this analytical tool to a college.

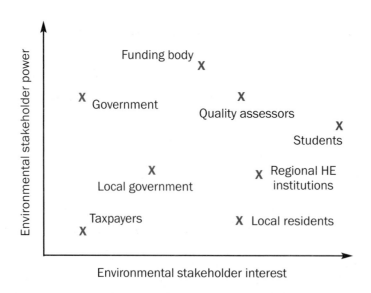

Figure 2.7 Stakeholder mapping: college of higher education

Activity 2.8

Can you think of any other indirect or external stakeholder groups?

Insight

At the other end of the spectrum, big tobacco companies are responding to the imminent outlawing of smoking in public places in England in mid-2007 and existing bans in Eire and parts of the United States. British American Tobacco has invested in developing new ways of giving people a nicotine hit. They are seeking to create a market for Snus, a form of snuff which is sold in teabag-like pouches that users place in the mouth. Snus is currently banned in the European Union with the exception of Sweden, where it outsells cigarettes and is credited with helping to reduce lung cancer to the lowest rate in the world. The EU is now reviewing its ban with a view to using Snus as a 'cessation aid'. Companies are also massively increasing their sales in the Middle East despite anti-US feelings. They formed lobby groups in the 1980s and used influential Arab contacts to win sympathetic press coverage and defeat anti-smoking legislation. When Muslim clerics issued fatwas against smoking, they even funded Islamic seminaries to promote alternative fatwas in favour of the habit. Much perhaps could be learned by Coalition policymakers from 'big tobacco's' intuitive understanding of the Islamic milieu.

Activity 2.9

You should actively relate the stakeholders defined above to your own organization.

Alternatively you could select another organization and relate the stakeholders defined above to your choice.

This will help you understand how interlinked stakeholders, whether direct or indirect, can be.

Insight: McDonald's – keeping stakeholders on side

McDonald's has felt the full brunt of its external stakeholders in recent years (see 'Cutting the fat at McDonalds' in the December 2003 paper). It misjudged the public surge of sympathy for a protesting local French sheep farmer who 'trashed' their restaurant in Millau. This case was widely reported by the media and compounded a 40 per cent fall in sales of McDonald's as consumer confidence in the safety of French beef all but collapsed following a spate of BSE (mad cow disease) cases. McDonald's also had to confront religious pressure groups in Italy where it was seeking to double its chain of

272 outlets. A Catholic newspaper attacked fast food as targeting the 'holiness of food' and fit only for other religious groups. Such coverage reflects the hostility of those who view McDonald's as the unacceptable face of American-dominated global capitalism. Profits have fallen sharply in the United Kingdom leading to closure of 25 outlets, and even in the United States, it faces threats from other fast food chains, such as Subway and Burger King for instance. Lawyers have also threatened the company's image by claiming that its Big Macs are not only unhealthy but also addictive. There is an increasing resentment that US fast food has usurped local, historic cuisines and helped to homogenize town centres. British high streets are now depressingly similar with big chains dominating nearly half of them. Whether this will deflect the general public from the convenience of fast food in the longer term remains to be seen. On a more positive note the British Hedgehog Preservation Society persuaded the company, after six years of lobbying, to re-design its McFlurry dessert pots to make them safer for hedgehogs.

This example demonstrates how even multinationals like McDonald's ideally need all stakeholders on side if they are to overcome the challenge of market diversity within the global economy as well as fight back within an increasingly competitive marketing environment.

Activity 2.10

Key skills – Using information

Draw up a stakeholder map for your own organization or an organization of your choice.

Consider the criteria you are using in assessing the relative power and influence of each.

It is clear that most organisations can no longer only focus on themselves. The behaviour of companies has become everybody's business and organizations must recognize that they are under the watchful gaze of all the above stakeholders from time to time. Pressure groups, for example, exert legislative and ethical pressure in seeking to change business objectives, policies and behaviour in various ways. For example, large firms should pay smaller ones more promptly, top executives should set an example in their remuneration practices and employ a higher proportion of women and minority groups in senior positions.

The stakeholders of any organization are unique, but may either threaten and challenge its objectives and operations or support them. It is therefore vitally important that the business 'knows its stakeholders', since from knowledge comes the power to deal with them effectively.

Question 2.3

In what sense are you a stakeholder in CIM and how might you seek to influence the organization?

Pressure groups

Pressure groups are one of the more important elements in which an organization may have actual or potential interest. Pressure groups can have a huge impact on the activities of an organization or its ability to achieve its objectives.

Usually pressure groups do the following:

◆ Represent subsections of the population organized on the basis of specific common interests or attitudes.

◆ Exert pressure on people, organizations or government for their own special purpose.

◆ Seek to influence the context of government decisions.

◆ Do not seek election to government office and are not political parties. There is a big difference between a political party (e.g. the Green Party) and a pressure group (e.g. Friends of the Earth).

◆ Exercise pressure both for the purpose of securing favourable decisions and for preventing undesirable ones.

It is important to make the distinction between a sectional or interest group, whose membership is based on the performance of a specific economic role, and a promotional or cause group, who are bound by shared values or attitudes and seek to promote a particular issue or prevent an adverse outcome. The latter may be formed to fight a specific issue and then disbanded when it has won or lost. For instance a pressure group consisting of local residents attempted in vain to prevent the project to build Terminal 5 at Heathrow airport. Some can be personally threatening as in the case of activists seeking to halt animal testing. Following a sustained campaign against Huntingdon Life Sciences they have recently sent threatening letters to thousands of small shareholders in drugs giant Glaxo encouraging them to sell their shares.

Activity 2.11

Key skills – Use information

List the pressure groups you have belonged to and classify them into the groups described in this section. Do the same for the following: Chambers of Commerce, the Mothers' Union, Campaign for Real Ale (CAMRA), British Medical Association.

Examples of sectional pressure groups include trade unions, consumer associations, trade associations and businesses themselves. Industry bodies such as the Nigerian Chamber of Commerce, the Ceylon National Chamber of Industries or the Trades Union Congress (TUC) are representative organizations.

There are numerous promotional groups. These have expanded rapidly in recent years. They fall into several groups and each country will have examples under the various headings. In the UK, these tend to be classified as follows:

Welfare	Age Concern, Royal Society for the Prevention of Cruelty to Animals (RSPCA), Action on Smoking & Health (ASH), NSPCC
Recreation	National Cyclists' Union, Ramblers Association
Cultural	Citizens' Advice Bureau, Lord's Day Observance Society
Environmental	International Fund for Animal Welfare (IFAW), Noise Abatement Society, Greenpeace
Political	Amnesty International, Campaign against Racial Discrimination
International	Oxfam, Médecins sans Frontières, Save the Children Fund, Red Crescent Society, Red Cross

Pressure groups are the activists of the stakeholder groups considered so far. They enable the individual to be heard on important issues by joining forces with like-minded people whether locally or nationally. Groups can arise to fight factory or hospital closures, ban hunting with hounds, challenge unacceptable business practices, or fight motorway proposals/airport extensions. They will usually use all means at their disposal to achieve their objectives:

◆ *Complain* (e.g. to the local media)

◆ *Inform and persuade* those likely to be affected

◆ *Debate and challenge* at local meetings

◆ *Lobby and petition* elected/representatives and state officials

◆ *Canvass and form opinion* among stakeholder groups

◆ *March and demonstrate* outside the factory gates/Parliament

◆ *Demand and negotiate* action and concessions from the company

◆ *Take legal action*

◆ Other means include alliances, information leaks, infiltration of the organization targeted, opinion forming, bribery and misinformation and blackmailing.

The formal channels through which pressure groups function are as follows:

◆ Pressure through government:

    ◆ Formal pressure may be applied when the group is invited to give evidence to commissions, or committees of inquiry.

    ◆ Government departments will consult directly with recognized and responsible pressure groups to sound out views on proposed legislation.

    ◆ Input at the initial drafting stage is an important advantage.

    ◆ Governments cannot legislate effectively without consultation with interested parties, and these are part of the routine relationships it maintains.

◆ Pressure through the legislature:

    ◆ Pressure groups will seek to recruit sympathetic elected representatives to their cause.

- These people are concerned with any matters affecting their constituencies and re-election prospects; they are therefore susceptible to particular issues and causes.

- Businesses often employ professional lobbyists to identify and mobilize such support for their interests.

- Elected representatives can introduce proposed legislation and ask questions during debates to publicize a cause, but this is normally much less effective than pressure exerted through government ministers and departments.

- The need to disclose earnings arising out of representation may also constrain such pressures.

◆ Pressure through public campaign:

- Educational and propaganda campaigns can be mounted to move public opinion in the longer term.

- Attention in the short term will tend to focus on raising public and stakeholder awareness and seeking to mobilize them against a specific threat using public meetings, demonstrations, petitions, newspaper advertisements and exposure in the media in general.

- This now includes the collection of electronic petitions and co-ordination of protests over the Internet.

- This may be relatively successful in the case of drink-driving, for example, but less certain in a campaign against fast urban driving.

Exam hint

Key skills – Improving your performance

Are you able to think of at least one or two more examples for each of the types of pressure groups disussed in the previous sections?

The examiner is going to be more impressed with your original examples, rather than re-reading his/her own!

The consumerist movement

The consumerist movement had its origins in America during the late 1950s when commentators like Vance Packard and Ralph Nader began to alert consumers to the fact that businesses were concerned more for their own profits than the welfare of the customer or of the environment.

In Britain, its development was slower. The publication and interest in the Consumers Association's *Which?* reports, comparing the relative performance and merits of rival brands from the user's point of view, served notice on the ancient maxim 'caveat emptor' (let the buyer beware), replacing it with 'caveat vendictor' (let the seller beware). Such associations are now to be found in most countries.

Customers are no longer willing to suffer in silence. Subsequently, companies have become increasingly proactive in adopting a marketing orientation towards these increasingly aware and demanding stakeholders. Accordingly, a more astute customer orientation has been displayed.

There is no one accepted meaning of the term *consumerism*. Definitions have however revolved around the following dimensions:

◆ The search for getting better value for money

◆ A social movement seeking to augment the rights and powers of buyers in relation to sellers

◆ Anything consumers say it is

In brief:

◆ Consumerism is clearly a force within the environment designed to aid and protect the consumer by exerting legal, moral and economic pressure on business.

◆ It has evolved over time and has embraced a number of issues ranging from unfair pricing and high credit costs through deceptive packaging and product labelling to poor value for money extended warranties:

　◆ The excessive use of packaging is a current issue with the average UK family spending the equivalent of £470 each year.

　◆ Supermarkets claim to be making progress in removing the excesses but argue that it is essential to protect many foodstuffs.

　◆ Consumers may not be so forgiving when they consider its direct cost and environmental consequences.

　◆ Future causes might include a UK scandal waiting to happen in the mass selling of self-invested personal pensions, payment protection insurance, Internet, junk mail and game show prize fraud and the issue of 'excessive choice'.

　◆ One has only to consider the number of shampoos on supermarket shelves, each with its own unique selling proposition. Interestingly psychologists found that shoppers were more likely to buy jams when only six varieties were on display, than when there were twenty-four.

　◆ However, economic historian Avner Offer has demonstrated that humans consistently underestimate the future costs of their actions, choosing instant gratification instead.

　◆ Self-control is especially hard in affluent economies where temptation constantly beckons. For example, faced with so much cheap and tasty food it becomes almost impossible to resist, leading to the obesity epidemic even though we know it will make us fat.

In 1962, US President J.F. Kennedy laid the foundation to consumerism by proposing the four basic rights set out in Figure 2.8.

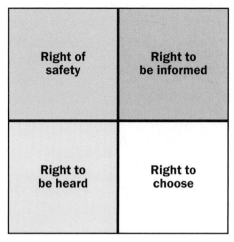

Right of safety	Right to be informed
Right to be heard	Right to choose

Figure 2.8 Consumer rights

◆ Safety:

  ◆ The right to protection against the marketing of any products that are hazardous to life, especially where hidden dangers may be involved.

  ◆ Products such as pharmaceuticals, cars, tyres, household appliances, insecticides and foods have been the source of many customer-related accidents or diseases and a major spur to consumerism.

  ◆ Current targets for legal actions include the tobacco, gun and drinks industries.

  ◆ Mobile phones constitute a new target due to microwave emissions, interference and in car usage.

  ◆ The long-term implications of food additives, irradiated and genetically modified foods, *Escherichia coli* bacteria and the transfer of BSE from cattle to humans are four further examples of such concern.

  ◆ Safe alternatives do not always cost more and may provide an edge for companies in the market-place. However, where extra cost is involved, as in fully effective air bags and ABS (anti-lock braking system), competition often prevents concerted action in the interests of greater safety.

◆ Information:

  ◆ The right to protection from fraudulent, deceitful and grossly misleading information and to be given the necessary facts to enable an informed decision to be taken.

  ◆ This impacts directly on the ethics of marketing departments since the consumer is a generalist lacking the expertise, the time and often the inclination to acquire the product knowledge necessary to make an informed purchase.

  ◆ Reliance for comprehensive and comprehensible information is therefore placed on the marketer in respect of advertising, promotional copy, personal selling, packaging, guarantees and service contracts. Timeshare, insurance and packaged holiday companies, for example, still seem to inhabit the lower reaches of the pressure sell and 'small print' jungle!

◆ Choice:

- ◆ The right to variety and a competitive service at a fair price.

- ◆ The customer should have the information and opportunity to make an objective selection and be able to distinguish between me-too and real competition in promotional offerings.

◆ A hearing:

- ◆ The right to express dissatisfaction over poor service and substandard product performance.

- ◆ Consumers should have easy-to-navigate channels for airing their grievances and receive full and sympathetic consideration. The need for a legal process and an external policing mechanism will be examined in a later unit.

Exam hint

Remember you are a consumer as far as the CIM and your college is concerned. You have a 'right' to expect a relevant syllabus, an applied approach, comprehensive information on examination requirements and feedback on performance.

Take advantage of your consumer rights and do not forget to regularly access www.cim.co.uk.

Consumers may follow many routes to make their thoughts clear. Some courses of action may be as follows:

◆ Consumers may refuse to buy on an individual basis or as part of a collective boycott.

◆ Consumers may engage in lobbying and media campaigns through 'Watchdog' type consumer affairs television programmes.

◆ Consumer groups and individuals are also registering their views on company websites, by e-mail, in chat rooms and through blogs.

◆ Consumer power has always suffered from diffusion arising from the variety of calls on available buyer purchasing power.

Agitating over dissatisfaction with a low-value or infrequently purchased good or service is often judged a waste of time and effort. A prime example of 'power diffusion' arises in the Common Agricultural Policy where nearly half of the total EU budget subsidizes farmers. They form a small but concentrated and vociferous pressure group, while unorganized households pay higher prices and taxes thought to average £1500 per household in Britain alone.

Business initially viewed the consumerist movement as a threat that created extra costs of compliance and inhibited their freedom of operation. Marketing-orientated organizations, however, soon learnt to listen to what consumers really required. For instance, Nissan recently recalled 2.5 million vehicles world-wide to rectify a potential safety fault despite the cost and potential impact on its reliability image. Sony was also forced to recall the faulty batteries that had caused Dell computers so much damage in their combusting laptops. Programmes such as 'Watchdog' are often leading to companies taking ethical courses of action in view of customer complaints about goods purchased in good faith.

A negative response was the formation of a US advocacy group known as the Centre for Consumer Freedom and funded by Coca-Cola, Wendy's and others. It promotes 'food liberty' as an area of personal choice fought for by the founding fathers and as a means of blocking State moves to serve healthier lunches and to ban vending machines in schools. Consumers vote with their money and, given acceptable choices, will shop elsewhere. Thus it is recommended that companies address the complaints and solve the problems of their existing and even potential customers before the latter turn to their competitors.

Insight: Are we being poisoned by our own food?

Read the following extracts from the Times and The Week and consider how the marketer should respond in practice to scientific studies which suggest that a significant range of everyday foods contain potentially dangerous levels of a cancer-causing chemical called acrylamide.

The US Environmental Protection Agency lists the chemical, which is used mainly in the manufacture of plastics, as a 'probable' human carcinogen and has limited the maximum permitted level in American drinking water to 0.5 parts per billion. In Europe, the permitted level for residues left on food from packaging is no more than 10 parts per billion.

Tests suggest that the chemical is produced whenever certain foods are baked, fried, microwaved or grilled at temperatures over 120C especially for long periods. Deep-fried and fast foods seem to have the highest levels with chips at 736 parts per billion and potato crisps at 4000 parts per billion. It has also been found at relatively high levels in some crackers, breakfast cereals and burnt meat.

The head of food safety at the World Health Organization (WHO) believes that a significant proportion of the 30–40 per cent of cancers linked to diet could be caused by the chemical. Modern food processing and cooking techniques could explain the rising trend of cancer in Western countries.

The WHO still maintains that the levels of the chemical that the average person consumes is not life threatening but it may not do too much harm on the precautionary principle to cut back on fatty fried foods and increase our intake of fruit and boiled vegetables.

Similar concerns attached to illegal food colourings prompted, in 2005, the largest food recall in UK history. The 420 types of contaminated ready meals gave a new meaning to the term 'processed' foods and all were traced back to an unwitting purchase of a batch of chilli powder that contained the banned additive Sudan 1 and sold on through the industry. Fortunately, the contamination was probably too small to induce sickness.

Environmentalism

There are an estimated 1400 environmental pressure groups in Britain alone. Demands they are making range over the following:

◆ Conservation of resources and energy saving

◆ Reuse, redesign and recycling of products

◆ Slowing of economic growth and elimination of eco-unfriendly products

◆ Protection of the natural environment, animal rights and endangered species.

Exam hint

Key skills – Improving own performance

You must get as much practice as possible at answering questions throughout the units. The exam questions are meant to test your specific knowledge about the questions as well as your ability to relate these to your understanding of the marketing environment.

Such demands imply economic and financial costs for business, potential redundancies and higher consumer prices. Despite a cyclical pattern to such pressures, they are likely to increase rather than diminish with time. Some industries such as pharmaceuticals research and development are more likely to be targeted than others but none are immune. Those most recently in the firing line include aerosols, agriculture, airlines, animal testing, chemicals, fertilizers, motorways, oil tankers, plastics, pulp and paper, refrigeration, tobacco, tourism, toxic waste and water. On the other hand, the environment has also been improving in a number of areas. Britain, for example, has more woodland today than it has had for 200 years, the air in London is better now than it has been for 300 years, plus its rivers and beaches are the cleanest they have been for decades. With entire bureaucracies in the European Union devoted to a better environment, the pressure groups have been forced to regroup and refocus.

Question 2.4

Key skills – Problem-solving

Take each of the industries listed above and suggest the environmental issue that has placed them in the firing line.

What responses have businesses in these industries made that you are aware of?

What other industries, not mentioned above, would you include as high-profile targets for environmentalists?

A number of possible threats arise if a business ignores its environment:

◆ The corporate image deteriorates in the eyes of stakeholders.

◆ Customers may prefer alternatives they perceive as less harmful.

◆ Shareholders may prefer to invest in ethically sound companies.

◆ Recruitment and retention of quality staff becomes more difficult.

◆ Unnecessarily strict legislation may be enacted due to failure to act.

◆ Loss of community support, hardening attitudes from authorities.

◆ Worsening competitive disadvantage compared to more proactive competitors.

◆ Cost penalties – higher energy bill, insurance, legal claims.

Activity 2.12

Key skill – Presenting information

In the light of the potential threats outlined here, make a case to your board of directors stating the potential benefits of becoming a more environmentally aware company.

Suppose the board is persuaded by the force of your arguments but asks you for guidelines to ensure that this new philosophy is adopted throughout the company. What would you suggest?

Although the natural environment is discussed in depth in Unit 4, two final aspects should be mentioned at this stage. Firstly, the importance of legal form, and secondly, the business response required to such pressure groups.

Sole traders and small limited companies normally face more intense competition and are less likely to have the resources to commit to achieving environmental standards in excess of those required by legislation. On the other hand, they will be owner-managed and do business in localities where they live. Such business people have traditionally filled many civic posts in the local community and may sacrifice profit to maintain their reputation and standing in this and other respects. Public limited companies, in comparison, will be well resourced and have a higher national profile. They will be more aware of developments with regard to the industry and its environment and are more likely to participate in government and other initiatives to bring about improvements.

Insight: Food waste – who's to blame?

Our waste mountain is growing at 3 per cent a year since a booming economy means that as we buy so we throw items away. An estimated £20 billion worth of food is disposed of annually, five times what we spend on international aid. Attitudes have changed dramatically and many now admit to profligate buying behaviour. However, there is a greater culprit, the supermarket and the associated disappearance of local stores. Large weekly shops, including many unwanted items, are now the pattern rather than daily visits to the local outlets. Supermarkets encourage wastefulness through two-for-one offers and confusing use-by dates. Farmers complain of leaving crops to rot because they fail to meet strict specifications on size or shape. Finally, there is the insane volume of packaging and plastic bags, none of which are necessary.

On the other hand, plcs are often in a position to relocate production activities to other parts of the world where legislation is less stringent. Small firms will find it less easy to justify the cost of meeting new environmental management standards such as BS 7750, although there are increasing pressures on suppliers to adopt these, irrespective of legal form.

Exam hint

Key skills – Metrics

All the exam questions are compulsory. If a question has four parts to it, you should allocate sufficient time to each part. Please ensure that you answer all the components of the questions. It is very important that you keep to the time allowed and not spend too long on parts you know more about. Give the examiner something to mark even in those parts where you are less confident.

The response

The final part is how business should respond to pressure from environmentalists. The organization must prioritize since it has insufficient resources to deal with all pressures and must assess which are significant and offer the greatest likelihood of impact on the business. The response may be framed in very simple terms, but each option requires considerable management effort and time to make it effective. Responses could be as follows:

◆ Listen/communicate to them and respond positively.

◆ Consult and liaise with them.

◆ Work with them to make the necessary things happen.

◆ Support them to work for you.

◆ Oppose them if all else fails.

Where a business is sensitive to the interests of relevant pressure groups, it is more likely to react more effectively to change in its marketing environment. Similarly, trust built up through a track record of public service is an asset and an investment to protect. Consumers are discouraged by brands where negative publicity arises, and insensitivity in one area can cancel out positive progress elsewhere.

Question 2.5

Key skills – Collecting information

Can you think of some recent 'negative publicity' for your or any high-profile company?

If not, scan the newspapers until you have some examples on file.

The characteristics of the product or service itself provide numerous cues to the various pressure groups and represent the litmus test of an organization's real commitment to its stated corporate values. Similarly, the promotional mix raises awareness and reinforces perceptions of a good business image or, alternatively, seeks to ensure that it is not undermined.

An organization may follow a range of options such as:

◆ The organization must decide its fundamental responsibilities and develop a policy towards each stakeholder group based on the values it considers important.

◆ Priorities must be established to ensure that limited resources are not spread too thinly. It should logically focus first on current and prospective legal obligations towards stakeholders.

◆ Due to the slow working of the legislative process and political manifestos, companies normally have advance warning of such developments (though not in the case of the US internet gambling ban). Organizations, or their trade associations, must therefore monitor proposed developments very carefully since they may wish to influence its detailed formulation in their own interests.

◆ The organization may wish to consider its moral responsibilities and where it stands on them (relative to its competitors). In these, as well as with projected legislation, it will concentrate its attention where the likely impacts on its business are greatest.

Exam hint

Key skills – Improving own performance

There is always a strong temptation in a time-constrained examination to start writing as soon as possible, especially when those about you seem to have done so already. It is more than likely, however, that such candidates will be writing unstructured answers which do not address what the question requires, and certainly not in a logical sequence.

As any effective marketer will tell you, it is the planning that goes into a campaign that is the secret of its success. The same is the case with exam questions. Understanding what the customer (i.e. the examiner) wants and then spending four or five minutes to plan how best to effectively satisfy these wants is what produces the excellent pass. You may wish to list your points or draw a web and map the links.

Writing it out in a form the examiner can comprehend is merely the mechanics of the process.

> Develop the habit of jotting down trigger word plans for all end-of-unit exam questions. Each 'word' represents an idea or factor you will introduce into the essay. Just one word will remind you of the idea and ensure you will include it at the appropriate point in your answer.

Organizations have to address a range of situations. For instance:

◆ Any organization can be confronted by a seemingly endless procession of stakeholder or pressure group issues in whose crossfire it threatens to be caught:

   ◆ Therefore it is important that the organization does not over-react to these issues since they can be double-edged.

   ◆ Politically correct behaviour, not least in the area of sexual harassment and the promotion of women into senior managerial positions, may also rebound if the result is a steep rise in the turnover of company-trained male managers.

◆ Performance against intended objectives must be measured and assessed (note the problems facing police forces in raising ethnic group representation in proportion to their population).

◆ Every effort should be made to frame objectives in such a way that progress towards them can be estimated.

Pressures for a positive organizational response

◆ **More knowledgeable/educated consumers** are aware of their rights and increasingly critical of irresponsible behaviour. They are more prepared to make legal claims which are costly in terms of time, money and bad publicity for the organization in question.

◆ **The threat of legislation** may inhibit behaviour that society considers unethical.

◆ **Rising affluence** increases social and environmental concerns.

◆ **Competitive pressure** as businesses seeks competitive advantage by emphasizing their responsibility towards stakeholders. Customers or investors who value such behaviour will wish to be associated with such ethical companies.

◆ **Stakeholder pressure** from those concerned with quality or their own corporate image. Many large companies insist their suppliers have implemented codes of good practice/industry standards.

◆ **European Union directives** ensure compliance with common standards across the Single Market. This may produce a ratchet effect on higher standards in food safety and so on.

◆ **Pressure group activity** crystallizes these pressures and provides support/legal backing.

◆ **The media** provide focus and attention on many areas of corporate weakness. Recent examples include allegations concerning the use of child labour in the manufacture of products for socially responsible organizations.

◆ **Demonstration effects** by high-profile organizations with close links to external stake-holders and responsive to pressure groups.

◆ **The power of the Internet** creates open information systems which readily link those with common interest in ethical business behaviour.

Summary

In this unit, we have seen that:

◆ Business ignores its environment at its peril.

◆ Marketers have a key role in identifying environmental change.

◆ Organizations have a number of primary stakeholders and influence is two way.

◆ Business must account/respond to wider opportunities and threats over which it has no control.

◆ Pressure groups are increasing in importance and can be classified as interest or cause groups.

◆ Pressure groups employ various means and channels to bring pressure to bear.

◆ Consumerism has become a force for companies to reckon with, especially as the causes pursued have broadened out from just narrow consumer protection issues.

◆ One of the important current issues for consumers relates to the claims and coun-terclaims of marketers regarding the eco-friendliness of their offerings.

◆ The scope of environmental concerns and the specific threats posed to busi-nesses are potentially serious (e.g. Sport Utility Vehicles have emission, fuel use and road safety concerns).

◆ The constructive response is not necessarily to confront pressure groups but, where possible, to understand their interests, listen to their point of view and work towards a common solution.

◆ Consumerism has provided many customer-orientated businesses with an oppor-tunity to make product strengths and socially responsible marketing a source of competitive advantage:

 ◆ It is a well-established feature of the marketplace and will remain so until there is scope for opportunist sellers to mislead and confuse consumers.

 ◆ Its concerns now extend far beyond consumer protection to issues such as pricing, design obsolescence and, increasingly, ecology, to which marketers must positively respond.

◆ Pressure groups' activities and influence are increasing. They are becoming more organized and professional in approaching both government and companies. They are now more adept at marketing their causes and highlighting the deficiencies of companies towards their stakeholder groups:

- Green consumers' guides and Friends of the Earth green con awards are examples of how a business' reputation can be soiled:

- To minimize such risks, a company must establish and apply values and beliefs conducive to a sustainable business.

- It must be aware of the threats and opportunities of enhancing its reputation in the eyes of stakeholders through effective and well-managed policies towards the environment.

- Unilever and the World Wildlife Fund for Nature, for example, agreed on a sustainable standard for fish products with a special logo if the product was from accredited fishing grounds.

Further study and examination preparation

Since the marketing environment links the organization with external constraints, opportunities and threats, it is unsurprising that questions frequently arise requiring you to explore the relationship between the two.

While the syllabus content of this unit is around 10 per cent, its significance extends much wider in terms of questions and part questions appearing at regular intervals on CIM papers.

Note though that Question 5 in the June 2006 paper referred to understanding of the micro-environment in contextual terms but was primarily concerned with marketing research and information sources.

It is also important to note that while the stakeholder concept is treated in more depth in the Marketing Fundamentals syllabus, part or even full questions will continue to appear in the Marketing Environment paper as seen in Question 3, December 2005. Pressure groups and how the marketer responds to them in practice remains an important element in examination terms.

Extending knowledge

Palmer A. and Hartley B. (2006) *The Business and Marketing Environment*, McGraw-Hill.

Chapter 1: Marketing, An Overview.

Chapter 2: Nature of the Marketing Environment.

Palmer, A. (2002) *The Business Environment*, McGraw-Hill.

Chapter 1: What is the Business Environment.

Chapter 5: On social responsibility.

Other suggested reading

Brooks, I. and Weatherston, J.(2000) *The Business Environment*, Prentice Hall, 2nd Ed.
Chapters 1 and 2.

Groucutt J. (2005) *Foundations of Marketing*, Palgrave Macmillan.
Chapter 2: The Marketing Environment.

Lancaster G, Massingham L. and Ashford R. (2002) *Essentials of Marketing*, McGraw-Hill Education.
Chapter 2: The marketing environment.

Jobber D. (1998) *Principles of Marketing*, McGraw-Hill, 2nd Ed.
Chapter 5: The marketing environment.

Bassington F. and Pettitt S. (2003) *Principles of Marketing*, Pearson Education Limited.
Chapter 1: Marketing dynamics.
Chapter 2: The European marketing environment.

Websites

www.ft.com and www.thetimes.co.uk for general up-to-date coverage of the marketing environment.

www.greenpeace.org for coverage of a host of environmental issues and links with other pressure groups.

http:/www.webdirectory.com/ is a directory of environmental organizations with a search facility.

www.tradingstandards.gov.uk take up consumer complaints over bad service.

www.fsa.gov.uk publishes fee and performance comparisons of financial providers.

Practicising past exam questions

Please see Question 4, June 2004 on the CIM website www.cim.co.uk

Please see Question 7, June 2004 on the CIM website www.cim.co.uk

Please see Question 3b, December 2004. Go to www.cim.co.uk for specimen answers.

Please see Question 4a, December 2004. Go to www.cim.co.uk for specimen answers.

Please see Question 3, June 2005. Go to www.cim.co.uk for specimen answers.

Please see Question 3, December 2005. Go to www.cim.co.uk for specimen answers.

Although past paper questions remain very relevant, students must understand that the format of the exam has now changed. Therefore you should also refer to the specimen paper to ensure that you are clear about the new exam format.

Please note that in September 2008 a new syllabus and assessment will be introduced. Referring to past papers is fine as the core syllabus content has not changed significantly but you should also refer to the specimen paper to understand the new exam format.

Unit 3
Analysis of the competitive environment

Study guide

This unit is concerned with the market environment of the organization and deals with an element that impacts continuously on most businesses – the competition. The marketer normally confronts this reality on a day-to-day basis.

The balance of the unit is concerned with information, a critical theme throughout this coursebook and one explored in detail in Unit 9. In this unit and again in Unit 4, we will develop your awareness and understanding of internal and particularly external information sources that contribute to the understanding and assessment of the marketing environment.

This unit accounts for around 12 per cent of the syllabus, but it represents a very important segment of the external environment. Subsequent units, that consider other environments, are mostly about their effects on competitive relationships. The activities should enable you to relate the material to your organization and work experience. They should also help you refine your understanding of the marketing environment in practice.

Monitoring competitors

You should re-read the material discussed in Unit 2 on actual and potential customers and competitors. In a dedicated section, the two-way relationship exists between them and the marketing function was explored clearly. To be fully effective, the marketer must appreciate the dynamics of markets, the behaviour of its rivals and the realities of customer preferences and customer behaviour. However, the relevance of the monitoring of competitors will vary according to the structure of the industry. The number of main players in the marketing environment, the type of players or competitors and their offerings will play a role in determining the level of competition within that industry.

Fragmented industries

Although fragmented industries cannot be completely generalized, there are however a number of underlying common characteristics:

◆ The number of participants is very large, but their average size is relatively small.

◆ Therefore there can be little to be gained by monitoring the competitive behaviour of all rivals. Hence the monitoring of only the main players, those that represent the closest competitors perhaps in terms of location or product/service characteristics, should be ideally conducted.

◆ Such industries are characterized by businesses competing for market share based on meeting buyer preferences rather than random selection among identical providers.

◆ The market is underlain by a diversity of incomes, attitudes, tastes and preferences so that sellers must discover the qualitative mix which best satisfies the needs of the target customer base.

◆ Companies must therefore make the most of their product's unique selling points before their competitors impede them from doing so.

Activity 3.1

Can you think of an example of a fragmented industry?

Try to identify the closest competitors.

Can you also think of smaller rivals?

Insight

Red Letter Days, the company behind adrenaline-filled trips and weekends such as hot-air ballooning, climbing Everest or flying to the edge of the stratosphere crashed into administration in August 2005. This resulted from suppliers boycotting the firm due to slow payment. It was doubly embarrassing for the founder and Chief Executive, Rachel Elnaugh, who had been recruited as a judge of budding entrepreneurs on the BBC venture-capital reality show Dragon's Den.

Market leaders do not tend to dominate because the scope for cost advantages from greater scale of operation is comparatively small. Advantage goes to those who are flexible and adaptable and such firms will seek to establish a competitive edge over their immediate rivals through innovation or successful differentiation of the marketing mix. Unfortunately, barriers to entry tend to be low in such industries, making new entry into the market likely especially when high profits are being made by existing firms. The extra supply this represents, combined with imitation of successful trading formulas, drives down margins and profitability over time. Any improvement in general demand conditions due to for instance changing tastes, rising incomes or unfortunate circumstances affecting substitute products will lead to initial improvement in sales and margins. However, subsequent and often rapid erosion of profitability through competition is the characteristic of fragmented industries.

Insight

One exception to this process was Google, inventor of the most powerful search engine, now used in more than half of all searches. It is a champion of open access to information and against state interference. Its mission was to organize the world's information and make it accessible by inventing a way for the Internet user to find relevant web pages in order of importance. The company grew by word of mouth and without promotional expenditure, and its services were free to the web browsers and incredibly useful. Its revenue derived from clicking on sponsored links to company websites found on every page. Because its revenues were kept secret before it was floated in 2004 for $100 billion it destroyed most of the competition. Since then, some strong competitors have also entered the market.

Question 3.1

Key skills – Problem-solving

Which of the following would you identify as fragmented industries?

◆   Health and fitness centres

◆   Restaurants

◆   Fast-food outlets

◆   Hotels

What factors account for the fragmentation?

Are there forces leading to consolidation in the fast-food sector?

One familiar situation to marketers, where competition is intense, is where the product has become a so-called 'commodity' as it enters the late maturity stage of the product life cycle. A saturated market dependent on repeat buyers, who are particularly knowledgeable with regard to desirable product and service characteristics, will make successful differentiation extremely difficult or costly to sustain. This produces a price-taker situation where the forces of market supply and demand determine the price which should be set, rather than the individual company. Potential customers will view product offerings as identical and rationally purchase the cheapest. Any attempt to set prices above what the market will bear will lead to drastic loss of sales and market share.

The development of e-commerce might make intense competition the rule rather than the exception due to the greater transparency it creates in pricing. Ready availability of near perfect knowledge will make it difficult for any business to charge more than the current price for standardized products.

Competitors who supply close substitutes (i.e. relatively undifferentiated products or services) are in a strong position to win customers by offering better value for money. Such firms, and particularly new entrants, will strive to win your established customer base by making it attractive to switch allegiance. The marketer, in such circumstances, must first recognize the threat (i.e. monitor close competitors) and then respond by making switching more difficult for their existing customers.

Activity 3.2

Can you think of some companies that offer close substitutes?

How do you think these companies attempt to make their product or service more attractive to their existing customers and even potential customers?

Possible strategies could include any of the following courses of action:

◆   Invest in relationship marketing to build long-term mutual benefits.

◆   Build other barriers to protect the market.

◆   Create the equivalent of a habitual or monopoly good by niche marketing, product differentiation and/or effective branding.

◆   Buy out or collude with the competitor. For example, Peng Travel, Britain's largest naturist travel operator, was bought out by Travelzest in 2006.

◆   Cut unnecessary costs in order to offer keener prices.

◆   Innovate to continuously distance your product or service offering from rivals.

Exam hint

Key skills – Improving own performance

Have you considered the advantages of 'differentiation' for your own examination script? An examiner is faced with marking scripts, literally in hundreds, all answering the same questions.

How are you going to make yours stand out?

What you require is a premium product that catches the examiner's eye at the outset.

Product differentiation and branding are the marketer's natural response to competition. If price rivalry is forcing down profit levels, they respond by mobilizing the marketing mix to differentiate the product either by specification or in the minds of the consumer. Branding will be particularly critical in business-to-customer (B2C) selling on the Internet. There will be a premium on established reputations since the easiest purchases for new consumers navigating their way through electronic shopping will be the products they know and trust.

The areas along which differentiation could de applied are by all means varied. Notwithstanding, some tactics and strategies may include any of the following choices:

◆ **Product** – Permutations of the *core, tangible* (e.g. design, quality, packaging) and *augmented* product (e.g. brand name, delivery, after-sales service). For example, America's fastest selling action toy in 2005 was a 5-inch plastic doll of a middle-aged librarian. Its only action was to raise a finger to her lips to request silence.

◆ **Price** – Credit and payment terms may vary, as can allowances and trade-in values.

◆ **Promotion** – To support the differentiation (e.g. sales force, advertising).

◆ **Place** – Offers opportunities through location adopted, coverage and, most importantly, service provided. Tesco, for example, is Britain's largest on-line retailer.

Businesses will segment the market in the search for a profitable niche that they will service with a product combining the optimum blend of characteristics that are clearly differentiated from competing products. Those who satisfy customer needs and wants most effectively will earn excess profits. The seller, in effect, obtains a monopoly of the branded product and is able to charge a premium price and still retain customers who prefer the product.

Question 3.2

Can you think of any example in any industry where small firms have innovated their product or service offerings and quickly been imitated by rivals or new entrants?

The strife of companies to differentiate themselves from their competitors is very important. However, what is also very important is what follows the attempts to create differentiation.

Several events could occur as a consequence of the search for differentiation. The following could plausibly happen:

◆ Returns associated with successful differentiation may and usually tend to attract imitation from existing firms (or former employees), wishing to expand sales, and new entrants, seeking profitable opportunities.

◆ The customer benefits as this imitation enables rapid diffusion of superior product and service ideas.

◆ New entrants also provide extra choice although there is a tendency to excess capacity in such industries as available customer demand is spread across the increased number of suppliers.

◆ There comes a point where attempting to utilize available capacity fully through extra promotion or discounting adds more to cost than to revenue. Hairdressers and restaurants are therefore seldom full.

Insight: Pottermania

The publication of the fifth in the planned series of Harry Potter novels underpinned a book, film and merchandise business worth £3 billion. Sales of Harry Potter and the Half-Blood Prince, the sixth book in the series, produced frenzied scenes around the globe with an unprecedented 10 million being sold on the first day. Clever marketing certainly contributed with jealously guarded plots, midnight launches, booksellers in wizard hats and the use of the J.K. initials to avoid putting off boy readers. On the other hand, it is unlikely that children or their parents would read a 600-page book because of the marketing magic. Despite J.K. Rowling being the highest paid woman in Britain with record advance sales in the history of publishing, the book will make little for retailers. This is due to large supermarket groups halving cover prices in feverish competition, to the cost of the smaller bookseller.

Therefore whatever strategies a company follows depends on its situation (i.e. its capabilities and its resources) as well as its mission and objectives.

Concentrated industries

The following characteristics underpin this type of industries:

◆ The number of competing firms is generally small but their economic size is large.

◆ In economic terms, this is known as high seller concentration and is typical in the so-called 'oligopolies'.

Activity 3.3

Key skills for marketers (i.e. metrics – carrying out calculations)

Seller concentration is defined as the degree to which production or sales for a particular market are concentrated into the hands of a few large firms.

With this definition in mind, calculate a *five-firm concentration ratio* for your own industry (i.e. add up the market shares of the five largest firms).

Alternatively, look up a Mintel report on an industry of your choice.

Oligopoly can be explained as follows:

◆ This is the typical market structure in mature economies.

◆ There is competition among a few main players. It arises where the largest four or five firms account for perhaps 70 per cent or more of total sales to the market.

◆ In 2004, there were 5475 tour operators and travel agents registered in the UK. However the industry was dominated by four major players: My Travel, Thomas Cook Ltd., TUI UK and First Choice. This four-firm oligopoly accounted for 46.5 per cent of industry turnover in 2004.

◆ In some industries, such as the aerospace or pharmaceutical industry, a 'four-firm' concentration typically represent 80 per cent or more of the industry turnover.

◆ Monitoring competitors is of critical importance in this situation because the marketing actions and decisions of any one of the main players depend crucially upon the reactions of its competitors. Their relative strengths and weaknesses must thus be evaluated and every facet of their marketing behaviour identified and assessed. The four major tour operators mentioned above undoubtedly keep a close eye on one another.

Question 3.3

Key skills – Using information

Is the company you work for in an oligopoly market structure?

Is the college you attend in an oligopoly?

Is the bank you use an oligopoly?

What about your supermarket or mobile phone operator?

Since each firm accounts for a large slice of the market any substantial change in the market share of one firm, whether achieved by lower prices, product innovation or successful advertising, will adversely affect the shares of competitors.

The activities of popular national newspapers often provide an interesting case study of such a market. Companies will watch each other very closely, producing a tension in the market between the *desire to compete* and gain in sales at the expense of competitors on the one hand, and the *desire to collude* in order to limit mutually damaging competitive activity on the other. However, the longer term future of many such newspapers is in some doubt as readers and advertisers migrate to the net and a new force of citizen journalists, bloggers and online alternatives spring up to fill the vacuum. With the exception of free newspapers, such as Metro and the Londonpaper and Londonlite, according to the Audit Bureau of Circulation and the National Readership Survey, most newspapers have shown declining circulation and readership in the UK over the past 30 years. The decline in readership is most evident among the 16 to 35 age group.

Reasons identified for declining readership include:

◆ The proliferation of TV and Radio stations.

◆ Increasing use of the internet for news, job advertisements, travel information, car purchases, property sales, entertainment information and numerous other marketing communication information sources once dominated by newspapers.

◆ Growth in the number of specialist magazines.

◆ Changing lifestyles. The 16 to 35 age group are spending more time watching TV, using the internet and playing video games.

Similar behaviour may however be observed in oligopolies throughout the world, whether it is the four big international oil groups, the five big car groups or Ghana breweries where ABC lager is competing head on with Kumasi Club beer.

In brief, the key features of an oligopoly market may be summarized as follows:

◆ Economies of scale and entry barriers tend to be significant.

◆ Customer needs are standardized and integrated through effective marketing and mass distribution systems.

◆ Dominant market leaders may emerge: for example Microsoft, Intel, Tesco or Nokia.

◆ High concentration rules with a tail of small firms, for example grocery retailing.

◆ Demand is uncertain because it is dependent on how rivals react.

◆ Outcomes are unpredictable when oligopolists have multiple competitive options. For example, if one of the main players cuts its prices, another may follow suit, or it may cut its prices more or less than the first firm. Alternatively, it may choose to do nothing, or respond with a large promotional campaign or launch a new brand.

Despite the variety of options available to companies operating in an oligopolistic market environment, a number of generalizations are however possible. For instance:

◆ Companies operating in an oligopoly tend to avoid the use of price as a competitive weapon. They are termed 'sticky' because the rivals often face a skewed demand curve. This suggests that the most likely rival reaction would be not to follow a price increase (thereby gaining market share/sales revenue at the expense of the organization), but always to follow a price cut (avoiding any loss of share/sales). Either way the firm will lose profits.

◆ Non-price competition, promoting carefully differentiated branded products, is preferred. For example, Procter & Gamble and Unilever market over 50 competing detergents worldwide.

◆ There is a tendency to occasional price war when a restructuring of market shares is in progress. For example, low-cost airlines have gained increasing share.

◆ Collusion is an attractive option but normally illegal. One recent example concerns the top 50 public schools such as Eton and Harrow in Britain who have been referred to the Office of Fair Trading for price fixing.

◆ Price leadership often occurs to reflect underlying cost changes (e.g. retail petrol, tobacco, car and beer prices).

Activity 3.5

Key skills – Observation and critical thinking

Watch the press for large firms announcing price changes, for example supermarket petrol prices or bank interest rates, and then look for their competitors' reactions.

Do they follow suit or not? If so, how quickly do their main competitors react?

New product development is recognized as the best strategy for achieving a sustainable competitive advantage. One worrying innovation currently being tested by British American Tobacco is a flavoured cigarette (e.g. vanilla or chocolate) which could make the product more attractive to younger smokers (their youngest target segments). However, the company insists that it is not targeting young people and has for long added undetectable flavourings to reduce tobacco harshness.

Insight: The future competitive shape of the UK grocery market

Following the successful takeover by Bradford-based Morrisons of the much larger Safeway, the resulting four-firm concentration ratio with Sainsbury's, ASDA and Tesco has 75.7 per cent of the UK supermarket market share according to the latest statistics released in October 2007. While Tesco accounts for 31.4 per cent of the market share, ASDA has 16.8 per cent, Sainsbury's 16.5 per cent and Morrisons 11 per cent. With top-line growth becoming difficult to achieve in the planning constrained and congested south, Safeway represented the last large player that the Competition Commission would allow to change hands. The takeover was expected to trigger a supermarket price war but Morrisons have only recently managed to integrate their acquisition, So, despite food prices falling in real terms since 2000 these retailers face not a price war but a third competition inquiry in seven years. Since 2001 the number of independent grocers has fallen by more than 22 per cent and the big supermarkets stand accused of predatory 'price flexing' (cutting prices locally to drive rivals out of business), excessively squeezing supplier margins and buying up land to prevent competitors expanding.

Exam hint

Key skills – Improve own performance

An examination question in this area will often state: in the context of an industry example, explain...

Make sure you know an industry example inside out, preferably your own.

Five-force analysis of competitive structures

Any organization that seeks growth and profitability in its existing market or perhaps is considering diversification into an emerging industry must carefully weigh future prospects. A competitive strategy to shape evolving competitive forces must then be determined to provide achievement of its objectives within a defendable market position.

Businesses earn profit by being more successful than competitors in creating and delivering value to the customer over time. Real success demands that the business:

◆ Offers value for money

◆ Achieves a competitive edge in delivering that value

◆ Operates efficiently.

The profit potential of an industry will be determined by the balance of supply and demand for the product in the short run, and industry structure in the long run. Long-run profitability will vary according to the strength of five basic competitive forces that govern the distribution of the added value created by the firm.

The model offered by Porter (see Figure 3.1) arguably identifies and illustrates the five forces that enables the structure of an industry.

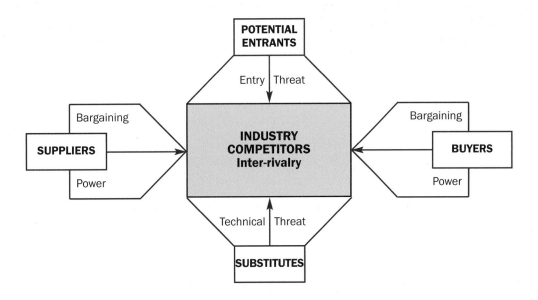

Figure 3.1 The five-forces model

Source: Adapted from M.E. Porter (1980) *Competitive Strategy*, The Free Press/Macmillan

Marketers must understand the nature of their competitive environment if they are to profitably exploit it. They must assess what is driving the competition and recognize that the collective strength of these five forces will set the present and future degree of market rivalry. This will determine the profit potential of the industry although each participating firm will seek to position itself so as to exploit maximum competitive advantage.

Question 3.4

Key skills – Problem-solving

Use five-force analysis to match fragmented and concentrated industry structures to two of the following combinations:

1   **Intense inter-rivalry** – High threat of entry, high buyer and supplier bargaining power, strong threat from substitutes

2   **Limited inter-rivalry** – High threat of entry, low buyer and supplier bargaining power, weak threat of substitutes

3   **No inter-rivalry** – No threat from substitutes or entry, no buyer or supplier bargaining power

4   **Intense inter-rivalry** – Weak threat from substitutes and entry, low buyer bargaining power, high supplier bargaining power.

Unlike market structure models, the perspective encompassed in Porter's Five Forces model provides marketers with a framework for analysing the complexity and situation of any industry. The approach is less rigorous but perhaps more useful in understanding the effect of structural and environmental change over time.

The intensity of inter-rivalry

Rivalry can range along a spectrum from non-existent (e.g. a powerful monopoly position protected by high entry barriers) to a cut-throat price war. In between are found gentlemanly understandings (collusive oligopoly) and normal marketing-based cut and thrust typically involving advertising and promotion, new product development and improvements to customer service.

Rivalry may either succeed in expanding the overall market and its profitability by drawing in new customers or increasing the volumes purchased, or undermine it by reducing margins or increasing marketing costs while serving only to redistribute static sales among the combatants.

Porter provides additional insight into this force by identifying the variables that help determine the degree of current rivalry and potential rivalry in the future. Key variables are:

◆ **The rate of industry growth** – Rapid growth reduces rivalry over market shares, while in maturity, firms battle over stagnant sales.

◆ **Use of expensive specialized equipment** – Pressure to fully utilize may lead to price war.

◆ **Volatility of supply and demand** – For example, if a new hotel opens in a locality, rivalry will sharpen.

◆ **The degree of product differentiation and brand loyalty.**

◆ **The significance of switching costs for buyers.**

◆ **The number of firms and their relative size** – Divergent corporate cultures: for example if one firm seeks dominance.

◆ **What is at stake** – If survival is threatened or big investment involved.

◆ **Misinterpreting competitor's intentions** – Unintended price wars.

◆ **The cost of leaving the industry** – This may deter exit of weak rivals.

The threat of substitutes

An industry is a group of firms producing goods or services that are close substitutes for each other. In practice, the nature of substitutability is complex and a range of widely differing offerings could compete for limited discretionary purchasing power which can only be spent once at any point in time. Package holidays compete with conservatories and new computer systems with upgrading the transport fleet. But more directly, they compete with independent travel suppliers (i.e. flights sold by airlines, accommodation sold directly to customers by hotels).

Insight: Is this the end of the Hollywood movie?

Box office receipts in the United States have fallen for three consecutive years despite blockbuster releases. Nearly three-quarters of Americans now admit to preferring movies at home using hi-tech wide screen TVs.

Many younger people are also opting for video games or surfing the Net. Film lovers don't even have to leave home to get a DVD since they can be delivered direct to the living room via cable or online rental services at a fraction of the cost of going to the cinema.

With remakes, prequels and sequels dominating the market-place, the studios may also have to refine their offerings if they are going to continue entertaining the public profitably.

Threats may materialize in many forms. For example in terms of different materials, an alternative technology (normal margarine versus cholesterol-reducing spread Benecol) or a new distribution channel (cinema versus DVD format).

Insight

On-line gambling was a substitute channel for visits to the land-based casinos of Nevada and elsewhere until the Unlawful Internet Gambling Enforcement Act was unexpectedly pushed through the US Senate. This triggered the biggest industry share price fall in living memory as up to 70 per cent was wiped of the value of companies like PartyGaming and Sportingbet. But, these substitutes were so popular and lucrative that as with prohibition they are likely to be driven underground or offshore until they are legalized again.

Key factors affecting the degree of threat involved may include the following variables:

◆ Relative price/performance ratio of the substitute: glass versus plastic containers for shampoos.

◆ Switching costs for customers to the substitute: switching from branch banking to internet banking.

◆ Buyer willingness to search out substitutes.

◆ The higher the price and profitability, the greater incentive for companies to search for and develop substitutes.

Question 3.5

Key skills – Using information and metrics

You have been asked to make the travel arrangements to Paris for your marketing director, who has an important morning meeting to attend, and a small group of friends who want a weekend of sightseeing. In each case:

> 1   What substitutes would you consider?
>
> 2   How close is their current relative price/performance ratio?
>
> 3   Why might the ratios be changing?

The threat from new entrants

Long-run profitability and market share will be damaged if significant entry occurs. Supply capacity will increase, putting downward pressure on margins, while extra competition for inputs will bid up costs. Any profitable industry is susceptible to this threat, particularly where returns are high. The dynamics of the competitive process ensure that forces are set in motion to eventually return profitability to levels that no longer attract further entry.

However, there are factors that may delay or even prevent this outcome, known collectively as barriers to entry. Their strength will vary from industry to industry. Where barriers are substantial, the threat of entry will be weak (e.g. nuclear reprocessing), whereas if they are virtually non-existent the threat will be ever present.

The factors to be considered with regards to barriers to entry include:

◆ **Capital requirements and economies of scale** – Entry will be deterred where the minimum economic scale or break-even point for an entrant is high due to plant costs (a modern microprocessor plant costs $1 billion), research and development expenditure (e.g. drugs) or promotional spending (e.g. branding in detergents).

◆ **Brand loyalty and product differentiation:**

     ◆ Promotional expenditure over time builds goodwill and customer loyalty for incumbent firms.

     ◆ Available product space may also be filled by a proliferation of products.

     ◆ Positioning of a new entrant's brand becomes difficult and heavy spending would be required to establish a new brand image.

◆ **Switching costs for buyers:**

     ◆ When considering an alternative computer operating system, the customer faces retraining costs, redundancy of equipment and knowledge, inconvenience and time lags as well as the risks inherent in adopting an untried product and supplier relationship.

     ◆ Prospective benefits must offset these costs.

◆ **Distribution channel access** – Existing firms may dominate existing channels (e.g. long-term contracts).

◆ **Absolute cost advantages** – Entrenched firms have experience and may control prime sites, patents or critical skills.

◆ **Expected retaliation** – Potential entrants will weigh the possible responses of existing firms very carefully, for example an extended price war could quickly remove the attractions of entry into the industry.

◆   **Government policies and regulation** – They may provide protection or encourage fair competition.

Activity 3.6

Key skills – Interpreting information

Examine the grid below and insert in each box an indication of the probable size and stability of returns to be earned; that is, you may designate one box *high and stable returns*, while another *low and risky returns*.

Exit barriers

	Low	High
Low	1.	2.
High	3.	4.

Entry barriers

Potential entrants must carefully weigh this high-risk strategy, particularly where start-up losses are high and reactions uncertain. Existing firms may reinforce entry barriers and reduce intensity of rivalry by merging. For example the £107 billion merger was conducted in pharmaceuticals between GlaxoWellcome and SmithKlineBeecham.

New entry into concentrated markets is not very frequent due to the high barriers. The main threat comes from cross-entry by a well-financed business in an adjacent industry or one using similar processes and distribution channels. For instance through product and brand extension of Dove, the company Unilever managed to penetrate many new markets such as deodorant and shampoo with new Dove products. However all these new markets were in fact for beauty products. Takeover by a foreign company of an existing firm, to provide a base for future growth in market share, is another possibility.

Insight

One entrepreneur has seized an opportunity presented by disaffection with American policies in Muslim communities and launched an alternative to Coke and Pepsi. This new cola was introduced into the French market and appealed to its three million Muslims. Branded as Mecca cola it has sold over 12 million litres to add to the half a billion litres sold in Islamic countries. Confident of the demand for anti-American goods there are now plans to enter the Italian market and extend the range of the initial product.

The bargaining power of suppliers

Where the relative power of an industry's suppliers is considerable and their behaviour aggressive, the rate of profit will be squeezed, but an ability to establish some control over supplies will offset this.

The main factors determining relative power are as follows:

◆ The number and relative size of suppliers.

◆ The ability to switch to rival suppliers and the cost involved.

◆ The threat of forward integration by suppliers. The four major tour operators mentioned earlier have strengthened their position of strength through vertical integration.

Insight: The four big players of the UK tour operator industry

The power of four main players has been strongly reinforced by the fact they are in actual fact all vertically integrated companies. A vertically integrated structure enables a company to achieve enhanced economies of scale and better control and bargaining power (within the constraints imposed by competition law) over product distribution and to present a brand image across the whole range of products offered.

The latter branding strategy is not always followed though, on the grounds that some niche markets are best targeted with individually branded products. For example, the main components of the MyTravel Group offering are: an airline, MyTravelAirways; an online travel website, www.mytravel.com; a retail agency chain, Going Places; and a number of MyTravel Tour Operations, marketed under a number of distinct brands, including Airtours Holidays, Tradewinds, Bridge Travel, Cresta, Panorama, Aspro, Manos and Direct Holidays.

The vertically integrated travel companies are also well represented among top retail travel agents. Thomas Cook Group has as its main subsidiary companies Thomas Cook Retail Ltd and Thomas Cook Tour Operations Ltd. Similarly, TUI UK, formerly the Thomson Travel Group, incorporates retail travel agent Thomson (formerly Lunn Poly). MyTravel has Going Places and First Choice has First Choice Travel Shops and Holiday Hypermarkets as their main high-street travel agency operations.

The four vertically integrated companies indeed have interests in many of the links in the supply chain, typically through their ownership or control of airlines, tour operators and retail travel agents. As a matter of fact, most of these operators have also added call centres, websites and online booking agencies to their portfolio.

The result of such integration has arguably led a heightened level in the bargaining power of the tour operators as buyers (see the model of Porter's Five Forces).

The bargaining power of buyers

Buyer power will also tend to reduce profitability and depends on two main factors:

1   **Price responsiveness** – This price elasticity of demand is determined by such things as:

   a   The importance of the product as a proportion of the total purchases of the buyer.

   b   The emphasis given by the buyer to product differentiation and branding.

   c   The profitability of the buyer, which may dull (or vice versa) their price sensitivity.

2   **Buyer leverage** – A number of factors also affect this:

   a   Buyer concentration and size

   b   Volume and the importance of purchases to the seller

   c   Practicality and costs of switching to alternative suppliers for the buyer

   d   Knowledge of the market and information available to buyers

   e   Existence of substitutes and/or threat of backward vertical integration.

Strategic and marketing implications of Porter's Five Forces

Porter's Five forces model and analysis is useful to the marketer in a variety of ways:

◆   It is a means of determining the attractiveness of an industry and its ultimate profit potential.

◆   It represents a framework for examining relationships in their micro-environment.

◆   It enables an evaluation of the probable degree of rivalry, now and in the future.

◆   It offers a justification for continuous monitoring of the micro-environment.

◆   It can represent the basis for formulating a strategy.

Strategy is about matching the resources and competences of an organization with the risks and opportunities afforded by its external environment. Competitive strategy is a search for sustainable advantage through a favourable market positioning. If such a market positioning is created, above average profitability may be achieved in the long term as well as in the short term.

In addition to offering a model to assess the situation of an industry, Porter also put forward a range of generic strategies. The four generic strategies are quintessentially different routes that a company can follow to achieve competitive advantage. These are: broad cost leadership, broad differentiation, focus cost and focus differentiations. It is not only not possible for any company to achieve all four strategies but just as importantly the worst possible strategy for a company is to be stuck in the middle.

Broad cost leadership

◆   The company chooses a strategy that will help it acquire a different position in the market-place. This will ideally be different from all its main competitors.

◆   This strategy needs to be implemented over time.

◆   Consistency is required so as not to confuse target audiences and the market.

◆   The strategy must also be able to respond to market change as shifting to another strategy is both risky and time consuming.

◆   The company will draw its competitive advantage from many sources.

◆   Intense and regular attention should be paid to competitors' products and services.

◆   Main competitors' costs, quality and communication should also be studied systematically.

◆   Such a strategy would emphasize efficient scale of operations and tight control of costs and margins.

Broad differentiation

◆   The company does not ignore the industry's structure but chooses a different strategy.

◆   To reduce the risk of imitation, the company must keep on being a moving target; this will sustain differentiation.

◆   The company will also have to dare to make trade-offs; choices have to be made and risks taken.

◆   Value is continually created for the customer.

◆   Value is readily perceived and viewed as most important by targeted customers.

◆   The company must communicate this value.

◆   This type of differentiation can be costly. Therefore the company choosing this strategy must be willing to invest while trying to minimize unnecessary costs.

◆   Differentiators also worry about cost; therefore everything that does not contribute to quality is taken out. With proximity in cost terms, a product or service perceived as unique and desirable by customers in terms of design, brand image and/or customer service is created.

◆   High marketing costs are offset by insulation from rivalry and mitigation of buyer power, while high margins cushion supplier power.

Cost focus

◆ Find segment with lower needs.

◆ A target segment, which in evidence has distinct needs, is chosen. The meeting of these specific needs will help create competitive advantage.

◆ Service that target segment exclusively.

◆ Companies should not be tempted to broaden strategy.

◆ Maintain consistency and dedication to the target audiences.

◆ Invest in the product or service when and where needed.

◆ Renovate and maintain quality of product and service.

◆ This strategy focuses on a narrow segment that is least vulnerable to competition.

Focus differentiation

◆ Create value that justifies premium price.

◆ Strategy involves more than the physical and actual product or service.

◆ The company should communicate the differentiation.

◆ The company should again be a moving target.

◆ Sharp focus on target segment and stay focused.

◆ Find segment with greater needs.

◆ This strategy is vulnerable to imitation or structural decline in demand. Broader-based competitors may overwhelm the segment.

Activity 3.7

Key skills – Identifying theory in practice

Can you identify a company, from any industry, for each one of the four generic strategies?

Justify your suggestion of these companies. Why do you think they are following the strategy that you think they are?

Question 3.6

Key skills – Presenting and interpreting information

Study the grid in Figure 3.2 and suggest companies that would fit into the strategy boxes for the following industries:

◆ Multiple groceries

◆ Travel agents

◆ Cars

Competitive advantage

	Lower cost	Differentiation

		Competitive advantage	
		Lower cost	Differentiation
Competitive scope	Broad	Cost leadership e.g. e.g. e.g.	Differentiation e.g. e.g. e.g.
	Narrow	Cost focus e.g. e.g. e.g.	Differentiation focus e.g. e.g. e.g.

Figure 3.2 Strategic grid

A shortcoming of the above strategies is that they all imply hostile options. In reality there are massive changes taking place in industry as businesses collaborate in partnerships, alliances (e.g. Delta Airlines, Air France, Alitalia and CSA Czech Airlines) and joint ventures (e.g. mobile phones). Another attractive approach is forming cartels since if successful the business would become the sole supplier to the market. Output could be restricted and market price and overall profitability would rise. The existence of restrictive practices legislation (see later) has ruled most forms of collective agreement illegal, but cartels still appear to operate clandestinely in some industries (e.g. sugar/concrete/PVC) and internationally: e.g. OPEC (oil), IATA (airlines) and De Beers (diamonds).

All cartels, however, are subject to instability in the longer term due to:

◆ Internal dissension over the allocation of quotas necessary to restrict supply and justify the higher cartel prices.

◆ The incentive for any cartel member to exceed quota for higher profits. This raises supply, making it harder to sustain the price.

◆ Internal policing is essential plus control over market entry.

◆ New producers operate outside the cartel at slightly lower prices, leading to rising excess capacity among cartel members.

An alternative to Porter's Four Generic Strategies has been offered by Johnson and Scholes. Their five competitive routes can be described as follows:

◆ **Route 1** – Cheap and cheerful:

  ◈ Reduced price of goods and reduced perceived value of goods.

  ◈ The company concentrates on price-sensitive customers.

  ◈ Customers recognize product or service as being of lower quality.

◆ **Route 2** – Reduced price while maintaining quality of product or service:

  ◈ Can be imitated by competitors.

  ◈ Price wars between competitors can ensue.

  ◈ Lack of innovation may be created due to low profit margins.

◆ **Route 3** – Hybrid, added value with low price:

  ◈ Cost base permits low price.

  ◈ Company has the ability to re-invest in company.

◆ **Route 4** – Added value or differentiation:

  ◈ Unique products and services are offered.

  ◈ Different from competitors.

  ◈ The company can achieve higher market share by offering better products and services.

◆ **Route 5** – Focused differentiation:

  ◈ The company offers higher value products or services at premium prices.

Activity 3.8

Key skills – Identifying theory in practice

Can you identify a company, from any industry, for each one of the five routes offered by Johnson and Scholes?

Justify your suggestion of these companies.

Why do you think they are following the strategy that you think they are?

Insight: Glass with attitude

The preciousness of the diamond is perhaps the world's most sophisticated illusion, a feat of marketing more dazzling than the gem itself. De Beers controls over 75 per cent of the world's rough diamond output and is the pivot of the world diamond cartel. It is not merely gems that De Beers is marketing, but enchanting symbols, myths and magic.

The clever slogan that a diamond is forever sells two dreams: that diamonds bring eternal love and romance and that diamonds never lose their value.

Control over supply allows price support in the bad times and the reaping of excess profits in good. The mystique of the diamond is also reinforced by clever manipulation of demand. Diamonds were associated with romantic rites of passage, such as engagements, weddings and anniversaries. De Beers continues to sell the dream with advertising copy such as: 'Is two months' salary too much to spend for something that lasts forever?' or 'Show her you would marry her all over again'. The latter campaign led to a fourfold rise in the sale of eternity rings in the United States.

The demise of the cartel continues to be predicted, particularly with accusations of cheating among members such as Russia and Angola, but with vanity, greed, envy, desire and even love, De Beers could scarcely appeal to more common human instincts. The diamond myth lives in a world slightly outside of logic and ordinary economics, and this allows us, the marketing sorcerers, to concoct glamour from carbon and fool us all.

Source: December 1999 examination case edited from 'The Diamond Business', *The Economist*, December 1997.

Activity 3.9

Key skills – Interpreting information

Consider the gondoliers of Venice. What enables them to charge such high prices (€200 per hour), earning around £7000 a month tax-free, for a glorified boat-ride? How do you think they manage to maintain these prices over time? Is clever marketing the explanation?

Insight: E-commerce impacts on the five forces in grocery retailing

Massive investment in ICT suggests that the driving force of future competitive advantage will be the exploitation of e-knowledge. Home shopping is more than an alternative channel to access customers, it is the substitute that will cannibalize sales from high-street stores. The bargaining power of the buyers will also increase since the Internet puts the consumer in control. They will be harder to reach, able to compare prices and able, in theory, to buy from anywhere in the world. E-commerce should also provide manufacturers with a unique opportunity to transform their eroded bargaining power with retailers (who had own brands, massive buying power and powerful EPOS systems that conferred in-depth knowledge of buyer habits) by dealing directly with end-users.

New entry into grocery retailing would be much easier since only a virtual organization would be required. Credibility and logistical cost would be the key success factors and just as multiple retailers have moved into complementary product groupings, so will any virtual organization with retail competencies, for example mail-order organizations.

Strategy demands heavy investment in e-shopping capability and its deployment to service potential customers in areas where its stores are thinly represented. Building and promoting a retailing brand image for quality, choice, value and trust in order to beat off potential entrants is vital as are renegotiated partnerships with key manufacturers to keep them on-board and divert any risk of disintermediation.

The nature of competition policies

Governments formulate competition policies for a number of reasons:

◆   They fear that market forces may be insufficient to prevent anti-competitive behaviour.

◆   They see a level playing field as fair and just.

◆   They desire efficient and effective use of scarce resources.

◆   Monopoly must be controlled as the natural outcome of the competitive process.

◆   They do not wish to see economic power abused at the expense of the consumer/taxpayer.

Making markets more competitive means creating the conditions associated with it. Policies have, therefore, attempted to achieve the following:

◆   Resist mergers and acquisitions which threaten to reduce the number of sellers to the point where consumer choice is restricted. The world-wide merger and acquisition activity was a record $1.93 billion in the first half of 2006.

◆   Keep entry barriers low so that supply, through new entrants, can respond.

◆   Deregulation of markets (e.g. domestic energy market and telecommunications).

◆   Encouragement of SMEs.

◆   Use regulators in natural monopoly and the law against anti-competitive behaviour.

◆   Improve the knowledge of the consumer through prevention of misleading advertising/promotion.

Legislation and competition

Firms facing intense competition may seek to form cartels and associations as a means of restricting output to raise prices and profitability. Equally, firms in concentrated industries may find collaboration and collusion more rewarding than rivalry. Large firms, including those that have monopolized their industry such as the big four supermarkets chains in the UK (Tesco, ASDA, Sainsbury's and Morrisons), might also abuse their power and position to discourage potential entrants.

All these put the customer at a disadvantage. Consequently, legislation governing such restraint of trade has been introduced in most countries more with a view to promoting more effective use of resources and to support a belief in the virtues of workable competition. Measures have included:

◆ **Restraint of trade** – Most agreements must not involve terms that restrict, or prevent a person from doing business.

◆ **Restrictive practices** – Legislation covers any form of agreement between the majority of firms in the industry that affects their freedom of action in disposing of their output. This is well known as anti-trust legislation in the United States but most countries have similar provision. It strikes a particular chord in Britain, where many durable consumer products, such as cars, tend to cost more than in the United States or the European Union. Increasing numbers of private motorists personally imported vehicles using for example the virtual showroom of Virgin cars at www.virgin.com/cars.

Note: A summary of the main points arising from the UK legislation is outlined later in this unit in the section "Fair Trading Act 1973". Non-UK readers should consult an intermediate economics text for a summary of your national framework for both restrictive practices and monopolies.

Insight: Mini case study – Microsoft

Microsoft, the world's largest software firm, was the subject of a long-running court case arising from its alleged abuse of its market power. Eight years after Sun Microsystems first complained that it was stifling competition, Microsoft is back in court appealing against the £345 million fine imposed by EU regulators for monopoly abuse. It is a crucial test of the freedom of dominant companies to keep enhancing products. The distractions of the legal proceedings and appeal prompted a worrying brain drain from the company while rival start-ups seeking to compete in Microsoft's markets are finding it easier to obtain business partners and raise finance. Microsoft was also frozen out of entire new industries such as smart phones and set-top boxes. The conclusion must be that use of the law was justified because market forces could not have dealt with Microsoft on their own. By shining a spotlight on the company's practices, the case forced it to restrain its behaviour towards customers and competitors on the one hand and emboldened business rivals on the other.

Question 3.7

Key skills – Problem-solving

Can you fill in the gaps in Figure 3.3?

Can you suggest what cartels do? Fixing minimum prices is one thing but what else?

Can you name any cartels?

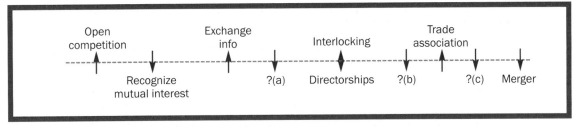

Figure 3.3 The spectrum of restrictive linkages between firms

Fair Trading Act 1973

◆ A Director General of Fair Trading is in overall control while the Competition Commission takes operational responsibility.

◆ Covers agreements on prices, recommended prices, terms, areas/businesses supplied and so on. The Office of Fair Trading has accused Britain's 50 leading independent schools of running an illegal price-fixing cartel. Schools like Eton and Harrow used to exchange detailed financial information, until they realized it was contrary to the 1998 Competition Act. However, fees have continued to rise from an average of £6400 to £7800 a term since 2003.

◆ Agreements must be registered and are presumed to be against the public interest unless the parties can justify it to the Restrictive Practices Court.

◆ Eight gateways can be used including protection of, or benefits to, the public, protecting jobs or export earnings, or to countervail competition or monopoly and agreements must not 'on balance' be detrimental to the public.

◆ Enforcement of minimum retail prices on distributors and withholding supplies with a view to coerce is also prohibited.

◆ The Director General of Fair Trading is empowered to investigate anti-competitive practices by firms with over £5 million turnover: that is, conduct that restricts, distorts or prevents competition in the production, acquisition or supply of goods or services. It includes discriminatory and predatory pricing (to force out rivals), vertical price squeezing (e.g. raise prices on inputs supplied to competitors), full line forcing (buy one item – must buy whole range) and discriminatory supply.

Insight: Designer versus imitation products

British supermarkets have lost their long battle to sell cut-price designer goods bought cheaply outside the European Union. The European Court ruled that it was illegal for Tesco to sell Levi jeans sourced from the United States and East Europe without the supplier's consent. Levi convinced the Court that it needed to ensure that its jeans were sold by trained staff and so justify prices being nearly double those charged by the supermarket. Tesco has retaliated by supplying good-quality unbranded jeans at very low prices.

Withholding supplies of perfumes to cut-price multiples was allowed by the British authorities on similar grounds. However, perfumiers in France are now having to close ranks under proposed EU laws that require lists of ingredients to be displayed on product labels. The information is thought necessary to protect consumers against allergies to traditional ingredients. Such information would be commercially sensitive and difficult to implement given the 100-plus ingredients in a perfume. The industry centred on the town of Grasse foresaw a plot to mastermind counterfeit products by their north European competitors who rely on synthetic ingredients.

Monopolies and mergers legislation

The methods adopted in Britain involve the following:

◆ A case by case judgemental approach.

◆ A cost–benefit framework to compare good and bad effects.

◆ A loose presumption that monopolies are against the public interest.

◆ A recognition that market dominance might reflect superior efficiency.

◆ Removing barriers to entry is preferred to preventing firms getting larger.

◆ Investigating horizontal mergers – More likely to be motivated by monopoly motives.

Both the Secretary of State and the DGFT (but not for mergers) have powers to refer a case to the Competition Commission. The legal definition of a referable monopoly is a 25 per cent market share while proposed mergers involving assets in excess of £30 million, or where they would create a legal monopoly or add to it, may also be referred.

Insight

Exxon's $76 billion takeover of Mobile to create the world's biggest company in revenue terms ($250 billion) means these qualifying sums are easily achieved. Despite the apparent scope for cost savings and extra market power, recent research by J.P. Morgan suggests that only 56 per cent of large European merger deals since 1985 have created value for the acquiring company. Who benefits if employees lose jobs and customers lose choice? Many mergers that appear to offer a 2 + 2 = 5 synergy opportunity end up as 2 + 2 = 3! Horizontal mergers of companies in the same line of business tend to achieve better returns, but at the expense of reduced competition, and the consumer.

In practice, only a very small proportion of qualifying monopolies or mergers are referred and then the Competition Commission may just report or will make recommendations. The final decision rests with the Secretary of State, who has been known to overrule Competition Commission recommendations. This is particularly likely when the benefits of greater size are thought to offer increased international competitiveness.

The Secretary of State has powers to seek appropriate undertakings, regulate prices, require the sale of controlling interests or prohibit the continuation of a practice. Offences are punishable under criminal law.

The 1998 Competition Act provides no excuse for the authorities not to act and sets much stiffer penalties, with fines of up to 10 per cent of turnover and permission for civil actions to be brought. The Office of Fair Trading has been given extra resources and an enhanced role to root out cartels, with attempts at obstruction made a criminal offence. British Telecom preferred to pre-empt an Office of Communications Act (Ofcom) inquiry and cut its broadband rental charges to less than a third of the former level. Rather than stifle competition, it calculated that more rapid growth would offset the negative impacts on revenue in the longer term. A similar effect may result if a proposed 60 per cent cut in the price of international mobile phone calls is fully implemented.

Activity 3.10

Key skills – Interpreting information

State five ways in which the Director General of Fair Trading is actively protecting consumers.

The promotion of free competition between member states of the European Union is fundamental to the success of the Single Market. Its legislation therefore overrides the national legislation of member states.

Some sections of its legislation relate to the welfare of the marketing environment. These sections are:

◆ Article 85 – This stipulates the prohibition of all restrictive agreements affecting trade between member states that prevent or distort competition.

◆ Article 86 – This relates to abuse of a dominant market position.

◆ Articles 92–94 – These three articles forbid government from subsidizing firms or industries which can distort or may threaten to distort competition.

◆ Co-operative agreements – These agreements stipulate that shared facilities, market research and consultancy are acceptable.

Directives have also been introduced governing such matters as ingredients in food and the introduction of sell-by dates. British law is only now coming into line with EU law and its tough fines of up to 10 per cent of domestic turnover for illegal anti-competitive agreements. Recent examples of EU fines include £95 million against Nintendo and £12 million against Sotherby's for their collusion and price fixing with Christie's, their fellow auctioneers and main rival. Their former chief executive was also fined $350,000 in the United States and narrowly avoided a prison sentence.

Other areas of legislation that affect the marketer

Patents

◆   This is a right given to the inventor to reap all the rewards accruing over a specified period, normally 20 years.

◆   To qualify, the invention must be novel and go beyond the current state of the art.

◆   A European Patent Office has been established as a cost-effective means of achieving coverage across member states.

Insight: The significance of patents

BlackBerry, the iconic mobile, faced closure following a US patent ruling. It failed to reach agreement with the patent holder resulting in a court injunction that could shut down its wireless e-mail service. BlackBerry users and shareholders were dismayed, but only if businesses have confidence that infringers will be dealt with by the courts will they patent and license their inventions for the benefit of wider society.

Trade marks

◆   There have considerable importance for the marketer who has invested heavily in a particular brand name.

◆   The Trade Marks Act in Britain provides exclusive rights to registered marks (words or symbols).

◆   Infringement may lead to an injunction and damages.

Insight: The significance of trade marks

Apple versus Apple is a long-standing dispute in that the Beatles' record label has claimed that Apple Computer have flagrantly violated a 1991 agreement not to use its logo to sell music. However this was before the digital revolution and the iTunes Music Store which accounts for 70 per cent of music downloads in the United Kingdom and the United States. Apple Computer claimed it was providing data transmission, not selling music, and won the case.

Monitoring the micro-environment

The following section discusses the sources of information on the micro-environment. You should complement your reading of this section with your reading of the discussion about the macro-environment in Unit 4. Both the micro-environment and the macro-environment form the context for consideration of environmental information systems in the final unit (Unit 9).

Collecting information is a key statement of marketing practice. So is the subsequent interpretation and presentation of the information collected and its analysis and the findings uncovered. It is also one of the key marketing skills that you require to develop.

Different types of information are required depending on the decisions to be taken. The following discussion identifies which types of information can be collected about which groups of people or organizations.

The following pieces of information can be collected about:

◆ **Competitors:**

- Set prices, discounts, credit terms
- Sales volumes by segment, product, region and distribution channel
- Market shares and key objectives
- Promotional activities, catalogues and distributor incentives
- New product development, expansion plans and changes in personnel
- Financial strength and relationships with key stakeholders

◆ **Suppliers, distributors and potential entrants into the market:**

- Set prices, discounts, credit terms
- Sales volumes by segment, product, region and distribution channel
- Market shares
- Main objectives (mission statement)
- Activities, catalogues and business-to-business incentives
- New product development, expansion plans and changes in personnel
- Financial strength and relationships with key stakeholders (clients and parties in the supply chain)

◆ **Industry:**

- Sales volumes by product, segment, region and country
- Sales growth and seasonal/cyclical patterns
- Production capacities, levels, plans and stock positions
- Technical change and investment plans

Information gathered through marketing intelligence and market research needs to be combined with that gathered internally before being classified, processed and analysed. Information databases are central to modern marketing. Collecting information on customers is one thing (*data collection* and *data storage*), but processing and utilizing the massive amounts of data captured by computers (*data analysis* and *data mining*) is much more demanding and pertinent.

Gathering customer insight through the collection and analysis of information can help companies is a variety of ways. For example:

◆ This may help create opportunities to explore new ways to create efficient information systems. Information systems can greatly help manage relationships with customers. As such, information systems represent a prime facilitator of relationship management with customers.

◆ This may help organizations shape the way in which they communicate internally as well as externally with others (B-2-B; B-2-C).

◆ This may help companies individualize and personalize their relationships with specific customers and customer segments through the providing of vital information at every point of interface with existing customers.

◆ Database related tools are used to interact with customers. They can help predict behaviour and help companies select actions to influence customer behaviour. The knowledge gathered through the analysis of information can help companies in their strategies for focused acquisition, tailored cross selling and even selective retention of their existing customers.

There are three crucial stages in database management or the management of information about customers. These stages are:

1   Consolidate all the data collected about a customer into a usable set of information:

    ◆ Conduct automated cleaning of data.

2   Analyse information about customers:

    ◆ To precisely target most attractive prospects.

    ◆ To discard suspects who do not meet profiling criteria.

3   Results of targeting of specific guests must be tracked to determine which customers responded to what campaigns:

    ◆ Step will identify profitable customers.

    ◆ Process will also indicate which promotions and campaigns have been successful.

In brief, the gathering of information can provide a critical element in the process of:

◆ Forming or deepening customer relationships and loyalty. For example one cruise line sends a 'best table' photograph award in a New Year's card to remind recipients of happy times spent on a recent cruise.

◆ Spotting emerging patterns and trends to provide focus for marketing campaigns.

◆ Segmenting customers for receipt of tailored offers.

Main sources of information

To complete this unit it would be useful to examine briefly the nature and requirements of an information system for effective competitor analysis. Attempt the following activity before reading on.

Activity 3.11

Key skills – Collecting and interpreting information

List at least four sources relevant to a competitor analysis under each of the following headings:

Internal sources (e.g. sales force records)

Company sources (e.g. company reports)

Industry/market sources (e.g. trade associations)

Government sources (e.g. censuses)

Commercial sources (e.g. A.C. Nielsen)

Academic sources (e.g. *Journal of Marketing*)

General sources (e.g. quality press reports)

Internet sources (e.g. www.strategy-business.com)

Select one source under each heading and explain how it would contribute to the analysis.

Competitor analysis involves the gathering and interpretation of intelligence from a range of sources, regarding key rivals, with the intention of achieving a competitive edge over them by:

◆ Identifying and exploiting competitor weaknesses.

◆ Avoiding actions that provoke aggressive and possibly damaging responses.

◆ Discovering moves that competitors are unable/unwilling to respond to.

◆ Avoiding any surprises that may give rivals a competitive advantage.

Actual and potential threats must be accounted for. Threats could be as follows:

◆ Companies that could overcome entry barriers.

◆ Customers or suppliers that could integrate backwards or forwards.

◆ Possible takeovers of existing rivals or foreign firms benefiting from tariff or regulatory changes.

There are literally hundreds of potential intelligence sources but these are useless unless meaningful information can be extracted. Data mining has been developed as a process of analysing and manipulating data so as to provide new and powerful insights into consumer and competitor behaviour patterns. To understand potential rivals, however, companies must first understand and appreciate their goals, capabilities, strategies and view of the future. Consequently, the spectrum of information needed could include the following.

Financial information

◆ Successive company annual accounts reveal information on performance and direction of growth.

◆ Future borrowing capability can also be ascertained. These may be accessed through websites or the Companies Registration Office.

◆ Business reference services and commercial databases provide detailed reports and comparative analyses on hundreds of companies in the form of graphs and ratios – Examples include the following:

1 Datastream holds 10+ years accounts on all UK quoted companies.

2 www.ft.com covers 50,000 listed companies in over 50 countries.

3 www.carol.co.uk links to the annual reports of companies in the United Kingdom, Europe, Asia and the United States.

◆ These allow companies to build a financial health profile of each competitor.

◆ Embracing indices such as turnover, debt, assets, growth and credit rating can give a very accurate picture of fellow companies.

◆ Credit reference agencies and your own company's treasury department may provide insight on bill payment habits and credit worthiness.

Organizational information

◆ The trade and quality press are up-to-date sources of such information.

◆ A variety of business periodicals often provide in-depth coverage of specific companies.

◆ Access is often eased through databases. For example, see www.europages.com or www.companiesonline.com or www.asiansources.com or Business Africa online at www.banks-r.demon.co.uk.

◆ Monitoring the comments of the chairman and the chief executive in consecutive annual reports and responses to questions at AGMs provides strategic background on goals, activities and corporate values.

◆ More detailed knowledge may be provided through the salesforce of suppliers or purchasing staff of mutual intermediaries.

◆ Stakeholder information networks are of general importance as are local papers and planning application records.

◆ To form an organizational profile for a competitor, the following might be tracked:

1 Key decision-makers

2 New appointments

3 Takeovers

4 Subsidiaries

5 Closures

6 Investments

7 New ventures

8 Current problems

Production and product information

- Patent application records provide clues to future plans and a rival's research capability as well as technical information.

- Research networks and the scanning of technical papers give warning of breakthroughs.

- The Consumers' Association provides independent product comparisons and reverse engineering can provide information on attributes and costs.

- Local chambers of commerce will be a useful source on facilities and employment.

- Intermediaries are in a good position to contribute product knowledge.

- Competitors should therefore be monitored in terms of the following criteria:

  1 Locations/size of facilities

  2 Breadth and depth of product line

  3 Costs

  4 Qualities

  5 Performance

  6 New product developments

There are many ways to find out useful information on troublesome rivals. Courses of action could include the following steps:

- Marketing information:

  - The field salesforce is a key source of marketing intelligence. Properly trained and with an effective recording and retrieval system they can generate vast amounts of information on new products, comparative prices and discounts, market shares, promotions and packaging. They are at the daily interface with customers who are in the business of comparing product and seller capabilities.

  - Other sources include the Marketing Surveys Index and product research organizations such as Mintel. See world market research abstracts at www.mra.warc.com or www.keynote.co.uk.

- Question job applicants for inside information. They might be keen to impress and probably would not have been warned about divulging secrets.

- Go on plant tours/monitor aerial maps/monitor staff and transport movements.

- Recruit staff from competitors.

- Quiz staff at trade shows/conferences/exhibitions. The informal atmosphere and easy conversation may greatly help.

- Commission academic research among relevant suppliers and intermediaries.

- Undertake reverse engineering on competitor products to determine performance/costs.

- There are of course many more less commendable courses of actions.

With markets often changing so quickly and dramatically, a formalized information system is required. It must incorporate procedures for the co-ordination and communication of intelligence to relevant decision-makers without delay. The existence of a system should encourage participation in the information-gathering process by all organization members. This important need for environmental intelligence will be developed further.

Activity 3.12

Key skills – reflection about current practices

Samsung, the world's third largest maker of mobile phones has banned the use of 3G camera phones in its factories, fearing industrial espionage.

Is the marketer failing in their duty, if they do not fully exploit publicly available information?

Some of these practices seem acceptable, some unsavoury – where would (a) you, (b) your organization draw the line that defines ethical behaviour?

Does the line move if corporate survival is threatened?

Summary

In this unit we have dealt with the following important aspects:

◆ The nature and implications of competition in fragmented and concentrated industries.

◆ The importance of monitoring the actions and reactions of competitors.

◆ An appreciation of the five forces required in a structural analysis of industry profitability.

◆ A practical framework for assessing the intensity of market competition and changes over time.

◆ Adoption of the five-force framework to allow consideration of collaboration.

◆ The regulatory framework relating to competition.

◆ The need for an information system and the important sources of information required for a competitor analysis.

◆ Competitive activity involves more than the price variable.

◆ Choice between alternatives is the key as firms compete on service, innovation and non-price variables.

◆ Large firms predominate in concentrated industries due to the importance of barriers to entry in which economies of scale figure importantly.

◆ Smaller firms are the product of more fragmented structures, although profitable niches can be found in most markets.

◆ Concentrated and fragmented industries also interact. In the UK between 1993 and 2000, an estimated one-fifth of all corner shops, high-street banks and post offices disappeared. The rate of this decline is accelerating.

◆ The need to monitor competitors, while providing some predictions of competitive response, only takes account of rival firms within the market.

◆ More thorough analysis requires consideration of several groups in the micro-environment.

Further study and examination preparation

The competitive environment confronts virtually all organizations in some way or another and is the bread-and-butter concern of the marketer. The examiner has a variety of question options available. These range from Porter's analysis to the competitive/co-operative relationships between a business and its suppliers or distributors, to assessment of the impact of policies relating to competition.

You must demonstrate not just an understanding of theories and analysis discussed in the unit but also an ability to relate to your own or a representative industry. You must be very clear as to the contribution of the marketer to shaping marketing forces and sustaining better than normal profitability over time.

This unit often provides part questions, although a very recent example of a full question is given in Question 4b/c, December 2004. Question 1a/b, December 2005 provided two parts of the section based on the Microsoft case. Don't bank on a five-force question coming up too frequently. Neither of the specimen papers provided contain one.

Extending knowledge

Johnson G. and Scholes K. (2002) *Exploring Corporate Strategy*, London: Prentice Hall International.

Palmer A. and Hartley B. (2006) *The Business and Marketing Environment*, McGraw-Hill (Chapter 6 on the Competitive Environment).

Porter M.E. (1980) *Competitive Strategies: Techniques for analysing Industries and Competitors*, New York: Free Press.

Porter M.E. (1985) *Competitive Advantage: Creating and Sustaining Superior Performance*, New York: Free Press.

Porter M.E. (1986) *Competition in global industries: a conceptual framework, in Competition in Global Industries*, Boston MA: Harvard University Press.

Other suggested reading

Jobber D. (1998) *Principles of Marketing*, McGraw-Hill, 2nd Ed.

Chapter 16: Analysing competitors and creating competitive advantage.

Lancaster G. and Massingham L. (2001), *Marketing Management*, McGraw-Hill Education.

Chapter 2: Analysing the environment: opportunities and threats.

Relevant websites

www.ft.com.

www.economist.com.

http://europa.eu.int/pol/enter/index_en.htm for EU competition policy.

www.strategy-business.com.

www.asia-pacific.com/ for news and data from this region. See also www.feer.com/ the *Far Eastern Review*.

www.europages.com.

www.companiesonline.com.

www.asiansources.com.

Practicing past exam questions

In September 2008 a new syllabus and assessment will be introduced. Referring to past papers is recommended as the core syllabus content has not changed significantly but students are also advised to refer to the specimen paper so that they can gather a clear understanding of the new exam format.

Please see Question 4b/c, December 2004. Go to www.cim.co.uk for specimen answers.

Please see Question 4, June 2004. Go to www.cim.co.uk for specimen answers.

Please see Question 3(i), June 2004. Go to www.cim.co.uk for specimen answers.

Please see Question 1a/b, December 2005. Go to www.cim.co.uk for specimen answers.

Please see Question 4, June 2006. Go to www.cim.co.uk for specimen answers.

Unit 4

The natural environment, the challenges of change and information sources

Learning objectives

This unit introduces the macro-environment while subsequent units consider the specific economic, legislative, social and technical environments in more depth. Accordingly, in this unit the natural environment, the challenge of change and information sources are discussed in depth. By the end of this unit, you will be able to:

◆ Appreciate the breadth and significance of the external environment (3.1).

◆ Undertake an identification and assessment of environmental threats and opportunities facing an organization of your choice (3.1/3.2).

◆ Appreciate the implications of the natural environment for marketers (3.6).

◆ Access and assess relevant data on the environment of business in a time- and cost-effective manner (3.2).

◆ Recognize the potential significance of emerging environmental challenges to effective marketing in the present and the future (3.7).

Study guide

This unit provides the framework for a section of the syllabus accounting for 40 per cent of the total. It is primarily concerned with the importance of monitoring and understanding changes in the wider environment. The main elements of the macro-environment were briefly defined in the first part of Unit 2 and you should refresh your memory of this before reading on.

This introductory unit is also a very good source of possible examination questions. These may test your general understanding of the macro-environment and its importance in the assessment of the marketing environment and in the development of marketing strategy. Another area addressed by this unit is how information sources can and do underpin the marketer's ability to monitor a changing marketing environment. The natural environment is also discussed.

It is vital that you seek to relate your studies to up-to-date and relevant examples and applications. By now you should have acquired the habit of scanning quality press or websites for these. It is very important for you to be able to relate theory to the practice of marketing management as the examiner will not only expect you to be able to do so but just as importantly, credit is given for the demonstration of your knowledge of relevant as well as current developments.

Understanding the macro-environment

Marketing is actively concerned with anticipating and then responding positively to changes occurring in the external environment. Although as discussed in depth in Unit 3, an organization cannot control its micro-environment, it can however do much to adapt to the

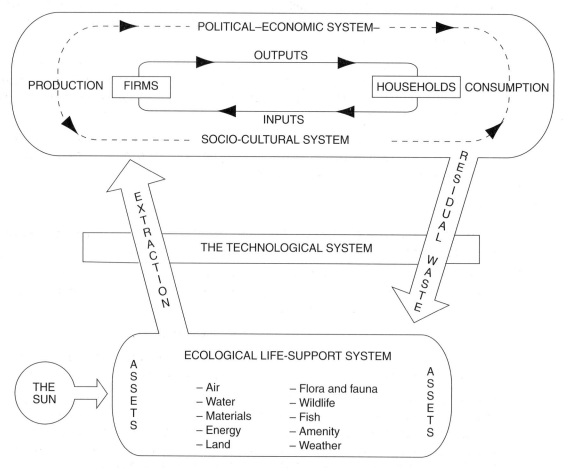

Figure 4.1 Business as open systems within the macro-environment

factors of the micro-environment. Organizations can also not control the forces of the macro-environment. Notwithstanding, the generally uncontrollable forces of the macro-environment can and do create a succession of potential threats and opportunities for organizations.

In Unit 1, the topic of the business as an open system interacting with its external environment was discussed. Figure 4.1 provides an appreciation of the linkages involved. The business, as an open system, competes for inputs that are privately owned by households. These inputs are converted into outputs of goods and services that are desired and purchased by households using incomes received from selling factor services to the firm. These transactions are not only conducted in the micro-environment of any given business, but also within the wider political, social and economic systems.

The political system, explored in Unit 7, provides for the election of a government on the basis of a declared manifesto. Some fundamental functions underpin most political systems. These are generally as follows:

◆ Broad policy objectives are set and legislation is enacted to implement it.

◆ An important political objective is to secure re-election. This by all means emphasizes the attractiveness of economic growth as the main driving force in the economic system. For instance, households living in relative poverty usually seek improved living standards while the rich seem intent to get richer. As such, if there is a need to choose a party, they are most likely to opt for the political party that offers sustainable growth.

◆ In line with the changing socio-cultural landscape, the number and structure of households are changing as populations alter. The attitudes and values of households also appear to change over time. Education and the media are generally seen to be strong influences.

◆ Firms also operate within a social and cultural system. Patterns of consumption reflect evolving lifestyles, and societal expectations impact on what is deemed to be acceptable behaviour within businesses.

The natural environment

Figure 4.1 shows the SLEPT factors, discussed in Unit 3, as part of a much larger system upon which they depend.

The natural environment forms the backdrop to our social and economic lives. As such a growing economy must draw part of its necessary inputs from this life-supporting system. Inputs can be divided into two categories:

◆ Renewable assets – For instance softwoods or fish stocks.

◆ Non-renewable assets – Inputs such as oil and minerals are effectively non-renewable assets accumulated through natural processes over very long time periods.

While some resources can be renewed, this can only occur due to an input of energy from another system (i.e. the sun can help trees grow; these in turn will provide softwoods). The environment also receives discharges from the economic system in the form of residual waste. Waste which exceeds what the natural environment can assimilate is referred to as pollution. This can impact air, water and land quality as well as the weather.

Insight

The UK produces about 430 million tons of waste a year. Over 30 per cent of food waste is in fact organic waste due to changing domestic habits, overly tight sell/use-by dates and demand for uniform fruit and vegetables. As two-thirds of this is biodegradable matter, this produces methane gas, a powerful greenhouse gas, as the food decomposes.

Although 70 per cent of household waste could be recycled instead of ending up in landfills, in the UK only about 17 per cent used to be recycled compared to 47 per cent in Holland and 64 per cent in Austria. However the UK's target was raised to 25 per cent for 2005. Since then, there has been a conscientious rise in awareness and initiatives.

Insight

Growth in the UK domestic waste has slowed from 3 to 2 per cent per annum and targets for 2020 are to increase incineration from 9 to 27 per cent, reduce landfill from 72 to 25 per cent and recycle the balance.

The European Union's recycling targets are forecasted to cost £10 billion or £400 per household. This said, no private company is likely to make the necessary investments without assurances of a market for recycled material. One seasonal solution to current problems was provided by the Emma Maersk, the world's largest container ship. While it brought 11,000 containers of Christmas goods from China to the UK, its return cargo was made up of British rubbish. Although UK residents and businesses are being encouraged to recycle, most of the recycling of plastic can unfortunately not be conducted in the UK but in China.

The real solution of course requires our 'throw-away culture' to be revised. Bins are filled with fast-food packaging, piles of paper and plastics. Plastic is treated as disposable, yet its output rose 50-fold in the last half century and products can last for 400 years. Getting households to become involved in recycling is indeed a big marketing challenge.

Some countries have however started a positive cycle of change. For instance, Ireland now taxes non-recycled waste and plastic bags. This has reduced the usage of plastic bags by 90 per cent. In the UK, 8 billion plastic bags and 500 million plastic bottles are thrown away each year. Supermarkets have so far prevented any action being taken over its vast packaging to transport food across the globe and supply ready-to-eat meals, but the political pressure appears to be mounting. Hence, supermarkets such as Sainsbury's have started to review the packaging of some of their convenience food ranges. Meanwhile although they still produce their traditional product ranges, Levi's have also started offering sustainable jeans made from organic denim. The buttons are coconut shell, the dyes natural, the label cardboard and all materials are European in an attempt to reduce transportation costs.

Insight

Electronic waste is one of the fastest growing forms of rubbish with over one million tons being thrown away each year of which 90 per cent goes to landfill. At current rates each of us will over a lifetime dispose on average of 12 washers, 10 fridges, 95 small kitchen appliances, 55 items of recreational equipment and 35 pieces of IT kit. However, under a new EU directive introduced in 2005 manufacturers and retailers will be held responsible for recycling used products.

The technological system can be double-edged. It can open up the natural world to the ravages of uncontrolled tourism or exploitative cultivation of the rainforests and also facilitate recycling and substitution. This said, reconciling the demand for economic growth with the protection of our natural life-support systems may indeed be considered to be the primary challenge of the twenty-first century.

Insight

Scientists have warned that rapidly expanding soya production, illegal logging and a $40 billion development project proposed by the Brazilian government will cause the rainforest to all but disappear by 2020.

The Advance Brazil scheme involves the building of new roads, railways and dams. Satellite imaging and computer modelling techniques can now identify selective logging of valuable trees and suggest that eventually only 5 per cent would be left intact. The region is already suffering from unprecedented drought due in part to tree loss. Accounting for 40 per cent of the world's tropical rainforest, 30 per cent of all plant and animal species and generating 20 per cent of the world's oxygen and fresh water, such an outcome would dramatically affect biodiversity, the carbon cycle, global climate and the greenhouse effect. In fact, the record 10,000 square miles which has already disappeared has caused environmental damage that could far outweigh any economic benefits.

On a brighter note the main producers, who produced 50 million tons of soya on 23 million hectares of former rainforest in 2005, have signed a moratorium on buying crops grown on recently deforested land, following a critical Greenpeace report.

Insight

The controversial £13 billion Three Gorges Dam, to block the Yangzte and supply the electricity for China's rapid growth, is now complete and has commenced flooding its 254-square mile reservoir. As China's largest construction project since the Great Wall this will, when fully functioning in 2009, have submerged 1200 communities and displaced over 700,000 people. However, failure of the dam would have catastrophic consequences for the up to 300 million Chinese living downstream of the 600-foot dam.

But, such reservoirs are also necessary to try and contain the accelerating melting from China's glaciers, which may disappear by the end of the century. Holding 15 per cent of the world's ice, this would dramatically worsen the current floods and raise sea levels.

Meanwhile China currently faces a water crisis as industrialization and drought have reduced water tables and polluted most watercourses. Consequently wheat production has been falling since 2000 and imports will soon dwarf global reserves leading to rising prices and further hardship for the world's poor. The turbines also supply over 18 k megawatts of clean power for its fast growing economy, but this will not affect its 15 per cent contribution to global greenhouse gases or the doubling in emissions expected by 2025.

Unfortunately China, like the United States, is predicted to be much less affected by climate change than India and Africa, making them very unlikely to introduce limits. It continues to average one new coal-fired power station a week (500 completions are planned by 2030) adding the equivalent of the UK's total capacity in one year.

Activity 4.1

Key skills – Presenting information

(The June 2005 mini-case study referred to a jet-set disease, a form of bird flu.)

Flu is one of the oldest diseases known to man and each year kills around 4000 people in the UK alone. However, since 1580 there have also been over 30 pandemics, of which the 1919 Spanish flu outbreak was the most catastrophic. Spread world-wide by soldiers (who had kept poultry in the trenches) returning from WW1, it killed 40 million, treble those lost in the war itself. Unusually, the strain particularly affected the 15–34 year olds rather than the old and frail.

The current strain of bird flu, despite some deaths, will have to mutate again before it can transmit between humans. But until scientists see what form it takes, they will not be able to design a vaccine for it.

Media frenzy has been widespread with as many as 150 million dead being predicted. Mass culls were conducted and the European Union banned live bird imports.

The fear of a pandemic sparked panic buying of everything from face masks to the antiviral drug Tamiflu produced by Roche.

This company is being encouraged to relax its patent and allow licensing to help countries where the drug is unaffordable. On the other hand, GlaxoSmithKline claim that they could produce a vaccine within four months of the pandemic.

Read the case material and press coverage to determine whether Roche should go for maximum profits or social responsibility.

The decline of the natural environment

The impact of technology

Economic growth has progressively inflicted a significant cost on the natural environment. This has arisen, in part, because of externalities that have been borne by third parties other than the producer or consumer involved.

Declining environmental quality has been the unavoidable result, unless the state has intervened to legislate or make the polluter pay. Technology and business activity have unquestionably affected the future of the environment.

Three fundamental constraints limit the pace and nature of technological change and the continuity of economic growth:

◆ **Social and institutional factors:**

  ◆ This is reflected in customs and legislation intended to curb the appliance of science in ways felt to be undesirable to society.

  ◆ For instance, a moratorium on nuclear programmes after Chernobyl was applied. However this attitude has been changing with nuclear being seen by Blair's government as the least bad option to meet the impending energy gap.

  ◆ Bans on animal testing, controls over GM foods, bans on human genetics may also go through due to the power of pressure groups. However, these are still being practised.

◆ **Depletion of non-renewable resources:**

  ◆ This includes fuels, minerals, fertile lands (through overgrazing), tropical rainforests and biological diversity in terms of animal and plant species extinction.

◆ **Pollution of the ecosystem:**

  ◆ Ecology is the study of plants and animals and their interaction with each other and the environment as a whole.

  ◆ Ecosystems include biodegradation processes that decompose wastes to provide nutrients for renewed growth.

  ◆ Problems arise only when their absorptive capabilities are overloaded due to the volume and/or nature of the wastes concerned.

Insight: Cloning the first human embryo

The first small step towards the most fundamental challenge to the natural environment – the world's first cloned human embryo – was announced by the US company Advanced Cell Technology in 2001. They replaced the DNA from a donated female egg with the DNA from the centre of a single adult male cell. The egg cell then divided as in normal development and could have potentially become a human being if implanted in a woman's womb. The Human Fertilization and Embryology Authority in the UK has since given a limited go-ahead for doctors to create 'designer babies', genetically selected to act as donors for their sick siblings.

This is a prime example of the general tension between technology as a force for good or a force for evil in its impacts on the natural environment. Certainly, the potential of therapeutic cloning represents amazing promise, but there is also the fear that nature is being violated and that a Pandora's box of irrevocable consequences is being opened. It may be well to remember that the so-called 'Black Death' that ravaged over half of Europe's population in the fourteenth century was more likely due to an unknown *Escherichia coli* type virus than the lowly black rat and its fleas.

Industrial impact

Effluents, emissions and solid wastes are often the result of industrialization. For instance, seven of the world's ten most polluted cities are in China. Similarly the Scottish salmon industry is threatened by rising levels of carcinogenic residues in the farmed fish and despite assertions by the Food Standards Agency that levels are within the safety limits researchers have warned that more than three portions a year could increase the cancer risk.

Toxic and chemically complicated wastes pose such a threat that Western governments have contributed $20 billion to fund their safe disposal. For instance, in Russia decaying armaments are posing a big problem for the government to dispose of. At present, an estimated 30,000 tons of enriched uranium and 780 tons of arms grade plutonium are stored around the country in often low-security military camps. This does not include abandoned nuclear reactors and submarines. Meanwhile, the UK does not have any agreed strategy for dealing with the 80,000 cubic metres of higher level waste which could grow six-fold as facilities are decommissioned. A government inquiry warned that suitable underground sites could take up to a century to approve and construct.

Consumer

Various factors can influence the impact of consumers on the natural environment. Despite the halving of noise and emissions in the new generation of aircrafts, the overall emissions of carbon dioxide are forecasted to rise due to an expected doubling of passenger numbers from 180 to 470 million. In fact, aircraft carbon dioxide emissions are predicted to rise from 8.8 to 18 million tonnes between 2000 and 2030 despite improved airliners like the Airbus380 super jumbo carrying 800 passengers from 2007.

In spite of increasing initiatives to educate consumers, half of all households do not appreciate that domestic power adds to global warming. As such, more than a million tonnes of greenhouse gas is released each year due to electrical appliances being left on standby. For example, when a consumer leaves a dishwasher switched on at the end of their cycle, 70 per cent of the power used when running is used.

Urban noise unquestionably increased tremendously. It has been said that it is now three times noisier than it was 30 years ago. Mobile phones, traffic and loud music are the most cited contributors of increasing noise pollution.

Human wastes have also added to the strain of the natural environment. For example, after Christmas, British households throw away an estimated six million fir trees, 85,000 miles of wrapping paper and 2.5 billion cards – enough to go around the globe nine times.

The introduction of the congestion charge on vehicles entering central London and the proposal to penalize gas guzzlers and offer a nil charge to cleaner engines have by all means affected the levels of car usage in London. Nonetheless traffic is still far above sought levels in the capital. In the rest of the country, with workers spending on average 90 minutes commuting each day, car travel appears to have grown so much that gridlocks are predicted despite proposals to extend electronic road charges.

Activity 4.2

Key skills – Interpreting information

Match the terms with their correct definitions:

1 Effluent

2 Emissions

3 Acid rain

4 Ozone-layer depletion

5 Greenhouse effect

a Carbon dioxide absorbs and radiates back heat that would otherwise escape into space, causing temperature rises.

b Liquid wastes discharged into seas or watercourses.

c Discharges of sulphur dioxide from power stations or vehicle exhaust gases combine with water vapour in the atmosphere.

d Release of gases into the atmosphere.

e Caused by the discharge of CFCs in aerosols, solvents, foam plastics and fridges allowing through dangerous ultraviolet rays.

Sources of the decline

The natural environment has found no difficulty in coping with the wastes created by our economic development, at least until recently. Natural disasters, or acts of God as they are legally referred to, have also been relatively easily accommodated (at a cost), be they Californian forest- or Australian bush-fires, Bangladesh floods, Java earthquakes or Caribbean/Pacific hurricanes, because their impacts have been both localized and reversible. However, the cumulative effects of the nineteenth century's industrial development has involved a different order of 'impact magnitude and irreversibility' in many of the effects created. Figure 4.2 shows the main factors responsible.

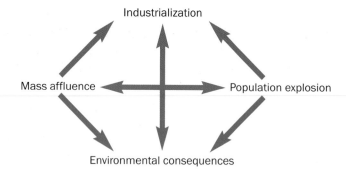

Figure 4.2 Key factors in environmental degradation

Although any one of the three elements will cause environmental problems, their combined and interdependent effects are much more serious.

Three-quarters of the world's population still live in less-developed countries and should they wish to emulate the high resource-consuming lifestyles of already industrialized countries, the environmental consequences are likely to be unsustainable.

If every Chinese or Indian household merely aspires to own a fridge, for example, then the impact on the ozone layer would easily offset successful international efforts to reduce CFC (Chlorofluorocarbon) emissions. The effects of the above are compounded by the pressure of competition, the pursuit of economic gain and the political imperative of economic growth in all countries. Many natural resources are neither privately nor corporately owned but are subject to common exploitation with little regard to environmental costs and benefits.

Insight

North Sea cod stocks have fallen from four million tons prior to mass commercial fishing to 53,000 tons today. The International Council for the Exploration of the Seas has recommended a total ban to the European Union for the fifth year running since merely reduced EU quotas (to help fishing communities) have not resulted in a recovery in fish stocks. Belated recognition of such consequences has mobilized both government and business interests to seek solutions. The immediate reaction of halting or even reversing economic growth has, however, quickly given way to a more pragmatic concern for achieving sustainable development.

Exam hint

The discussion about the natural environment is only a very short section, but still a very important aspect of the syllabus.

The natural environment will be one of the main business issues of this new century and therefore may occur as a question theme.

Sustainable development

Sustainable development involves meeting the needs of the present generation without compromizing the needs and requirements of future generations. In effect, the objective is to achieve a negative relationship between GDP (gross domestic product) and pollution through the introduction of viable controls for the achievement of sustainable development.

One highly specific threat involves the melting of Europe's permafrost due to global warming. Underground temperatures in the Alps have been rising five times faster than air temperatures. This has led to increasing landslides and avalanches. The implications for the Alpine sports industry and its marketing could be dramatic over the coming decades.

Insight

Recent developments like a mile-wide hole opening up in the North polar ice, a doubling in the ice flow from Greenland's glaciers in five years, a predicted ice-free Arctic ocean by 2050, the collapse of a vast Antarctic ice shelf and the progressive disappearance of Himalayan glaciers, are creating a sense of alarm and global warning.

If the land-based Arctic sheet ice melts, sea levels will automatically rise threatening to submerge some of the most fertile and densely populated areas of the world, for example Bangladesh and the Netherlands.

On the positive side, global warming is opening up a north-west trading passage from Europe to the Pacific. However on the negative side, the course of the Gulf stream is being disrupted and weather is becoming uncertain and more extreme.

The economic and environmental impacts of the latter are likely to be immense. For example the UK's average temperature could drop by five degrees making it similar to Iceland. Yet currently spring is coming 8–10 days early impacting on farmers and fashions alike. The opening of new trade routes could also lead to political disputes as Canada currently lays claim to Arctic waters while the United States believes they should be treated as an international route.

Since pollution and resource depletion do not observe boundaries, they are global problems that can only be solved by global initiatives. The Montreal Protocol, for example, agreed to cap CFC production but with reduced targets applying to less-developed countries. Scientists calculate that a 70 per cent reduction in greenhouse gases is required to halt global warming but the Americans, who alone are responsible for 25 per cent of greenhouse gases, refuse to implement even token cuts. The Bush Administration did admit that global warming exists and will inflict serious and permanent changes on the global environment, but did not recommend altering current policy or committing to Kyoto targets.

Insight: Climate change and sustainable development

The key to a poor country's development is access to energy. The International Energy Agency estimates global energy demand will rise 60 per cent by 2030 with developing countries accounting for two-thirds of the increase. If conventional energy sources are developed to meet demand, then high carbon dioxide emissions would result.

The Stern report assessing the human and economic costs of global warming stated that if unchecked, temperatures could rise by up to 5 °C by 2050 and catastrophically affect the natural environment. Climate change was described as the greatest market failure ever. Even full compliance with Kyoto targets would only succeed in postponing the warming by five or six years. Stern suggested that inaction would eventually shrink global economies by up to 20 per cent but remedial efforts would cost only 1 per cent of annual global GDP (gross domestic product). All governments must put an appropriate price on carbon, negotiate robust international treaties and invest more in green technologies. The only other alternatives appear to be either keep the people poor or a major switch to nuclear power.

Whether this report will provide the necessary political and business impetus and engender the necessary action is debateable. The UK is likely to meet the 12.5 per cent cuts required by Kyoto but not the 20 per cent target the government set itself to prove it was possible to meet green objectives while maintaining a healthy economy. Emissions have actually risen since 2002 due to increased car usage, airport expansion and congestion. Even if all emissions were eliminated overnight they would be nullified by two years of Chinese growth. Unfortunately, developing countries are taking no real steps to limit their own growing emissions and the co-operation required to secure the necessary 60 per cent cuts in emissions looks unlikely. It could even be argued that what the developing world needs most is peace, stable institutions and effective rules of law.

Sustainability may well be synonymous with a society that works. Business too requires a long-term policy framework if it is to respond positively. Many far-sighted companies see global warming as an opportunity. Since the climate change market is worth £500 billion saving the planet and serving the interests of shareholders is not necessarily mutually exclusive.

Insight: Nature versus technology – the challenge of GM food

This is food made from crops whose genetic code has been altered or modified in some way. The aim is to develop strains that produce higher yields with more consistent quality, nutritional value and appearance. Further objectives are to enable the crops to grow under hardier conditions with greater resistance to disease and parasites so that fewer chemical-based weedkillers or herbicides need to be applied. In effect, it is a high-tech development of what agriculturalists have been doing for centuries through selective use of crop strains/breeding.

Despite the risks to adjacent wildlife, it offers massive potential to developing countries, particularly those affected by soil erosion or unable to afford expensive fertilizers and chemicals. It replaces trial and error with control and systematization and if the fears prove unfounded it will be the poor who suffer. Despite widespread acceptance in the United States, the media label 'Frankenstein food' constituted a marketing nightmare for those promoting its acceptance in the European Union, and pressure led to hasty and emotive regulations on labelling.

Implications of the natural environment for marketers

◆ Business is central to the problem of environmental decline, but also to the solution.

◆ Environmental consciousness is rising, so the evolving green agenda needs to be monitored by companies.

◆ Few consumers budget on environmental performance alone.

◆ External stakeholders seek reassurance. Therefore at the same time improvement of performance and a risk-free future need to be emphasized.

◆ Agreed objectives need to be set by top management/trading partners. The latter will prefer to deal with a business applying environmental standards it is committed to.

◆ Seek a competitive edge via ethically sound practices. This could be achieved by means of the use of cleaner technologies.

◆ Assess the carbon footprint made by the organization and assess the possibility of carbon offsets from investment in cleaner technologies and products.

◆ Offset resource depletion through technical change, redesign, reduction, reuse, recycling and substitution, linked to quality initiatives.

◆ An environmental strategy needs to be based on sound ethical principles, an audit, impact assessment (see Unit 9) and action based on benchmarking of best practice.

◆ Stakeholders must be involved/educated into good environmental practice.

◆ Pay-off is in an increased sense of security, improved image/relationships, lower insurance premiums and avoidance of fines/litigation.

Insight

Mobile phones now pose an environmental threat and marketing challenge. One billion handsets are in use globally, with over 100 million discarded (upgrades average 18 months) each year in Europe alone. Containing lead and beryllium, they represent a threat to health if not disposed of properly. Currently most discards are crudely recycled for sale in less-developed economies but rising ownership suggests a challenge to come.

The challenge of change

Unlike the micro-environment, broad natural, political, economic, social and technical trends and changes do not directly impact on day-to-day operations but are extremely important in shaping the competitive situation and the actions and perceptions of relevant stake-holders.

How many businesses do you know that can afford to be purely production orientated? Ever since the beginning of the industrial revolution, change has been the predominant and enduring feature in both industry and wider society. The marketer is actively involved in the shaping and changing of consumer tastes but such effects are nothing compared to the evolving influences of educational expectations, the media, peer groups and travel.

It is also likely that the twentieth century will be best remembered for technological achievements that have put astronauts on the moon, transformed communication and automated industrial processes. Satellites, computers and supersonic aircraft laid the foundations for a 'global village' where events on the other side of the world are known earlier than those in a nearby town or village. Business must therefore be constantly alert to the challenges of new processes and technology, to possible substitutes and, increasingly, to competitive threats.

Question 4.1

Key skills – Problem-solving

Can you think of any businesses that face *static* market conditions? (This implies no change in both consumer tastes and the state of technical knowledge.)

The management guru Peter Drucker emphasized that companies need to continually and consistently keep themselves updated about the changes occurring around them so that they can embrace these. This contention by Peter Drucker underlines the reality of continuous change in contemporary marketing environments.

Although the size of an organization can safeguard it with regards to some factors, size is no longer an automatic defence against the forces of change. Indeed, only half of the companies listed in the *Financial Times Top 100 Companies* 25 years ago, are still operating in 2008. It is argued that the companies who are missing failed to meet the challenges and so fell victim to a number of misfortunes, which could have included:

◆   'Old economy' companies are increasingly replaced by 'new economy' Internet-related businesses.

◆   Acquisition by another firm: for example Safeway or Abbey.

◆   Spectacular failure: for example Enron, Rover or Farepak.

◆   Poor relative performance: for example Sabena Airlines.

◆   The state forced to take ownership: for example Railtrack in the UK.

Clearly, the larger business must stay alert to survive changing circumstances. However the weight of its bureaucracy may make this difficult. Smaller businesses may have the flexibility to adapt more effectively, but only if given access to sufficient resources. In brief, all types of companies must recognize that they are on the equivalent of a moving conveyor; they must therefore be prepared to move fast in line with changes as tastes, technology and competitive forces are evolving rapidly.

Although change is the characteristic feature of industrial and information societies, its pace and complexity appears to have increased. The 1950s and 1960s, for example, while still experiencing change, were relatively stable and predictable. Up to 1970, economic growth and development in many countries was almost continuous and fluctuated within narrow limits. There was no Internet or even computers or mobile phones. Unemployment and inflation were low in developed countries and a high degree of social consensus prevailed. Political parties had similar agendas and both technological and market changes were manageable. The oil crises of the 1970s replaced this comparative calm with turbulent change that has continued ever since. The market environment was even more turbulent in Asian economies such as Hong Kong or China, where rapid growth was compounded by critical political uncertainties and changes.

In less dynamic economies such change exposed previously sleepy market sectors to considerable threats since familiarity with previously established conditions had led to complacency. Similar effects have been felt more recently with world-wide privatization and deregulation, the introduction of the Euro, international trade disputes, a dot-com collapse, renewed oil price instability, the war on terrorism and in Iraq and so on. Dynamic and complex market environments demand that the marketer understands the future rather than rely on the patterns of the past. Accordingly, the marketer needs to follow some consistent yet continuous and systematic processes. These would invariably include the following:

◆   Scan their environment.

◆   Identify those forces relevant to the organization/its industry.

◆   Forecast political, economic, social and technical change.

◆   Respond to threats and opportunities by implementing strategies.

◆   Monitor the outcome of planned action.

◆   Continue to scan their environment.

Exam hint

Improving own performance

Specimen papers will give guidance on the question format and an indication of question style. The best preparation for this unit is to practise relating PESTEL elements to specific organizations or sectors then working through the case in detail as the exam approaches.

The response to 'uncontrollable macro forces' in terms of strategies requires more explanation. 'Standing still is the fastest way of moving backwards in a rapidly changing world' is a quotation attributed to the late Anita Roddick, founder of Body Shop International. Businesses cannot afford to passively accept change in the macro-environment but must adapt or suffer the consequences. This requires the marketer not only to scan and analyse threats and opportunities but also to develop positive strategic responses. This might involve lobbying for political change or managing the media in order to influence critical publics. Being proactive, even where scope for direct influence on events is limited, will always have more effect on the outcome of the 'game' than the pure spectator role. However, one of the first steps in effective environmental scanning is to identify the relevant sources of environmental data and it is to this task that we turn next.

Internal and external information systems

There are two main categories of existing information:

1   **Internal data** – gathered in-company as a result of operational activities (e.g. employment, cost and sales figures).

2   **Secondary data** – gathered from external sources (e.g. government statistics, published surveys – see Figure 4.3).

Figure 4.3 Secondary data for a business

A third source of information is *primary data* commissioned specifically through market research, for instance to fill knowledge gaps left by the much cheaper alternatives above.

Exam hint

Improving own performance

The examiner will always give credit to candidates who not only make a relevant point in answer to an examination question but can also cite the source. Since sources of information are an explicit part of the CIM syllabus; you would be well advised to link different information sources to different sections in your file, for example social trends linked to population changes.

Information required for adequate marketing

Many different types of information are required, depending on the decisions to be taken.

Economy:

◆ Main economic indicators – inflation, interest rates, labour market changes

◆ Business confidence indicators – capacity utilization and investment

◆ National income, output and expenditure patterns

◆ Government taxation and spending plans

Society:

◆ Demographic indicators – birth/death rates and interregional migration patterns

◆ Household and working patterns – change in cultural norms

◆ Leisure activities and ownership ratios for homes, cars, mobiles and so on

Similar factors could be identified in other areas of the SLEPT environment, underlining the diverse nature of information requirements in modern business today. In an environment of rapid change, where time and delay can cost a company dearly, the ability to obtain a clear and accurate picture of developments can provide the firm with a distinct competitive advantage. Information is power, but to achieve this requires knowledge not just of key sources of information but also of how to access them quickly and effectively.

Exam hint

Improving own learning

News analysis is one means of assessing the importance of current environmental issues. Editors have limited space and must make critical choices as to what/what not to include. They will tend to include subjects of current and future concern, but exclude those they identify as 'yesterday's news'. For example, one method of defining whether an economy is coming out of recession is to track the number of references to it in the quality press over time. As this index declines, so the economy must be picking up, since writers and editors no longer see articles on it as 'news'.

Internal sources

Many questions can only be answered by reference to internal records. The strengths and weaknesses of the business may be identified in this way, although this must be assessed relative to competitors. To be useful, records must be gathered in a form that is accessible, accurate and relevant to the forecast or evaluation required. The flow of information through a business should be analysed systematically to achieve these objectives.

Published material

Such sources are seldom used regularly or systematically by business decision-makers. The diffused nature of many of these sources makes collection, classification and distribution to interested managers an expensive and time-consuming process. The government is one of the main producers of primary data, published through the Office of National Statistics (ONS). Fortunately, many of the more important sources have now been produced on CD or the Internet, making access almost instantaneous and far more cost-effective. Increasingly, through intranets and extranets, much in-depth information can be acquired.

Published business information sources

Some larger organizations delegate a junior executive to undertake this task and circulate a regular summary to appropriate staff. Organizations such as McCarthy and Extel also grew by providing information on specific companies in a readily referenced format. However, while the value of such information in informing decisions has been recognized by perceptive marketing executives and planners, their use has been haphazard and on a need-to-know basis only.

As we discussed in Unit 3, information and communication technologies are now being applied to transform scattered data into quality information available whenever it is required by the appropriate decision-maker. The key skill for a marketer to develop is therefore to know what information is available on a particular issue and, most importantly, where to find it. Published material exists on most topics and is far cheaper than undertaking primary research. Marketing intelligence reports such as KeyNote and Mintel are also valuable sources of information.

Trade sources

The usual means by which managers keep informed of internal and external developments is through the grapevine. They establish and build networks of information sources that can be drawn on when the need arises. Regular conversations with colleagues, customers and other stakeholder contacts provide a moving tapestry of events supplemented with such things as sales records and consultancy reports. Much of the material gathered from the sources in Figure 4.4 will be sifted, cross-referenced and assimilated on a day-to-day basis.

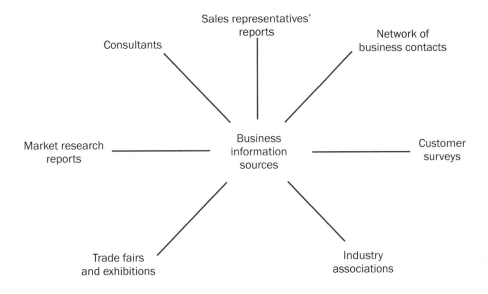

Figure 4.4 Trade sources and networks

Sources of information and assistance in the macro-environment

Social-cultural environment

◆ *Guide to Official Statistics* – overview of statistics available on the macro-environment

◆ *Annual Abstract of Statistics* – all major aspects of government responsibility

◆ ONS Census – population size, distribution and structural change

◆ *Social Trends* – annual survey of key societal indicators

- www.statistics.gov.uk/onlineproducts/default.asp#social (or economy)
- *Family Expenditure Survey* – annual statistical analysis of spending/lifestyle patterns
- ACORN/Mosaic – classification of local neighbourhoods for segmentation purposes
- Journals/quality press society sections, for example *New Society* – changing social patterns
- British Market Research Bureaux – research cases on lifestyle change
- UN indicators on population worldwide: www.un.org/depts/unsd/social/population.htm
- World Bank development data: www.worldbank.org/data/data, for example health/employment

Political-legislative environment

- Select Committee reports – monitor and report on political issues of the day
- JUSTIS online legal database – current legislative developments
- Legal digests – recent case law
- European Commission – EU directives and implementation timetables
- Mainstream media and news databases
- People's Republic of China site: www.moftec.gov.cn
- Malaysia government: mcsl.mampu.gov.my (gateway to agencies)
- Nigeria law: www.nigeria.law.org

Economic environment

- ONS National Income and Expenditure/the *Blue Book* – macro-economic analysis
- *Monthly Digest* – most recent figures on the economy, industry and labour market
- *Economic Trends* – changing economic structure and activity patterns
- *Bank of England Quarterly Review* – monitors monetary system/exchange rates
- *Regional Trends* – detailed annual data on social and economic change
- *Employment Gazette* – monthly publication covering wage and price movements
- *CBI Quarterly Survey* – measuring industry confidence and intentions
- *National Institute Economic Review* – quarterly commentary and comparisons
- Journals and quality newspapers/databases, for example *Economist, Financial Times*
- Bank reviews – articles and economic analysis
- Datastream provides economic data for Asia, Europe and the Americas

International environment

- Department of Trade and Industry – export credits/advice
- Chambers of commerce – advice/trade/contact networks, www.Srilanka.net/chamber
- Professional bodies, for example CIM, Institute of Exporters – networks of contacts
- Embassies and trade missions – on-the-spot advice/promotion/contacts
- Eurostat EU database: www.europa.ev.int/comm/eurostat
- Banks, for example HSBC, provide credit rating/market analysis
- International organizations, for example OECD/IMF/WTO/UN World Economic Survey
- International trade centre (UNCTAD/WTO): www.intracen.org
- Trade blocks, for example EU/ASEAN/NAFTA/Indo-Sri Lanka FTA-research studies
- Government departments, for example customs and excise/planning – specific sectoral data
- World Wide Web
- Quality press, journals and directories, for example *Kompass, Country Reports/Asia Week*

Technical environment

- Research journals and conference papers
- Trade press reports
- Channel intermediaries and ultimate customer need surveys
- Technical abstracts and databases
- Professional associations and industry networks.

Exam hint

Improving own learning

Don't be tempted to use report format for every answer you provide. This undifferentiated approach of producing reports when none are required wastes time and can deflect attention away from the actual answer content, which earns the majority of the marks. Where no specific format is required just break up your answer, where appropriate, with headings, white space and bullet points to make it examiner-friendly.

Summary

In this unit, we have seen that:

◆ Why it is crucially important for the organization to monitor change

◆ The impacts of change on the natural environment

◆ The implications of businesses as part of a larger system

◆ The importance of recognizing change in the macro-environment

◆ How the macro-environment can cause threats and opportunities

◆ How and why marketers can draw on internal and external information sources

Heightening concern for society and the natural environment requires that new technology is only introduced with care and foresight as to its likely impacts. While technology can help solve challenges and enable sustainable development through accelerated research and development, it also has shortcomings.

From the marketing point of view, the natural environment is a potentially valuable but not very consistent market as action-awareness gaps arise between what green consumers profess to want and what they actually buy. The Japanese, for example, buy 25 billion wooden chopsticks a year for cultural not environmental reasons. Awareness varies across market segments and even cultures. This however represents opportunities as well as threats for marketers across the marketing environment.

Finally, it should not be assumed that environmental impacts are primarily the concern of large firms and governments. It is in fact the concern of all the stakeholders in a marketing environment.

Further study and examination preparation

The importance of this area of the syllabus has been outlined earlier. It is central to the development of your marketing skills particularly with respect to the use of the Internet and presenting information. Similarly, it relates directly to the statements of marketing practice that are the primary concern of this coursebook: that is, collecting, interpreting and presenting information relevant to marketing strategy and planning processes. The first exam question is a challenging one and representative of general questions on the environment. Read it very carefully since the examiner requires an example (a charity) and is probing your ability to distinguish the two environments. Focus on why the macro-environment is important from a marketing perspective in the second part. The second and more recent exam question of this type relates a multinational food manufacturer to open systems (see Unit 1) and opportunities and threats.

Question 3(ii), June 2004 was referred to in the last unit. Here the focus is on changing macro-environment conditions in the haulage industry. Question 6, December 2005 provides a very context-specific question on the natural environment; however a choice of two from four macro-environments is provided. Questions 1c(ii) and 7e, June 2005,

Questions 7a and 7c, December 2005 and Question 5b, June 2006 are part questions on types and sources of information. It is always advisable to know four or five key information sources for each environment and be able to summarize their value to the marketer.

Extending knowledge

Palmer A. and Hartley B. (2006) *The Business and Marketing Environment*, McGraw-Hill.

> Chapter 2: The Nature of the Marketing Environment.

> Chapter 10: (this chapter also includes a section on the Ecological Environment).

Palmer, A. (2002) *The Business Environment*, McGraw-Hill.

> Chapters 1 and 5.

Other suggested reading

Jobber D. (1998), *Principles of Marketing*, McGraw-Hill, 2nd Ed.

> Chapter 5: The marketing environment.

Websites

The best Internet sites for keeping up with the news world-wide include the following:

www.cnn.com for serious international news reports cross-referenced and backed by video clips, photos, audio files and links to relevant websites. It is translated into several languages.

www.news.bbc.co.uk is also translated and offers in-depth reports.

www.washingtonpost.com many quality awards and can be customized to a specific region.

www.newsnow.co.uk provides international news updated every five minutes with a search facility that covers headlines if you wish to trace the origins of a story.

www.statistics.gov.uk/instantfigures.asp provides data on latest economic indicators.

http://earthtrends.wri.org/ is an environmental information portal.

africa.com is a gateway site to the African continent covering business, news and so on.

www.allafrica.com provides digests and reviews from 48 national news agencies including special reports on economics, technology and the environment.

www.chinapages.com, MyMalaysia.net.my and lanka.com for business news and information.

asnic.utexas.edu/asnic is an Asia-Pacific studies network information centre.

Practicising past exam questions

Please see Question 7, December 2003 and June 2006, on the CIM website www.cim.co.uk for specimen answers.

Please see Question 3(ii), June 2004. Go to www.cim.co.uk.

Please see Questions 1c(ii) and 7e, June 2005. Go to www.cim.co.uk.

Please see Question 6, December 2005. Go to www.cim.co.uk for specimen answers.

Please see Questions 7a and 7c, December 2005 and Question 5b, June 2006. Go to www.cim.co.uk for specimen answers.

Although past paper questions remain very relevant, students must understand that the format has changed. Therefore you should also refer to the specimen paper to ensure that you are clear about the new exam format from September 2008.

Unit 5

The demographic, social and cultural environment

Learning objectives

By the end of this unit you will:

◆ Have acquired an insight into key demographic changes and their marketing implications (3.3).

◆ Have recognized the interrelatedness of the socio-cultural environments (3.3).

◆ Appreciate the processes leading to the development of social and cultural values (3.3).

◆ Be able to assess the meaning and implications of socio-cultural change (3.3).

◆ Understand and apply concepts such as lifestyle, reference groups and social class (3.3).

◆ Have considered emerging trends and their potential impact on the marketer (3.3).

Study tip

A knowledge and understanding of demography and socio-cultural change is vital if the marketer is to truly appreciate the origins of buyer behaviour. Indeed, even though these are unquestionably uncontrollable by marketers, their appreciation and understanding is essential. Both evolve very slowly but their cumulative impact on market realities over time is considerable. Real living standards in the longer term are more likely to be determined by population changes, for instance, than the economic policy-making of governments.

Change in this environment is the most difficult to assess, yet the opportunities it offers must be grasped and exploited by the marketer. The relevant variables are usually inter-related. Therefore it is often difficult for marketers to assess and understand the contribution of any one element. As most of this is unspoken and unwritten, it poses in actual fact one of the greatest challenges to the marketing practitioner.

You will hopefully be able to identify with most of the different dimensions explored throughout this unit. However, you will also need to supplement your respective level of familiarity with these factors with more reading about the areas explored in this unit. The weekly periodical *The Economist* can be a useful source of information with regards to the economic trends. The periodical *New Society* can be very useful with regards to extending your knowledge of social trends. The government also offers national statistics online and publishes full reports of social trends (www.statistics.gov.uk/social-trends). International institutions such as the World Bank and the United Nations also have extensive comparative coverage on their websites. These are all readily available online.

Trends in population

Demography is the study of population trends. This study is important to marketers because of the latter's concern with the size, structure, composition and characteristics of the population. Indeed, segmentation and the assessment of the market potential of various segments of the population are of utmost importance to the marketer in view of the fact that a significant responsibility of the marketer is to target products/services adequately. Therefore an understanding of not only the breakdown of the population and the segments but just as importantly, an understanding of trends is also pertinent.

The Office for National Statistics, sometimes referred to as the ONS, is the government department responsible for the collection and publication of official statistics about the UK's society and economy in general. This department is the principal provider of official statistics about the UK.

The information it offers is used by government to make decisions about society and the economy. However, as impartial information is considered to be vital to an open and democratic society, this information is also readily available. This information is undoubtedly very helpful to the business environment too.

A ten-yearly census is carried out by the ONS. However sample surveys are carried out every five years. As explicitly detailed on its websites, timely updates are also conducted. These are referred to as amendments. The department is also responsible for the registration of vital events in England and Wales through the General Register Office (GRO).

A census is a survey of all people and households in the country. It is usually conducted by the government of a country. It is intended to provide essential information at national level as well as at regional and even area level for government, business, and the community. The most recent census was completed on 29 April 2001. Plans are being made to hold the next census in 2011. Although the Office for National Statistics holds a small number of data covering the census in Scotland and Northern Ireland, it is however not the main source of collection and distribution for these data. The ONS is also not responsible for the development of future censuses for Scotland and Northern Ireland.

The 2007 Census Test took place on 13 May 2007. The Test included approximately 100,000 households from within five local authorities. Processing of all completed questionnaires was concluded on 19 July and the analysis and evaluation of the test are currently being done. The results of all reports are available online soon after its official release.

Important trends uncovered by censuses in recent years, which are considered to be particularly significant to marketers, are:

◆ Current population levels and the future size of any given population

◆ The growth rates of developed countries versus developing countries

◆ The age and gender structure and its distribution by region/locality

◆ Migration within national borders and between international borders

◆ The demographic impact on world resources and the physical environment

Activity 5.1

Key skills – Collecting and interpreting information

It is important for marketers to appreciate the composition of a given population.

Use the Internet or your library to prepare a brief revision on the following:

◆ Total population, current and trend rate of change of the UK population

◆ Age, gender, marital status and location of population

◆ Occupational structure and ethnic mix

◆ Significant trends in structure (e.g. ageing, urbanization)

You may find it helpful to browse through the charts and tables in *Social Trends* or its local equivalent.

Insight

Russia is facing a demographic and societal crisis as its population of 149 million is currently being seen to shrink by nearly three-quarters of a million a year. The United Nations has even warned that its population level might fall to under 100 million by 2050. This is expected to cause dramatic impacts on its economy and security.

After the dissolution of the Soviet Union, the fertility rate within Russia was registered as falling from 2.08 babies per woman in 1990 to just 1.07 in 2004. In addition more abortions are being registered (1.6 million in 2004) each year in comparison with live births (1.5 million in 2004). Moreover, net outward migration is also rising. In contrast with many developed countries, death rates have also risen dramatically from a normal 10.7 per 1000 in 1988 to over 16 today.

Meanwhile, the economy is currently booming due to high oil, gas and commodity prices. However, the benefits have not been reaped by the bulk of the population. In fact, 15 per cent of Russians are considered to be living on under $2000 per annum.

Dismantling planning controls to bring the market economy to life after 1990 led to soaring prices, contracting real incomes and devalued savings. Economic uncertainty combined with unemployment and poverty led to numerous forms of social breakdown including alcoholism, increased suicide rates, marital breakdown, escalating HIV infections and loss of family cohesion.

In an attempt to counteract the declining birth rates, President Putin pledged significant increases in child benefits and a one-off bonus of £5000 for a second child. Although these offers by the state are bound to have some effect on some citizens, it is unlikely that this will address all the issues at stake. Indeed, these may be rather ineffective without the addressing of the basics issues at stake.

Implications for marketers

The implications of population trends are significant to the marketer on several levels.

These include:

◆ An increase in population levels could lead to an increase in the aggregate demand for goods and services.

◆ The level of demand will have a direct effect on the distribution of products and services. Regions, localities as well as market segments will need to be considered.

◆ The level of supply also needs to be considered. Is there adequate labour available to meet the new levels of demand?

◆ Changing levels of population have an impact on the usage of public services required. This increased level of need may have an impact on tax levels. The government will need to find the finance to create and deliver the necessary resources and services.

◆ Living standards can also be affected. The GDP is divided by the total population. Therefore standards of living may be altered. After the reunification of East and West Germany, many benefits traditionally offered to West Germans had to be curtailed by many of the regional administrations.

One of the most significant trends in mature industrial economies is the ageing of the population structure. Japan, Europe and, to a lesser extent, the United States are facing a sharp increase in the proportion of over 50s and this is just the leading edge of a global problem that will affect most economies in the next half century. Falling birth rates, greater longevity and the ageing of earlier baby booms are all combining to make the majority of the population older rather than younger. This trend is also shifting the centre of gravity of spending power in the economies affected. Development in the medical fields such as organ replacement and advances in genetics (e.g. stem cells) imply that even greater longevity may soon be possible.

Older, fit, healthy and relatively affluent pensioners are fast replacing the traditional old-age pensioner (OAP). Accordingly buying patterns of this age group are changing. Even though it has been said that one million remain on the poverty line, these numbers have been falling due to means tested pensions. Better educated, better off and better informed than their forebears, current and future pensioners have already started to command considerable purchasing power. This trend is set to rise.

Insight

Given current trends, by 2050 the median age in the European Union is forecast to rise from 38 to 49 and there will be some 70 million West Europeans aged 65+, representing over 20 per cent of the population. In Italy there are already more over-60s than under-20s.

Only greater longevity is preventing declining populations in many parts of Europe.

Activity 5.2

Can you think of any change in services that any government has had to offer because of the ageing of the population?

Activity 5.3

Within the marketing environment, can you think of any company that has taken on board the changes undergone by old age pensioners?

Evaluate how your selected company has altered its marketing strategies?

The effect of an ageing population on marketers

Ageing is an increase in the average age of the population and is a big challenge for the marketer.

Opportunities

Many opportunities can be reaped by marketers with regard to this younger disposed target audience. Many older citizens are not only fit and healthy but, even more importantly for marketers, they are intent on staying that way and enjoying themselves for as long as possible. The travel industry and health food shops (i.e. supplements) in particular have greatly benefited. Industries revolving around health-related products, security equipment and secure dwellings, quality furniture/other durable replacements, cars, financial services and nostalgia products have all also benefited from the change of image and disposition of this age group.

Activity 5.4

Consult a marketing intelligence report such as KeyNote or Mintel on any one of the industries mentioned about.

Evaluate if and how the older age groups are being viewed as a consumer group.

What are the trends associated with the segment?

What are the forecasts?

Threats

Although there are many opportunities to be reaped from an ageing population, one should also not ignore that this also represents a cumulative effect to any country and to any marketing environments. Thus, threats could also include the following:

◆ Companies run the risk of overlooking other important demographic developments at the expense of a focus on its ageing population.

◆ The dependency ratio is expected to continue to worsen in such countries as the UK. In the UK, forecasts predict an expected rise of 2.5:1 by 2015 and 1.5:1 by 2050. This implies that for every 2.5 people working, there will be an old age pensioner in 2015; in 2050 there will be an old age pensioner for every 1.5 working citizen.

◆ Those of working age would highly likely have less discretionary income due to the need to repay university loans, purchase expensive housing and provide for private pensions.

◆ Labour shortages could develop with a shrinking workforce unless working lives extend. This could prompt excessive immigration:

  ◆ This may lead to great disturbances in the social balance and cohesion of communities and even countries.

  ◆ This is already being seen within agricultural industries within the UK due to the lack of British labour.

◆ Savings ratios could fall progressively as a rising proportion of elderly would unlikely be able to have high levels of savings.

◆ Replacement of final salary with defined contribution schemes transfers pension risks to employees. Due to low funds, the state is increasingly not able to provide adequate pensions to its citizens:

  ◆ Hence employees increasingly need to learn how to fend for themselves.

  ◆ Notwithstanding, the 2004 Pensions Commission report stated that 9.6 million workers in Britain are not saving enough for a comfortable retirement (12 per cent of income is required if aged 25). Only half of full-time and 15 per cent of part-time workers have a private pension scheme.

The ageing population represents a range of significant factors for marketers. These could include the following:

◆ Emerging economies could gain a competitive edge by virtue of their younger and more energetic age structure. Current Eastern Europe migration into wealthier Western Europe has had a significant effect on not only the visitor economies (e.g. the UK) but also on the home economies (e.g. Poland), which have been left behind. This implies that both host countries and home countries will need to be both flexible and willing to change to adapt to these fluctuations.

◆ The centre of gravity of the population is increasingly forecasted to become the third age. Empty nest single or couple households (single parent or couple with no children living at home) and single households are increasingly dominating the landscape.

◆ The greying of the population may bring about a cultural shift within society. The Dutch are building a Senior City in Zeeland.

    ◆ This specifically created environment will be reserved for the over-50s.

    ◆ In line with being tailored to the needs of senior citizens, there will also be no provision for any facility that is not required by this market segment (i.e. schools).

◆ Consumer needs and wants change with age, and marketers must practise carefully researched age and life-cycle segmentation to exploit it. In the UK, Saga Holidays is now a specialist company which offers holiday breaks to senior citizens.

◆ The over-50s account for about 44 per cent of the population and own 80 per cent of the wealth. They therefore form a dynamic group in terms of spending power and significance of market segment. Discretionary spending power will be greatest among the 50–65 year group due to completed families, repaid mortgages, peak earnings and possible inheritance.

◆ Due to improving health and education, increasing life expectancy is anticipated. This makes this group a prime target for the leisure industries.

◆ The 2005 Turner report recommended extending the official retirement age to at least 67, restoring the link with earnings, scrapping means testing (to encourage savings) and introducing an 'auto-enrolled' national savings plan.

◆ Those approaching retirement will be encouraged by the government to keep working with promises of larger final pensions or lump sums and so on. Failing this, taxes would have to rise by £57 billion to maintain pensions at current levels up to 2035.

◆ Responsibility for ageing relatives may increase, reducing both time and income for spending. In 1950, a 65-year-old male could expect to live a further 12 years, compared to 19 years today and 21 years by 2030.

◆ An ageing market is not necessarily a mature market although the members may be age conscious. Value for money and quality may be important but so is the opinion that they are deserving of a little luxury. If so, then the marketing message must be altered accordingly.

Insight

Labour shortages are being countered by the use of alternative workforces, such as married women, immigrants and ethnic groups. African, Caribbean and Asian immigrants in England rose 40 per cent from 1991 to 2001 while immigration from Eastern Europe reached 600,000 between 2004 and 2006. Marketers need to embrace these changes in population dynamics. New technology, flexible contracts and a culture of continuous learning can help alleviate any skills gap. However partnerships with educational institutions, tailored and attractive recruitment packages and developing a positive image may help marketers position organizations as responsible employers.

Activity 5.5

As the number of retirees rises, so too does their power as an influential pressure group. More educated and articulate, they will possess the wit, the time and the means to use search and comparison technologies, and so constitute a demanding and service-orientated customer.

Marketers have no control on the changing demography. Notwithstanding, how do you think marketers can particularly attempt to tap into the increasing bargaining power of this market segment?

Question 5.1

Saga, the highly successful family-run business catering for the over-50s has been sold for around £1 billion. Founded in 1948 to provide value-for-money all-inclusive winter packages for older people, it was built upon a customer service ethos. It succeeded in turning 'grey hair into gold' by offering its eight-million customer database everything from travel to insurance, share dealing, credit cards, a website and magazine.

In the light of the ageing challenge above, suggest how and why the marketing mix of the new owners may have to be modified to meet its customer needs.

The dependency ratio

This is the ratio of the number of dependents in the population relative to the working population. Workers create the nation's material wealth and so support the non-working population either directly or through tax transfers. The ratio improves in the United Kingdom until around 2010, when lower birth rates and retirement of immediate post-war baby boomers will combine to reduce it continuously. Higher than expected inflows from new EU members and illegal immigration is expected to improve the ratio.

Insight

The biggest division in British society may be that between the 'baby boomers' of the late 1940s and the 'baby busters' of the 1970s. The boomers avoided major wars, enjoyed high employment, free tuition, accumulated wealth nearly continuously and look forward to a long and comfortable retirement on protected pensions and likely inheritance windfalls. Baby busters face a much bleaker future with the combined burden of higher taxes, steeper personal pension contributions, higher education fees and loan/credit debt repayments. They have to wait ten years longer to get on the property ladder but incur huge mortgages in the process. This will tend to depress disposable income among this age group and their attractiveness to marketers for some years to come.

Demographic changes have had significant repercussions on not only the marketing environment but also the general business environment. These also affect decisions and strategies adopted by governments. Some of the main situations and factors occurring in contemporary terms have been identified as follows:

◆ Labour shortages will be good news for the unemployed and those seeking career advancement and promotion, but bad news for taxpayers since real resources will need to be diverted to support those no longer contributing productively to society.

◆ Health services will need to expand continuously in real terms especially as life expectancies keep on rising:

◆ In the UK, health expenditure for the over-65s is already four times the average for the under-65s, while for the over-75s it is eight times.

◆ A doubling in the US population on retirement benefits by 2030 threatens the solvency of their social security and Medicare budgets.

◆ France plans to raise the pension age from 60 to 65 continue to meet with widespread demonstrations as thousands seek to protect their pension rights.

◆ For Austria to meet the levels of pension contributions they are currently committed to will involve either cutting other spending by 76 per cent or raising tax rates by 50 per cent. This puts the country in a quandary since they dare not implement austerity measures, but equally the single currency Stability Pact precludes excessive spending or inflating the national debt. This pension time bomb could therefore, in theory, force them out of the Euro.

◆ The fall in the number of births would seem to be a serious development for manufacturers dependent on this segment:

◆ The marketers of quality prams, for example, might have been expected to lose sales volume.

◆ In practice, married couples who were now delaying births were more likely to spend extra on their fewer offspring and, with established careers, could afford to do so.

◆ On the other hand, rising car ownership was shifting preferences towards a dual-purpose carrycot/pram, probably causing the demise of such companies. The marketer must therefore take nothing for granted in this complex area.

World population

Global population has grown exponentially over the last two or three centuries, as Figure 5.1 shows. This increase is set to continue in spite of lowering birth rates in many developed countries. The increase is directly linked with advances in health care and hygiene levels.

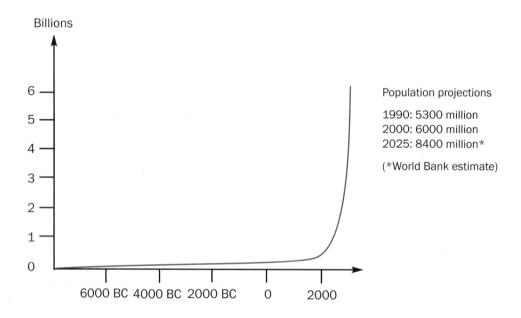

Figure 5.1 World population growth

As industrial economies matured, however, they enjoyed a *demographic transition* whereby customarily high birth rates fell to levels closer to already-reduced death rates. This process has yet to be completed in many developing countries, especially in sub-Saharan Africa. This means that the population of the world will arguably continue to rise, albeit at a reducing rate, at least until the middle of the century. However, the impact of diseases such AIDS cannot be ignored as these are reducing life expectancy. Consequently, these can be considered to be neutralizing some of this population growth.

Meanwhile, within the marketing environments throughout the world, successful economic development has enabled many developing economies to raise living standards and reduce poverty levels. For instance, population growth is still a challenge in China with the official population well in excess of 1.3 billion. However recent surveys by the Family Planning Ministry in Peking suggested that at least 200 million children were unaccounted for in the official figures. In spite of the state's attempt to monitor the rate of child birth, many poor families in relatively remote rural areas apparently ignored the one child per family laws. India is another country where unchecked growth rate is forecasted to result in an uncontrollable population growth if present trends persist.

Question 5.2

Key skills – Problem-solving

How can marketers help redress the balance sought by governments with regards to population stability?

Are the same strategies applicable within all countries?

Aggregate population

The record in population forecasting in many countries has been remarkably inaccurate, especially with regards to rates of birth as these can often fluctuate quite considerably. However across board, statistics are compiled as follows:

Population growth = birth rate – death rate + net migration

The British population is currently said to be around 60 million. Excluding any rise in illegal immigration, this figure is anticipated to stabilize at 64 million in 2035. Births per 1000 of the population exceed deaths by a small margin but the age-specific death rate, defined as the number of people (per 1000) of a particular age cohort that die in a year, is falling, especially for women.

The life insurance industry is built on this reliability with actuaries establishing probabilities to determine risk premiums for various customer age groups. The marketer must always be alert to the possibility of unexpected rises in the death rate, whether due to new contagious illnesses, hospital super-bugs (e.g. MRSA), extreme weather conditions, environmental deterioration or higher fuel prices as these will all have an effect on the behaviour patterns of the population.

The population in the European Union has grown by 20 per cent in the last 40 years to 415 million, but with the average European woman of childbearing age producing only 1.5 children (2.1 required for replacement), the long-run trend could be downward. However the population has been maintained stable and even increased in many countries due to immigration. As a matter of fact, a high percentage of the immigrants have come from countries and cultures (i.e. Turkey, Algeria and Egypt, sub-Saharan countries) where the rate of child birth is still much higher than that in West European countries. Accordingly, they have had a tremendous effect on the population of EU.

Improved economic performance not only tends to reduce outward migration but also increases attractiveness for economic migrants fleeing from the world's poverty or trouble spots. During 2005, 1500 immigrants arrived daily in Britain while 1000 emigrants departed, of which half were British nationals. Prosperous economies around the world attract similar flows of migration. However, most countries tend to maintain tight restrictions in an attempt to control the flow of population. Unfortunately, this in turn has created opportunities for illegal trade in human beings, whether from East Europe, Vietnam, the Balkans, Afghanistan or conflict-affected parts of Africa. In an effort to maintain tighter control on its population, the UK attempted to limit immigration from Romania and Bulgaria when these countries joined the European Union in 2007. Meanwhile, the Netherlands now requires a rigorous written test that examines cultural attitudes on sensitive issues. However, economies like Sweden and Spain with rapidly ageing populations may soon be anxious to receive rather than restrict such inflows. Indeed Spain granted an amnesty to existing illegal residents in early 2006. This could explain the current flood of African migrants trying to land in the Canary Islands.

To preserve the ratio of ageing pensioners to active working population that prevailed in the 1990s, the EU would require 130 million immigrants into Europe over the next 50 years. Just as European emigrants were a crucial resource in developing the Americas at the turn of the twentieth century, so the developing countries may be required to come to the rescue of the developed countries at the turn of the next century.

As a decline in the workforce would have serious implications for economic growth and funding social security programmes, so continued immigration, whether official or illegal, appears inevitable. Statistics now show that 1 in 10 people living in the UK was born overseas. This figure excludes illegal immigrants for whom records are understandably difficult to obtain. With immigration still on the increase in the UK in spite of governmental initiatives to control the influx of legal and illegal people, this percentage is highly likely set to rise.

Activity 5.6

What are the implications of such high rates of immigration to the marketers in the UK?

Population structure

While aggregate population may be stable this can seldom be said for the various dimensions of a population structure that include:

- Age
- Gender
- Marital status
- Region
- Ethnic group
- Occupation

Activity 5.7

Marketing skills – Using information and metrics

What marketing threats/opportunities arising out of age/gender will be faced in your country by the following organizations/businesses?

You can of course choose the UK as the country to examine:

◆   A university

◆   A cosmetic surgeon

◆   Private health insurers

Many businesses, particularly in services, have responded positively to economic upturn and labour shortages arising out of lower births and ageing. For instance initiatives or courses of action could include the following:

◆   More focused marketing of the business and its prospects to potential stakeholders. Potential stakeholders include both potential customers and potential employees.

◆   Building closer links with local educational establishments via the creation of networks.

◆   Using the Internet: creating a website to support operations in the market-place. Online presence can also be used to disseminate and even extend marketing communications.

◆   Tapping alternative workgroups using flexible employment patterns.

◆   Internal marketing for retention, retraining and promotion.

◆   Improving pay and incentives especially for flexibility.

◆   Moving to cheaper labour markets or using selective immigration. Many companies based in the West have shifted their product lines to Asia or the Far East (e.g. China, Indonesia and India) due to lower labour costs.

◆   One important means of compensating for contraction in the under-25s is by increased employment of married women and the older age groups themselves:

   ◆   Women account for 45 per cent of the UK workforce and there is ample scope to raise EU activity rates towards the 66 per cent found in Scandinavia and the United States.

   ◆   This solution will also have to be considered by developing economies as they encounter ageing, although there may be significant religious and cultural obstacles to overcome. For instance in many Muslim countries, due to cultural norms and religious beliefs, women are not allowed to work outside their homes.

Insight

Sunni Muslims live by a strict regime, which forbids most women to work or study, and either forces them to stay at home or cover their entire bodies and faces up using the burqa. The burqa or veil is a cultural phenomenon that will prove resistant to removal, particularly in traditional rural areas. However, religious dress codes that clash with prevailing cultural norms in Western societies are creating tensions and recourse to law to adjudicate on the fine line between human rights and implicit toleration of female oppression. Tony Blair recently supported the suspension of a teaching assistant who insisted on wearing the veil in class declaring that it made people feel 'uncomfortable' and because some women wore it as a mark of separation. A Commission for Integration and Cohesion has been established to question whether multiculturalism has produced the desired integration or the creation of separate communities in isolation from one another. Holland is planning to ban Muslim women from wearing veils in public. In an attempt to enhance integration, in Holland, the niqab and burqa were banned in state schools and on public transport in 2005.

Insight

Many school-leavers have opted to enter higher education in recent years. There has been a 75 per cent increase in EU students in the last 15 years to 11.8 million, implying a much better qualified and well-informed consumer group in future. The ratio of women in higher education is increasing although males still predominate in engineering, mathematics and computer science. Education is becoming internationalized with most exchanges being officially encouraged. Education for life is another important trend with increasing numbers of larger employers providing some form of continuing vocational training and professional development programmes.

Activity 5.8

Key skills – Using information and problem-solving

The youth-orientated society of the 1960s and 1970s has given way to a more conservative middle-aged culture. With the number of retirees booming worldwide, the face of marketing is bound to be affected.

What product values and characteristics do you think is and will be central to an effective marketing strategy focused on the over-60s?

Marital status and household structure

This is undergoing considerable change in many societies due to later marriage, rising divorce rates and remarriages, making the traditional marketer's assumption of two adults plus two children the exception rather than the norm. Additionally partners living together and sharing households without being married is becoming increasingly popular in many countries such as the UK.

Over 30 per cent of the male population is predicted not to marry at all, while divorce rates, despite an 8 per cent fall in 2005, are the highest in Western Europe especially among those marrying young. The average British marriage now lasts just over nine years although the greatest increase in divorce rates is highest among those married over 20 years.

Divorcees collectively spend an estimated £2 billion, mainly on legal fees, maintenance payments and setting up new homes. Earlier marriages have fallen sharply in recent years but cohabitation has increased, as have illegitimate births (one in four are raised by a single parent). Remarriages, already accounting for a third of the annual total, may produce 'composite' family groups combining different children in different ages from previous unions. The increase in single households is accounted for by the rising number of elderly, greater independence among the young, individuals staying single longer and rising divorce rates. This clearly forms a complicated tapestry for marketing analysis, but also a rich stream of potential segmentation.

Insight

The historically low birth rate of 1.64 in the UK has been linked to childless career women. Surveys suggest that more are delaying parenthood or forgoing it altogether. Two in five were concerned about its impact on career or finances. Less than one in eight believed that having children was necessary to achieve fulfilment, and one-third that had children felt no happier and registered a strong loss of independence.

Activity 5.9

How do you think this demographic factor affects the way in which marketers are targeting women between 30 and 40 years old?

Regional distribution

The marketer should be aware of the shifting distribution of population across regions and localities arising from both natural increase and net migration. The broad movement affecting all industrializing societies has been the steady drift from rural to urban living. Economic decline and depopulation has left a relatively old and poor residue from the south of Italy to the north of Scotland. For example, overall population in the United Kingdom has risen 11 per cent over the last 35 years, whereas Scotland's has fallen by 1 per cent.

There has been reverse flow from the inner cities to suburbia and the ribbons of development along the motorway and rail routes radiating away from city centres. As young couples move into these urban fringes to escape either inner-city decay or rural remoteness, so births increase to reinforce the process. However, rising suburban property prices and city-centre regeneration have recently put a brake on these flows, and the marketer must be careful to identify where the target populations reside, especially the retired.

The rising proportion of single households in Britain (doubling to a third, 1971–2006) and across the European Union is also creating opportunities for the construction industry but putting pressure on rural land. Over 4.5 million new homes are projected to be required in the United Kingdom alone by 2010. Another issue fuelled by the aftermath of Hurricane

Katrina in New Orleans, the French urban riots of late 2005 and Britain's July bombings is segregation in our cities.

This social fragmentation into ghetto communities, where ethnic minority groups are born, bred and educated in enclaves, is potentially destabilizing. While previous immigrant inflows eventually integrated, while retaining some cultural identity, many members of predominantly ethnic communities may have little contact with mainstream society. This can foster intolerance, alienation, suspicion and ultimately riots or terrorism.

Activity 5.10

How do you think marketers identify where their target audiences reside?

Question 5.3

Key skills – Using information

Many economies are characterized by dense urban conurbations interspersed by relatively sparse local communities. In the light of this or similar disparities in your own country, assess the implications for marketers seeking to serve the needs of these populations.

Ethnic groups

Many populations are diverse in their origins and therefore their buying patterns will be quintessentially different. Countries like Malaysia and Singapore will have a strong mix of Malay and Chinese, while the UK reflects its European and Commonwealth heritage. Ethnic minorities account for around more than 9 per cent of the total UK population. However this figure is continually rising. Indians, West Indians and Pakistanis comprise the largest groups but Chinese, Africans, Bangladeshis and Arabs are also well represented. Small ethnic minorities also abound. The percentage of Eastern Europeans is increasing rapidly and tremendously (e.g. Polish and Czechs).

Meanwhile the US census bureau predicts that the Caucasian population will fall from 70 to 50 per cent by 2050 while Hispanics will rise from 13 to 25 per cent. Such groups tend to be younger than the resident Caucasian population, producing a very different pattern of needs to be met by marketers and local authorities alike.

Although varied, ethnic markets can be very significant to marketers. For instance, through adequate marketing, the British Asian food industry has been extended to target many more target segments than the Asian communities.

Insight

The world-wide Islamic finance industry is estimated to be worth $750 billion. However for the marketer of financial services in the UK, the two million plus Muslim population represents a challenging segment. Shariah law forbids riba or usury, making both saving and borrowing difficult. Shariah-compliant Ijara mortgages have to based on sale and leaseback arrangements while Sharia-compliant savings accounts like that of the Islamic Bank may be operated where the interest is expressed as a share of the bank's profit or given to charity. Credit cards are considered acceptable as long as the monthly balance is cleared thereby avoiding any interest payment. Share dealing is acceptable but not speculation. Permitted investments necessarily exclude shares deriving income from pork products, alcohol and gambling for instance as these activities and products are forbidden by the Islam religion.

Question 5.4

Key skills – Interpreting information

Why have ethnic minority-owned businesses been able to exploit profitable niche markets among these populations without attracting substantial competition from established businesses?

Occupational structure

At the outset of an industrialization process well over 60 per cent of the employed workforce are engaged in the primary sectors of agriculture, forestry, fishing, mining and quarrying. This ratio can be as high as 90 per cent in some of the poorest nations of the world such as Albania or Nicaragua, dependent as they are on cash crops for the majority of their exports. Countries such as Malawi rely on foreign aid and traditional migration of the underemployed to the mines of southern Africa.

Industrialization is said to occur when 60 per cent of the employed population are engaged in manufacturing, construction and utilities such as electricity generation. Economies such as Malaysia now generate over 70 per cent of their visible exports from manufacturing, in marked contrast to their previous dependence on timber products and rubber. A further transformation into a service-based economy occurs when 60 per cent are employed in the tertiary sector, including transport, financial, retail and other services. This state tends to be achieved by developed post-industrial societies such as those in North America and Western Europe (e.g. the UK and Germany). It also includes island economies like Singapore and Hong Kong where financial services contribute over 13 per cent of the countries' GDP.

The next stage of the development is the full emergence of the information society, when 60 per cent of the workforce will be employed in activities at the interface with the final consumer, be that a customer, an elderly person, a patient, a taxpayer or a student.

The workforce in employment: some important trends

A number of important and interrelated developments in employment can be identified as economies mature and evolve from industrial into service and information societies. Some of the more obvious features are described below.

The decline in full-time employment

◆ The cultural norm of a standard work day, work week and work year is weakening.

◆ Whether this is an 8-hour day, 40-hour week and 48-week year as in Northern Europe, the trend is clear. This trend is partly due to the rise of more focused and flexible organizations wishing to meet the needs and wants at the convenience of the customer, rather than in a time slot favourable only to the producers.

◆ More and more organizations operate on a 24-hour, 7-day week, 52-week year basis and require a workforce to match. Manufacturers, retailers, transport fleet operators and by implication leisure and catering providers now open all hours and demand flexible employees willing to work whatever hours are necessary to get the job done. However, this trend should not be oversold since over 80 per cent of the British workforce remain in a permanent job and average tenure has risen from six to seven years compared to 1984.

The corresponding rise in part-time employment

◆ This has risen in the UK from just under 5 per cent to nearly 30 per cent of all employment in just 25 years.

◆ It largely reflects the entry of large numbers of married women into the workforce for whom part-time work is an ideal compromise with domestic responsibilities.

◆ It also reflects the growing needs of employers to cover service peaks and holiday periods.

◆ Organizations prefer the adaptability of a part-time workforce and feel better able to adjust to changing economic conditions over the business cycle. Nearly half of all women work part-time, although the percentage of males is also rising as attitudes alter and more seek to supplement income in early retirement.

Hours are lengthening for full-time workers

◆ This reflects not only the need for flexibility but also a cultural change, resulting in more intense and stressful lives for an organization's permanent workforce.

◆ Any organization dedicated to achieving competitive advantage and more than fully satisfying the needs of its customers, requires an equally dedicated workforce to achieve these ends.

◆ It also reflects income pressures on employees as they drive to achieve and maintain high-consumption and affluent lifestyles. This runs counter to the current vogue for achieving a work–life balance:

  ◆ A Prudential survey found that over 60 per cent of working adults and 70 per cent in Greater London are thinking of making a 'life-shift' allowing less stressful jobs and more time with their families. This may be an illusion for most who want to progress in their careers.

- In the United States, average working hours rose by 20 per cent, 1970–2002, while in France it fell by 24 per cent due to their adoption of the 35-hour week.

- EU legislation seeks to limit weekly hours to 48 per week, but many managerial and professional staff voluntarily work longer.

- Over 40 per cent of Britons regularly work more than the national average of 48 hours a week and half are working more hours than five years ago.

- The 35-hour week enacted by France in 1998 has backfired, with unemployment now around 10 per cent. Longer holidays of 5–6 weeks look equally unsustainable when compared to the one or two in Japan and the United States.

- Americans have longest working hours and less holidays, with the exception of South Korea and the Czech Republic.

- US working hours exceed those of the UK by 250 and Germany by 500 hours a year.

Self-employment is rising

- Self-employment is projected to increase by a quarter in the next decade although the incidence varies widely between industries.

  - Self-employment is especially high in services industries and in construction.

  - Hotels and catering are understandably above average while manufacturing records only half the overall rate.

- The primary drive is the opportunity created by information technology and e-commerce combined with the desire of organizations to outsource non-core activities.

- There is no organizational reason why most professional and information workers should not be retained on a self-employed basis.

A rise in contractual and temporary employment

- An increasingly competitive environment has forced many businesses to concentrate on core activities.

- Specialized resources must be fully utilized or it becomes more efficient to contract-out services or contract-in labour as and when required.

- The convenience of a large directly-employed labour force has become a luxury not even the public sector can afford.

- Transport and distribution may be contracted out to third-party operators while specialized marketing skills are hired or outsourced through specialist agencies as and when required.

Question 5.5

Key skills – Interpreting information

What do you think are the attractions of part-time employment to:

◆ A business?

◆ An employee?

◆ The government?

The emergence of flexible organizations

◆ More and more organizations employ a core of full-time scientific, technical, marketing and managerial employees with company-specific skills and proprietary knowledge to co-ordinate and direct the fundamental activities of the business.

◆ A flexible workforce makes up the non-core groups. These could include: high turnover semi-skilled full-time employees, part-time employees, temporary/ad-hoc workers, job sharers, employees on temporary contracts, student placements, individuals on apprenticeship or special training programmes and subcontractors.

◆ Call centres, employing an estimated one million employees in the UK, adopt just such a mix of flexible workers in order to keep the phone, fax and e-mail links operating around the clock.

Insight

The trend towards 24/7 opening hours is being repeated across other societal services, from proposals for doctors' surgeries to be open all weekend and evenings to the extension of drinking hours. Very few pubs have applied for 24/7 but many want longer hours at weekends and on holidays. Scotland has enjoyed such relaxation for two years without any great problems but concerns continue due to the rise of the 'binge drinking' culture. When hours were relaxed in countries with such a culture, for example Australia and Ireland, there was increased consumption, disorder and associated crime.

Employment stress

◆ This is said to arise from a variety of factors including changing employment patterns, competitive pressures, globalization, e-commerce, downsizing and deregulation of many public services, which has removed much of the slack in productivity performance.

◆ More women have work and domestic economy duties while many men work longer and more intense working hours.

- There is a growing segment of employees who do not do their share of work in many societies and not surprisingly stress and depression are on the increase.

- The Department for Work and Pensions figures state that over one million are too stressed to work. This represents 45 per cent more than when the Labour government came to power in 1997. This statistic shows how much more pressure employees have been under in recent years.

Activity 5.11

Attempt to uncover statistics about absenteeism due to stress in the UK for the past year.

Insight

Symptoms of depression now occur in half the UK population. This is about double the rate of 20 years ago and is rising fastest among females. Suicide rates have tripled over 30 years in the UK. In Japan, the number of suicides is twice that of the UK. Middle-aged men pushed aside in the economic slump are most likely to commit suicide in Japan.

As a result of stress there are now more than half a million therapists, mentors, grief counsellors, anger managers and lifestyle gurus practising in the UK alone.

Insight

The global call centre market is increasing in value as more and more organizations centralize their operations with regards to customer contact. It is calculated that this sector already employs 3 per cent of the North American workforce. This represents a higher percentage than those employed in the car, steel and coal sectors combined in the UK.

By receiving calls on behalf of businesses for telemarketing, sales/reservations, technical support or customer relations, they are inextricably linked to marketing. Such services can be readily contracted out to third-party companies that might be located anywhere in the world. Indian call centres in Bangalore, using well-educated English-speaking graduates, are growing at a phenomenal rate, serving customers ranging from American Express to Lufthansa to many UK-based banks. They are happy to work in well-appointed centres for one-fifth of UK rates. They are familiarized (using TV soaps) to regional accents and keep abreast of local news coverage. With the advent of the Internet, potential customers are much better informed before making a call to buy something. The call centre staff therefore must be equal to this challenge. As the only point of contact between the calling customer and the ultimate product supplier they must be more than just competent and personable. India is on course to win a big slice of the global market but must also bear the risk that fickle Western companies might quickly go elsewhere if the price and service is right. South Africa has been recently identified as an attractive new destination for call centres for UK-based companies due to the fact that British people tend to find the South-African accent easier to understand.

The rise of the knowledge worker

◆ Well over half the workforce can be designated as knowledge workers.

◆ They tend to produce, process, use and/or distribute knowledge as well as maintain the infrastructure for its transmission.

◆ Marketers are clearly knowledge workers because they perform all these functions, but even in manufacturing industry only a third of employees will normally be manual workers on the shop floor.

◆ Since most jobs will require some level of expertise, governments are rapidly expanding vocational and higher education in an effort to avert critical skill shortages from inhibiting high-technology growth opportunities.

◆ With the Japanese pattern of educating virtually all its highly motivated 18-year-olds being emulated by the other emerging countries of East Asia, they appear potentially much better equipped to effect the transition to post-industrial society.

◆ The concept of 'lifelong learning' has developed based around computer literacy and the systematic and continuous renewal of knowledge in a rapidly changing world.

Flexible work lives

◆ The need for flexibility to match working hours to operational requirements and produce a more effective work–life balance is producing a kaleidoscope of employment patterns for the marketer to observe.

◆ They can all yield higher productivity as well as lower turnover and absence rates:

Flexitime – This enables employees to plan their own time allocation.

Staggered hours – These lengthen but also spread the rush hours.

Flexible work years – These are used to match activity patterns to personal circumstances.

Flexible shifts and rosters – This is used by companies to effectively cover customer service requirement.

Longer days but shorter weeks – This is used in an attempt for employees to maximize their actual working time

2 × 12-hour weekend shifts – This is used by companies in an attempt to maximize the utilization of the site and the companies' resources (i.e. factory)

Working from home – Telecommuting through office intranet links has enabled more and more of this type of work

Planned reduction in hours towards retirement – In the UK, there has been a dramatic decline in labour market participation among over-50s males. The government has demonstrated concern by introducing a tax credit scheme for helping over-50s back into work and offering a £30,000 lump sum for those working five years beyond official retirement age.

Exam hint

Improving own performance

Remember that any question posed on the environment must be answered in context. Regurgitation of academic content alone is insufficient – shape it to fit the question context.

This is why it is inadvisable to prepare model answers to questions you think might be set in the exam. It is highly unlikely that the way the question is posed will match your preparation. Unless you are very careful, you will be tempted to make the question fit your prepared answer rather than the other way round! Better to be flexible: read and answer the question precisely.

Increased mobility

◆ Allied to flexibility are lengthened daily travel distances which have risen fivefold in the United Kingdom since 1950 from 5 to 30 miles.

◆ On present trends, they will double again by 2025 although mounting congestion or road pricing schemes may act as an inhibitor.

◆ Organizations require their knowledge workers to be mobile and they are often prepared to travel rather than to move in order to maintain their desired lifestyle or avoid disruption to partner or children.

The self-service economy

◆ Non-standard work patterns imply non-standard leisure patterns with more time being absorbed doing tasks that were previously undertaken by business.

◆ Self-service is already well established in most retail outlets while home-shopping cable and satellite systems take the process one step further.

◆ Interactive computer systems linked to databases offer dramatic potential to transform the way in which many services are currently marketed, sold and performed. Home banking, direct insurance and distance learning are just a sample of leading-edge applications.

Insight

The ultimate in self-service was the IKEA concept of the self-assembly flatpack. It eliminated the cost of shipping vast quantities of air and redistributed the task of assembly to the final consumer. It also meant that Ingvar Kamprad became one of the richest men in the world as owner of a company with 186 outlets in 31 countries and turnover of £7.6 billion. The company had 76,000 employees and was visited by about 310 million customers in 2003 alone.

Other companies such as Homebase and B&Q in the UK have also benefited from this trend and the still ongoing trend of DIY.

The changing role of women in work and society

The situation of men and women at work differs dramatically across different societies due to varying cultural norms, education levels and stage of development. Nearly three-quarters of Japanese women are university educated yet little more than one in four works after graduation. Frustrated at their failure to find sufficiently challenging jobs in the strong masculine culture of domestic companies, they turn to less discriminating non-Japanese multinationals. In the Middle East the position and acceptance of women has slowly begun to undergo some changes. The influence of Islam and its associated 'mutawah' policy continues to dictate conformity to traditional structures and customs with regards to what is considered acceptable and respectable female behaviour.

The UK remains a society where the different genders are employed in different sectors, different industries, different occupations and different levels in the hierarchy. Women usually have family responsibilities yet over half now go out to work, at least part-time. Domestic duties combine to ensure that they often work harder although the hours spent cooking and on other domestic activities have fallen drastically over the past few decades. However they are promoted less often and are generally less well paid than male counterparts. Women in Britain now earn, on average, 82 per cent of men's wages. This disparity is improving but is still less than in most other European countries. Two-thirds of women admit to being afraid to ask for a rise in pay. However, almost 40 years after the Equal Pay Act was introduced in 1970 women employed by local authorities in England are about to achieve parity with men for equal work together with up to 10 years of back pay as a result of a number of 'compensation cases' being upheld by the courts. The settlement could cost up to £10bn and might even result in some male pay rates being adjusted downwards.

Women are underrepresented in manufacturing but dominate in many of the expanding service industries. Although caring professions such as health and primary education register a high ratio in favour of women overall, men still dominate the top positions. The rising proportion (50 per cent +) of women in higher education, has contributed to an improvement in their representation in managerial and professional occupations. This is now well over 25 per cent but is not reflected in senior management since women fill only 15 per cent of the executive jobs and just three have headed up FTSE 100 companies. Still, this trend slowly changes. Women executives tend to predominate in people- or service-centred staff functions rather than line positions, contributing directly to profitability.

Activity 5.12

Identify the areas, in any organization of your choice, in which women appear to be underrepresented.

Investigate the causes of this situation.

Consider the ingredients of a 'positive action plan' to improve the utilization of women in that organization.

Organizations are missing out on a lot of talent by not thinking creatively about how to harness women's ambitions. Policy responses to tap this potential could include any of the following strategies:

◆ Setting targets for employing more women in senior positions.

◆ Offer nurseries within the workplace.

◆ Offer financial support for private childcare.

◆ Offer flexible working patterns and career break keep-in-touch schemes.

◆ Adopt women-friendly recruitment, selection, appraisal and promotion procedures.

◆ Implement processes which facilitate the retraining and training of employees in core activities.

◆ Implement schemes whereby common pay and conditions are achievable: equal reward for work of equal value.

When the Civil Service adopted similar policies to allow women to mix family and career, it resulted in an actual decline in those prepared to dedicate themselves to getting to the top.

Insight

According to segmentation research by Close Wealth Management, there are 200 000 single, rich and happy women in the UK. Unfortunately, this female affluence has little to do with workplace equity and much more to do with stressful personal lives and associated financial settlements.

One in five women (three in five executives) is electing not to have children and in many large companies, motherhood is considered a rather furtive activity that interferes with performance and constitutes exclusion from the job. However the high expectations made on employees are not only limited to female employees.

Recognition of so-called 'glass ceilings', preventing women's advancement, has begun to attract government resolution for more positive action. Pressure groups are also becoming more active and some shareholders are asking questions at AGMs. However, the most effective catalyst for fundamental change may remain a diminishing labour supply that ultimately confronts businesses with the choice between hiring more women or lower-quality men.

The social and cultural environment

Difficulties experienced by women in employment are largely a reflection of a combination of societal attitudes in general and male-dominated corporate cultures in particular. Culture moulds and regulates daily behaviour through constant conditioning and reinforcement. We learn what is and what is not appropriate behaviour in different social situations. Our attitudes, beliefs, values and language derive from such cultural influences as the family, community, religion and education. The former two are referred to as reference groups.

Understanding culture is particularly important to cross-cultural management and marketing in global organizations. Marketers, who seek to impose their own behavioural norms on customers or employees from other cultures, will fail. The marketer must recognize that:

1   Culture is built up through a system of values, beliefs and attitudes.

2   Culture is specific to one group.

3   Culture is not innate but is learned from one generation to the next.

4   Culture influences the group in uniform and predictable ways.

Hofstede (www.geert-hofstede.com) identified five dimensions along which cultures can be assessed with relation to national related values. These are:

◆   Power distance

◆   Individualism vs. collectivism

◆   Uncertainty avoidance vs. risk taking

◆   Masculinity vs. femininity

◆   Time-frame: long-term orientation vs. short-term values

Power distance

◆   This dimension refers to the extent to which the less powerful members of institutions and organizations expect and accept that power is distributed unequally.

◆   This does not reflect the actual difference in power distribution but the way in which people perceive power differences. In Europe, power distance tends to be lower in

Northern and Western countries (e.g. the UK, Sweden and Holland) and higher in Southern (Italy and Greece) and Eastern parts (Poland, Croatia).

Individualism vs. collectivism

◆   This refers to the extent to which people are expected to behave. Individualistic environments favour people standing up for themselves while collectivism prescribes that people act predominantly as a member of a bigger group or team.

◆   Latin American cultures rank among the most collectivist environments, while the USA is one of the most individualistic cultures.

Uncertainty avoidance vs. risk taking

◆   Cultures that scored high in uncertainty avoidance prefer rules (e.g. about religion and food) and structured circumstances.

◆   Mediterranean cultures and Japan rank the highest in this category.

Masculinity vs. femininity

◆   This dimension refers to the value placed on traditionally male or female values (as understood in most Western cultures). Masculine cultures value include competitiveness, assertiveness, ambition, and the accumulation of wealth and material possessions, whereas feminine cultures regard relationships and quality of life as being more valuable.

◆   Japan is considered by Hofstede to be the most masculine culture, Sweden is regarded as the most feminine culture.

◆   The UK culture is considered predominantly masculine although feminine values are also favoured.

Time-frame: long-term orientation vs. short-term values

◆   This dimension refers to a society's time horizon, or the importance attached to the future versus the past and present.

◆   In long-term oriented societies, values include persistence (perseverance and thrift).

◆   In short-term oriented societies, values include personal steadiness and stability, respect for tradition, and reciprocation of greetings, favours and gifts.

◆   China, Japan and the Asian countries score especially high (long-term) here, with Western nations scoring rather low (short-term) and many of the less developed nations very low.

Although some cultures have been traditionally associated with certain characteristics (e.g. Japanese culture with collectivism, while in the West, individualism is considered to be regarded more favourably), such polarity is no longer so obvious in contemporary terms, due partly to globalization and changing trends.

Culture is reflected in what people eat, how and where they live, their lifestyles and buying preferences, not to mention their mannerism, humour, art, religion and music. The international marketer must be especially aware of diverse social mores. Business and general societal customs should be carefully observed if offence is to be avoided. Language translation is another pitfall to beware of, particularly for global enterprises. Nescafé's 'blue' pack coffee would receive a negative reception in Kuwait as the name when translated means death. Similarly, Big Macs are not favoured by the Hindus of India or Sri Lanka as these cultures do not consume beef and pork due to their religious beliefs. The bank HSBC has with humour emphasized such subtle cultural differences in a series of advertising campaigns.

Activity 5.13

Key skills – Presenting information

The social customs or norms of accepted behaviour in many countries are radically different from those predominant in the UK.

Compare the culture of the UK with another non-European culture.

Can you suggest behavioural guidelines for an international marketer trading between these two countries? What should the marketer be particularly cautious about?

Exam hint

Many CIM candidates are women, so given that the examiner will wish to appeal to all constituencies of the target candidate market, from time to time, you may come across an occasional question on the role of women in the changing marketing environment.

The marketer should recognize that while many social mores and customs are deeply rooted, others are in the process of change, for example the cult of instant gratification and an emerging compensation culture has affected many marketing environments. The following dimensions have had particular significance to the marketing environment.

◆ Role of women:

   ◆ The primacy of the domestic and maternal role has declined relative to work and career.

   ◆ Smaller families and enhanced parental aspirations have freed resources for girls to pursue higher education.

   ◆ Changing female stereotypes are reflected in advertisements where the subjects are less likely to enthuse about the relative merits of detergents and more prone to be confident, assertive and pursuing an independent life.

   ◆ For the marketer, the working woman provides extra discretionary purchasing power to the household and has increasing influence over its disposal.

   ◆ Demand for property, consumer durables and holidays have been sustained by these incomes, while work and domestic pressures have put a premium on time and its effective management.

   ◆ Convenience foods, time-saving appliances and the combined versatility of the freezer and the microwave have transformed food preparation, with many meals being taken separately and 'on the run'.

- Traditional roasts are in decline while pizza sales have doubled in a decade.

- Central heating and instant warmth at the flick of a switch have extracted the drudgery from another basic household function.

- Lifestyle and mail-order catalogues and one-stop shopping are other necessary innovations to enable the management of a bigger house and enlarging household consumption within the declining non-work time available.

◆ **Religious values:**

- The same religion may be practised across national boundaries. For example Catholicism is followed by majorities in Ireland, Spain, Poland, Chile and the Philippines but culture varies significantly.

- Religion can also be idealistic and prescriptive. In many Islamic countries, religious authorities have far greater influence than in the UK for instance.

- Fundamentalist groups, in Egypt, Chechnya and elsewhere, are seeking to assert religious values over economic ones and they challenge the rights of governments to impose and implement a legal system. Such influences would certainly inhibit or may even enhance the effectiveness of the international marketer in the countries concerned.

- Church attendance in Britain has fallen sharply in the last 25 years to stabilize at around 7 per cent (compared to 40 per cent in the United States). This is reflecting declining religious values among post-war age groups and secularization. It also reflects increasing mobility of households, alternative family activities on Sundays and affluence.

- The rising ownership of cars and television and a parallel decline in the cohesion of many local communities have also contributed to this erosion.

- Eventual success in the Sunday Opening campaign in late 1993 was the culmination of these forces for change, opening a vast new market for large retailers and do-it-yourself stores.

◆ **Healthy living and fitness trends:**

- Natural foods were mainly the realm of eccentric hippies up to 20 years ago.

- Smoking was also the norm and thought to symbolize maturity and sophistication.

- Attitudes in high-income societies are markedly different today with widespread concern over heart disease, cancer, obesity and lack of exercise.

- Rich countries appear to be dividing into an overweight majority underclass and a super-healthy minority elite.

- Children growing up on high calorific diets of fast food and computer-based leisure activities have led the World Health Organization to predict that 50 per cent of British adults will be obese within 20 years. In Britain this is not helped by the fact that 10 billion bags of crisps are consumed annually, more than the rest of Western Europe combined, or the revelation that the current budget for school meals was just 37p as compared to between £1.50 and £4 in France.

◆ However, one school in Glasgow has discovered incentives encourage pupils to eat healthily. Fatty fast foods earn no points while salads provide 15. Points are accumulated and exchanged for cinema tickets (850 points) or even the latest i-Pod (4000). Take-up of school dinners has risen 40 per cent and healthy choices have increased by 60 per cent.

Activity 5.14

Scan the marketing environment and identify how marketers have been encouraging consumers to eat more healthily.

What strategies and what tactics are being used?

What market segments are being specifically targeted?

Insight: The boom in organic food

Organic means that no chemical fertilizer or pesticide is used in food production and that crops have been rotated and that animals are reared without antibiotics or growth hormones. However, to date there is no conclusive evidence that organic produce is healthier or tastes better than non-organic products.

With price premiums of over 50 per cent for organically labelled food, it is unsurprising that it has become one of the fastest growing segments of the UK grocery market. However, some market segments have been deterred by the high prices. Still, as product lines expand, sales have grown at 30 per cent per annum from virtually nothing to £1.6 billion in less than 20 years. However, four-fifths of all products are imported into the UK as only a minimal percentage of domestic farms are certified by the Soil Association as 'organic'.

Organic farming promotes greater biodiversity but is more land extensive. The concept may also be hijacked by businesses due to its profitability. In fact, minimal standards set by the European Union have enabled supermarket groups to exploit organic grey areas (e.g. source eggs from chickens fed with organic grain but in factory farm conditions!) Indeed, such has been the negative publicity that belief in the 'goodness' of such foods has been dented, especially among the young.

Activity 5.15

Attempt to make a comparative evaluation of how a range of supermarkets have been promoting their organic products.

Although jogging as an activity may have waned, fitness clinics and the pseudo-image provided by designer sports wear provide symbolic substitutes. Appearances are increasingly important to all generations and offer complex but profitable marketing opportunities. Note the 30 per cent annual growth rate of cosmetic operations in Brazil, second only to the United States, where 25 per cent of face fixing and stomach tightening occurs among men aged 19–34.

The younger age groups, in particular, have a strongly developed image consciousness although children may face lower life expectancy due to their dependence on convenient and trendy junk foods. Similarly, a Japanese research study has suggested that figure-conscious girls may develop smoking behaviour if they believe it encourages weight loss. Despite heavy advertising, fruit and vegetable intake in the age group up to 18 is half that recommended by nutritionists while salt intake is double. Marketers of savoury snacks, oven chips and fizzy drinks should perhaps beware of an eventual backlash. Schools in Connecticut have already been banned from selling fizzy drinks and junk food, a business worth $700 million to the soft drinks industry alone. These rules derive from the strict new anti-obesity bill recently passed in the Senate.

Activity 5.16

Identify how the marketers of some 'crisps' companies in the UK have addressed concerns about high salt intake.

Insight

A 2004 Commons report suggests obesity has risen 400 per cent in 25 years with one in two adults currently overweight and the same proportion in prospect for children by 2020 (worldwide the figure is 300 million obese adults including 32 per cent of the United States and 25 per cent of the Middle East population).

India, long associated with its starving millions, now has an obesity crisis affecting the rich in its cities. In Delhi about 75 per cent of women suffer as do 33 per cent of urban 15–17 year olds. In 2006 it was confirmed that Britain was the most obese in Europe with 23 per cent of adults and nearly 15 per cent of children both significantly ahead of France, Spain and Italy. Here it affects the poor and direct medical costs are £3.5 billion and rising along with the incidence of diabetes, hypertension and heart disease. The United States has double the rate of diabetes for the over-55s and health spending is 150 per cent higher. Causes range from sedentary lifestyles, eating more (junk food), overwork and stress and exercising less (800 less calories burned per day).

The marketing of junk foods in supermarkets also stands accused of promoting 'pester power', with up to 75 per cent of spontaneous food purchases being traceable to an insistent child. The government has, despite intense lobbying, belatedly introduced regulations banning junk food adverts during peak children viewing times. However, supermarkets have so far prevented the single 'traffic light' food-labelling system which makes clear which products are unhealthy. Instead of adopting the unified FSA guidelines for the traffic light system, different supermarkets have adopted their own traffic-light colour codes.

A Ministry of Fitness has been appointed to create a healthier nation in the run-up to the 2012 London Olympics and the government is introducing a data collection exercise to weigh and measure all primary school children with a view to policy making and shocking parents!

Insight

The average American is ten pounds heavier than a decade ago causing US airlines to spend an estimated extra $275 million a year on fuel. On the other hand, the number of Americans (11 per cent) on low-carbohydrate diets is so large that sales of eggs in Ohio are enjoying a boom while potato-producing Idaho is in crisis.

Social class

One way of classifying groups within society is according to the class or strata they occupy. A class comprises individuals with a defined status who share common characteristics including wealth, occupation, income level, educational background and various aspects of lifestyle. For the marketer, it is not always the actual social class an individual belongs to that is significant but rather the class they identify with or aspire to.

Open educational access, mobility and rising incomes have facilitated class movement. Even in a class-based society like Britain, studies find that more than 50 per cent had moved class through their lives.

There is, however, an 'underclass' at the bottom of society, from which few escape, especially the one-quarter of all children growing up in the 1990s in families with no adult in employment. Indeed, under global capitalism the gap between richest and poorest is getting wider and particularly in the United States where divisions can be along ethnic lines too.

Class and class aspirations are important since shared values, attitudes and behaviour will be reflected in purchasing preferences and form one of the most widely used methods of segmenting product markets. Examples of widely used categorizations based on class include the JICNAR social grade definitions:

Social class category	Occupation
A (upper middle)	Professional, administrative, top management (for example directors, barristers)
B (middle)	Intermediate professional, managerial (for example marketing manager, lecturer)
C1 (lower middle)	Supervisory, clerical and lower management
C2 (skilled working class)	Skilled manual (for example crafts)
D (working class)	Semi- and unskilled manual
E	State pensioners, long-term unemployed, and so on

An upper class based mainly on wealth is superimposed on this classification. Thus, it is important for marketers of luxury products and services to appreciate this too. They should also take into consideration the aspirations of their target audiences.

Question 5.6

Key skills – Interpreting information

Critically appraise the usefulness of the above classification system.

Is there a more appropriate approach to segmenting socio-economic groups?

Is buying behaviour of a consumer more related to his or her income level or to the social class to which he or she aspires?

In mass urban centres where people are unable to get to know one another with the closer intimacy possible in small communities, it is unsurprising that symbols are adopted to signal who we are and where we stand in society's pecking order. We classify those we meet on the type and quality of clothes they wear, the cars they drive, their sports and social activities, the houses and localities they live in as well as their manner, speech and the type of job they do. These are, in effect, badges of class membership and therefore vital pattern indicators for the marketer to recognize and mobilize in focused promotional campaigns.

Reference groups

Related to class is the concept of the reference group whose actions and behaviour influence the attitudes and values of large numbers of others who seek to imitate them. They include:

◆ The family

◆ Student peer group

◆ Work colleagues

◆ Club members

Since most individuals wish to 'belong' to certain preferred groups, they will tend to conform to the norms of dress and behaviour laid down by them. Those within the group whose influence over what is and is not acceptable is substantial are known as opinion formers or leaders. Their influence may be based on expertise, knowledge or perhaps a charismatic personality. If a business can persuade such leaders to adopt their product then 'opinion followers' will also tend to purchase. Little wonder that sports equipment manufacturers secure endorsements from top players (i.e. celebrity endorsements); use their product and you can be a winner too!

Movie makers are also getting in on the act, although Reebok's legal action arising from an altered film ending suggests potential conflicts between art and commercialism. It may therefore be reassuring to learn that Coca-Cola signed the biggest marketing promotion in history (so far!) when it paid £95 million for the right to use the Harry Potter logo on its cans. Already translated into 47 languages with sales of over £110 million in 200 countries, *The Philosopher's Stone* promotes a counterculture of modesty, fair play, sportsmanship and indignation with injustice.

Marketers must identify the relevant reference groups in the segments they have targeted. This is required especially where expensive purchases (relative to the group's income) involving conspicuous consumption are concerned. The need to 'keep up with the Joneses' or emulate members of a reference group to whom the consumer aspires is a powerful basis upon which to charge premium prices, not least to reinforce the implicit snob appeal involved.

Insight

One of the best examples of the power of promotion is that of modern-day Santa Claus. Notwithstanding pagan origins and the cult of St Nicholas, his modern-day appearance dates only from 1931. It was then that Coca-Cola Inc. decided to design a new Christmas advertisement campaign. Its inspiration lay in making over Santa in the company's corporate colours of red and white. A plump and bearded former employee was selected as the model for the campaign.

The family

The family is a close and influential reference group. It conditions behaviour and values from birth and continues to influence buying decisions throughout the individual's life. This led to the identification of a *family life cycle* made up of different stages or phases in family life with significant implications for buying behaviour:

◆ **Young unmarried:**

   ◆ Young with relatively high disposable income due to limited commitments. Fashion and entertainment orientated.

◆ **Newly married/no children:**

   ◆ Becoming outdated with a third of all cohabiting couples being unmarried.

   ◆ Dual income with expenditure focused on home building, consumer durables and holidays.

◆ **Young married or living together with children:**

   ◆ Again 40 per cent of babies are now born out of wedlock in Britain.

   ◆ Home and family expenditure orientated.

   ◆ Limited scope for luxury items.

◆ **Middle-aged married/teenage children:**

   ◆ Approaching maximum dual earnings

   ◆ High replacement expenditure on quality durables.

- ◆ Older married/children left home:
    - ◆ Disposable income at a peak
    - ◆ Focused on retirement planning and luxuries.
    - ◆ Well-established tastes and preferences.
- ◆ Older retired/single:
    - ◆ Reduced disposable income but increasingly numerous and affluent.
    - ◆ Conservative tastes and less susceptible to marketing campaigns.
    - ◆ Important purchasers of one-off items like cars, holiday homes and expensive garden equipment.

Activity 5.17

Key skills – Collecting information

Scan the advertisements in newspapers and magazines and classify their appeal according to (a) reference groups and/or (b) family stages.

In understanding the family and its spending decisions, marketers should seek to identify not only who makes the final purchasing decision but also the influence exerted by other family members. Only in this way can they be sure as to whom they should direct their promotional messages. Who is it that decides the type and location of this year's family holiday? Do parents decide on style of dress or their teenage children? Are changes taking place in the distribution of this decision-making power as more married women work and men share the domestic responsibilities?

Stereotyped notions of the male deciding the type of car and home improvements while the female decides the food and furnishings are increasingly suspect, and marketers and organizations must keep abreast of changes if the marketing mix is to remain relevant and effective. That said, a recent edition of *Social Trends* saw little evidence of 'New Man' emerging among younger age groups. The division of roles in households persists, with mothers spending six times as long cooking and cleaning and twice as long shopping.

The Japanese family, once the model of togetherness, is also disintegrating under the weight of multiple TVs, phones, video-recorders, Play Stations and PCs. Surveys suggest that like their European counterparts, Japanese children are no longer eating with their parents nor wish to participate in family activities. The longer-term consequences on culture of such social isolation remain to be seen. It may be an illusion given the fact that 89 per cent of 11–12 year olds, 58 per cent of 9–10 year olds, 24 per cent of 7–8 year olds, 13 per cent of 5–6 year olds own a mobile phone and a company has just launched one targeted on 4 year olds.

Lifestyle

Lifestyles are defined as the patterns in which people live, spend time and money and are mainly a function of the individual's motivation, prior learning, class and personality. They are measured by analysts, using *attitude, interests and opinions* alongside demographic factors to establish market segments with clusters of common characteristics.

The central idea is to identify behavioural patterns to build a picture of how individuals interact with their environment. This will then allow marketers to segment the market more effectively and tailor campaigns designed to appeal to particular lifestyle types. The presumption is that these groups will respond to different marketing mixes that can then be exploited to advantage.

Companies such as Laura Ashley and Next have used such analysis to drive their marketing communications and encourage readers of their catalogues to identify with a particular cluster and therefore focus their purchasing behaviour on the products offered. Websites exploiting segmentation opportunities include www.style365.com which specializes in luxury goods with links to 'gold pages' such as Aspreys & Garrard, while www.littleblackdress.co.uk delivers to your door within 24 hours. Selection is by mood or fabric with advisers available for a 'personalized' service. For multi-million celebrities, Dubai is creating 300 man-made island properties by 2008, designed like a map of the world and costing from £3.5 to £20 million each.

The marketer must, however, avoid oversimplified categorization. Individuals may exhibit multiple lifestyle characteristics or evolve from one type to another as time and circumstances alter. Companies may wish to customize their own lifestyle segments or use generic categories such as strivers, aspirers, achievers and succeeders. According to the University of Cambridge, one lifestyle choice that could add 11 years to the life expectancy of thousands of people involves giving up smoking while eating five portions of fruit and vegetables a day and taking moderate daily exercise. Every bit of positive activity has a measurable impact on health so even McDonald's is making a contribution following its new emphasis on 'healthy eating'. Sales are up between seven and nine per cent in the United States and Europe as a result of its new strategy, although it still sells eight double cheeseburgers for every salad.

Activity 5.18

Key skills – Using information

Consider the realism of the following lifestyle trends and their implications for niche furniture manufacturers and retailers:

Instant gratification	*Live now pay later*
Easy credit attitudes	*To finance the good life now!*
Time conservation	*Critical resource constraint on consumption*
New work ethic	*Working to live, not living to work*
Consumerism	*Concern for price/quality/service/environment*
Personal creativity	*Desire for self-expression/improvement*
Naturalism	*Return to nature but retaining material comforts*

What other lifestyle trends can you currently identify in society?

Summary

In this unit, we have seen the following:

◆ It is important for marketers to monitor and understand the implications of demographic changes:

   ◆ Demographic changes occur slowly over time but their cumulative impact over a period can have great consequences for buying patterns.

   ◆ Demography can help marketers predict size and change in target markets by population, age, gender, region, family size or ethnic group.

   ◆ The scope for demographic segmentation is considerable *and* is a means of adapting marketing approaches and product offerings to match changing needs at the different stages of life – Club 18–30 or Saga have a clear life cycle focus.

◆ How changes in population structure can affect market supply and demand.

◆ Employment trends can and do influence the need for greater business flexibility:

   ◆ Organizations must market themselves effectively in the face of potential skill shortages and target potential employees whose needs must be analysed and matched to the organization's needs.

   ◆ The changing role and impact of women in work and society.

   ◆ Marketers must respond to demographic trends and be more flexible.

   ◆ Advertising and promotion should reflect the changing patterns.

◆ Social trends and their impact on marketing and the marketing environment.

◆ The significance of social influences (i.e. class, occupation, lifestyle, reference groups) as bases for segmentation.

◆ Consumer markets can be segmented through:

   ◆ Geographic: region, climate, density

   ◆ Lifestyle

   ◆ Demographic (age, gender, race, nationality and religion; income and education; family size and life cycle; occupation and social class)

◆ The real meaning of culture and its relevance to international/regional marketing.

◆ Geodemographic segmentation is based on *neighbourhood and type of dwelling*:

   ◆ As a composite index of factors relevant to buying behaviour, this is thought to represent a more accurate assessment than those based solely on one factor such as class or income.

   ◆ A well-used example of this approach is the ACORN system (i.e. A Classification Of Residential Neighbourhoods), which classifies households into one of 11 major groups and 36 specific neighbourhood types and is used by companies such as IKEA, the Swedish furniture retailer, to analyse its customer base.

- Other examples of such databases include PIN (Pinpoint Identified Neighbourhoods) and MOSAIC.

◆ The real meaning of culture and its relevance to international/regional marketing:

- Culture is a complex blend of acquired values, beliefs, attitudes, customs that provide context, conditioning and behavioural guidelines in society.

- A national culture is usually composed of subcultures. This is based on origins, religion or some basis of shared outlook and values.

- Subcultures form important bases for segmentation whether regional (Welsh), urban (Bradford, Pakistani) or local (Jewish, North London).

- Marketer must recognize the degree to which purchasing behaviour is culturally driven. Individuals from different cultures are likely to respond to different imperatives in terms of what, where, when and how they buy goods.

- Ample data exist for analysis of purchasing variations related to regional cultural differences. *Regional Trends* is compiled by ONS and may be supplemented by market research derived from regional television companies.

- The South East with its concentration of higher-income households may provide useful insights into future buying trends in other less prosperous regions.

◆ Marketers should take care in classifying people into different groups/segments for marketing purposes, since many of the behavioural assumptions are generalizations and subject to change.

◆ If it is an individual's perceptions and aspirations that drive purchasing decisions, rather than their objectively defined status, then prediction is much more hazardous.

◆ Complex family structures rule out the use of the occupation of the so-called 'head of the family' as an indicator of purchasing potential.

◆ Society is becoming progressively better educated, with lifelong learning the dawning reality. Marketers must therefore adjust their attitudes and communication methods accordingly.

◆ Social, cultural and demographic factors influence incomes, tastes and preferences, all important demand determinants. Equally, they may inhibit purchase decisions.

◆ Distinguish a customer's beliefs (conclusions based on available objective facts and subjective experience) from their values. Values are more generalized, deep seated and enduring. Greens are good for you may be a belief, but vegetarianism values life itself.

◆ Products can acquire cultural meaning through the marketing process: for example designer clothes or a BMW in an achiever's lifestyle.

◆ The changing role of women is making more promotional spending gender specific, as seen, for example, in car advertisements.

Further study and examination preparation

Alternative forms of examination question provide ample scope for the examiner to select at least one factor or trend from the social, demographic and cultural environment.

Extending knowledge

Palmer A. and Hartley B. (2006) *The Business and Marketing Environment*, McGraw-Hill.

Chapter 9: The Social and Demographic Environment.

Palmer A. (2002) *The Business Environment*, McGraw-Hill.

Chapter 11.

Other suggested reading

Jobber D. (1998) *Principles of Marketing*, McGraw-Hill, 2nd Ed.

Chapter 5: The marketing environment.

Lancaster G, Massingham L. and Ashford R. (2002) *Essentials of Marketing*, McGraw-Hill Education.

Chapter 2: The marketing environment.

Websites

http://unstats.un.org for UN population data.

www.worldbank.org for World Bank population data.

www.intute.ac.uk is a gateway to the social sciences.

Practicising past exam questions

Please see Question 1d, December 2003 on the CIM website, www.cim.co.uk.

Please see Question 5, June 2004 on the CIM website, www.cim.co.uk.

Please see Question 1a, b, c, e, f, December 2004. Go to www.cim.co.uk for specimen answers.

Please see Question 6i, December 2005. Go to www.cim.co.uk/learning zone for specimen answers.

Please see Question 6, June 2006. Go to www.cim.co.uk/learningzone for specimen answers.

In addition to referring to past paper questions, students should also refer to the specimen paper to ensure that they are clear about the new exam format.

The economic and international environment

Learning objectives

By the end of this unit you will be able to:

◆ Understand the basic workings of the economy (3.4).

◆ Evaluate measures of economic activity and the limitations of economic indicators (3.4).

◆ Understand the nature of macro-economic objectives and the role of government.

◆ Assess the likely effects of alternative economic and trade policies (3.4).

◆ Evaluate economic impacts and implications for marketers in different types of organization.

◆ Identify the implications of the international environment (3.4).

Study guide

The economic environment is one area where we all have first-hand experience. Not only do we read the newspapers and listen to items on television or radio, we also feel the direct impact of economic events such as changing taxes at budget time, a rising interest rate or an accelerating pay freeze. Even though economic factors are not controllable by organizations, marketers nonetheless need to take these into consideration as such factors can have a direct or an indirect effect on consumer behaviour and consumer attitudes.

Activity 6.1

The 2008-2009 UK Budget in Brief

In March 2008, the Chancellor of the Exchequer Alistair Darling presented the new budget.

The first rise in duty on spirits in a decade was intended to take effect from midnight on Sunday 16 March, with 55p added to a bottle of spirits. Duty on wine rose by 14p per bottle and tax duty on cider rose by 3p a litre. A pint of beer now attracts 3p more duty. Alcohol duties are forecasted to rise by inflation plus 2 per cent for the next four years.

The planned 2p tax rise on a litre of petrol that was due to take effect in April has been delayed until October. But, on environmental grounds, fuel duty will rise by 0.5p in real terms from 2010. The tax break for biofuels is also set to end.

The Chancellor increased the tax on a packet of 20 cigarettes by 11p from 12 March 2008, while a pack of five cigars will cost 4p more. But the tax break on nicotine replacement products, with VAT cut from 17.5 per cent to 5 per cent, has been extended beyond June.

The Chancellor demanded that energy companies triple their spending on social tariffs to £150m a year in a move that will benefit the five million energy customers on pre-payment meters. Pensioners' winter fuel allowances will also rise by up to £100 this year.

What implications do you think these changes could potentially have on the marketing environment and on marketers?

Macroeconomics is about the aggregate behaviour of consumers, businesses and governments. Concern is with general price level rather than individual product prices, and attention focuses on total output, income and spending. The rate of economic growth is of central importance as are cyclical fluctuations around this trend.

Businesses must take very careful account of this environment since decisions on capital investment, the timing of a new product launch or hiring and firing, for example, will need to be set against the general economic background. Unanticipated movements in interest or exchange rates can quite literally convert expected profit into crippling loss.

Study tip

The economy is a complex open system and marketers who can master their consciousness of current and forecasted economic problems and anticipate the direction of policy changes will possess a competitive edge over rivals.

Likewise you would ideally learn how to appreciate these factors.

The international environment is also increasingly familiar to us, not only through our travels but also by membership of trade blocs. Some of the popular ones are:

- ◆ **EU** – The European Union is a political and economic community of member states located primarily in Europe.

- ◆ **AFTA** – The ASEAN Free Trade Area is a trade bloc agreement by the Association of Southeast Asian Nations supporting local manufacturing in all ASEAN countries.

- ◆ **SAARC** – The South Asian Association for Regional Co-operation is an economic and political organization of eight countries in Southern Asia. In terms of population, its sphere of influence is the largest of any regional organization.

- ◆ **NAFTA** – The North American Free Trade Agreement (Spanish: Tratado de Libre Comercio de América del Norte, TLCAN) (French: Accord de libre-échange nord-américain, ALENA) is the trade bloc in North America created by the North American Free Trade Agreement (NAFTA) and its two supplements, the North American Agreement on Environmental Co-operation (NAAEC) and the North American Agreement on Labor Co-operation (NAALC), whose members are Canada, Mexico and the United States. It came into effect on January 1, 1994 and (as of 2008) it remains the largest trade bloc in the world in terms of combined GDP of its members.

Civilizations through the mists of time have prospered as a result of trade. Recognition of the gains to be made from exchanging surpluses for scarce and desirable products from foreign lands has led to the development of international trading. International trading networks now form a tightening web of linkages between all corners of the globe.

Trade nowadays is more complex with multilateral exchanges facilitated by international finance. However, participating nations and businesses are also increasingly vulnerable to global political and economic influences. For instance the effects of the September 11 attacks in the US were both global and continuing. Consequently, the international environment presents the marketer not only with considerable opportunities but also with greater challenges than the domestic market.

Study tip

As with your own economy, it is important you have a clear appreciation of your country's international trade position.

Is its balance of payments in surplus or deficit?

What is its pattern of trade with other countries and the composition of its imports and exports?

Does your country belong to a trading bloc? If so, what regulations govern its internal and external relationships?

Exam hint

CIM is a qualification undertaken by students from around the world. The global environment forms a context common to all and may provide a range of questions as a result.

Government economic objectives

Governments, like businesses, have a number of objectives, ranging from social concerns to national security. In the economic realm, they have one overriding goal:

◆ To achieve sustainable economic growth ideally at a productive pace.

However, governments also tend to have three other significant objectives. Without these, their success may be constrained. These are:

◆ To maintain higher levels of employment or real jobs

◆ To control inflation: to keep inflation at very low levels and avoid deflation

◆ To achieve a favourable balance of payments averaged over a period

Subsidiary goals might include:

◆ To keep the aggregate tax burden below 40 per cent of GDP

◆ To restricting the budget deficit to 3 per cent of GDP (Euro-zone limit for members)

◆ To achieve a balanced regional development, resource conservation and environmental concern (e.g. target to reduce carbon emissions by 60 per cent by 2050)

◆ To distribute income to reflect equity and economic contribution

◆ To achieve a competitive exchange rate

Economic growth and development

This is the fundamental objective because a growing economy allows a government to achieve many goals. Through economic growth and development, resources can be acquired. These in turn can help resolve conflicts with regards to the allocation of resources.

An electorate that experiences real increases in purchasing power, job opportunities and spending on health, education, defence and pensions is more likely to vote for the return of the party in office. It is often said that oppositions do not win elections, but that governments lose them. Failing to deliver improvements in living standards is often hailed as the main cause of election loss.

Eurostat has reported that per capita income in the UK is now nearly 20 per cent higher than the EU average. While this has been more sustainable in recent years, in 2005 growth fell sharply to its post-war average of around 2.25 per cent. However it recovered against expectation to 2.5 per cent in 2006 and was even forecasted by the Chancellor to be 3 per cent in 2007.

The primary economic objective is to raise overall performance while limiting fluctuations around the trend. Sustaining continuous growth by better economic management, and so avoiding recessions, should create an atmosphere of investment confidence and more positive expectations for the future. This can be reinforced by encouraging entrepreneurship and innovation through tax incentives. In the UK, the economy has enjoyed an unprecedented 57 consecutive quarters of growth and despite predictions of downturn it continues to thrive on a diet of high social spending, high taxation and significant investment in public infrastructure.

Growth does not always mean rising consumption even though this accounts for two-thirds of aggregate demand. An export- or investment-led rise in output will do little to raise domestic consumption in the short term but is normally much healthier for longer-term competitiveness. Similarly, growth in GDP that is achieved by using unemployed resources should be distinguished from real growth. This is sustained by rising productivity through investment in skills, infrastructure, capital and new technology. Poorer countries are more concerned with economic development involving a transformation of economy from one based on primary production to one based on manufacturing, services and information technology. This will usually require external funds to finance the dramatic improvements required in both the skill base and basic infrastructure (i.e. production in China; services in India).

Economic growth as an objective has attracted growing criticism because of externalities arising from it. Concern as seen briefly in Unit 4 has focused on non-renewable resource depletion and greenhouse effects arising from the combustion of carbon fuels in power stations and vehicles. Projected growth, particularly in developing countries, is expected to expand greenhouse gases and raise the temperature of the planet. Acid rain, ozone depletion, oil and chemical spillages, industrial pollution and rising congestion are just some of the other side effects associated with economic growth. Adoption of the 1997 Kyoto protocol limiting carbon dioxide emissions has not been helped either by the re-election of President Bush or the observation by the French president that each American emits three times more greenhouse gases than a Frenchman. However international agreements such as the Kyoto protocol are attempting to curtail this.

Question 6.1

Key skills – Problem-solving

Is there a solution to the quandary outlined above?

If so, what are the marketing implications?

Key macro-economic concepts

Four macro-economic dimensions are significant to the economic environment. These are:

◆ The circular flow of income *(concept 1)*

◆ The multiplier effect *(concept 2)*

◆ The accelerator effect *(concept 3)*

◆ Inflationary and deflationary gaps *(concept 4)*

Each concept will be defined and discussed in depth in the following sections as their understanding is quintessential if a thorough appreciation of the economic environment is to be afforded.

The circular flow of income (Concept 1)

This is a simple model for understanding the workings of the economy.

Think in terms of flows between households and businesses, banks, foreigners and governments. These flows are either incomes or expenditures and circulate around the economic system. Figure 6.1 displays how households, as the owners of productive resources, receive a flow of income from firms who employ them to produce goods and services.

Households use income gathered through such means as wages, salaries, rents, interest and even distributed profit to purchase products and services from companies. This flow of expenditure creates the demand for the products of the companies. The revenue received by the companies from the households (and the consumers) is what is used by the same companies to meet the cost of inputs for the next round of production.

Therefore economic activity is like a circulating flow of spending power. This increases with injections of resources or finance or reduced by leakages of expenditure. If all income received by households is spent then the flow of activity continues period after period. However in reality there is also an element of saving. Unless any leakage is re-channelled into the circular flow, the level of the flow will fall because of lower demand for products and services.

Companies cut back on employment levels and labour costs, and as incomes fall households will save more as a precaution against potential unemployment. This will inevitably cause activity levels to fall further. The paradox of thrift suggests that saving is a good thing. However, saving without any corresponding investment may lead to lower income availability and even employment.

Flow of income/output/expenditure

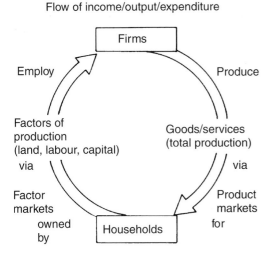

Counterflow of money

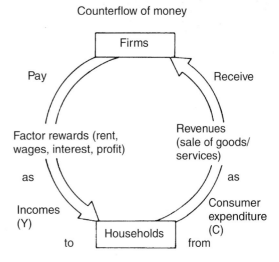

Figure 6.1 The circular flow of economic activity

Study tip

With regards to this syllabus, although all aspects of the environment need to be considered, only an appreciation of economics is expected. Accordingly, you will not be expected to reproduce a detailed analysis. However an understanding is important.

In practice, savings are not normally kept, but deposited in financial institutions to earn interest. These funds make it possible for such institutions to lend to households or companies. At other times, financial institutions can make investments. All the three options imply that funds are being re-injected back into the circular flow.

So long as the investment injection balances the savings leakage, the equilibrium in the flow is maintained. Investment may create additional demand for the producers of products and services. However it cannot be guaranteed that there will be increased and even sufficient aggregate demand to sustain production at the desired enhanced level. Unfortunately, those who invest are seldom those who decide on what to save.

Question 6.2

Key skills – Problem-solving

As a marketer, can you think of any mechanism that might bring savings and investment to equality at the equilibrium level?

Do you think that this mechanism will work quickly and effectively?

What is the condition for equilibrium or stability in the circular flow?

To complete our circular flow and make it fully realistic, flows to the government and the rest of the world must also be introduced (see Figure 6.2).

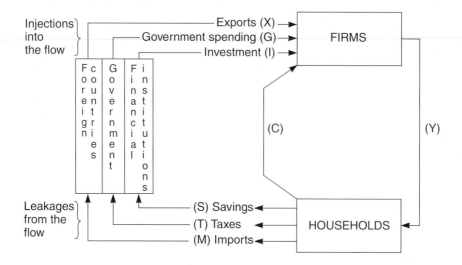

Figure 6.2 The full-economy model of injections and leakages

Households pay taxes on income and expenditure and these are leakages from the flow. Similarly, spending on imported goods and services creates demand for the output of foreign firms. Government spending and exports are injections of purchasing power into the flow, creating demand for domestic firms. However, if injections exceed leakages then income, output and expenditure is expected to rise until equilibrium is restored. Equilibrium is achieved by companies responding to excess demand by producing more and vice versa. Aggregate demand drives domestic activity levels. This also determines employment level and income.

The multiplier effect (Concept 2)

An extra injection from the government or other investment may increase the level of income in the flow by more than the initial expenditure. The injection creates demand for extra output. This in turn requires businesses to employ more resources provided that these are in fact available.

Extra output generates new incomes which are paid to households. Households receiving this income pay taxes, buy imports and save, but the rest is spent on domestic consumer goods and services at the second round of the process. As affected businesses produce more output to meet this demand, more resources are brought into the equation. The resulting incomes are paid out to households, and the process is repeated.

Activity 6.2

The decision by the Spanish and Moroccan governments to commission plans for a rail link under the Straits of Gibraltar would trigger such a mechanism.

Attempt to identify the flow that may be started by such a project.

Leakages reduce the power of the multiplier. The higher these are as a proportion of the circular flow, the lower the multiplier value and vice versa. The multiplier also works in reverse, as falling injections (e.g. reduced exports) can cause a cumulative fall in income, output and jobs down the supply chain. This in turn will create leakages and perpetuate the flow.

Exam hint

Key skills – Understanding of marketing or general business jargon/terminology

Example: What does the term 'multiplier effect' mean?

The accelerator effect (Concept 3)

The *accelerator* reinforces the effect of the multiplier. It arises from the fact that the value of the capital stock (i.e. plant/equipment) is, on average, four or five times as large as the annual value of output. For example, if capital has a useful life of 10 years and total car production of 2 million units is supplied by 10 similar-sized plants, then average replacement investment, equivalent to one plant, is required each year.

Insight: The real cost of the Athens 2004 Olympic Games

Facilities for the Greek Olympics Games of 2004 managed to be ready on time. However, this was at the expense of the budget. The final cost rose from £4.6 to £11bn or 5 per cent of Greece's GDP. This affected the entire Greek economy by pushing the fiscal deficit to double its Eurozone limit. This has now been reduced by revising upwards its GDP to account for the value of its informal economy to include less prominent services (e.g. prostitution). The games were deemed a success but as in Montreal's case, the taxpayers will unquestionably bear the effects of the increase in cost for many years. London has won the right to stage the 2012 Olympics. An estimated budget of £2.375bn in addition to the £7 billion of government funding has been allocated for vital transport infrastructure improvements. The National Lottery is expected to offer £1.5 billion, the London Development Agency £250 million and £625 million is expected to come from London council taxpayers. In order to meet this target, taxes in London will be raised as an annual levy over 6 years (extended to 8 years if costs overrun). Revenues are expected to be around £1.5 billion with ticket sales contributing to one-fifth. The balance is intended to come from licensing and sponsorship. For the UK, the impacts may be considered small in comparison to the size of the economy. However all these associated projects must be finished on time and within budget. Furthermore the Olympic Games are intended to help regenerate the standard of living and performance of a deprived part of the city. This said, the scheme is potentially over-ambitious. Although tourism is expected to be stimulated, it is questionable whether the transport system will be able to cope. 7000 skilled construction jobs could be created in the run-up to the games and many new homes and businesses should be created as a long-term legacy. The high streets are also expected to benefit from the public buoyancy during and even after the games.

After its hosting of the football World Cup, Germany's unemployment levels fell below 10 per cent while living standards began to rise after being having been static for four years. Consequently, it is expected that the same positive effects will be experienced by the UK economy.

Insight

Economic factors will have a distinct effect on different parties. For instance, a rise in interest rates might trigger a media headline *Interest rate gloom* and concerns from retailers. However, savers will be very pleased.

In the UK, far from saving more than spending, the average British household currently has been spending nearly £600 per week while earning under £500. This had led to much increase in debt levels and been detrimental to the savings ratio. Notwithstanding, the rate of inflation has been maintained low due to spending. Thus for retailers, this has been positive.

Inflationary and deflationary gaps (Concept 4)

If there is insufficient aggregate demand to enable all businesses to operate profitably while using available resources in an economy, a deflationary gap is said to exist. This will put downward pressure on producers and retailers to maintain low pricing structures. Alternatively, if aggregate demand exceeds the amount necessary to secure employment of available resources, an inflationary gap would be created. In such circumstances, when there is enough money in circulation to enable the process, general prices would tend to rise to even out the available supply of products.

Question 6.3

Key skills – Problem-solving

If your economy, along with other trading partners, is stuck in a deep recession with activity levels falling and unemployment climbing to disturbingly high rates:

◆   Which of the aggregate demand components would you expect to rise, fall or stay unchanged, and why?

◆   Which component(s) do you think could be altered?

◆   Would falling interest rates, exchange rates and wage rates increase activity levels in the short run or would these increase activity rates in the long term?

Insight: What is the short-term economic future?

Britain is currently said to be worth about £6 trillion. This is an increase of about £120 billion since 2005. This rise is equal to the entire output of Saudi Arabia. 60 per cent of this wealth is property. However, while the City of London and the South East are booming with rising house prices and stock market prices, the regions, high street retailers and many manufacturers are suffering due to unemployment rising to 1.7 million.

Despite buoyant growth projections, the current boom is largely fuelled by consumer and public sector spending. As this is financed largely by debts, it is mostly unsustainable. The price for excessive debt is generally slower future growth.

Interest rates were 5.25 per cent and were set towards 6 per cent in 2007 yet business investment has already fallen from 14 to 9 per cent of GDP. This was further weakened by wasteful public spending.

British productivity has therefore suffered and the trade deficit continues to widen. The economy is at an inflexion point and as the world economy is softening (e.g. falling house prices in the US), the UK might experience a period of prolonged slowdown or even recession. This is in fact already being reflected in the stagnating house prices in the UK.

Due largely to rising taxes and red tape, Britain was judged by the World Economic Forum to have fallen since 1997 from the 4th to the 13th most competitive economy. Consequently, the UK is now less well placed than it was in 1997 to deal with a recession.

Several economic factors can lead to a recession. These include:

◆   Rising interest rates in major economies to curb inflationary pressures

◆   Consecutive increases in the unemployment rate

◆   Personal and business bankruptcies reaching record levels

◆   Faltering consumer confidence

◆   Reductions in credit card debt levels

◆   Falling private sector pay growth

◆   Uncertainties arising out of the war on terror (i.e. war in Iraq)

◆   The EU curtailing levels of growth

A recession is considered to be long overdue in the UK. As companies face the need to fundamentally restructure their organizations to face new risks such as intensifying competition from India and from China, redundancies may be inevitable.

Notwithstanding, several current economic factors can also help prevent a recession. These include:

◆ Oil and gas prices have fallen by 20 per cent from their recent peak. Only if sustained at $85, according to a recent Morgan Stanley report, would they derail consumption and the world economy.

◆ Inflation is still close to the Bank of England's 2 per cent target.

◆ Internet sales have risen sharply to counterbalance flat high street sales. Sales figures about retailers in the UK released after Christmas 2007 showed a significant increase from 2006.

◆ India and China continue to provide the world economy with a major boost:

　　◆ Sales of mobiles have risen in India from 6 to 43 million in two years.

　　◆ China, after 25 years of sustained growth, is set to overtake the UK as the fifth largest economy.

　　◆ Its manufacturing power has produced cheap goods, helping to reduce inflation in the West over the last five years.

　　◆ Since 1995 women's clothing has fallen 35 per cent in real terms, home entertainment equipment 73 per cent and computers 93 per cent.

　　◆ China currently contributes about one-third of world growth.

　　◆ However interest rates are rising and the renminbi (the currency of mainland China) is coming under pressure to be revalued.

　　◆ Consequently the cooling down of the economy and the raising of export prices may occur.

The significance of gross domestic product (GDP)

The circular flow represents the value of goods and services produced in an economy. This is measured annually in three ways:

1 **National income** – Incomes created from producing the output, for example wages, rent, profit

2 **National output** – Sum of final output or the value added by each domestic firm

3 **National expenditure** – Aggregate spending on national output

Gross domestic product (GDP) differs from gross national product (GNP) in that this includes 'net income from abroad'. In the UK, this only represents about 1–2 per cent of the GDP. It is much higher in countries like India and Pakistan due to substantial remittances by nationals working in foreign countries.

Gross domestic product is not adjusted for capital used up in the process of producing annual wealth due to difficulties in agreeing on its value. Great care is taken, however, to avoid double-counting output or incomes. Only final output is included and transfer incomes such as pensions and student grants are ignored.

The three measures are defined in this way in order to be conceptually equal to each other. However, in practice a balancing item is required to ensure equality. Errors and omissions in data collection make this necessary. If capital consumption is removed from GNP (the gross national product), it is then referred to as the net national income.

Insight

With oil prices recently at record levels, refining might appear to be a profitable business. Consider, however, the classic perfume, Chanel No. 5. This retails at $246 per fluid ounce. The main ingredient of such a perfume is ethanol, which retails at just $40 a barrel. It appears that the marketers of this popular luxury perfume have achieved an astonishing mark-up on their product costs.

Exam hint

Improving your performance

Many economic concepts are of value in revision and examination technique. Time is the scarce resource and you must allocate it efficiently. Opportunity cost means that additional hours spent on one subject leaves fewer hours to spend on the others. Allocating time between questions in the exam requires the equi-marginal principle, which revolves around allocating resources equally.

Aim to achieve a position where you could not improve on your overall mark by trading more time on one question for less on another.

The uses of national accounting data

In the UK the Office for National Statistics (ONS) collects and publishes the data in the Blue Book. This information provides the basis for forecasts as well as for the analysis of the current state of the economy. The Treasury has developed a sophisticated computer-based model to predict the future path of the economy. The government is known to partly base its policy judgements on these predictions and analyses.

The GDP (gross domestic product) figures uncovered by the ONS can provide a measure of the following:

◆ The gross physical output of products and services of domestic companies

◆ The annual percentage increase or growth of an economy

◆ The productivity or GDP per head/capita by dividing GDP by working population

◆ The average standard of living by dividing GDP by the general population

◆ A comparison of performance between different economies

Question 6.4

Key skills – Metrics

If Sri Lanka's GDP is growing by 3 per cent per annum, and its population is growing by 0.5 per cent while China is growing by 9 per cent and its population by 1.5 per cent, which country is better off?

What is the GDP of your economy in local currency terms and how fast is it growing?

Does an increase in GDP automatically mean that you are better off?

Care is required when assessing the potential of overseas markets using national income data. Different countries have different values, tastes, needs and proportions spent on armed forces for instance. This will affect the amount of available disposable income. In general, Asian economies tend to have higher savings ratios than Europeans. The general consensus is that the United States' high energy-consuming lifestyle is more than double that of other countries.

The efficiency of governmental statistical agencies also varies widely and exchange rate fluctuations often make comparisons very difficult. Sometimes statistics may also be flawed due to human error or technological mistakes.

It has been uncovered that some poorer economies had understated their GDP to attract aid from international agencies while others have very wide disparities in income, making figures on average living standards very misleading. Less-developed economies also tend to have large barter economies, making many transactions difficult to record.

The true value of data

A further reason for caution over the accuracy of the statistics is that GDP data are normally expressed in nominal or current prices terms. If, for example, inflation in China in Question 6.4 was 8 per cent while only 2 per cent in Sri Lanka then the overall position is 0.5 per cent *real* growth for the latter and –0.5 per cent real decline in the former.

Consequently, it is always recommended that one checks whether the figures are expressed in nominal or real terms to avoid being misled; that is, GDP at constant prices adjusts for inflation by expressing GDP in terms of prices prevailing in a base year (e.g. at 1997 prices).

Notwithstanding, even if all the calculations were entirely accurate, problems could still remain with regards to statistical information and the interpretation of the latter. These concerns could resolve around any of the following factors:

◆ An increase in exports or investment will not necessarily increase *current* living standards.

◆ An increase in GDP may be due to longer hours or increased female participation rates and involve unaccounted costs in terms of stress, reduced health or less leisure time.

◆ No account is taken of *externalities* associated with growth such as emissions, effluents and waste:

◆ Economic activity to remedy environmental damage (known as defensive expenditures) is actually counted as part of GDP.

◆ Measurement of *sustainable* income would also have to take resource depletion into account.

◆ Gross domestic product increases when people pay for services they would have previously performed themselves. Although child-minding, garden maintenance and laundry are services associated with busy lifestyles, they however do not improve living standards.

◆ There is no valuation of leisure time or unrecorded activities occurring in the informal economy.

◆ There is no account of redistribution. Furthermore the share of the nation's wealth enjoyed by the richest 1 per cent has risen in Britain to over 23 per cent.

Gross domestic product is no longer the undisputed measure of economic progress. Although it was never intended to be a measure of welfare, its primacy with economists as a tool of analysis tends to obscure its limitations. Moreover, the GDP does not allow for the consumption of non-renewable natural assets or the subtraction of the impact of untreated pollution. The latter is in fact causing some interest groups to call for an environmentally adjusted measure. Meanwhile other financial institutions such as the World Bank may be leading the way by adopting a single *measure of welfare* that reflects indicators besides income. Indicators may range from the distribution of income, voluntary leisure time, environmental quality, the standard of health and education, crime levels, employment, informal activities and even suicide rates.

The underlying trend of real GDP growth for the world economy has been firmly upward since the Second World War. This has been particularly evident in East Asia. However, these predominantly export-orientated economies have not managed to avoid strong and irregular oscillations in their economies. This has been partly due to their interdependence with the main markets, which they supply. For instance, high specialization and a focus on a narrow range of products and market segments have exposed these countries to risks identical to those confronting companies within the competitive business environment. For instance, new EU quotas severely affected Chinese textile producers in summer 2005.

Study tip

The World Bank website offers a wide array of information about development economics and the environment. Please check www.worldbank.org.

Exam hint

Improving your performance

The marketing environment provides opportunities to illustrate your understanding of many subjects by using diagrams or charts. While these can be potentially useful, only use them if:

> ◆ You draw them correctly. Any axes or relationships shown must be adequately labelled. Nothing exposes ignorance of the marketing environment as obviously as an incorrectly drawn relationship.
>
> ◆ They are relevant to the question.

The business cycle

The business cycle refers to the periodic fluctuation in economic activity that occurs in industrialized economies. Economies tend to oscillate between periods of high activity, growth in employment and booming confidence, and periods of falling output, rising unemployment and general despondency. This is particularly the case with open economies like Singapore, Sri Lanka and the UK where a high trade (25–30 per cent) dependency prevails. This dependency makes these economies especially vulnerable to international shocks. In contrast, countries such as the United State and Canada, which have low export and import ratios (10 per cent), tend to have more stable economies. However, these economies are also not completely protected from adverse economic factors.

The business cycle represents the *average* of a multitude of individual industry cycles. Any one business may therefore be in advance of or lag behind the main cycle. Consequently, the marketer of a company must locate their own relative position since the published data always refer to the average. The duration of the cycle is also a variable. Up to 1945, it averaged 8 to 9 years in open economies while a less-consistent pattern has prevailed since. Figure 6.3 shows the typical stages of the cycle.

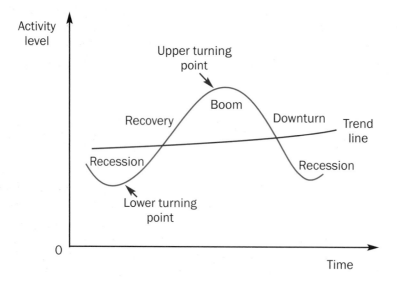

Figure 6.3 The stages of the business cycle

Recession is defined as at least two successive quarters of *falling* GDP. When economies are going through a recession, unemployment rises alongside spare capacity. As wage and price increases are difficult to achieve, inflation is moderated. These are also difficult times for marketers. As consumption spending falls, competitive forces intensify. At the same time budgets come under increasing pressure. Profitability falls during any recession. Subsequently, business confidence is usually low and any investment is reduced.

Question 6.5

Key skills – Interpreting information

Identify the key features of the following phases:

◆ Recovery

◆ Boom

◆ Downturn

The severity and duration of the phases vary from cycle to cycle. Central banks have become more skilled in taming cyclical fluctuations in output and employment but at the price of huge swings in asset prices. The best current rule of thumb appears to be 'the bigger the boom the bigger the bust', with excessive consumer and government spending still threatening a future upper turning point despite recent rises in interest rates.

Insight

The UK's last recession was in 1990–1992 but there have been a series of 'bubbles' in dot-com stocks, property, commodities and oil, as well as unsustainable balance of payments deficits. Property prices, for example, have doubled in the last five years making housing unaffordable for many public sector workers. These inflations may be defined as massive and sustained suspensions of disbelief and, if not positively corrected, threaten to end in tears.

Insight

Personal debt was, until recently, a taboo for most British families. This is no longer the case with an average personal debt of £5300 and rising at 14 per cent per year up to 2005. Since then, these figures have risen. Household debt (credit plus mortgage debt) now averages over £17,000, equal to total output of £1000 billion. Households typically owe 130 per cent of their annual income, 50 per cent higher than in the unstable boom of 1987–1989. However at the beginning of April 2008, many banks started limiting the number of mortgage offers they were to make to first time buyers with limited deposits. This move is bound to affect the housing market.

Historically, low interest rates have, until recently, kept debt service costs below 10 per cent of disposable income but seven successive rate rises signalled a new reality. As the borrowing stops so does the consumer boom but even with static house prices, it will take an estimated six years of sluggish growth or four years of zero growth to return debt ratios to a more sustainable 105 per cent of disposable income. Should a 'worst case scenario' of rising taxation, inflation and unemployment combine to detonate this unexploded bomb of accumulated debt, then expect mortgage arrears and repossessions to rise sharply.

The marketer must anticipate fluctuating economic conditions. Governments can underestimate the business cycle and other random influences. Thus, marketers should always be prepared for unpredictable economic changes. The upper and lower turning points are the key moments to identify as they signal a significant 'sea change' in economic conditions. Unquestionably businesses should actively and promptly respond to such conditions. The upper turning point often occurs more quickly than the lower one. Falling sales and confidence can be contagious in the downturn but slow to ignite in recovery. Once the turning point is passed, the multiplier-accelerator mechanism should reinforce the change in conditions.

If marketers expect cycles, they will be more prepared to deal with the changes. As such, cycles can sometimes be viewed as positive opportunities that can assist new product launches and market penetration. However, it is imperative that they are introduced at the right time. The key to success is in timing and the rule of thumb is that the higher and longer the period above the growth trend line, the lower and longer the subsequent period below.

Activity 6.3

Key skills – Problem-solving

For each phase of the cycle, attempt to set out the kind of policies a business should be pursuing.

For example, in the *boom* phase, the rate of growth of sales levels out as demand bumps along a peak. The firm must remain in stock but all expansion plans should be frozen. Any surplus plant should be sold at this time to realize top prices. New markets may be explored but emphasis should be on controlling costs to meet the gloomier times just around the corner.

Unfortunately for businesses, the prediction of turning points is not easy. This is clearly indicated by the poor performance of highly respected forecasting groups who failed to predict the 1997–1998 Asian recession or its length. They furthermore overestimated the speed of economic recovery.

Businesses may however be able to judge developments more effectively by using two monitoring techniques. These are as follows:

◆ Leading indicators:

   ◆ This was developed in the United States. These foreshadow change in the pace of the economy by identifying indicators that consistently give advance warning (8–12 months) of upward or downward movement.

- ◆ A composite index is used, normally including the share index, total dwellings started, rate of interest and aggregate financial surplus or deficit of all companies.

- ◆ Other less predictable indicators might include, for example, the sale of transit vans (a sign of small-firm confidence) and commercial vehicles crossing between Malaysia and Singapore.

◆ **Industry trends survey:**

- ◆ A representative cross section of domestic companies is surveyed in depth to measure changes in business confidence (e.g. CBI Quarterly Survey of 900 firms).

- ◆ Psychology is important and the famous British economist John Maynard Keynes suggested that the animal spirits of capitalism produced alternating phases of optimism and pessimism, both of which tend to feed on themselves!

- ◆ However marketers must always beware of being carried away by such over-wrought instincts.

Activity 6.4

Can you predict the real GDP growth of your country's economy or of the UK's economy for 2008–2009 by using these indicators?

Exam hint

Improving your performance

Apply economic thinking to your exam and focus on the marks attached to each part of the question and to each of the questions set.

This is the scoring system that should guide you to the achievement of best allocation of your time.

Remember that the exam will consist of eight compulsory questions, five short questions (each worth 8 marks) and three long questions (each worth 20 marks). Overall weighting within questions is: 40% for theory and 60% for evaluation, application and format.

If Question 1 is worth 8 marks while Question 6 is worth 20, then economic logic demands nearly double the time and effort be devoted to Question 6.

Your percentage of coverage of the questions should also reflect the corresponding weightage. The answer to a question that is worth 20 marks should ideally be twice as extensive as the answer to a question that is only worth 8 marks.

Investment takes time and is an act of faith in the future. The penalties of a wrong decision are considerable since if the firm commits resources and the market then fails to materialize, or if a company does not allocate any resources to product and demand booms, then market share will be lost to competitors.

Environmental changes will often influence expectations and competitive decisions which may be *self-fulfilling* in the short term. If a critical mass of households and businesses *believe* things will improve, and invest and spend on that assumption, then things will, in general, improve, *feeding back* into even more positive expectations. A 'feel-good factor' is the expression of such considerations, easy to visualize but economically less easy to achieve. The process can also lead to enormous over-investment, as in the dot-coms or buy-to-let housing.

Economic objectives

Full employment was the primary and explicitly stated goal of many governments after 1945. It was seen as a social as well as an important economic objective. Fast-growing economies in East and South Asia found it to be an automatic consequence of their developmental process.

This philosophy changed dramatically from the 1970s with the European Union suffering over 20 million unemployed by the late 1990s. Even Japan accepted this inevitability. Recognition of the need to control inflation was the cause of this loss in priority and unemployment remained high even during periods of economic boom. Success in the control of inflation has seen much higher employment levels in Britain and Ireland.

Insight

In 2006, the UK economy generated 223,000 new jobs but needed 447,000 to stop unemployment growing to 1.7 per cent. This should be seen in the context of large numbers of migrant workers, more women wanting to work and higher numbers working on beyond retirement age. The UK rate is still around half the Eurozone average but excludes a record 2.7 million registered for incapacity benefit. In contrast, Ireland's success has been fuelled by EU subsidies and low interest rates arising from participation in the single currency.

Unemployment is often referred to as a social and economic drawback which can and does impact negatively on businesses:

Economic drawback	Social drawback
Scarce resources not utilized	Loss of income, status and satisfaction
Tax burden of benefits reduces incentives to work/invest	Relative poverty compared to those in work with affluent lifestyles
Reduces mobility of labour	Alienation from society leading to crime, vandalism
Reduces purchasing power	Dual society of haves/have-nots
Depresses confidence/risk-taking	Young entrants to labour market are hard hit

Unemployment is a personal tragedy since work binds us to society and gives meaning to our lives. Not only is our income lost, but also our status, esteem and self-respect.

Long-term unemployment affects specific groups such as the young (as employers cease recruitment), the unskilled, ethnic groups and the over-50s, the disabled and those living in inner cities or areas of structural decline. The young are forced to move away from such areas, condemning the latter to unemployment rates double the national average and a downward spiral of economic and social decay incurs. This consequently produces much difficulty for marketers.

Question 6.6

Key skills – Using information

Are unemployment levels a detriment as far as your organization is concerned?

Think carefully about this question from the view of wage levels, recruitment, discipline and ease of achieving change.

The seeming inability of many governments to achieve permanently lower unemployment and their acceptance of a certain unemployment rate as being unavoidable can be a reflection of a number of factors. These include:

◆　A rapid rate of technological change: unemployment of those left behind by change.

◆　The adoption of technology (e.g. automated services).

◆　Customer orientation, changing tastes, intense competition and shortening life cycles cause rapid structural change that some find difficult to adjust to.

◆　Inflow onto the job market exceeding outflow as married women's and foreign workers' participation rises.

◆　Acceptance of a natural unemployment rate that is consistent with low and stable inflation.

◆　A more turbulent environment, which makes business focus on job flexibility rather than job security.

The factors identified above can be best understood in terms of four main types and causes of unemployment. These are described below:

1　Insufficient aggregate demand:

◆　Also known as cyclical unemployment.

◆　Businesses respond to lower orders in recession by cutting overtime, halting recruitment, curtailing the use of contractual labour, lay-offs and finally making redundancies.

2　Imperfect market forces:

◆　Prevent labour markets clearing at wage levels where no involuntary unemployment exists.

◆　Factors preventing a matching of the supply and demand for different types of labour skill include lack of qualifications, immobility, discrimination, restrictive employment legislation and poor management.

3   **Relative wages are too high:**

   ◆   If set too high to clear the market due to legal minimum wage levels or union bargaining power then unemployment will result.

   ◆   The productivity associated with the wage paid is also part of this equation.

   ◆   If European wage-for-productivity levels are too high then business will respond by moving operations to lower-wage countries (for example Dyson) and investing in technology as a substitute for relatively expensive labour.

4   **Technological change – new process innovations:**

   ◆   Typically associated with displaced low skilled manual and clerical workers.

   ◆   Now also threatening all grades including managers.

Insight

Ever since the Luddites in the early nineteenth century, technology has been viewed by workers as an enemy in the short term even though over time it has created clusters of *new product innovations* that allowed jobs to grow in line with the working population. So long as wants exceed our ability to satisfy them, human resources will be demanded. Machines will specialize in doing what they do best, as will human beings.

However, there is now a structural mismatch between those with unwanted skills and abilities in declining industries or where machines have a comparative cost advantage, and skill shortages in high technology and creative knowledge-based employments. Considerable investment in education and flexible skills will be increasingly required if a permanent category of the hard-to-employ is not to emerge. Little wonder that education policy is a key issue in election campaigns and one of the top spending priorities.

The alternative of large falls in the relative wages of the unskilled will be resisted by unions or prevented by minimum wage legislation as enshrined, for example, in the European Union's social chapter.

Exam hint

Preparing your answers

Providing unrelated information is worthless. Therefore, take time to make sure that you understand exactly what the question is asking you for. Then make a plan of your main points. A list or a mind map is usually favoured. Only then, should you start writing out your answer.

Activity 6.5

Key skills – Problem-solving

For each of the types of unemployment being discussed in the previous section, think about possible policies that can minimize its occurrence.

You should ensure that each one meets the following requirements:

◆ The policy will not lead to increased inflation.

◆ The policy will not lead to inefficiency or lack of competitiveness.

◆ The policy is consistent with people's needs and wants.

For jobs to be *sustainable* they must not be subsidized. Unemployment can only fall if the growth of GDP exceeds the net growth of the working population and its productivity.

Question 6.7

Key skills for marketers – Using information

From the point of view of the lower-wage economy (e.g. Indonesia, Bangladesh or China), assess the positive and negative business impacts of a multinational company transferring its operations there.

Inflation

Inflation is a general increase in the average price level that is sustained over a period of time. It is usually calculated by changes in the consumer price index (CPI). In 2003, the retail price index (RPI) was replaced by the consumer price index. The CPI is measured by a basket of representative products and services typically used by the average household. The products and services are weighted according to their importance in total spending.

In some countries, a distinction is made between the so-called 'headline rate' and the 'underlying rate'. The headline rates exclude exceptional influences such as mortgage interest as the latter for instance tends to inflate the index in times of rising rates. In late 2006 the CPI was 2.4 per cent; hence above the Bank of England target of 2 per cent. The RPI was 3.7 per cent; at its highest for eight years. The CPI has been criticized as being flawed because the index is overweight in cheap imported clothes and electronic products and underweight in services, transport, housing and local taxes.

Inflation has been a persistent problem in many countries for most of the last half-century. Governments were often seen to be happy to trade off a little more inflation for a little less unemployment. However, from the late 1970s both tended to rise together to unacceptable levels. This is considered to be the worst of both possible economic worlds. This economic situation is referred to as *stagflation*. Some Western economies including the UK are currently threatened by such an economic situation.

In contrast some Western leaders such as Dame Margaret Thatcher and Ronald Reagan strove to control inflation as the central priority even though this was at the expense of sharply rising unemployment. The battle to conquer inflation became a constraint on these governments' ability to achieve more growth and jobs.

A politically acceptable unemployment level was therefore sustainable without increasing inflation. This also enabled inflation not to significantly rise above levels in the major economies with whom a country competed internationally. This policy was an economic success in most countries with inflation falling to 30-year lows by 2004. Unfortunately national insurance benefits including pensions are tied to the inflation index in some countries and this causes politically embarrassing small rises when compared to average earnings.

Question 6.8

Critical thinking

Is inflation a problem from the marketer's point of view?

Creeping inflation, when associated with buoyant high demand, can generate buyer confidence and business investment. Since borrowings are repaid in gently depreciating currency and the value of stocks appreciate, it tends to enhance profitability.

Households experience 'money illusion', whereby they feel better off than they really are as nominal incomes rise. They fail to notice or account for the real value eroding through cost of living rises. This eases the process of change and is preferable to the continuously depressed economic conditions that may be necessary to keep prices from rising at all.

However, once inflation exceeds a critical rate the costs outweigh any possible benefits. This is because of a variety of reasons such as:

◆ A rapid fall in the value of money affects consumer confidence.

◆ Uncertainty over future price levels deters companies from entering long-term contractual commitments. This makes planning very difficult.

◆ Arbitrary and unintended redistribution of income occurs as debtors gain. Furthermore creditors/savers lose. Fixed income groups like pensioners suffer. Weak bargaining groups are unable to keep pace (e.g. people on benefits, low income hourseholds).

◆ Although rising nominal income means higher tax brackets, tax allowances can be eroded.

◆ Domestic marketers face competitive imports; rising export prices affect international sales.

◆ Frequent price rises upset customers – i.e. continuous adjustment to lists and packaging can be irritating.

◆ Prices no longer accurately reflect 'relative' values. Consequently, the consumer is confused. They can become more price-sensitive and less responsive to other marketing-mix elements.

◆ Investment moves to 'unproductive' inflationary hedges such as gold, antiques, property.

◆ Wage groups fight for income shares. Business activity can be disrupted with strikes, complaints.

◆ Price wars due to misinterpretation of rival intentions could be triggered.

Marketers must remember economic cycles. As inflation accelerates, so governments will be forced to drastically reduce demand pressures to restore stability. However, attempting to overcome inflation, with limitations on spending, is often worse in its effects than the inflation itself. Zero inflationary expectations also challenge marketers due to the effect on cost increases. Price resistance is reinforced through resort to transparency of the Internet. Businesses are then left with no option but to raise productivity (and shed jobs) to reduce the cost base.

The UK has, until very recently, been growing well above its sustainable non-inflationary rate of 2.25 per cent. Given Gordon Brown's ambitious spending programme as the previous Chancellor of the Exchequer, lax monetary policy, oil price fluctuations and rising costs in Iraq, intensifying inflationary pressures seem unavoidable. On the other hand, average take-home pay in the UK actually fell in 2006; the first time since the recession of the early nineties.

Exam hint

Exam questions on the macro-economic environment are frequently set to test your knowledge and understanding of current economic conditions. Accordingly, you should keep yourself informed about changes in growth, employment, inflation, the balance of payments and even more importantly about the effects of these factors on the businesses, the marketing environment and marketers. However, you need to ensure that your answer relates to the exam case study.

The causes of inflation

Marketers need to appreciate the causes of inflation in order for them to be able to conduct an assessment of the likely future path of general prices. This understanding and subsequent assessment is also needed by marketers in order to avoid being damagingly surprised by sharp changes in the pace or direction of prices. The sources of inflationary pressure may originate from the supply as well as from the demand side of an economy.

As discussed below, three scenarios may occur:

◆ **Demand-pull inflation:**

◆ This occurs when there is too much spending relative to available productive capacity.

◆ This leads to increases in the prices of both inputs and outputs.

◆ As wage costs rise, these feed into higher prices, prompting further wage demands and creating a wage/price spiral.

◆   Monetarist inflation:

◆   Money is the fuel that sustains inflation.

◆   If the money supply is not expanded to provide extra cash for higher wages and prices, then interest rates rise, real aggregate demand in the circular flow declines, goods are left unsold and businesses reduce their employment of factors of production.

◆   Inflation can only continue at the cost of rising unemployment. Money supply increased by 10 per cent in the UK during 2004.

◆   Cost-push inflation:

◆   This occurs when a cost element causes prices to rise but in the absence of any excess demand to justify it.

◆   Stakeholders such as employees may push up wages through militant action to increase their real income at the expense of profits.

◆   If businesses then raise prices to restore profit margins, this reduces the purchasing power of wages and the process repeats, producing a *wage/price spiral*.

◆   Competition between different wage groups to maintain *wage differentials* can also lead to a *wage/wage spiral*.

Insight: Energy shocks

Demand for oil had contracted with the 1997 Asian economic crisis causing prices to collapse to $10 a barrel. By the Autumn of 2006 global consumption was rising at its fastest pace for 40 years and the price was closer to $80, more than double the $30 of the immediate post-Iraq-war period. Demand was driven by uncertainty over the consequences of Israel's incursion into South Lebanon, deterioration in Iraq and fast-growing Indian and Chinese economies.

Oil is at the centre of the world economy and provides the lubricant for an advanced civilization. An attack on a tanker, threats to interrupt Saudi supplies, and hurricane Katrina that disrupted 10 per cent of US refining capacity, underline the vulnerability of Western oil supplies. The current oil price includes a 'terror premium' estimated at up to $8 a barrel.

Previous energy shocks had always been good predictors of a global recession to come (12–18 months later). The OECD (The Organization for Economic Co-operation and Development) calculates that a $10 rise adds 0.5 per cent to consuming country inflation and reduces growth by a similar margin.

It is not in OPEC's (The Organization of the Petroleum Exporting Countries) interests to provoke a global crisis. High prices trigger recession in the West which feeds back negatively on suppliers. However, the IMF (The International Monetary Fund) warned in 2005 of a 'permanent oil shock' over the next two decades due to the combination of a plateau in production and sharply rising vehicle ownership in China and in the rest of the world in general.

Insight

Due to structural shifts from heavy manufacturing industry to services and 'new economy' virtual activities, developed countries use only half as much oil per dollar of GDP as 30 years ago. However, the more consumers spend on transport, the less they have to spend on other goods, and even a weightless 'virtual' economy depends on logistics and just-in-time deliveries.

Emerging economies are hit much harder because of their industrialization programmes and increasing ownership of motorized vehicles causing rising oil use per dollar of GDP.

A low inflation environment makes it difficult to pass on rising fuel costs leading to lay-offs and a profits squeeze. Some countries with very high fuel taxes have witnessed unprecedented demonstrations as well as panic buying. However, high fuel prices make sense from an environmental point of view. In the UK a nationwide road-pricing scheme was proposed, with cars fitted with transponders to log their movements and a variety of rates being charged to match demand with available road space at all times of the day.

History suggests that high prices today produce low ones the day after tomorrow due to greater investment in oil production and energy efficiency. Indeed, energy is a baseline cost for all economies.

Low prices encourage wasteful consumption (gas guzzling SUVs/pick-ups account for over half the US market and add to fuel use/greenhouse gas emissions) and discourage conservation, exploration and development, for example drilling in the Alaska National Wildlife refuge (estimated 29 billion barrel reserve). Low prices might also destabilize countries like Saudi Arabia and Venezuela where breakeven is $28 a barrel.

Saudi Arabia dominates the world oil market with 25 per cent of global reserves (US 3 per cent), double that of the second largest producer, Iraq. It is the largest supplier to the United States (25 per cent of world oil consumption; imports 60 per cent of its requirements) but is becoming progressively less stable.

Insight

The world needs a non-nuclear alternative to fossil fuels and the potentially fatal dependence they have created. Until oil-consuming nations break their dangerous addiction to a gas guzzling lifestyle, they will never disarm the oil weapon. Oil is nearing the point where nearly half of all known reserves have gone. To avert a potential crisis, the markets need to be confidant that cost-equivalent substitute technologies are available. President Bush has called on America to end its addiction to oil and has set a target of replacing 75 per cent of Middle East imports by 2025. The Middle East currently supplies 17 per cent of US needs.

Increasingly sustainable and greener alternatives are being embraced (e.g. wind farms). However to date, their contribution is very limited compared to oil.

Nuclear or 'clean coal' technologies only affect electricity generation and have unre-solved social and political costs. Hydrogen fuel cells could run hybrid vehicles but required materials like platinum are currently too expensive and the gas is explosive. Ethanol derived from maize or sugar cane is an alternative and will run 80 per cent of Brazil's transport fleet by 2010. Sweden will also use it and has pledged to be oil-free by 2020. However, even though growers are subsidized, it is significantly more costly than oil.

When inflation becomes rapid and uncertain it creates net costs for business and society. It poses difficult marketing-mix problems for the marketer, especially those serving seg-ments most seriously affected. In the extreme, *hyperinflation*, defined as price rises in excess of 50 per cent per month, causes all confidence to be lost in paper money and barter re-emerges.

Governments have also learnt that *expectations* adjust as actual inflation is experienced. No permanent trade-off of a little less unemployment for a little more inflation is possible. Inflation would accelerate instead.

Insight

Café owners in 1923 in Germany were forced to raise coffee prices while customers were sitting and waiting for their bills. At one stage during the German hyperinflation, prices were rising by 5 per cent per hour.

Activity 6.6

Consider the recent situation in some war-affected countries of Africa.

Balance of payments

The balance of payments is the systematic annual record of all exchange transactions between the residents of one country and the rest of the world. Exchange transactions include:

◆　　**A visible balance of trade** – This is made up of foods/fuels/materials/semi-manu-factured/finished products.

◆　　**An invisible balance of trade** – This is made up of financial/travel/other services, government transfers, net earnings.

The visible balance and invisible balance of trade combine to make up the *current* account. A *capital* account reflects net short- and long-term capital movements. A *balancing item* is included to adjust for data collection errors. The balance of payments must balance. However, there is a final balance for official financing which either adds to, or draws from, official currency reserves and borrowing depending on whether a net surplus or deficit arises.

The current account is the best indicator of the long-run health of an economy since it reflects whether an economy is trading successfully. No country can run a persistent current deficit since its reserves would eventually run out. In such cases, the confidence of its foreign creditors will also be eroded.

Action would have to be taken well before this point. Alternatively actions will be forced onto that country as a condition for a loan from the International Monetary Fund (IMF). However, since the world balance of payments must logically sum to zero, some countries cannot avoid being in deficit at times.

This said, what is more important is the cause for this deficit. Accordingly, it is necessary to identify whether the deficit is manageable. The direction of change is also required to be justified. If a developing country, such as Nigeria, incurs a deficit in order to import investment goods to develop its oil and gas deposits, this will increase its productive potential and exports in the future. The IMF or World Bank loans often support such a rise in productive potential. This is a very different case from a country importing conspicuous consumption goods and living beyond its means.

Insight

The United States and the UK had record trade deficits of $729 billion and £65.5 billion respectively in 2005. The UK's trade deficit is due partly to becoming a net oil importer for the first time since the 1970s. Its current account deficit was £32 billion or 2.6 per cent of GDP. The United States is feeling the impact of higher oil prices, Chinese imports and the Iraq war that has already cost $291 billion and might eventually total around $700 billion.

The balance of payments is not a desirable objective in itself, but rather, as a deficit worsens, it will become a tightening constraint on the government's ability to achieve other macro-economic objectives. In the short term, a deficit can be financed by willing foreign creditors, currency reserves or by raising interest rates to attract foreign capital flows. However, this will only succeed if creditors believe an offsetting fall in the exchange rate is not imminent. Higher rates will also tend to depress consumer and investment spending, reducing aggregate demand and therefore sales.

Exam hint

Make sure that you know and memorize the current values of the main economic indicators in your own country.

Questions on the macro-economy frequently ask for a discussion on current or future situations.

Economic indicators

Governments use a wide range of economic indicators to decide on policy changes. Governments also use a range of methods to monitor their effectiveness. An independent central bank will also assess the economic indicators before deciding interest rate policy. Stock markets react quite strongly when publication of such figures diverges from expectations. Such reactions may cause a fundamental reassessment of the underlying health of the economy. These indices are equally important for businesses in determining their future marketing plans and policies.

Governments have a number of objectives and find that the achievement of one goal may sometimes undoubtedly conflict with the achievement of others. Consequently, governments must have as many policies as objectives if they are to be mutually accomplished.

Key economic indicators to monitor include the following:

◆ Activity, growth and unemployment rates

◆ Inflation and interest rates

◆ Trade figures and exchange rates

Activity 6.7

Key skills – Collecting and presenting information

State three specific indicators you would monitor under each of the above key indicator headings.

Economic policies

The main types of policy available for use by a government are as follows:

◆ Fiscal and budgetary

◆ Money and credit control

◆ Physical policies – wage and price controls

◆ Supply-side

◆ Trade and exchange rate

Study tip

As the current syllabus requires an appreciation rather than an in-depth understanding of these policies, the objective of this coursebook is to discuss their influence on businesses and the implications for the marketing environment and marketers.

Exam hint

Start giving serious thought to the forthcoming examination. One important key to planning a revision schedule is to try to determine possible topics. Note that your paper is set up to a year previously due to the administration required in approving it and ensuring efficient distribution to centres around the world.

What questions would you choose based on the syllabus and relating it to a dynamic environment?

Why don't you brainstorm some possibilities with your tutor?

Look at previous papers and think about 'topical' issues when the paper was prepared (and still relevant 12 months later).

Some past exam questions specific to each unit have been listed towards the end of each unit.

Fiscal and budgetary

Taxation is the main source of revenue for any government to finance its budgeted expenditures. Often accounting for 40–50 per cent of national expenditure, the government has important impacts. However, with similar tax revenues the overall effect is broadly neutral. Both taxation levels and areas for national and regional expenditure are decided in an annual budget. Marketers should monitor these levels as well as the pre-budget statements.

Government spending and taxation offers a relatively quick and effective means of changing the pressure of demand and therefore activity levels. Extra spending on health and education for example, impact on demand for a wide range of products and services. Therefore marketers should carefully consider the implications of spending plans as well as actual policy changes due to the following:

◆ As they reflect performance, spending plans and policy changes are closely aligned to government economic forecasts/objectives/plans.

◆ Policy actions may be inferred from the objectives set by governments.

◆ Tax and spending changes have a direct impact on the circular flow at different points in time.

◆ Targeted changes affect specific segments. For example child tax credits or new pension rules will only affect the concerned segments as opposed to the general public.

◆ Tax on specific product groups can have serious and selective consequences. For example an increase in tobacco duties implies that unless price is increased, the profit margins of retailers will be constricted.

◆ The scope for lobbying activity by special interests: for example incentives for North Sea exploration.

◆ Measures have ramifications for trends in other macro-environments.

The key requirement of fiscal policy is sound public finances and the avoidance of any danger of the government sector being a source of adverse shocks in the economy. The British government borrowing has risen more than expected. Consequently, to counteract, higher taxes and spending cuts may be required if growth is slower than expected in 2008. Such actions can also support monetary policy in controlling inflationary pressures or providing the scope for interest rates to fall. Marketers must appreciate the broad intention of these policies while recognizing that projections also do involve considerable uncertainty.

Insight

By 2007 Britain had enjoyed its longest period of sustained growth since records began in 1870. The economy averaged close to 3 per cent growth per annum in recent years, well above its long-term average of 2.4 per cent. Until recently, the country also had one of the lowest levels of unemployment, the steadiest inflation and the smallest national debt of the world's major economies.

Plans to increase government spending/pledges while not raising income tax or VAT depend on such growth. It should be noted that each 1 per cent shortfall in growth represents an £8 billion drop in tax revenues.

To meet its golden rules, the government's borrowing should only be for investment and the budget should balance over the economic cycle.

The UK cannot afford to lose its reputation for having the most flexible labour markets or being most tax competitive. Yet businesses in the UK have suffered most of the recent tax increases. In contrast Germany radically cut income taxes by 10 per cent in an effort to re-energize its ailing economy. Economic activity ensued and the unemployment level fell below 10 per cent.

Money and credit

This involves control of the supply of money and the credit-creating power of the retail banks. The central bank exerts control if it fears that its target for inflation will not be met. Control can be exerted by means of any of the following actions or even by a combination of actions:

◆ Controlling the supply of new money and changing base rates of interest.

◆ Controlling existing money supply by open market operations. Buying/selling government securities injects/withdraws money from the banking system

◆ Cash/liquidity ratio requirements to limit the size of the credit multiplier effect

◆ Quantitative controls to ration credit

◆ Lending as a last resort to enforce base rates.

Such measures can be used to expand or contract money and credit as required, but with a long time lag of up to two years. Marketers must estimate the full impact of successive interest rate changes since it takes time for consumers to react in terms of demand for housing or durables. The strength of the reaction is also often unpredictable.

Anything that might affect the stability of money needs to be carefully monitored. Success in reducing inflation to very low levels in recent years suggests that monetary stability has now been achieved. However this cannot be taken for granted. The key is to make intermediate targets for money supply growth, government borrowing and exchange rates consistent with growth desired in nominal GDP and inflation, and then stick to them. Marketers must learn to interpret signals such as:

◆ Why are base rates reduced on fears of recession or negative shocks like stock market crashes?

◆ What is the link between interest rate changes and the exchange rate?

Question 6.9

Which types of companies tend to be most affected by a credit squeeze?

Prices and incomes policy

Such policies were mainly used during the 1960s and 1970s in an attempt to achieve lower unemployment without incurring higher inflation and consequent balance of payments problems. If wage groups could be forced or persuaded to moderate their pay settlements and companies could be persuaded or even forced to moderate their price increases, despite demand pressure to justify them, then employment and output would rise.

Governments are still prone, particularly in boom times, to introduce public sector pay restraint as a means of controlling public spending and to set a 'good example' for the private sector to follow. For example, below inflation public sector pay rises were offered in 2007. In practice, such policies normally prove counterproductive or short-lived due to shortages or pay explosions.

Study tip

You need to ensure that you are clear about the differences between a slowdown, a recession, a deflation, a slump and a depression in an economy.

Although this is all part of the economist's jargon, they also affect marketers.

The above discussions should help you come up with your own definitions and differences.

Supply-side policies

Supply-side policies grew out of disillusion with demand management policies to achieve the macro-economic objectives. The standard response to low growth and rising unemployment had been to stimulate consumer, government and investment spending on the assumption that domestic firms would raise production and resource use. Multiplier and accelerator reactions would then stimulate businesses to invest in extra capacity and productivity improvements.

The business response in practice was as follows:

◆ To improve margins and profits instead of raising output

◆ A reluctance to invest due to stop-go patterns of demand

◆ Marked by an inability to respond quickly enough leading to import penetration

Resulting inflation and payments deficits would then force a policy reversal. Supply-side policies aimed instead to promote higher growth and employment, without triggering inflation, by relaxing constraints on productive capacity and efficiency. The policies involved:

◆ The reform of trade unions to ensure that their reduced power was used responsibly and democratically (with strikes at a minimum)

◆ The removal of tax distortions and disincentives to work and invest

◆ Implementation of measures to improve quality, quantity and relevance of training

◆ Improving job information and measures to encourage mobility and flexibility

◆ Encouraging employee share-ownership and self-employment

◆ The reduction of red tape and regulations inhibiting business

◆ Greater competition and the removal of minimum wages

◆ The privatization and the opening up of state services to private competition or internal markets

◆ The deregulation of markets to reduce entry barriers and increase competition

Insight: The flat tax revolution

Flat taxes would mean everyone above a set income threshold would pay the same tax rate. 'Progressive' taxes with all their exemptions, allowances, loopholes and tax accountants would be swept away. If the threshold was set relatively high then poorer people would pay nothing. Hong Kong has had such a system since 1947. This is often linked to its spectacular economic success. Jersey has a similar system in place with 20 per cent income tax and no capital taxes. More recently the Baltic States, Russia and Poland adopted this system. Its strengths are its simplicity, the reduced incentive for tax evasion or black market activity, and greater incentives to work and invest. Evidence is less clear, since while revenues did increase initially, for example in Russia, this was not sustained. Equally, other reforms may have caused the dynamism of the Baltic States. Weaknesses include the fact that less well-off taxpayers must subsidize the very rich (the top 10 per cent of taxpayers currently provide half the revenues) and large numbers pay no tax at all. Millions of taxpayers would therefore lose out in Britain making it political suicide to introduce. Western economies may be prepared to cut and simplify its taxes but not remove the 'progressive principle'.

Improving your learning and performance

Undertake a SWOT analysis of your economy.

Draw up a balance sheet of its strengths and weaknesses and then identify opportunities and threats. This formed the basis of a recent case question on China.

Trade and exchange rate policies

Many open economies operate a flexible exchange rate system that acts as an automatic two-way adjustment mechanism to keep the balance of payments in approximate balance. Should the payments position worsen then the exchange rate should fall relative to trading rivals, making exports cheaper in foreign currency terms and therefore more competitive. Imports become relatively more expensive so favouring home-produced products. Export receipts rise, import payments fall and the balance of payments position is restored. Unfortunately, this process is just a little too good to be true.

Marketers should recognize these criteria:

◆ Short-term and speculative capital movements can occur on a massive scale in the global economy:

  ◆ This can drive exchange rates rather than fundamentals like supply/demand for products.

  ◆ Relatively high interest rates will attract flows and tend to maintain an uncompetitive rate.

◆ The exchange rate is an important 'price' but takes time to work through:

  ◆ A lower rate causes a deficit that worsens before it improves since the now more expensive imported materials must be paid for before extra exports can be produced and shipped.

◆ The strength of reaction to a falling exchange rate may be uncertain:

  ◆ How big will the demand increase be in foreign markets?

  ◆ How will foreign competitors react?

  ◆ Can we meet the extra demand?

  ◆ Won't costs rise due to higher import prices?

  ◆ Will businesses gear up for extra production or merely raise export prices and make higher profit?

◆ Unplanned exchange rate movements create risk:

  ◆ A transaction negotiated at one exchange rate may become unprofitable by the time it is fulfilled.

◆ Currency appreciation is a serious threat to foreign sales (and domestic markets), as many international marketers have found to their cost:

◆ Is the solution cutting export prices in foreign currency terms, reinforcing product and promotional policies to reduce price sensitivity, or sourcing overseas? For example, Marks & Spencer's sourcing policy had to change as the rising pound has forced them to turn their back on long-standing domestic suppliers and move production to the countries where labour costs are much lower.

Many governments prefer to aim for exchange rate stability given the uncertainties and costs associated with exchange rate fluctuations. This may cause it to manage its exchange rate or shadow the value of a critical currency such as the euro or the dollar. Another alternative is to join the currency bloc and accept the disciplines of an exchange rate set collectively as Ireland did with regards to the Euro.

Insight: Trade barriers: making the poor poorer!

The Live8 concerts, timed to coincide with the G8 summit at Gleneagles, sought to 'make poverty history' by mobilizing public pressure. In the event, some progress was made on 'dropping the debt' (writing off $40 billion for the 18 poorest nations and doubling EU aid to $80 billion by 2010) but little progress on trade justice and reduced carbon emissions. Also, there were no real plans to improve governance, combat corruption or increase the respect of human rights although these problems have blighted the development efforts of many developing countries.

Aid and debt relief is clearly not the total solution to Africa's woes, not least because of the $500 billion that has poured into the continent over half a century without positive outcome. Millions still live on less than $2 a day. Yet for every dollar spent in aid, $2 are recouped in trade tariffs. EU dairy cows, for example, are subsidized by $2.20 per day making them richer than 40 per cent of the world population. Surplus milk is then dumped on the world market, driving small African producers out of business.

The pattern is repeated across other basic materials and processed goods. US cotton subsidies totalling $4 billion and the dumping of surpluses ensure that low-cost, high-quality producers in Africa cannot compete. The OECD (the Organization for Economic Co-operation and Development) calculates that farmers in the West receive $300 billion state help annually, six times the level of aid given to poor nations. A 1 per cent increase in Africa's share of global trade would produce seven times more income than is received in aid. Unfortunately, attempts by the World Trade Organization (WTO) to address unfair trade since 2001 through the Doha trade round have ended in failure, bringing the cause of free trade (and future of the WTO) into doubt. Lobby groups in the EU have already succeeded in maintaining the CAP at £28 billion until 2013 although export subsidies will be phased out. However, none of the big issues were resolved and a drift into protectionism threatens.

A lasting policy response to correct the problem may be painful because only two policy options exist:

◆ **Expenditure reduction:**

   ◆ Higher taxes reduce household incomes causing demand, including import demand, to fall.

   ◆ Falling domestic sales encourage firms to export more as well as putting downward pressure on wages and prices, so improving competitiveness.

◆ **Expenditure switching:**

   ◆ Resources and expenditure are switched away from imports to domestically-produced goods.

   ◆ Policies include various types of protectionism and incentives for exporters.

   ◆ The other means is devaluation which implies sacrificing the stable exchange rate (or leaving the currency bloc).

   ◆ The first two policies deal with symptoms of a deficit at the expense of trading partners, rather than with the basic cause.

   ◆ International trade agreements also limit their scope.

   ◆ All governments seek to promote exports by providing information, advice, assistance and often insurance against bad debts.

   ◆ Aggressive use of hidden subsidies to obtain unfair trade advantage, however, is not internationally acceptable.

The impact of international trade

All countries are open systems and must deal with the realities of the international environment. Some economies, such as the United States, are so large that the domestic economy is the dominant influence. Most, however, are like the United Kingdom (accounting for just 5–6 per cent of global output) and are export-orientated and always susceptible to outside shocks.

Several factors encourage many countries in their eagerness to expand their international exposure. These factors include:

◆ World trade brings diversity of choice. This is in evidence in any sizeable supermarket at any season.

◆ National differences in culture, human skills, resource availability, ingenuity and technology lead to product, cost and price differences.

◆ A global market rewards specialization and allows the exploitation of comparative advantage.

◆ International trade curbs monopoly power, increases competition, lowers prices.

◆ World markets offer scope for economies of scale and can significantly reduce costs.

◆ Access to world markets spreads risks and can counterbalance domestic activity.

- Trade or distribution networks encourage as well as enable the rapid diffusion of new ideas and inventions.

- Trade equals contact, mutual interest, cultural understanding, interdependence, co-operation.

- Liberalization of planned economies allows integration into the world trading system.

- Growth in world trade has been continuous and offers expanding opportunities.

- Trade liberalization agreements encouraged emerging economies to open their markets. In 1946 only 5 per cent of world GDP traded internationally, today it is closer to 25 per cent.

- The WTO was established in 1995 with a mandate to enforce world trade laws.

- Development of the Internet, travel and trade links are producing a global culture.

- Continued expansion of multinational enterprises and development of global companies.

Globalization

This is a process by which the world economy is becoming a unified interdependent system based on internationalization of companies and the progressive lowering of trade barriers. It involves multinational businesses adopting world-wide strategies that apply the same or similar marketing mixes in all markets. The process is facilitated by the progressive development of electronic commerce and enabled by mass media and travel creating similar patterns of consumption in otherwise diverse cultures.

The International Monetary Fund (IMF) has predicted the global growth will accelerate to nearly 5 per cent in 2006 due to unprecedented growth in the poorest countries. Living standards have increased rapidly, reflecting a fall from 472 million people living on under $1 a day in Asia-Pacific in 1991 to a projected 19 million by 2015. Sub-Saharan Africa is the exception to this trend, a situation unlikely to improve given the recent famines and continuing atrocities in Darfur.

Globalization is characterized by international flows of capital, information and increasingly mobile labour. The key agents in the process are international firms, who conduct a significant proportion of their business in foreign countries.

A global marketing perspective implies a centrally co-ordinated plan directed towards a world-wide audience rather than the usual decentralized focus on local or regional markets. The original multinational was the East India Company established 400 years ago with a charter from Elizabeth I to import Asian spices. Its present-day successor is Exxon Mobil, which has just become the first company to register sales of over $1 billion a day. It earned $10.4 billion on second quarter sales of $99 billion in 2006. Global products now include the likes of Rolex, Coca-Cola, Sony, Nike, McDonald's, Airbus, Xerox, Virgin and Microsoft.

Dramatic growth in the last half-century means that large multinationals now account for a staggering one-fifth of world output and 70 per cent of total global trade, with the UK now the leading foreign investor spending $132 billion or 25 per cent of the global total. Global revenues of the largest multinational exceed the GDP of all but the largest country. Many other factors may account for this trend. They include:

◆ Continuous progress in reducing tariff barriers through trade rounds and the WTO.

◆ 146 countries in membership and a new system for settling disputes.

◆ Development of regional free-trade zones where countries with similar interests obtain the benefits of free trade while retaining some protection against the outside world. These may represent the building blocks to eventual global free trade. For example the EU (European Union), NAFTA (North American Free Trade Agreement), APEC (Asia-Pacific Economic Co-operation) and SADC (Southern African Development Community).

◆ Many emerging countries in Africa, Latin America and Asia now see open economies and direct investment as a better route to development than protectionism.

◆ An infrastructure of international institutions is in place to support sustainable global growth:

◆ IMF – The International Monetary Fund is responsible for supervision of the world financial system. It provides lending support and structural reform programmes for countries in difficulty.

◆ The World Bank – Provides long-term capital for development purposes.

◆ The Organization for Economic Co-operation and Development – The OECD represents the richest and most powerful governments. Its main role is to co-ordinate economic policies to avert any mutually reinforcing inflation or deflation that would damage trade.

◆ WTO – The World Trade Organization encourages multilateral trade and seeks to resolve trade disputes.

◆ Others include the Arab League, the Organization of African Unity, the Organization of American States and the Commonwealth of Independent States.

Advantages of globalization

◆ Enhanced scope for specialization.

◆ Enhanced scope for the standardization of production and distribution.

◆ Cost-effective R&D, product design and promotion.

◆ Attractions of universal image advertising combined with the scope to adapt to suit local conditions.

◆ Shorter new product planning cycle via learning/comparison from global experience.

◆ Faster reaction to general customer preferences.

◆ Superior marketing potential.

◆ Transport cost savings.

◆ Improved supply chain efficiency and leverage.

◆ Direct investment gives tariff-free access to trade blocks if local content requirements are met.

◆ Direct access increases local market knowledge and customer confidence.

◆ Rivals derive competitive advantage out of their network of global activities.

◆ Greater political stability: web of multinational subsidiaries and 'common' commercial interests.

◆ Pressure on governments to conform to stable economic management as a condition for continued direct investment and a favourable reaction from global financial markets.

Disadvantages of globalization

◆ Cultural sensitivities force changes to global products: for example Big Macs in India.

◆ Divergence in language.

◆ Stage of economic development requires differentiation.

◆ Concern over the American/Western cultural domination undermining national identity.

◆ Risk of strategic dependence on multinationals whose strategy is globally not nationally driven.

◆ Powerful companies can play one country off against another to secure incentive packages: Western countries able to fairly easily move production from one Asian country to another.

◆ Multinationals may use leverage to obtain favourable treatment and avoid profits tax via transfer pricing. Set prices on components can vary internally and be transferred between subsidiaries.

◆ Political tensions between the developed and developing countries: for example, over debt relief or write-offs making slow progress, while rich nations refuse to cut their massive subsidies ($47 billion European Union) that distort world markets and destroy farming in developing countries through unfair competition. Milk and cotton have attracted much criticism.

◆ The gap between the world's richest and poorest has doubled since 1960, suggesting an unfair trading and financial system.

◆ Subsidiaries may be closed for political reasons. For example Peugeot Ryton plant despite high productivity and assurances to keep open till 2010 actually closed.

Significance of globalization to marketers

◆ The marketer must monitor a world-wide market-place and the global environment.

◆ The threat of competition in domestic markets is significantly increased.

◆ Interdependence creates the potential for rapid communication of shocks through the system.

◆   Slower growth may produce protectionist responses since governments are concerned with national competitive advantage and face pressure from affected interest groups.

Trading at the micro level

Although the principle of comparative advantage holds across a range of commodities, in practice equivalent consumer and industrial goods are imported and exported by many countries. Traded goods like cars and computers are differentiated products and the consumer desires a wide choice. Households do not want identical telephones or saloon cars and each manufacturer gains competitive advantage and economies of scale by producing one main brand for an international market rather than lots of brands in low volumes for a purely domestic one. Gains from trade in this case do not necessarily derive from relative cost differences but rather from brand diversity and effective marketing.

Although large numbers of small and medium companies either do not participate in international trade or engage in only a peripheral way, the advantages for them to do so can be substantial. Such advantages could include:

◆   Providing a wider market for specialist niche producers

◆   Additional volume to reduce the cost base and secure economies

◆   Escaping from a saturated or threatened domestic market

◆   A possible means of extending the product life cycle

◆   A source of volume growth to support expensive research and development (R&D)

◆   To counter a depressed home market and maintain capacity

◆   As a competitive strategy to counteract and deter foreign rival market entry into the home market

◆   As a means of spreading risks over different markets

◆   To exploit the scope for e-commerce

Entry into foreign markets requires a serious commitment. It is a strategic decision since the implications of subsequent withdrawal due to lack of preparation would be expensive in terms of cost, brand image and even credibility.

Insight: European Union enlargement

Hungary, Poland, Slovakia, Slovenia, Estonia, Latvia, Lithuania, Malta, Cyprus and the Czech Republic joined the European Union in 2004 followed by Bulgaria and Romania in 2007. This expands the Single Market 40 per cent by area and 75 million by population, and opens up new marketing opportunities for new and existing members alike. Stability and rising prosperity for former Soviet bloc members is seen as a political gain. Studies suggest a modest economic benefit of around £6 billion for existing members and two to three times that for new members. This is due to a regional aid package for the poorest regions of only £23 billion over the first 3 years and farm aid to new members at just 25 per cent of the normal level in 2004 rising to 100 per cent in 2013. There is also a 'transition' period (e.g. 7 years for Poland) before freedom to travel and work is allowed. New members had to demonstrate economic and environmental stability together with a fully functioning democratic market economy. Compliance with 80,000 pages of EU legislation, including the Social Chapter, was required and in the first two years after entry the European Union reserves the right to take purposeful measures if it feels that new entrants are distorting the Single Market. Doubts have already been expressed about corruption and organized crime in Bulgaria. The Centre for the Study of Democracy estimates Bulgarians pay 130,000 bribes a month, 50 per cent more than in 2004, and believes that any EU development funds will go straight into the pockets of corrupt politicians and their client companies. Controls introduced to regulate the numbers entering Britain are unlikely to bite since proposed fines are currently unenforceable and the self-employed can't be stopped. The European Union agreed the budget for 2007–2013 under which the UK will give up £7 billion of its annual rebate in return for a promised review of farm subsidies in 2008. The UK's net contributions will also rise by 60 per cent from £3.5 to £6bn as the EU budget expands to help fund the development of new member states. This gesture may put pressure on France for reciprocal concessions on subsidies.

Frictions in the international environment

Notwithstanding the powerful forces encouraging ever-greater participation in the emergent global market-place, there are numerous reasons for conflict in international trade. Although these can appear arbitrary to the marketer, they can nonetheless be extremely damaging. Producers threatened by imports are organized, concentrated, supported by their unions and very vocal compared to the exporters or consumers who stand to lose from such controls. Developed-country farm protection, for example, is estimated to cost poorer countries over $100 billion a year; this is in fact double what they receive in aid.

Russia and Taiwan are especially vulnerable to US trade sanctions because they are not members of the WTO. China has recently joined although it has had to agree to a number of reforms to open its economy to fairer trade. One resulting friction is America's $200 billion trade deficit with China which it blames on its undervalued currency (China blames US credit-fuelled over-consumption). For example the US responded to a surge in imports of bras, evening gowns and knitted fabrics from China by imposing quotas on Chinese textiles. Unfortunately, such actions can trigger trade wars and China is hugely important to the global economy. Resolution might be difficult since an appreciation that is too sharp would impose severe financial strains and cause severe hardship, not to mention export inflation to the rest of the world. At the same time, the dollar might be overvalued. However, the current situation of overproduction by China is not sustainable and adjustment must be progressively if painfully made.

Exam hint

By now, you should know the meaning of the many acronyms used in this subject. These might arise in the examination paper, so make sure you revise the meaning of GATT, WTO, GDP, ICT, SWOT and SLEPT.

Activity 6.8

Key skills – Using information

Match the terms with their correct definitions:

1   Tariff

2   Quota

3   Embargo

4   Non-tariff barriers

5   Terms of trade

6   Customs duty

a   Taxes on imported goods aimed at reducing their competitiveness with domestic equivalents

b   Various standards and regulations to which imports must conform

c   Tax imposed on imports in order to raise revenue

d   The index of average export prices compared to average import prices

e   A quantitative limit on the volume of imports per time period

f   Export prohibition on a particular good to certain countries, usually for political reasons.

Dumping involves goods sold in foreign markets at below cost of production and is viewed as an unfair trading practice under WTO rules. However, interpretation is difficult and lower prices might reflect superior efficiency. Recently, the United States lodged a complaint with the WTO over subsidies for the Airbus A380 super jumbo. The European Union has responded, alleging massive illegal US subsidies in the form of tax breaks and government contracts to Boeing.

Implications of economic factors for marketers

◆   Marketers must monitor the international environment for advance warning of threats.

◆   A deflationary scenario encourages protectionist instincts and threatens global prosperity.

◆ A tension exists between free trade advantages to the world as a whole and self-interest. One country can always gain from controls if all others continue to trade freely.

◆ Successive trade talks have ended in recrimination and accusation over multinational influence.

◆ Fear of international retaliation is often the main force against protectionism.

◆ Protection of infant industries is frequently used as a defence in developing nations.

◆ International marketers still face tariffs and quotas protecting domestic interests.

◆ Non-tariff barriers involve environmental, quality, health or safety standards and so may require expensive product modification.

◆ The marketer may also find a far from level playing field as domestic producers receive preferential assistance: for example tax breaks, supports and patriotic attitudes.

◆ The failure to agree on an agenda for future trade liberalization might harden attitudes.

◆ Many charities promote the cause of 'fair trade' for poor producers by encouraging consumers to purchase only products produced according to certain criteria, such as grown on family-run farms, without the use of pesticides and at higher prices.

Insight: The European Union clothing mountain

In January 2005, the European Union lifted the Multi-Fibre Agreement which had controlled the inflow of cheap textile imports for nearly 40 years. By mid-2005, Chinese clothing exports to the European Union reached £5 billion, equal to the total for the whole of 2004. Lobbied by European manufacturers, the European Union introduced transitional quotas till 2008 to give them 'breathing space', despite having already allowed them 10 years to prepare. However, since the millions of Chinese goods already en route now exceeded the new quotas, massive stockpiles built up. EU retailers who had already paid for these goods warned of empty shelves for Christmas and losses of around £1 billion. Bringing forward some of next year's quota is only a temporary compromise. The losers are the poor Chinese textile workers and the EU consumers deprived of cheap clothes. This represents the first of a number of trading challenges between the European Union and China. Its frenetic investment in steel capacity, for example, augers impending over-capacity and excess supply on world markets. How long before Chinese laptops and cars swamp Western markets? The first 4x4 arrived in the market in late 2005 at well below EU prices.

Exam hint

The international environment has global candidate appeal.

Remember, the examiner will be influenced by current events as well as syllabus content and its coverage over a run of papers. If anything of major global importance happened recently, it could be the basis of a question in your examination.

Summary

In this important unit, we have done the following:

◆ Analysed key aspects of the macro-economic and international environment.

◆ Focused on the need for marketers to appreciate the meaning of economic indicators. A grasp of future economic conditions will provide an important edge over rivals.

◆ Assessed each of the main macroeconomic objectives

◆ Investigated the circular flow to understand changes in income, output and expenditure

◆ Examined concepts such as the multiplier and the accelerator

◆ Looked at the meaning and measurement of GDP

◆ Identified the phases of the business cycle and how it might be managed to advantage

◆ Focused on the key indicators for marketers to monitor

◆ Outlined the impact of the main policy weapons on business and the marketer

◆ Examined the benefits and implications of expanding world trade

◆ Considered frictions in the international trade process

In brief:

◆ No marketer can remain insulated from this dynamic global economic system.

◆ The global economic system represents a major arena for profitable opportunity but equally a significant source of potential volatility and threat.

◆ Either way, the international environment cannot be ignored but must be closely monitored and carefully assessed.

◆ International institutions collect a wealth of information on the evolving state of the world economy and its constituent blocs, providing a database for marketing research on both trade potential and competitive risk.

Further study and examination preparation

The economy is always going to be an important part of the macro-environment and the origin of major impacts on the business. Given its day-to-day importance for the marketer it would be surprising if questions based on the content of this unit did not occur with some frequency.

A sound knowledge of your own national economy is therefore very important and should be summarized under headings such as: inflation, unemployment, balance of payments, economic growth, phase of the cycle, investment activity and the economic policy stance. The use of statistics, drawn from some of the mentioned sources, would be expected by the examiner.

Question 5, December 2005 provides an interesting question that combines coverage of the business cycle with methods of forecasting the turning points.

Extending knowledge

Palmer A. and Hartley B. (2006) *The Business and Marketing Environment*, McGraw-Hill.

> Chapter 7: The National Economic Environment.
>
> Chapter 13: The International Marketing Environment.

Other suggested reading

Jobber D. (1998) *Principles of Marketing*, McGraw-Hill, 2nd Ed.

> Chapter 5: The marketing environment.

Bassington F. and Pettitt S. (2003) *Principles of Marketing*, Pearson Education Limited.

> Chapter 1: Marketing dynamics.
>
> Chapter 2: The European marketing environment.

Lancaster G, Massingham L. and Ashford R. (2002) *Essentials of Marketing*, McGraw-Hill Education.

> Chapter 2: The marketing environment.

Groucutt J. (2005) *Foundations of Marketing*, Palgrave Macmillan.

> Chapter 2: The Marketing Environment.

Websites

Economic trends, www.statistics.gov.uk.

www.feer.com for Far Eastern Economic Review.

www.ft.com.

www.economist.com.

www.worldbank.org.

www.wto.org/index.htm.

www.oecd.org.

www.adb.org for the Asian Development Bank.

http://europa.eu.int/euro/html/entry.html for the Euro site.

Practicising past exam questions

Please see Question 1, June 2004 on the CIM website, www.cim.co.uk.

Please see Question 4, December 2003 on the CIM website, www.cim.co.uk.

Please see Question 1d, December 2004 and 1a, c June 2005. For specimen answers please go to www.cim.co.uk.

Please see Question 5a, June 2005. For specimen answers please go to www.cim.co.uk.

Please see Question 5, December 2005. For specimen answers please go to www.cim.co.uk/learningzone.

Please also check out the specimen paper to ensure that you are familiar with the new exam format.

Unit 7
The political and legislative environment

Learning objectives

In this important unit, we will explore the interface between two significant and closely interlinked aspects of the macro-environment. The societal agenda is set within the political environment, and enacted and applied within the legislative environment. By the end of this challenging unit, you will have:

◆ Consolidated your understanding of the political environment and its organizational impacts (3.5).

◆ Reinforced your grasp of the points of political pressure and influence (3.5).

◆ Distinguished between different forms of regulation (3.5).

◆ Appreciated the essential features of a complex legislative framework (3.5).

◆ Assessed the significance of legislation for marketers and key stakeholders (3.5).

Study guide

This unit considers a political environment that embraces institutions, agencies, laws and pressure groups. These elements may influence and constrain both organizations and individuals in society. They also define freedom in terms of what can, and cannot, legally be done by companies today. Pressure groups have been previously explored in Unit 2. These are now discussed in relation to lobbyists and the media.

Marketers are mainly influenced by the political dimension in general terms and by the legislative environment in detail. General legal issues – in particular the role and objectives of law and regulation, the methods available, an outline of the legal system, the costs and benefits of compliance as well as the impacts involved – will all be discussed.

Although marketers cannot control these, an appreciation is however quintessential. As a brief appreciation of relevant areas of the law, British statutes will be used as examples. Students from Asia, Africa, Europe and the Caribbean should please refer to their own legal system when examples are cited in examinations. Different countries have different legal traditions and systems. Even in the UK, the law applying to England and Wales is different in many respects from that applying in Scotland.

The political environment

The political environment might produce a variety of emotions ranging from apathy to out-right cynicism, but it is one that marketers ignore at their peril. Its impacts on business activity and international trade are both numerous and potentially damaging.

Insight

As seen most vividly on 2 November 2004, the world's most powerful democracy con-firmed a second Republican victory. Both contenders had 10,000 lawyers on standby in 'swing' states to contest close results following the last election 'debacle' in Florida but were not required. Election outcomes produce very different policy outcomes for key interest groups both within and outside America and, although Democratic successes in the midterm elections have curtailed the influence of the Bush administration, the stakes are high. Refusal to accept the result of democratic elections is becoming a fash-ion.

In Mexico, the left-wing candidate Obrador also refused to accept an election lost by a half a percent margin. After a recount the electoral commission ruled the result fair but it is still contested.

Even more surprising was Bembe's refusal to accept the victory of the incumbent Kabila in the Democratic Republic of Congo's presidential election, despite polling only 42 per cent of the vote and previously agreeing to accept the outcome and co-operate in the task of national regeneration.

Elsewhere, political elites have been responsible for considerable corruption, as seen in the transfer of a staggering $60 billion to foreign bank accounts from 1996–1999 in Brazil. This represented a quarter of the country's national debt and compares to the 9 per cent of GDP thought to have been 'stolen' by the Santos government in oil-rich Angola between 1997 and 2002.

A new political dimension to account for is the potential magnitude of the threat posed by terrorism and suicide attacks. Bloody bombings on the Madrid rail system appeared to 'swing' the Spanish elections in March 2004. Hostage taking in Iraq has similarly been used as an attempted lever on Italian and British political decision-making.

The role and significance of government in a market economy is considerable. The follow-ing points illustrate the role and significance comprehensively:

◆   The government has full political power and executive authority to pursue its chosen policies.

◆   The public sector, including executive agencies, accounts for a significant percentage of jobs, direct spending and total expenditure when transfer payments are accounted.

◆   The government is able to influence overall economic activity levels as it influences most key decisions, such as to work, train, save, spend and invest (see Unit 6).

◆ It enacts legal and regulatory frameworks that limit business freedom in the wider interests of society. Well-conceived regulation is accepted as a key role of the state. Most aspects of marketing activity are covered by some form of control.

◆ Governments help to shape standards of public behaviour and conduct.

◆ Democratic governments must present their executive and legislative records for electoral scrutiny at prescribed intervals.

◆ Day-to-day practice of government relies on gathering feedback from interest groups within the environment. As such, governments are susceptible to pressure and influence.

◆ Present-day governments operate in an open global system that may constrain its to their freedom of action. Governments must recognize the power of the markets: the need to keep national performance in line with rivals; the influence of trading partners and the rules of international club membership, for example, the WTO, UN, IMF.

◆ They must also recognize the latent power of the Internet reflected in the ability of individuals and groups to circumvent political control over the media and co-ordinate activities.

Activity 7.1

Do you remember what the acronyms WTO, UN, IMF stand for?

Exam hint

It is politically expedient to regularly consult the syllabus, examination reports and the CIM Code of Conduct (see www.cim.co.uk/learningzone) since these define and comment upon the rules applying to your examination.

There are still exceptions, but the trend towards international 'acceptability' of political outcomes has strengthened since the collapse of Communism. Examples include the following:

◆ Iran and North Korea continue to operate in relative isolation (Note: recent tensions over nuclear activities and tests).

◆ Bolivia has unilaterally re-nationalized the country's vast oil fields and plans to re-distribute up to 20 per cent of its land to indigenous peasants.

◆ Argentina is doubling the royalties that foreign oil companies pay and increasing income tax rates by 50 per cent.

◆ In China, as a communist one-party state, power is formally held by a Central Committee elected by the Party Congress:

  ◆ The Committee in turn elects a seven-member Politburo headed by a supreme authority.

- It has encouraged foreign investment in special economic zones, introduced market forces and joined the WTO.

- However, China has emerged from relative isolation and gradually improved relationships despite other human rights criticisms.

- Its recent economic growth has been rapid and sustained and it has been said that China could overtake the United States by 2025. However the country still has unresolved political contradictions such as high unemployment and widening inequality of income.

Insight: China woos Africa

While Western governments are preoccupied with the Middle East, China is purposefully extending its influence across the African continent. Its President and Prime Minister each visited 15 major African nations within three months offering aid and finance. Its investment is already significant and because of its endless drive for raw materials to sustain its own economic boom, its state-run enterprises are prepared to outbid most Western companies and come with no strings attached. African trade with the European Union and United States has been declining while trade with China has risen fourfold since 2000, to some 10 per cent of the total, helped by zero import duties. China is clearly motivated by its need to import raw materials. But this demand has driven up world prices for African commodities. Correspondingly, the price that Africa pays for manufactured imports from China have dropped sharply allowing Africa to grow at rates of up to 5 per cent a year.

The downside for Africa is its increasing dependence and vulnerability to sudden swings in global prices. Labour intensive industries like textiles have been hit by cheap Chinese imports. In Nigeria unemployment is adding to existing tensions. China provides aid and support to regimes with human rights issues such as Zimbabwe and Sudan. China's no-strings approach to aid has also undermined recent attempts by the G8 conference to bring greater transparency and accountability to business and governance in Africa. Given that China's investments are through state-owned companies that respond to long-run objectives not short-run profit, it is difficult to escape the conclusion that Western influence on the continent will continue to wane.

Insight

President Putin, elected by a massive majority for his first two terms has vowed to respect the Russian constitution and not seek a third election victory in 2008. He accurately described Russia as 'a rich country full of poor people' since it controls 13 per cent of the world's oil and 36 per cent of its natural gas yet saw its GDP halve from the fall of Communism to the collapse of the rouble in 1998, since when it has recovered, and especially as commodity prices have boomed. Putin promised to create a strong state and a 'dictatorship of law' to confront those previously above or beyond its powers. One marketing consequence of his attempt to foster family values and the belief that Russia can regain its former greatness is a ban on the sale of Barbie dolls and other Western toys for encouraging consumerism in children. There are some who worry that Russia might return to the kind of system that has taken hold in many developing countries, namely an elected autocracy with the power to stifle the independent media and enforce change. Notwithstanding, Putin's popularity is high particularly due to his willingness to conduct annual phone-ins with the public.

Activity 7.2

How do you think the intention to ban the sale of Barbie dolls and other Western toys may affect the marketers of toys produced in Russia?

Insight: American and British Democracy?

The US House of Representatives is the key policy maker, yet the majority of biannual elections are foregone conclusions. As in the last three elections when 98 per cent of Congress was re-elected, the incumbent nearly always wins. This arises from the long-established practice of 'gerrymandering' wherein most state politicians fix the boundaries of electoral districts. (In Britain, it is the non-political Boundary Commission that adjusts for population change.)

California, with 53 districts, has only one contest where the outcome isn't taken as inevitable. Despite a sharp rise in turnout to 60 per cent in the latest election, the overall trend is downward as voters increasingly believe that they have no influence. Although constituencies cannot be manipulated for senatorial (two per State) and presidential elections, the situation is still polarized with only 17 or 18 'swing' states.

As good marketers, the presidential contenders (brands?) concentrate their time and resources on these states and ignore the rest. The candidate who wins the popular vote in a state wins all its electoral college votes. This 'winner take all' system can, however, result in the one who loses the popular vote winning the presidency, as was the case with Bush in 2000, but not in 2004.

If the share of the vote in the UK had been equal on 5 May 2005, Labour would have had 140 more MPs due to the failure of boundary changes to keep up with demographic change. As it was, Labour achieved 3 per cent more of the popular vote and 159 more seats. In fact Labour won 13.5 million votes in 1997 but less than 10.7 million in 2001 and just 9.6 million in 2005. Despite this representing just 35 per cent of the vote the party won 55 per cent of the seats, a reflection of the skewed electoral system, not Blair's leadership powers.

Legislation and the decisions of public authorities clearly have a continuing influence on business activities. Accordingly, they must be monitored carefully in order to:

◆ Alert management to impending legislation.

◆ Mobilize efforts to represent stakeholder interests to the legislators.

◆ Develop awareness of public agency intentions and decisions affecting business.

◆ Identify likely changes arising out of electoral shifts.

◆ Assess political manifesto implications and philosophy of ministers.

The government also controls the macro-economic framework where decisions affect both its position as a major customer of the private sector and the political distribution of the tax burden. Business has a collective interest in the relative burden of business taxes and rates as well as trends in the size and composition of government spending on goods and services. Governments now aim to create overall stability and this is usually reflected in spending despite the pressures exerted by the demands of social security, health and education.

Insight

In the UK, the government has added 50,000 public sector jobs, boosted spending by over 60 per cent and raised average civil service pay by 20 per cent over four years. Public spending has risen from 39.8 per cent to 43 per cent and will converge with the EU average of 49 per cent by 2009 based on current trends.

The public sector itself has undergone a fundamental transformation in recent years with policies of privatization, deregulation and the contracting-out to private tender of more and more local authority and civil service functions. Much investment in Britain's public services is undertaken through the Private Finance Initiative.

In contrast, economies like Sri Lanka have adopted liberalization and privatization policies to promote growth and the re-emergence of the vital tourism industry.

The market solution or pure capitalist policies of the political right, based on the values of private ownership and an enterprise culture have, however, been blunted and moderated in social democracies, like the European Union, by counterforces promoting responsible capitalism and its attendant codes of good conduct.

Insight

Even David Cameron, the new leader of the Conservative Party in the UK appears more concerned with the health of the planet than with tax cuts or market freedoms.

The middle way is indeed a partnership of private initiative and responsible public enterprise to promote the welfare of all members of society, not just the rich and economically successful.

Activity 7.3

Key skills – Interpreting information

Match the terms with their correct definitions:

1   Privatization

2   Deregulation

3   Enterprise culture

4   Party manifesto

5   First-past-the-post

a   The candidate with the most votes cast is the election winner, irrespective of the distribution of votes to other contenders

b   Removal of rules and requirements restricting competition

c   A programme of intended policies, if successfully elected

d   A climate that encourages self-reliance, entrepreneurship, individual wealth creation

e   Transfer of 50 per cent or more of the voting shares to private hands.

The political framework

Political systems are located along a spectrum ranging from totalitarianism to popular democracy. The main features of these two systems can be outlined as displayed below.

Totalitarianism/autocracy	Democracy
Single leader	Universal suffrage
One ruling party	Periodic free elections
Official ideology rules	Freedom of speech/media
Opposition parties repressed	Open political competition
Power is concentrated	Pluralistic; the power is spread throughout society
Central direction/command; government controls media	Majority rule;minorities are protected and equal under the law
Minorities persecuted	Pressure groups free to lobby between elections

Political power is the ability to bring about change through influencing the behaviour of others. All organizations are affected by politics because people have different views, ideals and interests. Disagreements naturally arise over such matters as objectives to be pursued, decisions to be made and, perhaps most importantly, resources to be allocated. These must be resolved. Otherwise conflict would result and organizations, and indeed society, would cease to function effectively.

Political stability arises out of the identification and effective resolution of disputes through a mixture of authority, enforcement and compromise. Political stability is important, not least to investors who wish to minimize their risks. Multinationals, for example, are reluctant to invest in any economy experiencing political or labour unrest.

Insight

The Tiananmen Square incident in Beijing in 1989 had serious and long-lasting repercussions for China.

Mugabe's seizure of white farms caused the IMF and World Bank to suspend lending. This frightened much foreign investment away.

Question 7.1

What are the areas and issues where politics are involved for the marketing department?

How can political factors affect relationships between marketing and finance?

What sources of information should marketers consult to keep themselves aware about the political environment?

Are there cost-effective means of keeping abreast of national and supranational legislative developments?

The inputs into the political system originate in wider society and arise out of their changing attitudes, values, perceptions and demands. These will be diverse and conflicting and tend to coalesce around support for alternative party manifestos at election time (between elections they will be channelled and given focus by pressure groups and lobbyists). These could include lower taxes, devolution of power to the regions and more education spending. Political parties seek to differentiate themselves from their rivals. However they also need to appeal to a sufficiently wide constituency so as to gain election to government.

Insight: The cult of the personality

An interesting website for the marketer is www.number10.gov.uk as it gives an insight into political leadership and how political parties seek to distinguish themselves by focusing on the prowess and vision of their leader.

The website shows Blair as central to every issue and initiative as he markets the credentials and achievements of the Party. This approach can however have its limitations. For instance the cash-for-peerages (made illegal in 1925) scandal had serious repercussions.

The focal point of the criminal enquiry is Blair's pivotal role in the £12 million in loans made to Labour in early 2005 by four businessmen all of whom were later nominated for peerages. Neither the public nor the Labour Party auditors nor the Lords Appointments Commission were informed of the loans. When three of the millionaires were turned down, one admitted he had been asked to loan rather than donate to avoid the rules on transparency that the Labour government had itself in fact set up.

Interestingly the 83-year-old scrutiny committee responsible for stopping political parties rewarding its donors with honours was axed in 2005 by the Prime Minister's Office.

Elections are the ultimate democratic control over government. They provide the electorate with an opportunity to pass judgement on its performance. It is also an opportunity to judge the pledges and proposals of the opposition. Fear of defeat at an approaching general election, or a very strong wish for a second term, should encourage any government to consider the public wishes.

Question 7.2

Key skills – Using information

Since voters are very much like customers as far as political parties are concerned, what advice could a marketer offer to the following:

◆ The election campaign manager of a party currently in office

◆ The election campaign manager of the main opposition party

◆ The campaign manager of the Green party looking to establish a base in Parliament

The United Kingdom has a first-past-the-post electoral system that produces a number of characteristics:

◆   A simple majority of seats gives one party the power to form a strong government.

◆   Governments seldom win a majority of votes cast; the opposition vote gets split.

◆   Fewer smaller parties: they tend not to see their proportion of the vote reflected in seats won.

◆   The compromises and vulnerability to interest groups found in coalition government is avoided.

This may seem unfair but elections are held to produce governments and avoid the uncertainties of an indefinite outcome. There is always considerable resistance to change in political systems because of the uncertainties involved and disruption of established vested interests. Alternatives exist, as in Europe and Australasia, but these involve proportional voting systems. Although these systems produce a more representative electoral outcome, this may also potentially be at the expense of strong and effective government. A succession of weak coalitions had, for example, created a frequent absence of government in Italy, and one susceptible to bribery and corruption.

The politics of coalition are important to the stability of most economies, not least to those with a strong ethnic mix to their societies. The consequences of civil war are all too clear in countries like Sri Lanka and many African states. Sectarian violence can flare up along many fault lines as seen most recently in the Sudan. Similar ethnic or religious flashpoints in Israel, Nigeria, Iraq or Indonesia still persist.

The main concern of business is for stability in political decision-making, a dependable planning horizon and a positive climate in which they can operate. This is not possible if corruption is draining the strength out of the country's development process or if civil war is depleting a country's critical resources. Thus, the political environment is of vital importance to effective marketing. Yet, the political environment is one that can easily be taken for granted in times of stability. The Russian stock market plunged when hardliners arrested Khodorkovsky, the country's then wealthiest businessman, on corruption charges.

Changes in government in a polarized system can cause serious discontinuity as established policies are reversed, institutions abolished and legislation amended to reflect the new political philosophy. At election time, as in the United States in 2006, business companies carefully pondered the implications of alternative policies and pledges being implemented.

Insight: Gibraltar

After a succession of votes, the community of Gibraltar once again voted decisively (99 per cent on an 88 per cent turnout) to reject joint sovereignty with Spain. The legitimacy of the vote was rejected by Spain, which is in turn refusing an arguably more legitimate demand to return Olivenca to Portugal.

Activity 7.4

Key skills – Using information and problem-solving

With Tony Blair having won a record third term and Gordon Brown now firmly established as the Prime Minister, review the pledges and key policies of the Labour Party.

Assess the marketing implications, arising from the achievement or non-achievement, as appropriate of the pledges and policies.

Please apply a similar analysis to your own political environment if you are not based in the UK.

The electoral cycle

The other source of political instability is the tendency for elections to 'influence' business cycles. Governments know that reducing taxes and increasing spending, as an election approaches, will create a temporary sense of well-being. Disposable income rises, as does employment and business activity. This will be short-lived if prices and imports also tend to rise, since action will have to be taken to reverse the resulting inflation and trade deficit. However, since there will be a lag before such effects are felt, the government may well win re-election and be in a position to apply the economic brakes. These can then be released as the next general election approaches.

An adversarial two- or three-party system also tends to widen the credibility gap between politically nurtured expectations on the one hand and actual performance of the economy, on the other. Accordingly, marketers should also be able to gauge the pertinence, feasibility and sustainability of the ideals and objectives advertised and promoted by the various parties in general. This should also be done for those of the government in particular. Politics is often hailed as being the art of the possible but politicians including governments often deliver less than what is expected or even promised.

Central and local government

Parliament is the supreme legislative authority in the UK. Although private members of the Parliament can propose bills, the vast majority of the bills that become law are government sponsored or supported by the government; whatever the actual make-up and workings of the legislature. The marketer should appreciate the origins of new laws as well as appreciate how businesses might influence their form and content.

The table below illustrates some key features and stages within legislature.

Stages	Influence
1. *Origin* (about a popular issue, committee of inquiry recommendation, election pledge, pressure group, government initiative to close loopholes)	Trade association may press for legislation
2. *Green Paper* (government puts ideas on paper for discussion)	Monitor and contribute if industry interests are to be affected
3. *White paper* (government sets out definite proposals)	Comments from parties affected will be accounted/included
4. *Draft bill – first reading*	
5. *Main debate – second reading*	MPs can be lobbied to speak in support
6. *Committee stage* – studies the details	
7. *Report stage – to full House of Commons*	
8. *Final debate and amendments – third reading*	Last opportunity to lobby support
9. *To House of Lords – process repeated*	
10. *Possible reference back to Commons*	For example, restrictions on right to trial by jury
11. *Royal Assent – the law is enacted*	

It should be noted that it is vitally important that the views of businesses on proposed laws are made clearly and persuasively. If legislation is inevitable, then businesses and other organizations must ensure that it is workable and no unintended disadvantageous side effects may result. Emotional legislation in response to a public outcry is to be avoided through active lobbying.

The process is long and complicated, placing a limit on how much legislative business can be completed. Virtually all government-sponsored bills become law although the opposition can use delaying tactics. Case law, in contrast, evolves through independent judicial decisions and is not susceptible to influence by business, although the right of appeal exists.

Insight: Anti-terrorism laws

The Labour government was defeated for the first time in November 2005 in its attempt to extend the detention of terrorist suspects from 14 to up to 90 days. They argued that the rights of the public to be protected against biological, chemical or nuclear attack outweighed those of suspects and that in a hi-tech world, the police requires such powers to pre-empt terror strikes. The July 7 attacks on London transport yielded 80,000 CCTV videos, 1400 fingerprints and 160 crime scenes and it may take weeks to decode encrypted computer files or scan mobile messages. The new legislation allows the arrest of those preparing to commit terrorist acts. The opposition argued that detention without charge was contrary to habeas corpus and the government's own Human Rights

Act. Such a law could push moderates into the arms of extremists and civil liberties might be curbed. Experience of its nearest equivalent, 'internment without trial' in Northern Ireland, was even acknowledged by those who introduced it as providing the best 'recruiting sergeant' the IRA ever had. It has however not prevented the Chancellor and others from continuing to press for 90 days.

Activity 7.5

The ability of business lobbies to influence legislation that affects them is considerable. The transport industry lobby campaigns successfully against carbon taxes and cuts in greenhouse gases. The farm, supermarket and defence lobbies are other notable examples.

Select a topical bill (e.g. road pricing or ID cards) affecting a strong business lobby and assess their effectiveness.

Pressure groups, as discussed in Unit 2, represent a channel through which individuals and groups can make their views known to governments between elections. They are much more important than political parties in terms of membership and represent numerous, overlapping and competing influences within society.

Pressure groups' effectiveness requires *commitment, cohesion, organization, resources* and *strategic positioning*. Those who decide government policies need pressure groups. They often have a statutory duty to consult and require advice, information and feedback of views and reactions from those affected. They favour those groups with the ability to deliver on bargains and compromises made and who provide support in return. They also need co-operation in the implementation and administration of new laws.

Study tip

Marketing skills – Working with others

The marketing environment is a large diverse syllabus, so why don't you pool resources with a fellow student and actively compare notes and ideas?

Your combined strengths will produce synergy and help to reduce the overall workload. It may also offer both of you a different perspective.

Businesses are strategically well positioned to obtain political support when right-wing governments are in office but they are not always as successful when left-wing governments rule. However, effective pressure group activity tends to stimulate the development of counter-pressure. Accordingly, the countervailing action between rival coalitions limits the influence of any one grouping. Ministers may also be in a position to play one group off against another.

Government through devolved powers

A brief mention should be made of other dimensions of government with which the marketer might interact. Very close to home are local or city authorities whose political representatives are often protective of their independence and may even represent opposition parties and policies. The appropriate decision-making authority has therefore to be identified and lobbied.

Local government in the UK has undergone radical changes in the last ten years. Their powers to set business rates, raise taxes independently and decide expenditure totals have all been constrained by central government actions such as spending caps. Setting of national standards in education and other social services have also limited local autonomy.

Local government officers are now service facilitators rather than direct providers because of the requirement on them to offer contracts out to competitive bidding. This has made them more marketing-orientated in pursuing value-for-money services for ratepayers although formerly free services, such as leisure centres, are now often run on a more commercial basis. Consumer needs are identified and services provided, priced and promoted in order to cover costs and make a contribution to council funds. Apart from bidding for council contracts in such areas as street cleaning, parks maintenance and refuse disposal, there are also opportunities for working jointly on projects combining civic improvement and commercial development.

Local authorities are important stakeholders since they undertake urban planning and redevelopment, decide planning applications, control the supply of school-leavers, maintain local roads and infrastructure and provide a variety of inspectorates that impact on local business. It is an aspect of the environment, therefore, where businesses should build positive and mutually beneficial relationships. This is even more the case with Scotland and Wales who now enjoy devolved powers.

One final area to note is that of government agencies and other quasi-government bodies. The intention of many governments is to raise productivity and accountability by transforming government departments into executive agencies. These are free from day-to-day control from the central government. Therefore they are usually better able to focus on the achievement of long-term performance objectives. However as such agencies are unelected, questions may be raised over their independence and accountability, especially given the potential spending power and influence that some of these organizations command.

Supranational bodies – the European Union (EU)

The European Union is the most integrated and economically powerful bloc of countries in the world. Its members represent a combined market of over 400 million affluent consumers. As such, it is a magnet for marketers from around the world.

The Single European Market (SEM) initiative originated from concern over Europe's declining competitiveness in relation to the United States and the emerging nations of the Pacific Rim. Despite the Common Market, Europe remained fragmented into culturally differentiated markets protected by an array of non-tariff barriers to trade. A common desire for increased competitiveness and employment opportunities was the driving force behind the idea of a truly free market, which, it was hoped, would release a dynamic and revived spirit of enterprise within European businesses.

Insight: Consequences of the French 'Non' to the EU Constitution

Rather than face the challenge of open, global markets, the French have rejected the EU enlargement policy and opted to continue economic decline rather than reform. Unlike countries like the UK who made the painful reforms necessary to meet the dynamic Asian and East European competitors, and an IT-driven United States, the French appear to have retreated into the protection of their expensive welfare systems and inflexible labour markets. Their farmers are equally entrenched, with the Common Agricultural Policy providing £6.3 billion every year to prop up the sector. Agriculture accounts for just 5 per cent of EU jobs, 4 per cent of GDP but 40 per cent of the budget and provides one of the main distortions and obstacles to freer international trade. For years the average EU cow has received about $2.20 a day in subsidies, twice the daily income of the average African though this might change in the 2008 review.

Activity 7.6

Key skills – Collecting information and problem-solving

Use CD-ROM databases or newspaper summaries to locate any surveys assessing progress to date in implementation of the SEM (the Single European Market) and the new Constitution.

Membership of the SEM (the Single European Market), the European Monetary System and the Euro creates economic and legal obligations that imply a progressive loss of national sovereignty. The institutions relevant to the exercise of this transferred legislative authority include:

◆ **The European Parliament:**

◆ This is an elected body (MEPs) with widening powers.

◆ Originally, it was primarily consultative, supplying advice through the workings of various standing committees.

◆ More recently, it has acquired and flexed its powers to reject proposals, veto the budget and even vote out the entire incoming commission, for example, over the Buttiglione appointment. In May 2005, it voted against Britain's Working Hours Directive opt-out.

◆ **The Council of Ministers:**

◆ This is where the real decision-making power lies. It is composed of representative ministers, according to the issue under discussion.

◆ To speed up the process, the Nice treaty proposed increasing the voting power of the larger countries but ending the national veto in 39 new policy areas.

- More and more of the voting is on a qualified majority basis. This implies that marketers wishing to influence outcomes must broaden their lobbying base and/or co-operate with other sympathetic interest groups.

- **The European Commission:**

  - This is the executive body of the European Union.

  - It has drafted regulations and directives to promote the SEM and achieve a level competitive playing field.

  - It has the power to impose punitive fines for contravening competition rules.

  - Membership is decided by 25 governments and its role is to co-ordinate national policies and secure the adoption and execution of the EU policies.

  - The outcome has been a large number of measures and directives to facilitate the evolution of an integrated market.

  - Compliance costs have arisen for business in the process, but so too have the opportunities for greater trade.

  - One recent regulation (still requiring assent) requires local authorities to collect, strip down and recycle all electrical devices. Presently, 90 per cent of this waste is either dumped in landfill or incinerated. The cost will be borne by the electrical manufacturers.

  - Another regulation might require the re-labelling of most British yoghurt as 'mild alternate-culture, heat-treated, fermented milk' since it does not conform to their standardized definition of a Euro-pudding.

- **The European Court of Justice:**

  - It deals with any actions a business may wish to bring against EU institutions.

  - It also provides a means of individual redress where member states are not fully complying with their legal obligations.

  - Both national governments and organizations have learnt to their cost the consequences of referral to this final court of appeal.

Several main issues currently confront the European Union. The main ones are:

- The future of the single currency (Sweden, Britain and new entrants remain outside).

- Breaches of the now diluted stability pact (France/Germany).

- The implementation of the enlargement and confirmation of a Constitution to streamline decision-making.

- Enlargement raises real concerns, not least over pressures on the budget and endemic corruption in much of Eastern Europe, but also the escalation in language translation costs which already stand at over €1 billion.

- Enlargement is also linked to the proposed Constitution, creating as it would a European president, foreign minister and justice department.

◆ Economic policy, foreign affairs, trade, agriculture, fisheries, immigration, employment policy, environmental protection, home affairs and space exploration would all be primarily European Union governed.

◆ However, despite some votes in favour (e.g. Spain), the clear rejection by France and the Netherlands diminishes the prospect of ever-closer union. The UK has shelved its own plans for a referendum and the new Constitution appears to have been set aside.

The marketing challenge of a single currency

The Euro became the major transaction currency for the 13 participating countries on 1 January 1999 following a massive marketing campaign. Although it was introduced to world financial markets as an accounting currency in 1999, it was only launched as physical coins and banknotes on 1st January 2002. The single currency aimed to complement the Single European Market, facilitate open and free intra-EU trade and encourage European unity.

The UK ruled out joining until a clear case could be made. The government officially supports entry 'in principle' but the issue appears to be off the political agenda.

Uncertainties

◆ The government will recommend monetary union only if five economic tests are passed.

◆ Following 'exhaustive' Treasury assessment, only one test was passed by mid-2003. The test was that the City and financial institutions were ready to adjust.

◆ The tests are very broad and open to interpretation but failed tests included:

  ◆ Business cycles and economic structures are insufficiently compatible.

  ◆ Insufficient flexibility for adjustment to shocks.

  ◆ Creation of better conditions for making long-term decisions to invest in Britain not assured.

  ◆ Insufficient convergence to assure higher growth and a lasting rise in jobs.

◆ Public opinion, the Conservatives and the media are currently against it while the TUC (the Trades Union Congress) is for it. A positive government recommendation could move the balance of public opinion closer to acceptance.

◆ The European Union's 'one policy fits all' only works if convergence is achieved.

◆ If the pound is overvalued on entry, it will impact negatively.

◆ The political tone remains pro-Euro but with continuing review of the five tests.

Advantages of a single currency

◆ Currency uncertainty and transaction costs are reduced.

◆ The most powerful trading bloc with over 400 million largely well-off consumers.

◆ Independent European Central Bank (ECB) should stabilize inflation/interest rates.

◆ Members will be forced into deregulation/structural changes to put their economies in order.

◆ Competition should improve productivity, reduce costs and expand trade.

Disadvantages of a single currency

◆ Lack of adjustment mechanisms for individual countries may cause tensions. The introduction of the Euro caused sharp price rises in Germany and Greece.

◆ A unified monetary policy cannot meet the needs of up to 25 separate countries.

◆ Europe is not as open, mobile or flexible as the US. Therefore limited fund transfers to poor regions may occur.

◆ Unresolved structural problems: for example state ownership, subsidies, rigid labour markets.

◆ Pressure is developing to unify other aspects of policy: for example taxation.

◆ There is no mechanism for leaving the Euro and the stability pact is suspended.

Significance of a single currency

◆ Winners are businesses with high cross-border revenues.

◆ Losers are those pricing above EU levels. Euro 'transparency' allows comparisons.

◆ Winners are those who adapt most successfully. Relocation and restructuring will be required.

◆ Local markets will become Euro-wide markets and marketers in small firms must face up to more competition.

◆ Market extension strategies must be considered to exploit niches.

In brief, there is continued uncertainty regarding the UK's entry and the ultimate prospects for the Euro. Meanwhile, the Euro presents a marketing challenge whether the United Kingdom enters or not.

Lobbyists and the media

Lobbying may be defined as influencing members of a relevant legislature and soliciting their votes. This important activity has attracted adverse publicity but most lobbying activity comes within accepted definitions of ethical behaviour. To be effective it must be exerted where and when the decisions are being made.

The value of professional lobbyists to a business may be described as follows:

Monitoring	an early warning service on forthcoming legislation
Interpreting	the implications of proposed legislation
Identifying	political figures with a special interest in your issue
Informing	political decision-makers about (your) industry developments
Preparing	background briefs and cases for busy legislators
Co-ordinating	constituency protest letters to political representatives
Advising	the business on strategy and tactics to adopt

While there is little likelihood of stopping proposed legislation, the lobbyists seek to persuade those with political power to re-evaluate details, clarify ambiguity, gain assurances and secure legislation the industry can live with.

Insight

The best single measure to raise the EU's potential growth rate, a directive to create a free market in services across Europe, was seriously diluted at the Brussels summit following pressure from special interests.

Even more dramatic was the Brazilian referendum in 2005 to ban the general sale of firearms, which initially had majority support but was defeated by a two-thirds majority. Despite having the world's second highest murder rate, after Venezuela, massive promotional expenditure financed by gun manufacturers and a fear of being defenceless against criminal gangs swung the vote.

Exam hint

The mini-case given in advance is a critical aspect of the examination. Avoid the temptation to write out blocks of text as answers to questions. The case often provides themes, clues, hints and/or examples but you must process and re-express the information in the light of your syllabus knowledge.

You need to learn to display reflective and analytical skills as opposed to merely descriptive skills.

The pre-budget period is a busy one for lobby groups. Businesses, unions, consumers, heritage, environment and an array of other interest groups wish to make their presence felt. However, public perceptions and public opinion are also important inputs into the political process. The climate the government seeks to create through its policies and laws is an output intended to positively influence these opinions. Putting a positive 'spin' on events will, if successful, make the public more likely to re-elect the government concerned.

The mass media, including press, radio and television, are important influences on these perceptions and opinions. They supply awareness of political issues and scrutiny of government behaviour and performance. As with pressure groups, they can influence decision-makers and their policies through their campaigns. Investigative journalism, in particular, can have serious impacts on businesses as well as politicians. Exposure of malpractice can lead to damage to image, loss of sales, resignations and even policy changes.

Public relations (PR) is another important aspect of marketing management and special skills are required to create and maintain mutually beneficial relationships with the media. It is a two-way relationship based on principles similar to those between a minister and a pressure group. PR aims to influence both the media agenda as well as the tenor of any debate that results. Issues and outcomes must be monitored through market research to assess shifts in public opinion.

Insight

Interest groups may apply pressure but New Labour employs press officers to counteract such efforts. Since 1997 their numbers have risen tenfold to over 3250 while the budget of the Central Office of Information has tripled to over £320 million. The Internet age where the public expects to be constantly informed coupled with the need for more explanation in a complex policy world could have led to this increase. Still, this is mostly due to the desire to bury bad news and hype up the good. Such political marketing or public relations may have proved largely unproductive, as a Guardian survey recently suggested that barely a quarter of voters now trust ministers to tell the truth.

Activity 7.7

The most important issue confronting southern Africa – the politics of AIDS

◆ Of 42 million people with HIV worldwide, 28 million live in sub-Saharan Africa.

◆ An estimated 25 million have died so far worldwide (3.1m in 2006). 15,000 died in the UK (MRSA, the hospital superbug, killed 5000).

◆ Russia has the fastest growth rate but India may have most cases by 2010.

◆ Unlike other epidemic diseases that affect the old and young, AIDS mainly hits those aged 15–49.

◆ More teachers in Zambia and Swaziland are dying of AIDS than are trained.

- The US census report suggests that life expectancy in the relatively rich Botswana will fall to 26.7.

- Senegal, Kenya and Uganda have managed to avoid the general trend through intensive education campaigns and strong advocacy of condoms.

- The spread of AIDS from high-risk to low-risk groups in many parts of Africa is facilitated by poverty, ignorance, cultural mores and lack of treatment.

- Some epidemiologists are suggesting that 100 million could become infected in the next decade as HIV spreads across India and China.

How can the political environment make a positive contribution to a solution? What could marketers contribute to defeat the spread of AIDS?

Marketers should continuously reassess the political landscape. Inertia ensures that much of the environment remains constant but pressure to set and implement a policy agenda means there will always be shifts and impacts, particularly in the medium to long term.

A pluralistic society ensures that political change is often the product of compromise and consensus. Business interest groups can influence decisions but only if they understand the real nature of the political agenda. This may be driven by considerations of tactical or party advantage, especially approaching election time.

The legal framework

Legal issues and cases involving businesses are regularly in the news. Seldom a week goes by without mention of such things as a music copyright infringement, an advert being withdrawn, an out-of-court settlement for negligence, a case of insider dealing, an accusation of sexual harassment or a fine imposed by a government inspectorate. Law was initially based on a concept of natural justice while parties to a transaction were treated as equals. Each party looked to their own best interests and suffered the consequences of any poor judgement. Consumers were faced with the reality of 'caveat emptor' (let the buyer beware) but the growing power and size of businesses relative to individual consumers made this untenable. Pressure grew for legal protection that tilted the scales by increasing the rights of buyers and the duties of sellers.

Similar principles will apply to those organizations that thought the Internet would allow unlimited, inexpensive access to consumers without regulatory restrictions. Democracies monitor sites endangering vulnerable groups, while China employs 50,000 security officers to 'police' the web (on the other hand 100,000 Chinese go online for the first time every day). The Internet is no more a borderless medium than the telephone and a country has every right within its territory to check and redress harm. It can, however, only act against companies with assets in its territory and those that find local regulations repressive can choose not to do business there.

Question 7.3

Key skills – Collecting information

How does the law influence or affect you during a typical working day? This may not be directly, unless you get a speeding ticket! But how does it affect your day indirectly?

The framework of law is the product of both legal and political influences. An independent judiciary is normally responsible for the interpretation of common law. These are broad, comprehensive principles based on ideals of justice, fairness and common sense. The term 'common' means that it applies to all subjects. The way that common law is interpreted and applied changes over time through the effect of legal judgements made in higher courts. They then become precedents that must be applied by lower courts. Such judgements adapt the law to reflect current attitudes and values within society.

One recent judgement awarded damages to asbestosis sufferers who had grown up in close proximity to the plant manufacturing the product. This exposed the company to substantial liabilities arising from potential claims from other victims. Coca-Cola was fined $68 million in Mexico following attempts to prevent small shopkeepers from stocking a cheaper Peruvian substitute.

Governments introduce new laws in the form of statutes in order to implement their political manifestos. These acts reflect political philosophy as well as a growing pressure from society and pressure groups on government to regulate undesired activity or behaviour.

Recent actions include:

◆ The European Union has confirmed that its laws against discrimination do not protect smokers and could only be applied on grounds such as race, age, disability and sexual preference. This appears to make it legitimate for employers to sack workers because they smoke.

◆ In the United States a health benefits administration company gave their employees 15 months to give up. Three that failed a nicotine test at the end were fired. This may be extreme but a growing number are refusing to hire smokers in order to avoid annual costs per smoker of over $3000 in lost productivity and medical bills.

◆ Meanwhile, the European Union has introduced new laws that put the onus on employers to protect employees from a wide range of harassment. Penalties include heavy fines. This was designed to combat the macho culture of the Mediterranean but also has the side effect of making companies think twice about organizing office parties or ignoring inappropriate individual or even organizational conduct.

As society becomes increasingly more complex, the resulting rise in workload will continue to force governments to concentrate on enabling legislation, delegating authority to government departments, agencies or local authorities to fill in and administer the details. These are issued in the form of statutory instruments, regulations and bye-laws.

These authorities are normally responsible for the following roles:

◆ **Rule making and their interpretation** – for example regulations.

◆ **Standards setting** – emissions, food and hygiene for example.

◆   **Inspections** – these are usually unannounced spot checks due to complaints.

◆   **Enforcement** – various sanctions from fines to closure.

Entry into economic unions also makes member countries subject to its regulations and legal provisions. Directives from the European Union require implementation by member states, superseding national laws. They affect business, particularly in the area of competition policy, where fines of up to 10 per cent of turnover may be levied. The European Commission has recently ruled that television coverage of football can no longer be monopolized by one organization (i.e. Sky). The games will be divided into groups in future and no organization can buy all six groups.

Role and objectives of legislation

Legislation involves a delicate process of balancing the diverse, and often conflicting, interests of the various stakeholders involved. Some of these processes may be summarized as follows:

◆   Governs exchanges between parties: this is the foundation stone of the market economy

◆   Ensures a level playing field between individuals and companies

◆   Counterbalances the economic power of business

◆   Settles disputes between stakeholders

◆   Denies market access to certain groups: for example alcohol to children

◆   Balances the rights of the individual company with the collective rights of wider society

◆   Prohibits certain goods or activities: such as hard drugs or pornography

◆   Seeks to prevent abuse without imposing excessive regulation

◆   Governs what business can and cannot do

Unfortunately, the law is a relatively blunt weapon in the achievement of such objectives, not least because society's attitudes and concerns can often change rapidly whereas the law tends to lag behind. There is a limit to what the legislature can amend or enact each year and many worthy legal bills fail to become law because of lack of parliamentary time.

The activities of the media and community pressure groups such as the consumer's associations have, however, made buyers more aware of their rights and more willing to initiate action to seek the redressing of issues. Attitudes have changed dramatically in recent years with much more demanding consumer expectations of the service they believe they have a right to expect from business. A hardening compensation culture (though Britain still has the lowest tort costs at 0.6 per cent of GDP – one-third the US level) also demonstrates a stronger willingness to seek redress malpractice.

As the Figure 7.1 below illustrates, not all the pressure on businesses to deliver the adequate products and services comes from the law alone.

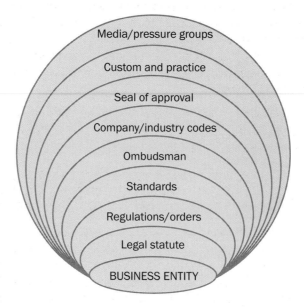

Figure 7.1 Regulatory pressures on business – a broader view

Activity 7.8

Key skills – Applying business law

Match the terms with their correct definitions:

1   Caveat emptor and caveat vendictor

2   Standards Institute

3   Code of practice

4   Legislation

5   Statute

6   Ombudsman

7   Seal of approval

a   Let the buyer beware (no legal obligation to notify defects) and let the seller beware

b   The process of making laws

c   Voluntary guidelines to encourage desirable modes of behaviour

d   A quango established to set product safety/quality standards

e   An official appointed to investigate individual complaints of maladministration

f   Law laid down by government legislation

g   A mark, given by an expert, to confirm or guarantee a product

The government has the primary responsibility for the establishment, updating and operation of the legal framework. The law provides a means by which it can constrain business activities by defining the powers and responsibilities of owners and management. Many governments have sought to curtail the amount of regulation in recent years. They have launched successive campaigns to reduce bureaucracy and red tape especially where it impacts on smaller businesses.

One notable regulation that the Singapore government has recently relaxed is their ban on chewing gum (also lap dancing and bungee jumping). They have allowed some imports as part of a free trade deal with America.

Insight

The Dutch calculated that red tape costs them over £11 billion, of which half originates from the European Union. They have targeted 2500 of the estimated 100,000 EU directives for removal and also deregulated a number of industries, such as telecommunications and transport services, in order to increase competition and release their latent potential for productivity improvements where inefficiency had accumulated. On the other hand, they have had to establish a large number of quangos to regulate and oversee these operations.

Study tip

Make sure that you engage in all the activities and questions set throughout this coursebook. These have been included to help you broaden your understanding of the various topics and sub-topics as well as to help you refine your level of critical thinking.

Exam hint

Ensure that your answers actually address the question that you are being asked.

Also make sure that you are addressing all the components being asked by a question. Some questions may ask you about more than one aspect of marketing management.

One area of marketing in which such extra legal bodies operate is in advertising and promotion. With the development of online interactive multimedia using digital broadband technology, not to mention e-commerce, increasingly more advertising is or will become cross-border. This raises the question of compliance with different national regulations.

Insight

In the UK, the Advertising Standards Authority was set up by the industry to counter the need for legislation by ensuring that all who commission, prepare and publish advertisements comply with the required codes. It adjudicates complaints from the public and other interested parties. Other bodies, like the Broadcasting Standards Council, govern specific media like TV. The Independent Television Commission, however, licences commercial services, whether terrestrial, cable or satellite, and regulates advertising and other standards through its code of practice. Ofcom is the regulator that covers broadcasting, telecommunications and the Internet. One notable regulation it has introduced is the banning of junk food advertising when younger viewers predominate.

The World Wide Web creates big challenges in terms of regulation. It is interesting that the EU plans to widen their tax taken from e-commerce by requiring companies with over £100,000 in sales to register for value added tax in order to ensure a level playing field. However, in practice why should an online trader from, say, East Asia register? Won't EU customers use non-EU billing addresses to avoid payment? In effect, the new tax may prove, as with many regulatory initiatives to govern the Internet, to be unfair, costly to police, difficult to collect and easy to evade.

Question 7.4

Key skills – Applying the law

What do you understand by the term 'red tape'?

Survey your organization for examples.

Impacts and influences on business

There is something of a pendulum effect operating with regulation since fresh societal concerns regarding certain business activities will bring calls for the government to do something about it. However, the costs of regulation and ensuring compliance must be balanced with the benefits to stakeholders and society of the legislation in question.

Some of the drawbacks of legislation and regulation include the following:

◆　The extra costs of purchasing and installing required equipment.

◆　The extra costs incurred for training staff to conform to standards.

◆　Costs involved in recording, reporting and taking action where deviations arise.

◆　Conforming to legal requirements adds to costs and reduces foreign competitiveness.

◆　Conforming to safety standards (e.g. testing required on new pharmaceutical products) delays introduction and returns. Thus investment and innovation may be deterred.

◆ Complicated regulatory procedures may be an entry barrier to small companies.

◆ Legal and insurance costs: for example fines and adverse publicity.

◆ Reduced consumer choice: for instance, the loss of the right to buy as we wish.

◆ Employment or environmental legislation may drive businesses to relocate to developing countries. In so doing, they take jobs, investment and potential exports with them.

◆ Threat of publicly damaging product recalls. For example Dell was forced to recall 4.1 million laptops and suffer brand damage despite the fact that it was Sony battery technology that was faulty. Sony suffered a 60 per cent cut in profits.

Environmental laws and regulations vary widely across the global economy. Predictably, it is the affluent economies which are most concerned about the quality of their environment. Poorer countries, such as China, India, Russia and Brazil, give more priority to the developmental process. Multinationals therefore find it difficult to develop standard environmental policies and are forced to tailor their general aspirations to local regulations. This undoubtedly creates scope for double standards and media exploitation to the disadvantage of the business.

Small companies are harder hit by regulations. Compliance costs will be a higher proportion of total cost, they lack form-filling expertise and the time involved is a diversion from real business. Since small firms tend to be single-product or single-market operations, regulation is more likely to affect the whole business than in a large multi-product organization.

Virtually, all marketing activities are subject to a wide range of laws and regulations. These may originate from or even overlap at supranational, national, state, regional or local levels. They are often in a state of flux and may change unexpectedly at the whim of public pressure or a change in government thinking. It is therefore hard work for marketers and organizations to keep up with important changes. Subsequently, some organizations may have to outsource this information role.

Compensation culture is the corrupting notion that someone must be financially liable for anything that goes wrong. Originating in the United States, it has resulted in hospital lawsuits becoming commonplace. Firing incompetent teachers has become a legal nightmare while many professional workers are ceasing to practise due to high insurance premiums. When pharmaceutical companies halt research into potentially life-saving drugs (e.g. new antibiotics made quickly obsolete by smart bacteria) because liability has become disproportionate to economic return, then only one thing suffers – society at large. President Bush has blamed the high cost of healthcare on this culture and is fulfilling his campaign pledge to cap damages for pain and suffering.

Exam hint

Improving your performance

Questions will focus, at least in part, on the impact of the law on the activities of the marketer. So refer to Figure 7.2 for examples from recent legislation to demonstrate your awareness.

While many businesses complain that they cannot compete fairly or profitably with current or proposed legislation, others seem unable to compete without it. Consequently, the government is being pressured to put in place tariffs and quotas or longer periods of patent protection for the products they develop. Suppliers of branded goods, such as Coca-Cola and Nescafé, are seeking stricter regulations to stop retailers using 'me-too' packaging for their own-label products. Others such as Levi are constantly lobbying to prevent non-approved retailers from selling their grey products.

In actual fact, the law is present to achieve three primary goals:

1   To protect businesses from one another (see Unit 3)

2   To protect consumers from business exploitation

3   To protect the interests of wider society against damaging business behaviour (see Unit 3)

However, legislation can clearly be double-edged. In some cases markets are made more competitive while in other cases, new entry barriers can be created. Thus, it is strongly advisable for organizations, businesses and even industries to actively lobby for workable legislation when the government proposes change.

The impact of legislation on the marketing environment

Some positive impacts on the marketing environment can be engendered by legislation. These include:

◆ **The facilitation of desirable social change:**

  ◆ Regulation sets norms of acceptable behaviour, alters behaviour, promotes change and can influence attitudes and perceptions.

  ◆ Legislation in the areas of equal pay, equal opportunities and sex discrimination has underpinned increasing female participation rates in the labour force and rising proportions in higher managerial positions.

◆ **The correction of market failures and assurance of fair markets:**

  ◆ Legislation to deter restrictive practices and the exercise of monopoly power produces workable competition to the benefit of consumers in the form of lower prices and wider choice.

  ◆ It provides a framework of control that accounts for externalities and acts on the structure of incentives to limit choices or protect certain interests.

◆ **Encourages further knowledge:**

  ◆ New environmental standards provide opportunities and rewards. These therefore encourage research into problems like the greenhouse and ozone effects.

  ◆ Regulation can provide leverage on the pace of change.

  ◆ Regulations can also influences the direction of effort by promoting or prohibiting certain technologies.

◆ **Reassurance of the public at large:**

   ◆ The introduction of more stringent vehicle tests. For example tests can reduce safety concerns and improve emission standards.

   ◆ Complex regulations cover food safety and new product development, encouraging greater consumption.

It should be noted that the beneficial impacts of regulation are both difficult to measure and more likely to be understated. Businesses may also tend to be more inclined to measure the costs of compliance and to a much greater degree than society will be inclined to calculate the benefits of such compliance.

One critical area for future legislation or industry self-regulation will be the Internet. There is increasing concern about the rise of fraud, junk mail or spam and the potential intrusion to privacy. Thus, while the Internet offers tremendous potential as a global marketing channel, it must also be monitored and controlled within acceptable codes of conduct that apply world-wide. Failing such supranational action (e.g. by the WTO), the full benefits of the Internet may not be achieved if negative customer and corporate attitudes build up.

Activity 7.9

Can you think of specific areas of concern for your organization with regards to the Internet?

Evaluate how legislation could help address these concerns.

Appropriate action

The relevant legislation that impacts on businesses in general and marketers in particular is clearly illustrated in Figure 7.2.

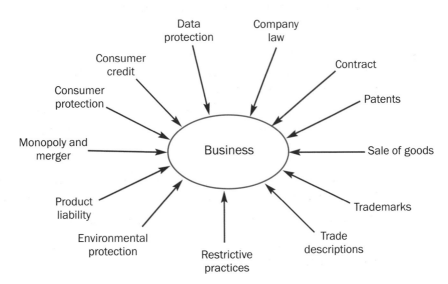

Figure 7.2 The potential impact of legislation on a business

Management needs to formulate a coherent policy in respect of legal matters. Primarily, management must seek to avoid liability under the various laws and regulations that affect the organization. This includes establishing policy guidelines and processes to ensure that at least minimum standards are attained. It also requires a policy regarding whether to take legal action against others and, if so, in what circumstances. This may involve competitors infringing patents (as in the case of multimedia products where copies are available at a fraction of the cover price very soon after release), or bad debts, or even a libel action against environmental activists maligning the company product.

In all but the simplest of cases, an organization should hire professional legal advice and representation. The law is extremely complex, not least where precedents are involved. Lawyers may deal with out-of-court advice and small claims, such as recovery of bad debts, and specialists will probably be retained where highly technical matters are concerned. This said, government departments such as the Ministry of Trade can also offer advice to businesses. Trade organizations such as the Institute of Hospitality also offer legal advice to its members.

Notwithstanding, a number of considerations need to be taken into account:

◆ The expensive nature of legal actions.

◆ The effect of actions on the company image.

◆ Longer-term interest in ongoing business relationships may incline companies to tolerate some situations rather than resort to law.

◆ Business contracts should therefore ideally include the means of resolving disputes: for example the use of mediators or arbitrators.

◆ Regulatory agencies may be content with assurances over future standards.

◆ Voluntary codes may be preferred to regulation and legal processes:

  ◆ These are standards of practice all businesses in the industry are expected to follow.

  ◆ They are difficult to enforce and may be replaced by law if widely ignored or flouted.

  ◆ The UK retailers have agreed on a code to promote Internet retailing.

◆ Industrial tribunals are quasi-judicial bodies used for cases of unfair dismissal, discrimination and related matters. To avoid liability in such cases, a business must ensure that it meets all its obligations by establishing the required internal policies and procedures and monitor their operating effectiveness: for example, by adhering to verbal and written warnings prior to dismissal of employees.

◆ Smaller companies are often exempted from certain legislation because of the high costs of compliance: for example employee protection.

Exam hint

Improving your performance

You have now undertaken over three-quarters of the syllabus.

Are you attempting the end-of-unit questions while the material is fresh in your mind?

It is advisable to review activities and questions answered again at a later stage so that you can gauge your knowledge and ideas as your confidence and understanding of the subject grows.

Study tip

The syllabus requires you to achieve a general understanding of the influence of legislation on marketing. Detailed and specific knowledge of statutes or cases is not required. However a broad grasp of their implications on marketing is not only expected but necessary if you intend to be able to demonstrate your understanding of an assessment of the marketing environment.

Exam hint

There will not be specific questions on, say, the finer points of contract law, but there may be general questions on the current legal position of the consumer and the possible scope for future legislation.

Fair trading and the consumer

Study tip

The remaining section of this unit provides a brief appreciation of the main English legal areas impacting on the marketer. Non-UK students should please relate these points to their own national legal context.

Contractual relationships

Contract law is the legal cornerstone regulating exchanges between buyers and sellers. Without a contract, there is no direct relationship between the parties and hence no rights and obligations. A contract, in effect, exchanges promises. The buyer may promise to pay a certain sum of money in exchange for a specified product or service.

A contract comprises a number of elements. These include:

- **Offer** – Whether by word or deed, it is legally binding on the stated terms.
- **Acceptance** – Must be voluntary and genuine on both sides.
- **Intent to create a legally binding contract** – Most commercial contracts assume this.
- **Consideration** – Something of value is exchanged for it to be enforceable. For example, cash could be exchanged.
- **Capacity** – Parties must have the capacity to make a contract for it to be binding.
- **Legality** – Contracts are deemed illegal if an existing law is contravened.

Activity 7.10

Key skills – Interpreting information

Make time to study the 'terms and conditions' attached to products or services supplied by your company.

Compare these to the elements outlined above.

Alternatively, study those you have to agree to when making a major purchase (e.g. an 18-month contract for a special mobile telephone rate).

Exam hint

If you are a non-UK candidate you have the option of relating your answers to the UK or your own country's legislation.

If you decide to select your own country, you must familiarize yourself with the equivalent legislation. You should strive to achieve at least the same level of exploration as encompassed within this coursebook.

Remedies for breach of contract include injunctions and award of damages. Any award will only be to compensate the injured party for damages incurred. All reasonable steps must be taken to mitigate the extent of the damage sustained.

Activity 7.11

Key skills – Critical thinking and reflection

A small painting and decorating company is confronted by difficult judgements where a customer challenges an invoice by claiming that the work done was not performed as specified or agreed.

If the sums involved are small, is it worth the time and effort involved to take the case to court?

Given the highly technical issues in judging whether a contract has been satisfactorily completed, is the risk of an adverse judgement worth the considerable legal costs involved?

What of the impact on the image of the company if it is seen to be taking its customers to court over relatively trifling amounts, not to mention the need to retain the goodwill of large customers in the longer run?

Activity 7.12

Key skills – Collecting information

An effective method of extending your knowledge of the special difficulties confronting the sole proprietor or small business is to talk to them directly.

Survey a cross section of such businesses you have dealings with.

Ask them for their three greatest legal challenges.

Protecting the consumer

This area of the law has grown incrementally in recent decades.

Since the Fair Trading Act 1973, the British consumer has enjoyed the protection afforded by the Director-General of Fair Trading (DGFT). In effect, the Director-General of Fair Trading is like a 'consumer watchdog'. His or her role is to gather information on the activities of suppliers, identify those detrimental to consumers and recommend action to be taken. This covers terms and conditions of sale, selling and promotional methods, packaging and supply as well as payment methods.

A permanent Office of Fair Trading (OFT) provides a pool of expertise and experience in consumer affairs and represents a considerable deterrent to dishonest traders. As a statutory body, it can deal with suspected abuses as they arise and prosecute actions against persistent offenders on behalf of the public. It has recently been given new powers to clamp down on loan sharks and the advertising of charge rates.

Local authorities are responsible for most of the day-to-day enforcement of consumer protection legislation and their knowledge in areas such as weights and measures, trade descriptions and trading standards are complementary.

Insight

The recent scandal in Italian football was as much about fair play as fair trading. Having just won the World Cup, Italy's top clubs were found guilty of match fixing after the exposure of a pyramid of corruption throughout the $6 billion industry. Penalties were severe, especially on the league champion Juventus.

Areas where consumers require positive assurance of the good faith of suppliers are discussed in the following subsections.

Assurance on labelling and description of goods

Acts govern how food can be stored, described and sold. Accordingly:

◆ It is a criminal offence to falsely describe goods or services offered for sale. This applies to physical features and fitness for purpose.

◆ Similarly, prices must not be misleadingly stated.

◆ Quantities and contents in pre-packaged foods must comply with the stated amount. A current issue in this area is the labelling of genetically modified foods.

Insight

Such assurance was most certainly absent on counterfeit vodka containing brake fluid and other poisons that killed over 50 Russians over a two-month period.

Ironically, demand had been created due to a new government excise system that made the genuine product too expensive for ordinary consumers.

Assurance on quality and expected performance

◆ Goods supplied must be as described by the vendor and be of merchantable quality. This means fit for purpose with due regard to price and description for instance.

◆ Similar protection extends to services where consumers have a right to expect that such services will be delivered with reasonable care and skill, within a reasonable time and at the agreed price, or at a reasonable charge where none was previously agreed.

◆ Any consumer contract clauses intended to limit liability in this respect are void.

Assurance of safety

◆ Acts regulate the sale of dangerous goods in terms of availability, packaging and labelling. Retail chemists, for example, must be under the supervision of a registered pharmacist.

- Product liability is where a manufacturer can be shown to be under a duty of care to the customer to avoid acts or omissions that could reasonably be expected to harm.

- A 1985 EU directive makes producers, including importers into the European Union, liable for product defects. One important defence is where the state of scientific and technical knowledge at the time was such that the producer might not have been expected to discover the defect.

Restraint of objectionable sales promotion

- False statements in adverts are an offence under the Trade Descriptions Act.

- 'Voluntary' codes have evolved as a means of more flexible regulation. Health warnings on cigarettes are the result of voluntary agreements between the government and the industry concerned.

- The Director-General of Fair Trading may seek an injunction (i.e. a court order) from the High Court to prohibit false or misleading advertisements. However, the All England Club were unable to promote a more professional dress code at Wimbledon in 2006 due to Adidas winning an injunction that there must be 'no restriction on the size of logos'.

Assurance on fair payment terms

- Acts provide comprehensive protection and enforcement on consumer credit and hire agreements. This includes disclosure of the real interest rate (the % APR) and total to be paid plus full awareness of transaction rights and liabilities (e.g. the right to repay debt early).

- A 'cooling-off' or cancellation period also applies if the credit agreement is drawn up away from the business (e.g. at home). This is intended to help reduce the consequences of high-pressure sales techniques.

Question 7.5

Key skills – Applying business law

Recent scandals over misleading selling of pension policies and endowments, payment protection insurance (PPI), upfront commissions and individual voluntary arrangements led to Abbey being fined £0.8 million.

How do you think legislation responded to the fact that recent surveys suggested that 30 per cent of life insurance policies are terminated within two years at considerable financial loss to the consumer?

Since customers now have the option of settling a dispute with the supplier concerned or going directly to the authorities, it has forced even reputable companies to review and formalize their trading standards. Companies who have prospered by guaranteeing quality, no-quibble exchanges and refunds must now codify their excellence in practice.

Insight: Farepak Christmas

Fair Trade protection means very little to the 150,000 low-income savers for Farepak Christmas hampers who expected their hampers in time to celebrate Christmas 2006. They have collectively lost £40 million in weekly subscriptions when the parent company went bankrupt. They stand to receive just 16p in the pound despite a £2 million donation by HBOS, the company's bank. Although the company attempted to blame the bank for rejecting five proposed rescue packages the fault is clearly poor management. The shares were suspended in July 2006 but the company continued to take customer subscriptions until mid-October. It took advantage of a regulatory loophole allowing it to treat members' money as cash flow. The scandal has prompted a much needed inquiry into savings regulations.

Companies may increasingly be forced to resort to law to counter the damage to their brand image from adverse media coverage. Individuals, often supported by pressure groups, are now bringing more civil suits on a 'no win-no fee' basis.

Insight

The State of New York has filed a lawsuit against major gun manufacturers accusing them of 'public nuisance' because of failure to introduce safety controls. Smith & Wesson was absent from the suit because it had voluntarily agreed to subscribe to a new code of conduct.

Voluntary industry codes are clearly a way forward for businesses:

◆ These are both encouraged and monitored by the authorities.

◆ Voluntary codes are tailor-made to the needs of the industry concerned. Therefore they can be effective if gaining membership is conditional on compliance.

◆ Normally, such codes include a means of resolving disputes with customers through a process of arbitration.

◆ They may also provide a marketing edge to participating companies where the customer looks for a mark of service or quality assurance.

While legislation is unlikely to be reversed, it can be viewed positively in defining the areas within the boundaries of the law and voluntary good practice where the firm has the 'freedom to market'. It has:

◆ The right to market any product given compliance with health and safety requirements.

◆ The freedom to price products provided it does not conspire or discriminate.

◆ Discretion in the marketing/promotional mix adopted providing it does not mislead or misrepresent.

Laws therefore represent freedoms as well as constraints; rights as well as obligations.

Question 7.6

Key skills – Using information

The tobacco industry has been under considerable pressure in recent years arising out of the habitual nature of consumption and its links to cancer, heart and respiratory diseases. The Canadian health authorities introduced a hard-hitting advertising campaign depicting images of diseased hearts and cancerous tumours on cigarette packets and a written warning that they lead to sexual impotence. Despite premature death for one of every two users, the tobacco industry has vowed to fight them in court.

If there is a proven link to these diseases, why do you think that although there is a rising trend of consumption among younger age groups, smoking has not been made illegal?

Why do think major retailers, who profess to be socially responsible, continue to sell such products?

Summary

In this unit, we have dealt with important aspects of the closely-linked political and legal environments for marketers. In brief, these are:

- The political process is complex but pressure groups and some processes are available to help business lobbies.
- The political environment is a source of uncertainty.
- The authority of supranational bodies, like the European Union, must now be accounted for and monitored.
- The media plays an important part in setting the political agenda.
- The influence of lobbyists is less readily detected but of greater potential importance to business interests.
- The law represents an evolving framework to reflect societal concerns and enable commercial activities to take place in a fair but effective manner.
- There can be an underlying tension between the needs of business to innovate and deploy resources efficiently over time, and the health, safety and equitable treatment of various stakeholders.
- Quasi-legal means of regulation, such as codes of practice, serve an important function.
- There are many considerations to weigh before an organization initiates legal proceedings.
- Failing to comply with at least the minimum legal requirements is bad business.
- Being forced to resort to law is potentially costly and time-consuming.

◆ Systems must be in place, plus staff suitably trained, to ensure compliance.

◆ Proposed legislation should be monitored and a proactive approach adopted.

◆ Employee legislation can highly likely reduce marketers' flexibility and freedom of action.

◆ Voluntary codes, if perceived as fair to stakeholders, can be cost-effective.

◆ Marketers can use superior legal standards as a source of potential competitive advantage.

◆ Compliance with exacting consumer legislation may put foreign competitors at a disadvantage and help create an image of 'best practice'.

Further study and examination preparation

Given the number of questions on the paper as a whole, you cannot guarantee that a full question will always come up on this environment. There is a strong likelihood, how-ever, that it would form at least part of a question, particularly within a section A case as seen below.

The examiner will be aware that candidates come from different national backgrounds and will set questions accordingly. The focus is much more likely to be on the impact of this environment on marketing than on political or legal specifics. Question 4, December 2005 provides a very good example of the level of generality expected.

Extending knowledge

Palmer A. and Hartley B. (2006) *The Business and Marketing Environment*, McGraw-Hill.
Chapter 11: The Legal Environment.

Palmer A. (2002) *The Business Environment*, McGraw-Hill.
Chapter 9.

Other suggested reading

Jobber D. (1998) *Principles of Marketing*, McGraw-Hill, 2nd Ed.
Chapter 5: The marketing environment.

Websites to scan

www.gold.net/ifl is an index of legal resources.

www.open.gov.uk is a gateway to a diversity of government information.

www.ft.com.

www.economist.com.

www.the-times.co.uk.

www.Europa.Eu.Int for information on the European Union.

www.labour.org.uk.

www.conservative-party.org.uk.

www.parliamentlive.tv features political debates.

Practicising past exam questions

Please see Question 1d, June 2004 on the CIM website, www.cim.co.uk.

Please see Question 4c, December 2004. For specimen answers go to www.cim.co.uk.

Please see Question 6d, December 2003 on the CIM website, www.cim.co.uk.

Please see Question 2, June 2004 on the CIM website, www.cim.co.uk.

Please see Question 4, December 2005. For specimen answers go to www.cim.co.uk/learn-ingzone.

Please see Question 1a, and b, December 2005. For specimen answers go to www.cim.co.uk/learningzone.

Please also look at the specimen paper to familiarize yourself with the new exam format.

Unit 8

The technical/ information environments

Learning objectives

This unit examines the all-embracing effects of the technical and information environments, as well as the dynamic and complex nature of change itself. By the end of this unit, you will have:

◆ Understood the role of business in the development and diffusion of new technology (3.8).

◆ Appreciated the factors driving and limiting change in the technical and information environments (3.8).

◆ Recognized the importance of monitoring and forecasting technical change (3.8).

◆ Explored the role of information, and the significance of the information revolution (3.8).

Study guide

We live in a technological society whose effects impact on all aspects of our life. Our working environment is particularly subject to such influences. Many major transformations have occurred in recent years in the majority of industries and occupations. So too have our means of transport, how we shop, the ways we spend our leisure time, how we learn, the houses we live in and the way our health is monitored. Only our sleeping habits seem relatively unaffected, although new drugs, insulation, bed designs and environment control are affecting the lives of many in this respect too.

Internet-based UK retail sales are said to have been rising by 50 per cent a year. Meanwhile multi-tasking teenagers now absorb more than 8.5 hours of media a day through watching TV, surfing the web, communicating on their mobile phones and e-mailing.

Marketers must strive to understand the changes taking place and be sensitive to new developments. The necessary skills must be acquired and continuously updated so that change is prepared for and promoted. Individual and organizational survival may depend on it.

Much of marketing is underpinned by technology. For instance:

◆ Advertising relies on communication technology.

◆ Logistics relies on transport technology.

◆ Market research relies on information systems.

Study tip

While this unit will concentrate on general themes, you will be left with the responsibility to find relevant applications from your own experience and reading.

Bear in mind that the technological environment is an area which can generate a diversity of examples as context for examining its impacts.

Exam hint

The examiner may require you to select technologies of your own choice and discuss their effects in context.

Relevant applications from your own working environment are more likely to interest and impress the examiner, as it shows that you are seeking to relate your studies to your work situation.

Make sure, however, that you have a working knowledge of technical terms affecting the work of marketers.

Definition of terms

The successful development of new technology comprises a number of distinct stages.

These are portrayed in Figure 8.1.

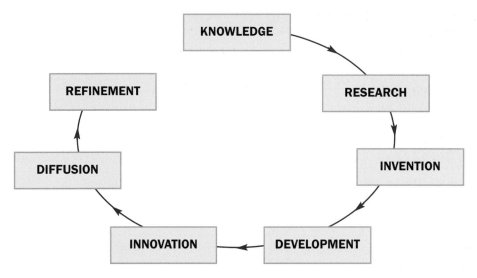

Figure 8.1 Stages in the development of new technology

The state of technology is a function of resources and of the knowledge and skills needed to use such resources. Technology can achieve a variety of functions. For instance:

◆ New technology enhances production possibilities, thereby satisfying consumer needs and wants more efficiently and effectively.

◆ Technology enables more and better value-for-money products and services to be produced with given resources.

◆ Technical change is the result of changing resources, increased product and process knowledge and the accumulation of applications experience.

◆ **Knowledge** of the current state of technology is the foundation upon which research takes place. New ideas and developments in sciences often form the basis of advance and synthesis in other areas.

◆ **Research and invention** is the generation of new ideas, or improvement of existing ones.

◆ **Development** is their useful application to specific products or processes.

◆ **Innovation** relates to the commercial exploitation of a development or new idea.

◆ **Diffusion** refers to the rate of its adoption through the potential target population concerned.

◆ **Refinement** exploits the full potential of the technology. It often forms the basis of product differentiation in the growth and early maturity stages of the life cycle.

Continuous innovation provides the fundamental drive and dynamics of capitalism. It is probably the only strategy that, if successfully implemented, will ensure an organization earns excess profits over time. New products that more effectively satisfy customer needs and wants will increase profits. Cost-saving processes and technologies will also have an effect on profits. However, only by re-investing profit back into the maintenance of techno-logical or design leadership can companies ensure long-term profits. Competitors will seek to enter the market and imitate the innovations, but they will always be aiming for a moving target. Similarly, anything that inhibits this creative process may threaten the economic growth and development of the system.

Activity 8.1

Identify some examples of innovation that have had a direct or indirect effect on your organization.

Insight: Laptop prototype

A cheap, wind-up laptop was unveiled at a UN summit in Tunis. This green machine should cost as little as $100, and will be sold on a non-profit basis to the developing world. Powered with a hand-crank, it has a seven-inch screen for basic word-processing and Internet use. It uses a flash memory rather than hard drive like that in a digital camera. It comes with a Wi-Fi radio transmitter designed to knit machines into a wireless mesh so they can share Internet connection. It would offer a self-learning route out of poverty for the young of the developing nations.

Characteristics of technology

The technological environment is not just about hi-tech and computers, it is all-pervasive. Some advances are relatively simple, such as 3M's adhesive message pads or Wrigley's non-stick chewing gum. Others such as the new packaging technologies or Siemen's wafer-thin TV screens are more complex. Still others, like the Dyson computer-controlled vacuum cleaner or dual tub environmentally friendly washing machine, may transform aspects of housework and therefore have significant effect on the way we may live.

Question 8.1

Key skills – Problem-solving

◆ Give six examples of industries with big cost-saving innovations over the last five years.

◆ Can you think of any industry that had no significant cost-saving innovations?

As one of the major macro-environment variables, technology has a breadth of impact that affects all the others. Stock market crashes, for example, can be triggered by automatic computer 'sell signals'. Increased employment of married women has been facilitated by the development of labour-saving, controllable and convenient technologies in the home.

This has led to a culmination of 'intelligent domestic environments' controlled by information and communication technologies (ICT). The politically complex Eastern Europe and China have altered beyond recognition as their citizens have become exposed to a wider world through telecommunication channels. Still, perhaps the biggest potential impact of all arises from our increasing dependence on technology.

Insight: The Achilles' heel of technology

The millennium bug may not have materialized but computers are susceptible to viruses and glitches that may involve significant costs.

Over 6500 viruses were detected in the first half of 2004 alone. One e-mail virus was unleashed in the Philippines and within hours had swept through Europe and America attacking five million machines and causing an estimated $1.5 billion of damage.

More recently, the Sasser and SoBigF variant of the Blaster virus each infected almost one in five computers causing serious damage to many companies. The e-mail, entitled ILOVEYOU, had an irresistible selling proposition that paralysed thousands of organizations. Disrupting both US and UK legislatures, it demonstrated the vulnerability of open electronic systems to cyber warfare. Only a few incidents come to light because companies are anxious to protect their image and share prices.

The first mobile phone virus called 'Cabir' detected in 2004 was able to steal phone numbers and text messages. Computer problems have also plagued government agencies. For example the £500 million IT system installed at the now defunct Child Support Agency is still not providing payments to thousands of single parents even two years after installation. Similar fears surround a £15–30 billion project for centralizing 50 million NHS patient records (original estimate of £6.2 billion) following the problems at iSoft, the lead contractor.

With most of the world's essential systems controlled by computer software, such vulnerability brings the risk of critical failures in air traffic control, nuclear plant, medical facilities, defence and the financial systems. Furthermore human error can also not be eliminated. The problem might be a simple 'fat finger' as in the case of a Tokyo trader who sparked panic selling when he inadvertently sold £1.6 billion worth of shares in a company worth £50 million.

System breakdown can easily lead to economic disruption and probable public disorder. It is clearly important that organizations plan for such contingencies since the potential commercial damage arising from some form of computer breakdown is almost inestimable for businesses such as travel companies or financial institutions.

Meanwhile hackers continue, almost as a matter of course, to gain access to 'secure' facilities despite massive investments to improve systems effectiveness. How long will it be before their services are co-ordinated by revolutionaries or rogue governments? Such thoughts should at least prompt the marketers to audit their information systems, ensure backup is in place and that manually-based contingency plans are potentially operational. Similar actions should be encouraged in the value chain.

Other threats arise out of the unregulated development of genetic modification which could allow the spread of even more deadly viruses than that of the species-jumping AIDS contagion. Even global air travel poses threats as demonstrated by the in-flight spread of infectious diseases and cases of malaria reported near British airports, caused by mosquitoes having hitched a lift on the aeroplanes arriving from malaria-infected regions. Severe acute respiratory syndrome (SARS) was spread by this means leading to widespread panic and disruption especially in Hong Kong where retail sales fell by 50 per cent as shoppers stayed at home. The final official death toll of 800 was statistically insignificant compared to the millions who die each year from common diseases. Yet it produced reaction out of all proportion to the probable risk. This signals global vulnerability to a modern plague such as avian flu, which like Spanish flu in 1918, could kill millions while paralysing commercial activity. Official measures in the face of such pandemics would include travel restrictions, compulsory health checks at ports, closure of schools and workplaces, together with the banning of large public gatherings.

Insight: The human genome project

A collaboration of scientists from the UK, China, France, Germany, Japan and the US enabled the understanding of the precise genetic code that makes us human. This is arguably one of the greatest scientific breakthroughs in human history. It heralds the era of biomedicine that corporate biotech giants can exploit. Genomics may indeed open up enormous commercial opportunities for biotechnology companies.

Potential advantages of this project include:

◆ More rapid development of treatments for cancer, birth defects and common ailments. (This includes development of Delta 32, the so-called 'survival gene', which is one of 10 mutant genes carried by those who are resistant to AIDS.)

◆ Life expectancy could be doubled by curing those previously incurable with personalized body repair kits.

◆ Despite private sector involvement, this may be freely available to everyone.

◆ Genetically-based antidotes to Spanish flu-like viruses are now being developed.

◆ Health care with gene therapy could revolutionize medicine.

◆ Cancer could be viewed as a chronic but manageable illness within 20 years.

Potential drawbacks of this project include:

◆ The temptation to engineer human beings (i.e. designer babies).

◆ Possible invasion of privacy (discrimination against genetically disadvantaged).

◆ Insurance/loan restrictions on individuals known to be susceptible to disease.

◆ Companies may demand genetic tests before recruiting new employees.

◆ Lack of ethical guidelines (i.e. human cloning from harvested embryo stem cells).

◆ No guarantee that genetic testing will be affordable by the poor (healthcare gap).

◆ Excessive control over life-saving diagnosis/treatment by firms patenting genes.

- Development of 'white plague' diseases genetically engineered to kill specific bio-logical groups.

- Development of GM primates for medical research viewed as unacceptable.

Technology progressed in phases until industrialization, when a marked acceleration occurred. Technology has always extended human capabilities and industrialization revo-lutionized this extension. Just three or four generations have seen transformation from agri-cultural through industrial to service economy. The pace is not slackening as developed countries enter a post-industrial information/communication society.

Several factors have acted as the basis or even catalysts for this increasing pace of tech-nological progress. They include:

- Technology is inherently a primary driving force for social change.

- Computer, telecommunications and mobile media technologies are increasingly con-verging.

- There is a high and rising proportion of communications and information technology ownership:

  - For example by the end of 2007, 2 billion people, or a third of the world's pop-ulation were said to own a mobile.

  - Up to 50 billion e-mails were said to have been sent each day during that year.

  - This is expected to double by 2015 with mobile phones becoming increasingly cheaper, simpler and more likely to be carried around than even laptops. Market forces are already putting them in the hands of even the poorest in the world.

- Development of digital superhighways unifying information, communication and mul-timedia:

  - Mobile phones are becoming integral to our lives with location software, multi-media and messaging readily used. Internet access on mobile phones frees us from our PCs.

  - Linking wirelessly to the Internet will transform the mobile into a device that is always on, always connected and with the speed and applications of a lap-top. One-sixth of the world's population is now online.

- Credit transfer rather than cash-based society, with Switch/Visa cards the global cur-rency.

- A diverse, decentralized and differentiated society is increasingly made up of knowl-edge workers.

Question 8.2

Key skills – Using information

What products and services that are taken for granted today did not exist 30 years ago?

Think in terms of organization.

Think in terms of your personal life.

The role of business

Business is the main conduit by which science and technology impact on society. Most change is incremental and progressive in nature, but breakthroughs can and do bring sudden and dramatic change requiring organizations to monitor their technological environment more closely than others.

If a rival succeeds in achieving a technological advantage, it is a much more significant competitive edge due to the time, difficulty and resource commitments required to counter it.

Insight

The Japanese microprocessor-controlled timepieces severely impacted on the Swiss watch industry. More recently Amazon.com and Direct Line severely affected traditional booksellers and insurance brokers respectively. Similarly, DVD prices fell by 80 per cent in the five years from their original launch, while non-digital cameras are no longer sold in major retail chains.

There are also potentially survival-threatening risks as discovered by the successful bidders who gambled €110 billion on 3G licences to develop high-speed mobile networks with Internet access. It has been calculated that recouping start-up costs would require revenues of €500 from each individual in Europe. With competition from rival technologies such as wireless LAN, the investors are already beginning to write off a large part of their investment.

Exam hint

Improving your performance

Information communication technology has been an area of weakness for some candidates. Since the CIM explicitly require candidates to develop information and communication technologies (ICT) skills, you should make every effort to be as up to date as possible.

The drive to seek innovation depends on a number of factors. These can be summarized as follows:

◆ **Stage of the product or technology life cycle:**

    ◆ The introduction and growth stages of any new invention will be characterized by creative product innovation that will continue until the technology matures.

◆ **Size of the firm:**

    ◆ Studies suggest that small firms provide a more productive climate for invention but lack the resources and organization to diffuse it quickly and effectively.

    ◆ Small firms tend to specialize and the risk of failure is high.

    ◆ Even large firms must beware of over-commitment. Remember the case of Airbus 380.

◆ **Nature of competition in the market:**

    ◆ The drive is powerful in fragmented markets but the resources and size to exploit them successfully are often lacking.

    ◆ Financial resources and control of the market exist in monopoly but innovation would make previous investments obsolete.

    ◆ The ideal combination is in concentrated industries, where size and market share are combined with considerable rewards if innovation can undermine rival product offerings.

    ◆ Interdependence, therefore, ensures that each company will maintain considerable research and development capability as a precaution against rivals obtaining such an edge.

◆ **The pace of change in consumer tastes:**

    ◆ If the existing market is static then new products supplied to new consumers in new ways may be the only strategy for growth.

Activity 8.2

Scan advertisements in newspapers, magazines and the trade press or even TV and Radio or the Internet for products or services which are being marketed on the basis of their technical sophistication or innovativeness.

Evaluate how the said products and services are being promoted.

What are the technical imperatives?

We live in a technological era where knowledge and expertise confer status and societal approval. The Japanese and other Asian economies are admired for their ability to emulate and improve on Western technology. In turn, European and North American companies have invested staggering sums in robotization and computer-integrated manufacturing in an effort to counter the lower wage costs and team-based productivity of Asian competitors. *Global competition* is clearly one of the imperatives forcing technological change.

The rate at which technology and competitive strategy dominance occur within different industries depends partly on the stage of evolution of that industry and partly on the type of technological and competitive forces at stake within and outside organizations in that specific industry. Advances in one sphere of science provide the catalyst for a dozen others in adjacent fields where time, money and human expertise provide the only limits to the expanding frontiers of knowledge.

Key marketing skills: using information and communication technologies (ICT) and the Internet

With wireless connections to the Internet now established within many business environments, an estimate of over one billion plus Internet users worldwide does not look unreasonable. America's 200 million online consumers spent £120 billion on the web during 2004–2005 while nearly two-thirds of UK share transactions were online. These figures have more than doubled since then. However access in some developing countries is still inhibited by limited Internet service provision or unreliable and costly phone links. For example, China has been described as the 'world champion of Internet censorship' by the pressure group, Without Borders. However, even with the show of co-operation shown by service providers like Google and Yahoo, technical loopholes are there for dissidents to exploit and undermine the controls.

Depending on the competence of the user and the power and speed of the recipient's computer, the potential uses of the driving technology that the Internet represents are as follows:

◆ An international source of information:

  ◆ Most constraints of national boundaries are eliminated allowing students, researchers and companies of all sizes to access vast databases.

  ◆ The amount of information stored on computers has doubled since 1999.

  ◆ The majority of US car buyers are said to consult the Internet before deciding what to buy.

  ◆ Gucci provides a sophisticated information-only fashion site whose high definition pictures make it one of the most elegant virtual arcades. Users can click on highlights of the latest collection and essential accessories.

◆ A communication tool:

  ◆ It offers a value-added and cost-saving means of promoting corporate or brand image.

  ◆ It can also help manage the supply chain by linking subsidiaries and stakeholders to a private intranet.

  ◆ It enables true interactivity between the customer and the organization. Communication is facilitated from the organization to the customer as well as from the customer to the organization.

- ◆ **A channel for marketing activities:**

  - ◆ E-marketing tools include: brand websites, online advertising, online events and seminars, advergames and online games, viral marketing (i.e. online networks and communities), online contests and sweepstakes, e-sampling and e-coupons and e-mail marketing.

- ◆ **A channel for e-commerce:**

  - ◆ Several benefits are driving the development of digital information super-highways. These include: speed, convenience and interactivity.

  - ◆ These channels are capable of delivering a myriad of business services using text, sound and vision, both business to business and business to consumer.

- ◆ **A major engine of potential future job growth:**

  - ◆ In particular with regards to technical skills.

- ◆ **An escape into virtual reality:**

  - ◆ Second Life is one of the hottest places to be in cyberspace with over one million subscribers signing on for a virtual world where you can create a new identity, buy a home, start a business and form relationships.

Activity 8.3

Can you think of any other potential or actual uses?

Voice over Internet protocol (VOIP) is a disruptive technology par excellence in that it undermines existing technology, and creates difficulties for companies like BT who are dependent on the status quo. In this case, its offer of free calls using networks based on Internet technology (e.g. Skype) implies a downward spiral for the existing trillion-dollar traditional telephone market.

The initial dynamics of e-commerce has found its focus on B2B applications (80 per cent of global revenues), where the scope for savings through electronically-driven purchasing, stock management and logistics is greatest. Business-to-consumer growth is fastest in product or service groups where e-commerce produces comparative advantage in ease of transactions and value-added online service, for example book extracts and CD demos. The customer's familiarity with a certain product or website is another critical determinant.

Despite ongoing concerns over the security of e-transactions and profitability of dot-com stocks, the future still looks very positive. It should be remembered that there were as many as a thousand US car producers in the 1920s yet only a handful survived. Of the Internet companies launched since 1995, precedent would suggest that over 90 per cent will end up as nearly worthless. Only the fittest survive in this intensely competitive process, but initial diversity normally ensures that all alternative approaches to the market are explored. For example, e-Bay, after 10 years, is now a global giant with 150 million users and $40 billion of traded goods a year.

E-commerce transfers key functions to the customer who must access the site and complete online ordering procedures whereas the website must passively wait for a customer to click on it. Traditional marketing therefore has a critical role in organizations like Amazon and AOL, since millions must be spent in advertising and sales promotion to get their sites and services known. It is not sufficient for traditional companies to add a website as an electronic equivalent of their sales brochure. The whole business must be redesigned to exploit the cost-saving and communication-easing properties of this forcing technology. It must be open and responsive to shifting demand in an online environment where the pace of change is fast, competition is fierce and entry barriers low for an innovative organization.

Despite the fact that Internet mania unquestionably propelled technologically-driven tactics to almost spiral out of control in the 1990s, the initial enthusiasm associated with the World Wide Web appears to have slowed down. This is due to the fact that companies are increasingly realizing that hype is not enough. Consequently, they are increasingly thinking about long-term strategy and evolving relationships. Although this new cautious approach to the Internet could have engendered a reduction in investment in Internet-based technologies, market intelligence reports such as Mintel and KeyNote provide evidence of the contrary. In fact, they reveal that expenditure on the Internet and its peripheral technologies has been steadily growing. It is anticipated that Internet services, rather than hardware, will be the main growth area. Such statistics not only implicitly confirm that strategies are increasingly becoming technology-driven in the context of the dynamic environment afforded by the Internet, but they also shed light on the growing role of peripheral technologies such as intranets and extranets.

Fifty-year innovation cycle

Another technology imperative may be provided by this long-wave cycle. It has been observed that economic development since the Industrial Revolution has progressed in 50-year cycles based on successive clusters of critical innovations, for example textiles, steam power, railways.

Businesses initially responded to downturns by cost-cutting and retrenchment, but as depression continued, were forced to consider more radical solutions to declining sales and profitability. A new wave of innovations was created as businesses became prepared to risk resources on new or existing inventions; for example, digital communications, biotechnology, lasers and nanotechnology are currently state-of-the-art.

Activity 8.4

Key skills – Collecting information

Taking these state-of-the-art technologies, brainstorm as many product innovations based on them as possible.

Can you think of any product or process innovations that represent fusions of these separate technologies?

Creative destruction

Innovation can be viewed as the source of creative destruction whereby dominant established firms and industries based on mature technology are challenged by new firms, using substitute products or processes, often from a different industry. Such entrepreneurial initiatives constantly threaten to shake up monopoly and oligopoly market situations, keeping them attentive.

Technological change is part of the *dynamics of capitalism*. The expectation of new and improved products is part of the culture and businesses are rewarded when these needs are satisfied. Businesses are motivated by the need to survive and make profits. Governments are motivated by the need to promote economic growth. People are motivated by the need to improve their lives. These needs in turn produce a drive for technology that feeds on itself, rippling through society as one advance triggers another in a technological *multiplier-accelerator effect*.

New generations of products are introduced with progressively reducing lead times, stimulating the planned obsolescence of current offerings. The power of appeal conferred on pioneer consumers and the requirement for followers to keep up through emulation reinforces the treadmill of constant novelty and change.

Question 8.3

Key skills – Using information to contribute to the strategy process

What are the opportunities and threats of technological change as far as the business environment is concerned?

What steps can the business take to minimize the threats and maximize the opportunities?

Microprocessors

Microprocessors became by far the most important technology of the late twentieth century. Despite a progression from valves and transistors, it represents a technological leap in innovation. This has allowed the enhancement of design and performance in a diversity of products and services.

The technology has also significantly contributed to the efficiency and effectiveness of communication systems, information services and other infrastructures (i.e. computerized traffic signals and electronic-based road-pricing systems to relieve congestion).

Microprocessors both extend and increasingly displace a wide range of intellectual and intuitive skills. In effect, it constitutes the most rapid and dramatic industrial change in history. It is still proceeding rapidly with the latest generation chips manufactured by Intel.

Characteristics include reliability, robustness, speed, cost economy, dependability and accuracy. When applied to manufacturing processes, these characteristics have led rapidly towards the development of computer-integrated semi-automated plants. These are small, self-organizing systems that learn from their environments as well as from their experience and adapt accordingly. The limits of power and performance that can be packed on a chip are, however, being approached, although alternatives include parallel processing and even DNA-based 'living' computers.

Question 8.4

Marketing skills – Interpreting information

Suppose that an unusual electrical storm unaccountably disrupted the workings of all microprocessors that have ever been produced.

What do you think would be the immediate effects on the following:

◆ A motorist?

◆ A household?

◆ A marketing department?

Exam hint

Working with others

As the examination or assessment deadline approaches, you must manage time effectively and use your marketing skills of working with others.

You will probably need the help and support of your family, your partner and your boss in these critical days.

Don't leave the preparatory work until too late, thus creating overload on you and those around you.

The technological diffusion process

The rate at which firms adopt innovations is the rate of diffusion and involves cost and risk as well as the prospect of return.

As can be seen in Figure 8.2, the process is similar to the product life cycle.

Factors that determine whether the rate is rapid or slow include the following:

◆ **Profitability** – The larger the innovation's impact on critical costs and revenues relative to what is currently the case, the more rapid the diffusion.

◆ **Deterrence** – This measures the consequences of *not adopting* the new technology. If a serious loss of sales is likely due to the superiority of the new technology then diffusion will be rapid as producers are forced to jump on the bandwagon or go out of business.

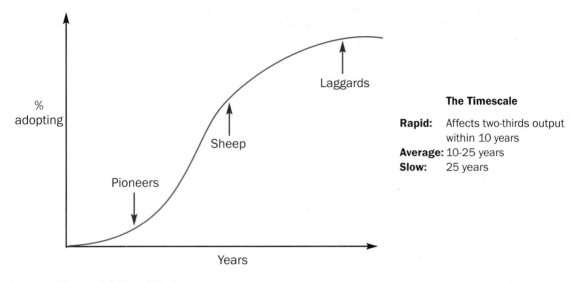

Figure 8.2 The diffusion process

◆ **Scale of investment** – Hi-tech generally means high financial outlays on both hardware and software aspects of operations. If internal resources and access to external risk capital are limited this will slow diffusion.

◆ **Market structure** – An oligopoly is probably the most effective structure for rapid diffusion. Multinationals have the organizational ability and resources to achieve this globally.

◆ **Characteristics of the new product or process.**

◆ **Potential range of applications** – More means greater profitability and sales potential.

◆ **Environmental acceptability** – Actual/perceived impacts of a new technology affect diffusion due to legislation/liabilities that arise. For example, rising costs of verifying drugs have halved Research and Development spend in 20 years.

◆ **Change agents:**

　◆ For a new idea to succeed in a business, it needs a champion to challenge the status quo and persuade decision-makers of the need for change.

　◆ Much is invested in the current way of doing things and resistance to change occurs among management, customers and the workforce.

　◆ The government is often a change agent through initiatives to support innovation or willingness to place orders.

The Internet is attractive as a channel of commerce due to a variety of reasons. Consequently the fast pace of its diffusion has been associated with a variety of factors. These include:

◆ **Low entry cost:**

　◆ Gaining a web presence (i.e. a website) costs a fraction of the price associated with entering the market-place.

◆ **Rapid return on investment:**

  ◆ Within months, this can be achieved. Eliminating paperwork and providing customer support can be very speedy.

◆ **Investment is flexible:**

  ◆ Open networks and standards support trading relationships with a multitude of business partners.

  ◆ Switching costs are minimized compared to specific electronic data interchange (EDI) systems.

◆ **Connectivity and ultra-rapid communication:**

  ◆ E-mail links save time and cost in communication, order and delivery confirmation.

◆ **Meets information needs:**

  ◆ Use a browser to identify market trends, competitors or opportunities.

  ◆ Information is readily available 24/7.

◆ **Critical mass:**

  ◆ Attracts more users/providers of business solutions.

  ◆ Stakeholders are increasingly connected.

  ◆ International participation by governments reinforces user confidence.

◆ **Technology-driven innovation cycle:**

  ◆ Established companies/start-ups create new opportunities.

  ◆ This can attract new entrepreneurs/reinforcing the virtuous circle of development.

◆ **Spin-off from other applications:**

  ◆ Although a high number of sites is associated with pornography, it is still an adequate channel for business.

  ◆ Many organizations have completed their operations in the market-place with online presence and activities.

Technological transfer

Another aspect of diffusion is the transfer of technology from:

◆ Basic research to practical applications

◆ Military/aerospace applications to industrial products

◆ Hi-tech to consumer goods and services

◆ Developed to less-developed countries

Fundamental new technologies originate from a number of sources, including universities and research institutes, military establishments, government agencies as well as businesses.

Technology may be licensed from the inventor, or leading-edge multinationals may be encouraged to locate subsidiaries and transfer expertise into an economy. For example, American and Japanese computer companies were attracted into central Scotland, providing opportunities for third-generation indigenous companies to prosper.

Many developing countries rely on foreign multinationals in banking, oil, textiles or food processing to provide a similar driving force to their industrialization process. Such companies often form an integral part of a dual economy that brings much-needed exposure to cutting-edge technologies, management methods and information technology.

Question 8.5

If your organization has invested large sums in developing a revolutionary new product or service idea, what actions would you advise it to take in order to generate maximum returns?

Technological forecasting

Successful managements have always kept a cautious eye on the pace of change in both their own and adjacent industries. However, this has tended to be a defensive outlook on the danger of being overtaken by substitute technology rather than with a proactive intention to achieve competitive advantage. Governments can be significant catalysts in starting the research process through grants, subsidies and tax allowances, particularly when external security or national competitive advantage is being sought.

A technological forecast should be the foundation block of long-term plans, based on effective collusion between the technologist, designer and marketer. This is necessary to achieve the essential balance between creating and satisfying the needs of the customer. Alternative or substitute product or process technology is more difficult to forecast than core technology, and requires a more qualitative analysis.

Exam hint

Improving your performance

Make short notes on other technological developments in each element of the marketing mix:

◆ Product (i.e. design cycles)

◆ Place (electronic data interchange (EDI) systems with intermediaries, satellite tracking of vehicles)

◆ Promotion (interactive TV, computer-designed samples, database marketing)

◆ Price (bar code scanning, electronic pricing)

The progress of technology can be assessed in three distinct ways as follows:

◆ **Evolution of the current technology:**

  ◆ Existing trends are identified and then extrapolated.

◆ **Morphological:**

  ◆ These types of analysis explore technological opportunities by systematically defining the basic features of current technology, identifying the known alternatives to each and then looking for feasible alternative combinations. For example, a car can have alternative fuels: petrol, diesel, battery, gas, solar, hydrogen fuel cell. It can have alternative body materials: steel, plastic, aluminium, fibreglass. It can also have alternative braking systems: friction disc, air, cable, and so on. These three components can then be combined in different formulas to produce alternative concept cars (hybrids are also possible, e.g. diesel/battery).

  ◆ This provides a fresh perspective on customary technologies and a fruitful basis for brainstorming feasible product alternatives. One recently developed example is Glasphalt, which resembles traditional road resurfacing materials but contains 30 per cent crushed glass. This conveniently combines recycling, reduced extraction of new materials and diminished pressure on landfill sites.

◆ **Scenarios:**

  ◆ These provide broader views of the future and insight into more diverse developments.

  ◆ For example they offer alternative personal transportation systems, such as microlight aircraft systems. Equally, developments in interactive video, teleworking and virtual reality might make many such journeys unnecessary in future.

Insight: Google talk?

Google, the Internet search engine floated onto the stock exchange in 2004, was valued at $100 billion despite profits of only around $150 million. Responsible for half of all web searches, the company was only formed in 1998. Used by over 100 million customers per month and processing 3000 searches a second, it generates its revenue from ads placed on the website. Launched with a higher rating than even Microsoft, the company does not, however, have an equivalent monopoly. So with open standards any rival with a better search engine will cause its customers to switch. Thus, the company is launching Google Talk, a web-based open platform for voice calls and messaging. This will pose a direct threat to closed networks operated by Yahoo, AOL, BT and MSN. It is not yet clear how Google will make money from this free service.

One key concern with Google is privacy since every search is logged, stored and traceable as are gmails. The latter enables the company to place targeted ads.

Several processes must be conducted by organizations if they are to achieve a consistent appreciation of technological factors. These should include the following:

◆ Potential impacts must be identified, not only for the industry itself but also for channel intermediaries and end-users.

◆ Feasible technologies are then screened to remove improbable options due to cost and environmental safety for instance. A timescale should be determined for the remainder. This might be done by drawing on the expertise of practitioners in the field.

◆ Possible technologies must be set against marketing forecasts of what the demand will be.

◆ Timing is also critical in achieving innovative success and avoiding technological failure. An innovation which is right for its time must not only have all the requisite technical building blocks in place but also receptive users, with the need, income and strength of preference to demand it in profitable volumes.

◆ Unanticipated consequences should also be considered. These include impacts on current methods as well as complementary effects. There were also 21 billion items of junk mail in 2006, up 66 per cent on 1997, of which 40 per cent are not read. In spite of increased attempts for precision targeting, these figures are expected to rise.

Question 8.6

Key skills – Using information and problem-solving

These were all in the future, five years ago. Where are they now?

◆ A chequeless society

◆ Virtual reality holidays

◆ Drive-by-wire electronic systems for congestion-free 'intelligent' motorways

◆ Speech-responsive computers

◆ Windscreen maps in cars

◆ Digital signatures for transactions

Study tip

You should keep abreast of any developments that potentially improve the marketer's performance.

Information technology and marketing applications

In this section, the main applications for marketers arising out of information technology will be briefly summarized.

The logical order to consider this is from product conception through to after-sales service and eventual disposal. German companies like Mercedes, for example, must now maintain computerized records of all vehicles sold so they may be tracked and accounted for in compliance with recycling legislation.

◆ **Product development:**

  ◆ This is based on forecasting and the use of various databases to assess customer requirements and tastes.

  ◆ Marketing research is facilitated through computerized analysis packages such as SPSS.

◆ **Product design:**

  ◆ The time needed for product development is increasingly falling due to the flexibility, versatility and time-saving afforded by computer-aided design, manufacture and engineering.

  ◆ Virtual reality offers further possibilities in terms of computer simulation.

  ◆ New cars which once took seven years from drawing board to production line now take much less than half that.

  ◆ The main implication is a shrinking maturity and decline stage for many products combined with a geometric expansion in models and parts numbers.

◆ **Mass customization:**

  ◆ This is enabled by computer-integrated manufacture.

  ◆ It offers an opportunity for marketers to deal not only with population segmentsbut with individuals. Technology now allows for marketing solutions tailored to the needs of the specific customer.

  ◆ The car buyer can specify the precise design components they wish to be incorporated into their new vehicle and the computer will do the rest. The ultimate expression of the marketing concept is to provide a bundle of benefits honed to the complete satisfaction of a customer's specific needs and wants. However until information communication technologies enables it, this was only economically feasible for high value B2B or for high-end products or services tailored to B2C customers (e.g. tailor-made finishes of a Bentley – oak dashboard, leather seats and steering wheel).

  ◆ E-commerce businesses do not have to content themselves with product differentiation in broadly segmented markets. Tesco is able to customize its grocery deliveries to specific households. Levi Strauss utilizes in-store booths to yield a three-dimensional laser measurement that can be downloaded to the computer-controlled cutting machines for a perfect fit.

◆ **Database marketing/management:**

- ◆ This is a necessary corollary to mass customization and precise targeting.

- ◆ Information communication technologies allow the marketer to capture, store, process, mine and communicate vast amounts of information through customer databases. This opens up massive opportunities for the far-sighted marketer to anticipate and identify their changing needs as well as build and maintain effective relationships.

- ◆ Database marketing involves the fusion of information gathered on actual and potential customers and competitors. This can be used to screen, then select and target potentially valuable customers as well as precisely create and target the marketing mix offered. The aim is to achieve maximum profit contribution in the light of operational and financial constraints.

- ◆ Significant benefits accrue from the ability to use previous purchasing history to identify requirements and target promotional messages accordingly.

- ◆ Such cost efficiency and targeted effectiveness is essential to the direct marketers using mailshots, telesales, personal selling or e-shopping.

- ◆ Database analysis is more versatile in identifying new or pre-existing lifestyle segments. Profiles of cruise customers or hotel clients can be used to identify and target the like-minded for mailshot purposes.

◆ **Manufacturing operations:**

- ◆ Integrated computer control delivers flexible manufacturing systems.

- ◆ Although cost efficiency used to demand large production runs due to long set-up times, these can now be altered in seconds.

- ◆ Waiting time is eliminated and small batches produced at near-equivalent speed and cost enable rapid response to changing demand, for example promotional initiatives.

- ◆ The spread of the just-in-time (JIT) stock control concept from Toyota has also transformed volume production and distribution systems. Responsibility for delivery of parts onto the shop floor, as they are required for assembly or processing, is transferred to suppliers allowing work in progress to be minimized. Similar systems have been adopted by retailers, in order to extend range, maximize selling areas and maximize sales per square metre.

◆ **Warehousing and logistics:**

- ◆ Service levels for fast-moving consumer goods are improving through the automation of storage and handling facilities.

- ◆ Maximum availability and rapid response to changing tastes and preferences now require a system which can instantly capture changing sales trends and translate them into the necessary supply and stock adjustments.

- ◆ Electronic point of sale (EPOS) systems using product bar codes and increasingly sensitive laser readers provide the sales data for stock control, sales analysis, automatic replenishment or new-order placement.

- More and more businesses are linked through electronic data interchange systems to facilitate such automatic computer linkage.

- Linked systems allow interrogation of stock and order status together with the transmission of marketing mix details.

- Delivery now often takes place around the clock to avoid traffic congestion and conform to Just in Time requirements.

- Computerized transportation programmes plan optimal routes while satellite beacon systems and radio links allow flexible redeployment.

- Digital technology similarly eases the delivery of a wide array of home services and offers opportunities for targeting customer segments.

◆ **Point of sale:**

- Electronic funds transfer at the point of sale (EFTPOS), from the customer's to the retailer's account (e.g. Switch), has transformed the potential of retail outlets on several levels, namely: additional sales area; demand-related stock ranges can be frequently replenished; speedier and more accurate customer transactions are engendered; shorter queues; improved cash flow; enhanced security.

- Some supermarkets have introduced automatic processing enabling customers to scan and pay for purchases without supervision (e.g. Sainsbury's).

- E-shopping orders will be picked in-store and either delivered directly to the home in an agreed time frame or collected from the store.

- The Internet is transforming direct marketing as well as improving customer relationships through accessible websites.

Insight

A microscopic speck of dandruff recently led to the arrest and conviction of a violent armed robber 10 years after the incident. The case, which relied on advances in DNA technology, prompted a national advertising campaign featuring the case by shampoo makers, Head and Shoulders, using the slogan 'Don't get caught with dandruff.'

Exam hint

Please see Question 5, December 2004 (www.cim.co.uk).

Plan out an answer as you work through the remainder of this section.

Future applications of technology

From information to commerce

E-commerce is facilitated through the World Wide Web. The World Wide Web is an open global system that allows access to anyone in the world with a computer, modem and telephone line. Companies initially provided informational and promotional web pages that users could surf for information and advice. These soon became interactive and increasingly enabled two-way communication flow; from the organization to the customer and from the customer to the organization. Increasingly websites have shifted from merely providing information to enabling interactivity and two-way communication. Increasingly websites enable not only marketing but also the sale of products and services. All that is most often requested are a credit card details and a delivery address. This has prompted many traditional retailers to follow suit to offset any decline in traditional channels and even more importantly to reap the opportunities offered by this added channel for sales and marketing.

Insight: The marketing challenge of e-business-to-business

Few challenges have received more attention than the growth of B2B exchanges on the Internet. The pace was set by Covisint, the consortium of car producers led by General Motors, Ford and Daimler Chrysler and followed by a succession of other industries, including aerospace, chemicals, energy and food. The three automotive manufacturers alone annually purchase nearly $250 billion of supplies.

Horizontal trading exchanges cater for buyers and sellers across different industries with common requirements, for example paper and office furniture, with savings averaging 20 per cent.

Vertical exchanges, including all contributors to the supply chain, are far more important and offer dramatic scope (up to 40 per cent) for rationalizing procurement in fragmented industries such as construction. Predictions suggest these will grow exponentially until virtually all chains are covered.

B2B trading exchanges are as old as commerce itself, but online globally organized trading exchanges between buyers and sellers using tenders, auctions and combined buying on the Internet is revolutionary. This can massively improve procurement for organizations of any size.

E-procurement through trading exchanges uses technology but is still founded on relationships between suppliers, intermediaries, market makers and buyers. Software compatibility is obviously important but trading standards are critical, particularly given the dramatic collapse of online energy traders like Enron. Intermediaries are emerging to provide assurance on the identity and trustworthiness of global Internet partners, but fees and possibly costly experience may be required before such networks can be established.

Despite its high rate of diffusion, not least due to the deterrence factor, there is considerable resistance to moving operations online. Its introduction may require cultural and organizational change due to the high risks of displacing existing supply relationships with electronic trade for materials and components crucial to the quality and success of its product offering. Notwithstanding, these supplies may offer the greatest potential for significant savings for buyers and sellers alike.

Opportunities may include:

◆ Collaboration with business partners can become more effective and flexible.

◆ Competitive advantage can be provided for the whole supply chain.

◆ An underlying strategy to enable the whole business to exploit the opportunities can be provided.

◆ Capturing and analysing information can help an organization improve its spending patterns and buying power.

◆ Small firms can secure deeper discounts from pooled purchasing (i.e. acquiring economies of scale).

◆ Operational efficiencies reduce transaction costs in the move from paper-based to web-based transactions: minimum administrative effort and more effective use of staff time.

◆ Improved feedback makes suppliers more responsive to customers' needs. The ability to meet their expectations is improved. However turning data into information and in turn converting information into knowledge requires not only effective data collation and filtering but pertinent data mining.

◆ Potentially global network of suppliers widens choice and reduces cost.

◆ Smaller suppliers can be integrated into supply chains at minimal cost. Sometimes all that is needed is a computer and connection to the Internet.

◆ Balance of power shifts to buyers due to price transparency. The bargaining power of buyers can be greatly increased.

As with every business challenge, there will be winners and losers as the e-business-to-business concept diffuses and matures across a succession of industries. The marketer must strive to ensure that their organization harnesses the potential benefits of this new form of electronic collaboration between business partners. The era of global electronic trading is upon us and many businesses will succeed or fail according to their competence in exploiting its potential. Indeed just having online presence is not enough.

Internet banking is rapidly increasing its share of the overall market along with travel bookings, share trading, tax returns and other financial services. These are rational rather than personal purchases and are therefore well suited to the Internet. Many organizations are offering incentives to encourage online usage, for example high interest Internet accounts or zero postage on goods supplied. Employment in the area of digital media, including home shopping and other Internet-based services, are predicted to expand exponentially over the next few years. One less recognized benefit is the recent development of Universal Network Language by the UN, which provides intelligible translations for the first time. This software will soon allow users to surf websites written in any language (currently 80 per cent are English), thereby encouraging the global dissemination of languages such as Mandarin Chinese, Swahili, Bhasa, Urdu and Russian.

On the downside, there are concerns regarding confidentiality, privacy of data, consumer protection and the fact that the Internet potentially puts children at risk and spreads bugs and viruses very rapidly. Successful attacks on large US websites, by flooding targeted companies like Yahoo and Amazon with fake messages, undermines trust in the Internet (600,000 reverted to phone and branch banking in the first eight months of 2005). If hackers can close down key sites, what might become of the e-commerce revolution? This has increased interest in open source software such as Linux, which unlike proprietary architecture such as Microsoft, allows anyone to get involved in removing bugs and improving the system. Governments are also increasingly concerned over the global diversity of legal regimes where products may be bought and the corresponding evasion of sales taxes. These issues may only be resolved by international agreements.

Question 8.7

Marketing skills – Presenting information

Identify four product areas where you think restructuring due to the rise of Internet sales has been the greatest so far.

Identify four product/service areas where you think the impact of the Internet sales has been the least.

E-commerce may, however, by eclipsed in potential scale by 'closed system' e-business-to-business. Influential factors include the following:

◆ Developments in telecommunications (digitalization) and the ability to overcome the problems of incompatible computer systems opened the way for electronic data interchange systems (EDI) on a dramatic scale.

◆ While final consumers may still prefer the impulsive attractions of the high-street store, B2B sales and service should expand without limit.

◆ Legal difficulties over the status of electronic documents have also now been resolved through the development of trading data communications standards.

◆ Benefits of automated systems arise in terms of:
   ◆ Improved accuracy
   ◆ Lower stockholding
   ◆ Accessibility
   ◆ Lower costs when transmitting credit/delivery notes
   ◆ Price/product information
   ◆ Availability status

◆ Expansion in such networks offers scope for improved relationships and customer service levels:
   ◆ Most industry supply chains are expected to follow the example of banking and vehicles in automating a high proportion of total transactions.
   ◆ The ultimate objective is indeed to keep downward pressure on costs and prices.

Teleworking

Alternatively known as telecommuting or the electronic cottage, this involves working from home or the car using telecommunications and computing equipment. Occupations expected to figure in future plans are data entry, sales or marketing work and computer-based activities.

The main benefits of teleworking include:

◆ Flexibility and reduced cost

◆ Convenience and a solution to travel problems

◆ Retain skilled staff and employ those with care responsibilities

◆ Space saving and ability to work in preferred locations

◆ Savings in travel time

◆ Greater productivity due to fewer distractions

◆ Reduced stress levels

◆ The falling cost of technology

◆ Increasingly versatile broadband equipment

◆ An attractive option as office and non-labour costs soar in urban centres

Global telecommunications also allows teleworkers from less-developed countries to compete with high-wage equivalents in affluent nations. Telework may be processed in India or Pakistan at one-tenth the cost of London.

There are, however, a number of drawbacks to teleworking:

◆ Management and communication difficulties, for example lack of face-to-face meetings.

◆ Social isolation and losing touch with the organization.

◆ Technical and security problems may also arise.

◆ There may be difficulties in ensuring quality control .

◆ Many employees find work discipline a difficulty.

◆ Employees may miss the creative spark provided by fellow workers. Employers have therefore often taken steps to increase social integration by providing more communication with colleagues, managers and customers.

Question 8.8

Key skills – Problem-solving

Technology now allows a vehicle to be fitted with the equivalent of the electronic office (laptop, fax, carphone modem, etc.)

With regard to marketing, do you think the future lies with mobile or residential teleworkers?

Justify your reasoning.

Teleconferencing/electronic meetings

Meetings can take up to two-thirds of a manager's time making its productive use essential, especially where clients are involved. If, say, ten people meet for an hour then the average contribution of each is just six minutes. Since 20 per cent of those present tend to speak 80 per cent of the time, the contributions of the majority are actually restricted much further.

Technology cannot substitute for brain power and human interaction but it can vastly increase contributions. Given appropriate technology (an ISDN line can support broadcast video conferencing, text and graphics), participants can type their ideas and contributions onto a network of screens and react to those provided by the others. Brainstorming and evaluation can take place quickly and anonymously, if necessary. Videoconferencing using broadband technology allows participants to see one another while videophone developments will enable the customer and the telesales operator to see each other. Texting and e-mails also appear to be transforming the nature of personal relationships with actual 'dating' taking a back seat to the mobile phone.

Virtual companies

These organizations have few or no assets but they provide services through the use of third-party contractors. They will use computers to co-ordinate activities. They are expected to become increasingly successful in the future.

Insight: National identity cards

Tony Blair declared in 2005 that identity cards were an idea whose time had come. The cards holding biometric verification data and costing over £90 each will be phased in from 2008 as passports are renewed. It is argued that they will counter 'identity theft' and terrorism as well as enforce security and immigration controls and check eligibility for public services. However, the validity of all of these claims has been challenged. Many see this as a costly move (£5.8 up to £18 billion estimated by the London School of Economics) towards a surveillance society, where the technology is error-prone and the advantages contentious. Every use of the card will leave an audit trail of personal information and yet the government's record in IT projects and their security leaves much to be desired.

The Dutch are planning to compile a vast database of their citizens in order to identify troublemakers and reduce crime. From 2007, a 'cradle to grave' file will be created for every baby with details of family, health, education and brushes with the law added as they grow up.

Another card-based idea being considered is for each citizen to be issued with a personal swipe card that records their annual carbon allowance. Points would be deducted for purchases of flights, fuels and domestic energy consumption. Those exceeding their allowance could trade for units from those who had under-spent. The annual allowance would be progressively reduced to encourage efficiency and economy and cut emissions. Despite complex administration and fairness issues this could be more equitable and empowering than traditional methods of regulation.

Mobile or wireless marketing

Mobile marketing includes all activities that are conducted to communicate with customers through the use of mobile devices. Activities could include:

◆ Promoting products or services.

◆ Providing information or offers. Typically marketing communications consists of commercial or sales promotional messages sent to mobile phones.

◆ Permission based SMS or MMS (multimedia messages).

◆ Messages can consist of digital pictures, audio tunes and even videos.

Advertising or WAP/i-Mode advertising is expected to be more productive and useful to marketers in the near future. Several factors will enhance the use of this communication channel for marketers. For instance:

◆ The mobile phone is a very personal device. It is much more personal and engaging as a communication channel than e-mail.

◆ One mobile for one user: therefore precise targeting could be more easily achieved.

◆ Accompanies the user: therefore a message can reach a potential customer anytime and anywhere.

◆ Faster dissemination of information: instant delivery of message.

◆ The recipient can respond straightaway: therefore lead times are greatly reduced for marketers.

◆ Wider reach than email: more people own mobile phones than are connected to the Internet.

◆ Production costs to marketers are negligible: cheap and effective but can be intrusive and irritating. Therefore Opt-in (*permission based*) or Opt-out options are recommended. Opt-in strategies are equivalent to permission marketing. Consumers must give explicit consent to receive messages. Clear opt-out options could also be included.

◆ Excellent for reaching young adults: however, older customers are also catching up.

◆ Internet advertising can be viewed by internet connection of mobile device.

◆ Time-based information and location-based information as well as real MMS are increasingly becoming more widely available and popular: location-based advertising message; wireless coupon for a restaurant in your town/neighbourhood.

◆ Precise targeting can be facilitated.

◆ It is expected to create 5-10x more click-through rates compared to internet advertising messages.

◆ As messages including alerts, SMS messages and voice calls are proactively sent out to users. A push strategy is followed: However, caution should be used and this tool should ideally only should be reserved for companies that have an established relationships with the specific customers or companies that have obtained permission to push communications to wireless users. It should be noted that privacy issues imply that push strategies are seldom used to acquire new customers. Instead messages are shown to users when they are navigating WAP or wireless sites and properties.

◆ As mobile phones primarily favour a two-way communication, companies should incorporate two-way aspect in any of their M-campaigns.

◆ This is still a novelty. As there are less companies using this form of communication, there is less clutter.

Push and pull strategies should both display some characteristics. For instance:

◆ They should be carefully targeted. A message must be of real value to each recipient.

◆ They should be relevant to customer. This will improve customer response and acceptance. Every useless message leads to an intrusive connotation.

◆ The user should never feel this is costing them airtime.

◆ The sender must be clearly communicated.

Digital (broadband) television

This development is expected to transform the nature of advertising and promotion and possibly supplant the PC for e-shopping. Digital or interactive television encompasses a range of properties. For instance:

◆ Viewers can interact with programmes and use interactive services:

◆ Already there are a range of interactive services being broadcast. These include: T-government, T-banking, T-commerce and T-learning.

◆ This technology is interactive. Therefore it enables the following:

◆ E-mail

◆ Home shopping

◆ It also allows significantly more programmes and on-screen peripheral information to be broadcast.

◆ It also offers much more flexibility:

◆ For instance, a viewer only has to click on an advert icon for more information.

◆ Access will be by customer choice giving the ability to view in real time or to customize viewing.

◆ This arguably leads to more audience fragmentation.

◆ It can also lead to the enhanced ability to target audience segments with adverts and direct response promotions.

◆ The ability to filter out adverts may lead to more programme sponsorship:

◆ For example, shopsmart.com sponsored mid-evening movies.

◆ This medium offers new possibilities for marketers:

◆ With one push of a button, customers have accessed to a variety of communication messages.

◆ Consequently, marketers will be able to move buyers through the entire buying process. Viewers can view information, then they can ask for extra information about specific products or services. When they receive coupons or samples, they may even buy products or services via this channel exactly in the same way that transactions are conducted online via the Internet. In turn, the behaviour of customers can help marketers understand the attitudes and indeed the behaviour of specific target groups.

◆ Tailored interactive advertising content such as the following can be used:

◈ Programmercials (programme sponsorship)

◈ Messages on the electronic programme guide

◈ Linking with t-services

◈ Bannering during programmes

◆ The technical properties of this medium can help marketers to build relationships with viewers. Subsequently, offerings can be precisely tailored and precisely targeted.

Automated customer handling

Automated customer handling is increasingly being used within the marketing environment and within businesses. However, some fundamental criteria are associated with this. These include:

◆ Customer relations management has been transformed through personalized mass communications.

◆ These can facilitate the building of trust and long-term relationships with stakeholders.

◆ Touch-tone phones and automated exchanges direct customer contacts through a series of prompts (and classical music) to the right person in the right department or an automated message.

◆ FAQ is a convention used in such systems and on the Internet, to compile a list of 'frequently asked questions' and responses typically encountered by an organization.

◆ Basic information can be acquired quickly, providing savings for both parties.

◆ The technology offers several advantages to customers. For example:

◈ It can make customers feel closer to the organization.

◈ It can help increase customers' participation.

◈ It can also help improve service levels.

◆ However, as with most information technologies, care must be taken to minimize or avoid alienation arising from the lack of human interface and other potential frustrations.

◆ It remains to be seen whether the development of videophone technology, with pleasing digitalized 'human' images, will resolve some of these problems:

◈ Such an image has already been programmed for potential use in news-casting and weather reports.

◆ Similar developments for direct marketing and customer care cannot be far behind.

Resistance to change

Technology has been the major engine in the development of mass affluence yet there is always some resistance. From the Luddites, who smashed the knitting frames that threatened their livelihoods at the outset of the Industrial Revolution, to the print workers displaced by computer typesetting or coal miners made redundant by cheaper alternate fuels, the outcome has always been the same: beneficial progress may have been delayed but it cannot be prevented.

The short-term impact of technologically-induced unemployment has frequently been considerable, not least on communities dependent on the industry in structural decline. In the long-term, however, there has been a growth in demand for labour broadly parallel to the growth in the labour force.

Process technology has substituted machines for labour to minimize costs but new *product technology* has created employment opportunities. The e-Bay site, for example, has created employment for an estimated 10,000 online traders. Adaption has been difficult, however, because the new jobs have generally required higher-order skills than the ones they replaced.

It is not only employees who resist change, but also consumers, distributors and managers themselves. Changes in method and organization are as readily resisted as in technical processes, although change in one normally requires change in the others.

Question 8.9

Key skills – Problem-solving

Management is about the efficient allocation of resources to match changing consumer needs and wants, yet British management has frequently been criticized for its reluctance or inability to bring about change.

Identify factors that may account for this weakness.

Identify conditions that enable managements in your own country to become effective change agents.

Customers may resist product changes because of several reasons such as:

◆ Out of force of habit

◆ Prejudice

◆ Conservatism born of age

Product revivals may succeed on similar grounds as adults relive their youth or bring their children up consuming equivalent goods and services. Market understandings may also make the business reconsider introducing changes that disrupt competitive relationships.

Change may also be resisted by external forces such as pressure groups, concerned with the impact on the environment. Laws and regulations also constrain what is possible. The Data Protection Act, for example, required that mailing list organizations register and abide with its provisions, so limiting the scope for use by direct marketing businesses. Provisional EU legislation will forbid unsolicited fax transmissions unless prior permission is obtained. This will inhibit the activities of many direct marketers and limit the growth in corporate junk mail.

Question 8.10

Key skills – Problem-solving

Identify some unintended consequences of the following product developments:

◆ The car

◆ The telephone

◆ The television

◆ The CCTV camera

In your opinion, how have these developments changed the nature of marketing?

Summary

In this unit concerning the technological environment:

◆ Some of the main characteristics of technology and its main phases were identified, culminating in the information or communications era, which developed economies are currently entering.

◆ The critical role of business was examined and the factors encouraging innovativeness.

◆ Technical imperatives driving the pace and diversity of technological change were identified and explained.

◆ The diffusion process was explained and the need for technological forecasting emphasized. Sources of information by which a business can keep track of potential developments were outlined.

◆ Various applications to sales and marketing were discussed with reference to the supply chain. Some future applications were assessed including telecommuting and marketing databases.

◆ An exploration of M-technology and digital communication was also offered.

◆ Technological change is very much a double-edged phenomenon.

◆ Its accelerating pace has accommodated rising populations but produced future shock challenges among many seeking to cope with the myriad changes involved.

◆ It has provided convenience through increasingly intelligent products and services but also unforeseen consequences as the effects have rippled through society.

Further study and examination preparation

Technology is an all-pervasive aspect of a business environment that knows no boundaries. Companies of every nationality will be seeking to exploit its potential for competitive advantage. It is therefore likely to be a popular aspect of the macro-environment for examination questions, given its general applicability to all CIM international centres. Expect a compulsory question on the technology area from time to time (e.g. December 2001). However, even on a non technical case there is the possibility of part questions as in Questions 1(iv) and 1(v), June 2006.

Extending knowledge

Palmer A. and Hartley B. (2006) *The Business and Marketing Environment*, McGraw-Hill.
Chapter 5: The Information Environment.
Chapter 12: The Technological Environment.

Palmer A. (2002) *The Business Environment*, McGraw-Hill.
Chapter 4: The Internet Environment.
Chapter 12: The Technical and Information Environment.

Zahra S, Sisodia R. and Matherne B. (1999) Exploiting the dynamic links between competitive and technology strategies, *European Management Journal*, **17**(2) 188-201, April.

Tapp A. (2001) *Principles of Direct Marketing*, Prentice Hall, 2nd Ed.
Chapter 2: The database.
Chapter 3: The customer database: analysis and applications.

McDonald W.J. (1998) *Direct Marketing: An integrated approach*, McGraw-Hill International Editions.

Jobber D. (1998) *Principles of Marketing*, McGraw-Hill, 2nd Ed.
Chapter 5: The marketing environment.

Websites

www.amazon.co.uk as an example of how Internet technology may be harnessed to the provision of innovative customer service.

www.what is.com is a directory of Internet terminology.

www.cyberatlas.com for a business perspective on Internet developments.

www.fpmg.co.uk and www.eyuk.com are consultancy company sites often offering free reports.

For e-business see: http://www.brint.com/Elecomm.htm as a portal and http://www.ebusi-nessforum.com as an Economist Intelligence Unit forum for news, issues and so on. Also http://www1.oecd.org/dsti/sti/it/ec for OECD reports.

Practicising past exam questions

Please see Question 5, December 2004. For specimen answers go to www.cim.co.uk.

Please see Question 6b, June 2005. For specimen answers go to www.cim.co.uk.

Please see Question 5a, June 2005 on the CIM website, www.cim.co.uk.

Please see Question 6(iii), December 2005. For specimen answers go to www.cim.co.uk/learningzone.

Please see Questions 1(iv) and 1(v), June 2006. For specimen answers go to www.cim.co.uk/learningzone.

A new syllabus and assessment will be introduced in September 2008. However, it is recommended that students still refer to past exam papers, as the core syllabus content has not changed significantly. Just as importantly, it is advised that students should also refer to the specimen paper. The specimen paper is intended to help students gather a clear understanding of the new exam format.

Unit 9
Environmental information systems – coping with the challenge of environmental change

Learning objectives

This unit is intended to consolidate your knowledge of marketing information and its use in organizations, particularly in meeting the challenges of environmental change through its application in the strategy and marketing planning processes. By the end of the unit, you will be able to:

◆ Appreciate the complex nature of the marketing environment and how its challenges might best be managed in marketing terms (3.10, 4.1, 4.2).

◆ Understand the role of a marketing information system (MkIS) and the importance of information to organizations (3.10, 4.1, 4.2).

◆ Explain the nature and importance of marketing research (3.10, 4.1, 4.2).

◆ Understand the key problems associated with forecasting change in the marketing environment (3.10, 4.1, 4.2).

◆ Appreciate the continuing impact of information communication technology (3.10, 4.1, 4.2).

Study guide

This concluding study unit focuses on the effective management of the future marketing environment. It deals with Element 4 of the syllabus, Environmental Information Systems, accounting for 15 per cent of the total.

We have already dealt with Sections 4.4 and 4.5 in Units 2 and 4 so now we will consider the remaining aspects of information systems.

317

The first aspect concerns the importance of information and the need for organizations to develop an effective marketing information system. The second introduces marketing research and the benefits it can provide. The third considers key problems in dealing with the dynamism and uncertainty of future change. The fourth surveys the tools and techniques available to the marketer in establishing the nature and significance of the environmental challenge. The final aspect considers the continuing impact of information communication technologies on environmental information systems.

We also consider the all-embracing nature of change. Multi-faceted, and in most cases interactive, change in one part of the system causes reactions elsewhere. It is complicated and turbulent, requiring marketers to understand the complex processes at work and, if possible, be part of the change itself rather than merely responding belatedly to its confusing effects.

This unit draws together the various strands of the marketing environment syllabus and provides focus on all the relevant statements of marketing practice. It is concerned not only with the collection, presentation and effective interpretation of important marketing information, but also with the creative manipulation of that information into a form that is useful for the strategy and planning processes of the organization.

Monitoring the marketing environment

Systems thinking discussed in Unit 1 helps to provide an integrated view of the world. Organizations compete and collaborate with a variety of primary stakeholders and interact as interrelated parts of the wider marketing environment. This environment is subject to continuous change but organizations are also adaptive. This causes them to seek greater understanding of their environment in order to plan or react more effectively.

To be effective the business organization must possess the following subsystems:

◆ **A sensing system** – This is used to access information and appraise developments using secondary sources or market research to acquire sufficient market understanding.

◆ **An information classification system** – This is needed to convert raw data into potentially usable information. Unanalysed facts and figures are converted into information.

◆ **An information processing system** – This gives information meaning via feedback and so on.

◆ **An information database and retrieval system** – This is used to collate and store data and thus is usually referred to as a data warehouse. When required, data mining can be conducted. This stage occurs when data is retrieved to be converted into information and subsequently knowledge.

◆ **A control system** – This helps to establish any deviations from established objectives. Accordingly, tracking, monitoring and evaluation can be conducted. Strategies can be altered if need be.

◆ **A planning and policy-making system** – The decisions are based on choices identified and evaluated by the marketing information system (MkIS).

◆ **A communication system** – This is needed to receive information from internal and external sources. Information also needs to be distributed to relevant parties, decision-makers and stakeholders.

The significance of new business orientations

Although as discussed in the previous units, the strong association between the development of various orientations and the practice of marketing has been established, the understanding of the evolution of marketing as a discipline would remain somehow unclear without reference to additional concepts. In recent years new business philosophies have been proposed by leading academics. Accordingly, the societal marketing concept has been offered as the fifth business concept. Other emerging marketing philosophies, namely corporate social responsibility and ethical marketing, and sustainable marketing, have also been suggested.

The societal marketing concept not only favours the notion that an organization should identify the needs, wants and interests of its target markets and deliver the desired satisfactions more effectively and efficiently than its competitors, but the concept also prescribes that these needs, wants and interests must be met in a way that maintains and even improves the wellbeing of consumers and society in general.

In proposing corporate social responsibility and ethical marketing as an alternative business philosophy, it has been advocated that companies should not only take into consideration their customers and the profitability of their business, but that they should also take into consideration the good of wider communities, local and global, within which they exist.

There is no set theme and no working definition has been agreed upon. Instead, corporate social responsibility and ethical marketing reflect differing perspectives, which are based on perceptions and implementations in companies. Thus, corporate social responsibility (CSR) sometimes implies engagement of non-governmental agencies. Sometimes CSR is equivalent to charitable donations from companies. At other times, it is akin to the treatment of employees. Additionally, it has been said that CSR is a tool for companies to market themselves. As such, CSR is sometimes used to enhance image of brands. At other times, CSR provides a framework which dictates just the right way for companies to behave.

The ethical standpoint or social responsibility position implies that companies expect nothing for their efforts. Instead activities benefit customers, society and the world at large. In direct contrast, as a business strategy, CSR is used to boost a company's self-interest. In the latter case, CSR can help with image refining (as part of public relations activities) or even with achieving return on investment. Consequently, not only is an organization's CSR agenda directly aligned with its vision, mission and objectives, the CSR agenda can also strongly impact the vision, mission and objectives of the company.

Sustainable marketing business philosophy instead argues that companies should not only just revolve around concerns about environmental and ecological issues but just as importantly be concerned about the social, economic and cultural development of society.

In summary, the emerging philosophies seem to advocate that the current challenge to marketing thinking is to broaden the concept of exchange in order to extend the realm of marketing to incorporate the longer-term needs of society at large rather than simply maintain a focus on the short-term pursuit of individual gratification and consumption of individual companies and businesses. Consequently, the short-term focus ultimately centred on gaining market share or profitability favoured in varying degrees by all four of the established philosophies is expected to shift to more long-term objectives, which would revolve instead around society at large rather than on individual companies. This said, it is also important to emphasize that the emergence of social marketing as an increasing trend has been instrumental in establishing the social values associated with CSR. As such, marketers cannot ignore the significance and implications of the newer orientations discussed above.

Insight

Despite the focus within the hotel industry remaining predominantly short-term in terms of sales and occupancy, hotel companies can already increasingly be seen to have been making progress towards the adoption of more environmentally-friendly approaches to operations.

In an attempt to regulate its energy consumption, Thistle Hotels, a hotel group operating solely in the UK, set up energy committees within their business units. The aim of these committees is to identify how possible savings can be made in terms of both energy costs and usage. Accordingly, many of the hotels within the company's portfolio have introduced energy-efficient light bulbs, joined recycling projects for the disposal of glass and paper within the establishments, and have even been striving to reduce the amount of detergents used in the servicing of dirty laundry.

In terms of the wider community, many hotel companies now not only support the UK's government initiatives such as the New Deal Project but also initiate fund-raising activities aimed at offering financial support to selected charity organizations. Although the engagement in such activities may be commendable, it is nonetheless pertinent to also highlight that the motivation of many hotel companies may not merely lie in environmental, societal concerns and indeed corporate social responsibility, but rather revolve more around an effort to reduce their own operating costs and hence increase profitability. Notwithstanding increasing attention is being paid to environmental issues and corporate social responsibility. Although these are still largely self-regulated, increasingly regulations and legislation are being put in place.

The importance of information

To be useful to marketers the collected facts and figures needs to be analysed then present in a pertinent format to the relevant parties. For example, data from point of sale has to be collated, ordered, processed and analysed into a form that is helpful to marketing decisions. Consequently, sales trends can be used to inform future ordering, delivery and stock control. In brief, data collected needs to be converted into information. The knowledge that can emerge from this information is what is intended to help marketers and organizations as well as all parties concerned.

Information, like communication, is said to be the lifeblood of the modern organization. One implication of the proliferation of information communication technologies is the need to learn continuously about marketing information systems and their potential to provide marketers with more and better information.

Activity 9.1

Key skills – Using ICT and the Internet

Brainstorm a list of information communication technologies of relevance to the marketer that you think have already been mentioned in the coursebook so far.

Then check to see how many, if any, you missed or weren't actually there!

Information is also power. However, this power can only be unravelled and harnessed when certain conditions are met. The focus is not on information gathering, since competitors can do that equally well, but on ensuring that the correct information is collected as a first step. Thereafter organizations need to ensure that the information and knowledge engendered is utilized effectively to achieve competitive advantage.

Indeed, information is of limited value unless it meets the following criteria:

◆ Data must be collected from the right sources.

◆ Data must be accurate enough to form the basis of effective decision-making.

◆ Data should be collected at a time relevant to decisions to be taken.

◆ Data should be processed into market intelligence.

◆ Information should be made available to the appropriate people/parties to discuss and act upon as required.

◆ Information should be accessible to key internal and external stakeholders and partners. The resulting information should be distributed to the right business level

◆ Data should be collected, processed, stored and distributed in a timely and cost-effective manner.

◆ The information should be presented in a concise format and to adequate depth. There should be no overload when providing the details appropriate to the decision needs.

There are three crucial stages of database management:

1 Consolidate all the data collected about a customer or organization or what is being assessed into a usable set of information. The automated cleaning of the data needs to be automated to ensure the same level of quality and depth of data input.

2 Analyse the data: at this stage, data is converted into information. The aim could be to target precisely most attractive prospects and to discard suspects who do not meet the profiling criteria.

3 Results of targeting of specific guests must be tracked to determine which customers responded to what campaigns. At this stage information will be converted into knowledge. This step will identify profitable customers. The process will also indicate which promotions and campaigns have been successful for instance.

Exam hint

Key skill – Consolidation of your learning

Have you visited the CIM website and consulted past papers? Have you reviewed the Senior Examiner's comments on these and been attempting sample questions under examination conditions? Have you also consulted the specimen paper?

At this stage, it is all about preparing SWOT and PESTEL and revising theory with relevance to specific cases. This is also part of what you are expected to do with the mini-case study given before the exam during your preparation.

Quality information needs to be collected, processed and communicated for four important marketing purposes:

1   Planning

2   Strategy formulation

3   Decision-making

4   Control

Information from the marketing environment is clearly an important input into the assessment of strengths and weaknesses, opportunities and threats in the strategy process. This requires communication with, and interrogation of external systems as the preliminary to decision-making.

Control, on the other hand, relies on the comparison of feedback on actual performance to planned performance using internally and externally generated information.

Information communication technologies are the primary mechanisms through which change can be managed and the means of providing the necessary information to relevant decision-makers, so ensuring more effective outcomes compared to competitors. Through dynamic technological developments, such as the Internet, teleconferencing, e-mail, intranets, extranets, digital TV and WAP technologies, there are numerous advances to be realized. These include:

◆   Improving connections, dialogues and relationships with important stakeholders

◆   Improving an organization's ability to learn from others and to learn from past trends and patterns

◆   A strengthening bridge of open communication between the organization/its environment

◆   An online view of changing environments through an explosion of secondary sources

◆   Perhaps a new element in the marketing mix, P for processing quality information

◆   Allowing instantaneous customer-focused response to complaints, and so on

◆   Increased speed and cost-effectiveness of research

◆   Readily-accessible communication channels between customers and the organization

Question 9.1

Key skills – Presenting information

In Activity 9.1, you brainstormed a number of information communication technologies and some have been referred to in this section.

What others can you think of?

Can you arrange them into a classification?

Marketing skills: information at your fingertips

Keeping in touch with what is going on in the marketing environment is essential if one is to be able to have a constant assessment of the marketing environment. This has been the traditional means for the marketer to keep informed. However, this may not always be effective in times of rapid change. The information may either come too late or not be available at the time when the decision-maker requires it. The volume of potentially useful data often appears boundless. As information expands, the need to manage it more effectively becomes even more pressing. As identified briefly earlier, converting data into information is a crucial stage. Converting data into marketing intelligence to profitably use the results is even more important. Excellent companies must work more smartly if they are to survive and prosper, and this raises demand for better-quality information to support decisions. Sophisticated databases and data mining procedures are called for.

Marketers need information at their fingertips to manipulate and add value to, just as professionally managed organizations now need marketing information systems. Marketers need not only a personal information system but also a network of business contacts. Building a matrix of stakeholder and organizational contacts is one of the keys to working effectively.

A changing economic structure has shifted the emphasis towards knowledge workers and knowledge-intensive sectors such as financial and public services. Our society is becoming increasingly information-based. Even small firms are adding to the demand for value-added information services from government and consultancies. Mass markets are becoming increasingly fragmented into specialist niches as tastes become less standardized and predictable. Consequently, sophisticated marketing information and analysis is required to take advantage of the opportunities presented.

The explosion in business-focused information is a reflection of these forces. There are 3500 business-to-business magazines in the UK and similar diversity exists in other countries. Collectively, such sources are termed the business press.

The marketing information system (MkIS)

A marketing information system is made up of the people, equipment and procedures to gather, sort, analyse, evaluate and distribute needed, timely and accurate information to marketing decision-makers. This succinctly summarizes the above discussion of the importance of information. Information is now too important to be left to chance and the marketer must ensure that the information needs of stakeholders, of the organization and perhaps even of shareholders are identified, anticipated and assessed as the basis for systematic provision through well-designed systems.

Question 9.2

Key skills – Working with others and collecting information

List the roles of the marketer in formulating an effective marketing information system (MkIS).

Activity 9.2

Key skills – Information search

List the types of information on competitors that will not be available in published sources.

What methods are available to obtain this information?

Information may be obtained from a variety of sources such as: internal records, marketing intelligence or marketing research. This then needs to be processed into a useful form. Then, the resulting analysis needs to be distributed at the right time, in the right format to the right people (i.e. the decision-makers): information on strategies, product developments, planned promotions, future intentions, likely reactions. Methods range from industrial espionage to debriefing former employees to questioning associated stakeholders.

The information that comprises the marketing information system (MkIS) comes from three main sources. These are:

1   **Internal data:**

◆   Day-to-day company activities generate a tremendous amount of operational and control data. These can be processed to assess marketing performance and help identify strengths and weaknesses. The significance of revenue flows, orders and sales records to the 'Price' variable or customer service data to 'Product and Promotion' could be considered as an example.

◆   Such data is available and accessible. However it may be in a form that is better suited to accountants rather than marketers.

2   **Marketing intelligence:**

◆   This refers to the information gathered and distilled through personal information networks.

◆   This tends to cover a diverse range of employees and stakeholders and trade sources.

◆   This may be complemented by competitor research using cross-referenced secondary sources to provide understanding of the evolving competitive environment.

◆   Marketing intelligence reports may also be purchased from specialist suppliers, such as Nielson, KeyNote and Mintel.

◆   Distilling value from such intelligence is a time-intensive but potentially rewarding activity.

3   **Marketing research:**

◆   Marketing decision-makers cannot always wait for the right information to turn up and should take positive steps to identify what they require.

◆   In fact, this information links the customer and public to the marketer and the organization.

◆ Marketing research can be conducted for a variety of objectives. These include: to identify and define marketing opportunities and problems; to generate, refine and evaluate marketing actions; to monitor marketing performance; to improve understanding of the marketing process.

Organizations that have the ability to sense environmental change and proactively respond tend to perform better. Change often signals the need for re-organization and reformulation of marketing strategy, but there is no guarantee of the appropriate response being made in time. This vitally depends on the quality of the available information systems and the degree of management's understanding of the complex and often interacting changes taking place.

Exam hint

Improving your performance

To manage your performance and future on this course, you must manage your information.

How is your folder shaping up?

Have you been processing information unit by unit or does it just contain data?

Have you tested your 'outputs' on your tutor/boss/colleague and used their feedback to fill any gap?

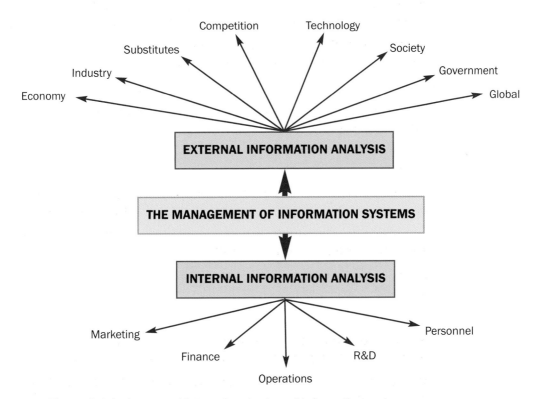

Figure 9.1 An integrated internal and external information system

As Figure 9.1 shows, any business needs an integrated internal and external information system to provide the means for dovetailing organizational and marketing developments with environmental change.

An efficient information system must be able to programme information into the 'corporate memory' of organization members in much the same way as a computer. The objective is to make the information accessible and usable by the relevant decision-maker when required. The power and flexibility of state-of-the-art networked computer database systems now offer this capability and can support the more human networks mentioned above.

Online business information

Databases are revolutionizing management information systems. A database is simply a file of information in electronic form providing ease and speed of access and manipulation. Online means that the database is stored on a remote computer but can be accessed directly by business users through phone lines. Real-time systems mean that they are constantly being updated with new inputs of information, while CD-ROM systems are millions of pieces of information stored on compact discs, updated on a regular basis (see Waterlow Directory: Multimedia and CD-ROM) and accessed flexibly by the computer. The rapid development and take-up by business of fax machines, scanners and intelligent printers is also expanding the potential of such information sources by providing hard copies to remote locations when required.

Some of the main types of databases currently available include those shown in Figure 9.2. By keying in a competitor's name, for example, such systems can search out all available published material. Search engines provide the largest databases with websites such as

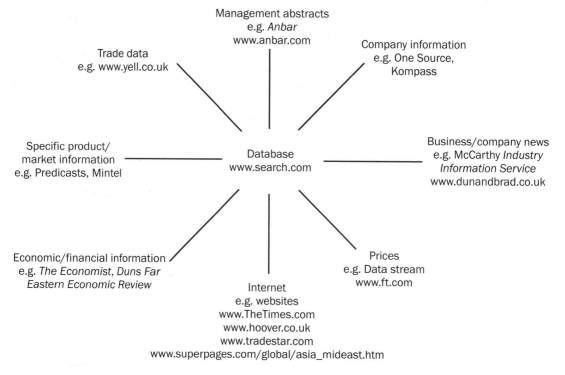

Figure 9.2 Relevant database sources

Google processing over 200 million search requests each day and scanning three billion web pages in an average of 0.2 seconds. This involves a system embracing 54,000 servers, yet it only covers half the World Wide Web. Despite a doubling of information stored on computers since 1999, the majority of human knowledge continues to be stored in books. It also should be remembered that a search engine 'records' what you searched for, and when, so revealing possible motives. Under America's Patriot Act, the US government can compel access if it is deemed part of a terrorist investigation.

Insight

Over the past ten years, the UK has increasingly become a surveillance society in which personal privacy is under threat:

◆ Over four million CCTV cameras – more than the rest of Europe combined

◆ Plans for a biometric identity card

◆ Plans for 'face recognition' software to link CCTV with identity cards

◆ A £14 billion computer system linking GPs, hospitals and medical records by 2014 (this information is readily available to police and security services)

◆ Plans to introduce more intrusive questions in the next census on income and sexuality

◆ World's largest DNA database (3.6 million profiles or 6 per cent of the population) with 40,000 added monthly as a result of the 2003 Criminal Justice Act extending coverage to anyone arrested even if not subsequently charged

◆ Spy-in-the-sky satellites/GPS/road pricing technology to track and store vehicle movements and monitor how we drive

◆ Recording of phone messages, e-mails and mobile phone conversations

◆ On-line purchases, till scanners, loyalty card histories and credit card transactions

Computers, combined with communications technologies, are making business information available at rapidly falling costs. Global knowledge brings global competition as Asian and other emerging economy companies assess the competitiveness of Western markets as a prelude to exports or direct entry.

The benefits of online searching compared to traditional methods may be summarized as follows:

Online features	Benefits
Speed in searching	Time saving
Selectivity in searching	Quality data
Flexibility in searching	Comparative data
Interactive searching	Flexible scope
Data manipulation	Usable statistics
Up to date	Best available data
User-friendly	Will be used
Charge on actual use	Economic access
Professional methodology	Competitive edge

Business database applications should ideally include:

◆ Market research and marketing plans

◆ Marketing presentations and customer relations/communications

◆ Market/sales analysis and sales force co-ordination

Some final words of warning must be noted regarding computer databases as a panacea for marketing solutions. There is a considerable *learning curve* involved in the effective use of such systems and many commercially available databases are expensive to subscribe for any but the largest company. More crucially, the most important information, namely that relating to future plans and developments, is not normally available even on real-time systems.

Similarly, there are limitations on the potential of information and communication technologies (ICT) in allowing the marketer to respond flexibly to the changing product and service demands of the customer. These limitations could revolve around the following criteria:

◆ The need to balance the requirement for information against the cost of obtaining it

◆ The dangers of information overload on managers

◆ Reliance on experience and intuition rather than cross-referenced reliable knowledge

◆ Ultimate dependence on human interpretation/judgement of the information no matter how fully or speedily provided

◆ The reality of physical and psychological communication barriers and resistance

Exam hint

Key skills – Improving learning and performance

The most common cause of poor examination performance is the failure to address the question. To prevent this:

◆   Practise on as many questions as possible.

◆   Conform to the format and context requirement

◆   Underline the instructions: for example explain/compare/give implications/illustrate/discuss

◆   Double underline and define key words that represent the central issue of the question

◆   Produce a trigger word structural answer plan and compare it to the specimen

◆   If you have misunderstood, carefully consider why, and learn the lesson.

Once you have understood the question, make a list of your main points and check these when you write your answer. You may choose to do a mind map instead. Do whatever works for you.

Once you have completed your answer, go back to your main points and verify if you have addressed all of them.

While you are writing your answer, if any more points come up, you can quickly add these to your list and then go back to where you were with your answer.

The importance of marketing research

The quality of marketing decisions are directly related to the quality of information that underpins them. Key questions for the marketer in terms of 'who are my customers' and 'what are their needs and wants' must be addressed before decisions on product, price, promotion and place can be made. Marketing research is important because it can generate the specific and tailored information required to answer these questions:

◆   It is an important marketing tool in terms of the information it generates.

◆   It underpins marketing decisions that need to be based on an in-depth understanding of the market in general and the behaviour of the consumer in particular.

◆   It systematically collects, researches and analyses information about specific marketing problems or in order to take advantage of marketing opportunities.

◆   Examples include calculation of market potential, assessment of market trends, competitor analysis and short-range and long-range forecasting.

◆   It is problem-orientated and a continuous process in an environment of change.

◆ It feeds into the marketing information system (MkIS) through environmental scanning of the PESTEL factors and monitoring change in the behaviour of customers and competitors.

◆ It improves the ability of the marketer to make timely decisions.

The information benefits of marketing research

Information is inherent in many stages of the marketing research process. In fact, as indicated below, information features in many of the key stages in the marketing research process.

The following functions outline the key stages in the marketing research process. The role of information within these stages has been indicated:

◆ Define the research problem.

◆ Set specific research objectives

◆ Design a research plan

◆ Determine information needs. The type and level of information that is needed needs to determined clearly.

◆ Define secondary sources and gather information. Information at this level will be mainly from other sources such as reports, documents, previous studies etc.

◆ Plan quantitative and qualitative data collection. Information at this stage will be collected by the organization or party leading the research project. What specific data is required will need to be ascertained.

◆ Select research techniques and implement research plan

◆ Data analysis, interpretation and reporting of findings: at this stage, the specific data collected will need to be collated and analysed in line with the needs determined previously. Data is converted into information. This information is then converted into knowledge to be used by the organization, hence meeting the objective of the research.

Exam hint

English is not the first language of many CIM candidates. Examiners take this into account. However please note that CIM employs specialists to screen papers for potential language confusions.

Take your time to make sure that you understand what a specific question is asking of you. It may be a good idea to explain your interpretation of the question at the outset of your answer. The examiner can then make an informed judgement in the light of your justification.

Also remember to ensure that you answer all the components of a question.

The information benefits that flow from the market research process include the following:

◆ Focus on your organization-specific information requirements

- Assistance in defining the nature of your marketing problems

- Detail that is unavailable from mere scanning of secondary sources

- Information tailored to current and future needs of the organization

- Information unavailable to competitors and a potential source of competitive advantage

- In-depth survey of secondary sources and identification of primary data needs

- Adoption of appropriate and cost-effective research approaches to gather primary data

- Objective interpretation of timely information that can form the basis of appropriate action

Activity 9.3

Key skills – using information

Can you match up the definitions to the marketing research terms?

1   Exploratory research

2   Observational research

3   Causal research

4   Descriptive research

5   Qualitative research

6   Quantitative research.

a   Test hypotheses regarding cause–effect relationships.

b   Gather primary data by people, behaviour and situations.

c   Gather preliminary data to help define problems or suggest relationships.

d   Collect interview data in sufficient volume to allow statistical analysis.

e   Help describe markets and marketing problems, for example market potential.

f   Uncover customer motivations, attitudes or buying behaviour using personal or small group techniques.

Much of the value of market research is that it helps to define future possibilities so it is to the future and its prediction that we need to turn. The future is essentially unknown in other than general terms and the further forward we attempt to peer, the more uncertain our view becomes.

We will first review the problems of forecasting. Some of the techniques available to forecast future demand will then be considered.

Coping with the environmental challenge: the key problems

Future determinants of the market for a product may be significantly different from the past, so most forecasting techniques that rely on historic information or the forward projection of past and current trends will tend to be misleading. Even highly sophisticated forecasting based on computer models, as used by the UK Treasury, has been prone to considerable error. One cynic suggested that economists had successfully forecast nine of the last five recessions!

The long-awaited green shoots of recovery from the last serious UK recession, for example, took 18 months longer to germinate than predicted and led to the resignation of the Chancellor of the Exchequer. The long-term consequences of the sharp tax rises required and the persistence of the 'feel bad' or at best 'feel insecure' factor that ensued led to a change in government at the following election.

Businesses may fare little better. Many have a planning horizon of 5–10 years. These are known as long-term strategies. However, make strategic plans over such a time period implies a reasonable degree of certainty regarding significant environmental trends and developments. Thus, as turbulence frequently undermines predictability, such an approach becomes questionable.

Insight: The budget for London 2012

The London Olympics, with a planning horizon of just over five years, had its original cost of £3.4 billion. This was revised upwards in a 'new budget' announced in March 2007 of £9.375 billion, nearly triple the original estimate of two years before. Since Sydney cost £3.1 billion, Athens £6.3 billion and Bejing is forecast at £8.4 billion, it is not surprising that some are predicting that the London 2012 Olympic Games would cost much over that amount; particularly when the organizers are talking about social regeneration and a long-term vision for London.

Insight: A wholly predictable energy crisis!

Having denied for months that the UK is in danger of running short of natural gas, there was a sense of panic as temperatures dropped in November 2005. Prices to industrial users trebled.

The National Grid predicted that in the event of a Siberian type winter (one every 50 years), industrial consumption would have to be halved for up to two months while a one-winter-in-ten freeze would require a 30 per cent reduction for up to 40 days. This impending crisis was entirely predictable with known depletion rates of North Sea supplies turning the United Kingdom into a net importer. The only political consolation of this worrying state of affairs is the support it will give for new nuclear build.

Accurate forecasts are critical here due to the long lead time for planning, constructing and commissioning. The exhaustion of high-grade uranium deposits and much higher processing costs of lower grade ores, together with terrorist threats (as in Australia) and the unsolved problems of safe decommissioning and waste disposal, make the economics of this greenhouse-friendly fuel source much less predictable.

The potential consequences of bad forecasts are so significant that organizations need to consistently consider a few factors. These are:

◆ **Which are the right forecasts?**

  ◆ Organizations should consider a variety of independent economic forecasts.

◆ **How significant are the different trends?**

  ◆ For example, organic food sales are growing 40 per cent per annum but only account for around 5 per cent of total sales.

  ◆ How long does it take before a pattern of events becomes a trend? Is tele-working a trend yet or not?

◆ **Where are the turning points?**

  ◆ Failure to anticipate and prepare for growth, maturity and even decline will result in either lost sales or unsold stock, depending on the error.

◆ **Which are the discontinuities?**

  ◆ Forecasting is most difficult when the 'rules of the past' no longer apply causing a trend to reverse or disappear: For example cheap to dear energy in 1973–1974 and 2001–2005 was a discontinuity. After a phase, the cost of energy resumed previous rates. A change in government with a very different economic philosophy can also have this effect. The demise of the nuclear family (2 adults + 2 children) as the norm is another.

◆ **What is the pace of change?**

  ◆ Knowing the direction of change is one thing, but knowing the speed of its development is the key to an effective response. Who predicted the frightening pace of contraction in the British coal mining industry? Who predicted the halving, and halving again of EU cod quotas?

  ◆ Suppliers and local traders who failed to anticipate and adjust will also have suffered the consequences.

  ◆ Similarly how rapidly will e-B2B expand in various sectors, and how rapidly will the new 3G videophones take off also need to be considered.

Question 9.3

Key skills – Contributing ideas to the strategy process

1 Why must a business forecast?

2 When must a business forecast?

3 What must a business forecast?

Many distinctive trends have reversed or discontinued in recent years. The power and significance of trade unions have declined greatly in many developed economies, share prices and even house prices have fallen, at least temporarily, while inflation, in general, has decreased to negligible rates not seen for over 25 years. With falling birth rates, youth culture has also given way to an affluent ageing one. Increasingly consumers as well as organizations are becoming conscious about environmental issues.

Activity 9.4

Key skills – Using ICT and the Internet

Identify three strong patterns or trends in a market of your choice that you consider will reverse or discontinue in the next 20 years.

Give reasons for your choice.

Coping with the challenge of environmental changes

Disagreements over the answers to the key problems outlined above can produce very different views of the future with no guarantee as to which will turn out to be the most accurate one. Possible business responses to such forecasting problems could include the following:

- **Abandon all forecasting pretensions:**
  - This would be a naive response to such difficulties.
  - Every action involving strategic plans or preparations for tomorrow requires some forecasting to be effective.
  - The essence of managerial decision-making involves forecasting future conditions.
  - Even day-to-day operational decisions with a much shorter time horizon require a clear view of the future if stock levels, sales targets or advertising budgets are to be effectively set.

- **Concentrate on short-term adaptive planning:**
  - The further marketers attempt to predict the future, the more hypothetical the view can become. Consequently, it is best to focus on the year ahead and on the short-term and medium-term.
  - However, a flexible management system that allows rapid adaptation to environmental change should be established. This may be possible for some businesses in relatively static markets, but what about a utility company, a telecommunications supplier or a pharmaceutical business, which is operating in a more volatile environment?
  - A new reservoir or nuclear plant must be planned over 10 years ahead, while technological change is so rapid in telecommunications that a reaction strategy, no matter how effective, would come far too late.
  - The companies within the pharmaceutical industry must be planning its product life cycles and research and development in the knowledge that testing and verification procedures may take a decade.

◆ All companies considering acquisition, modernization or diversification must forecast the medium- and longer-term future, if only in broad terms.

◆ **Improve the quality of conventional forecasts:**

◆ Forecasts normally refer to objective, quantitative techniques that seek to extrapolate historical data into the future.

◆ Effective forecasting involves the following stages: selection of the critical environmental variables as future indicators; identification of relevant sources of information on the variables; evaluation of forecasting techniques; integration of forecast output into strategic plans on a continuous basis; monitoring and evaluation with particular reference to possible discontinuities.

Exam hint

Improving your performance

Questions are seldom essay style, but they are set to test your communication skills by requiring a brief, presentation or report.

Up to 10 per cent of the marks may be awarded for presentational effectiveness. If a report is required, do not get carried away with format and forget to answer the question itself which counts for at least 90 per cent of the marks!

Provide a title, introduction, findings and conclusions/recommendations, but concentrate on setting the points out clearly and break up the text using lists of short, key statements rather than long sentences. The use of headings and sub-headings can greatly help structure your answer.

The problem with forecasting is not a lack of the necessary statistical techniques but rather the quality and availability of the necessary data. As with database management, the principle of garbage-in garbage-out applies. The resulting projection will only be as good as the data input. Sophisticated statistical methods such as multiple regression, moving averages and exponential smoothing will be of little value if the data collected is suspect. Consequently, organizations should evaluate from where they are collecting their data and just as importantly what and how they are inputting and reviewing their primary information.

Use the combined view of experts (Delphi technique)

◆ This is a subjective and qualitative technique relying primarily on human judgement rather than on statistical method.

◆ It is essentially an intuitive technique, deriving from the expert's blend of knowledge, experience and judgement.

◆ The experts may include academics, consultants, relevant stakeholders as well as key directors in marketing, operations, finance and non-executive board members.

◆ Each may make an independent forecast of sales, for example, or respond to an initial prediction.

◆ These may be fed back for further comment in the light of each expert's contribution.

◆ The resulting forecast reflects the collective 'informed view' of those who are in the best position to judge developments.

◆ The consensus achieved will smooth out extreme views and should carry credibility with those who use it.

◆ It is a time-consuming and costly process, which may also fail to capture the possibility of radical change due to a similar mindset of the experts involved.

Activity 9.5

Key skills – Using information

Match the terms with their correct definitions:

1   Demand function

2   Depth interview

3   Multiple regression

4   Moving averages

5   Exponential smoothing

6   Probability

a   Best estimate of the outcome of each decision alternative.

b   Unstructured, usually face-to-face and intended to elicit meaningful information from a respondent.

c   A technique used to calculate the explanatory value of a number of independent variables affecting a dependent one.

d   The factors that determine the quantity demanded of a good per period of time.

e   Change in the average of, say, sales values over a number of time periods, by adding the most recent value and dropping the earliest in the series.

f   When weights used in the averaging process decrease progressively for values further into the past.

Use judgemental analysis to identify a desired future:

◆ We all engage in goal-orientated planning if we wish to progress.

◆ It is a relatively successful approach so long as the world around us remains relatively stable and predictable. A young person who aims to be a doctor will plan to get good grades, particularly in maths, so they can progress to secondary school or college level where good results are required in the various sciences if they are to gain entry to a university with a record of excellence and so on towards their goal.

◆ The organization may also map out its future towards a desired goal, given the environmental landscape.

◆ Lack of perfect foresight, unexpected obstacles and changing conditions might force changes in direction along the way, but the goal is clear and an outline map is better than no map at all. In any event, change for most of us is not all that revolutionary. Taxes, terrorism, temperatures and sea level may rise a bit, but will mostly carry on much like before.

Activity 9.6

Key skills – Improving your learning and performance

Have you identified your desired future and made a map?

The fact that you are reading this coursebook suggests that you have given some thought to your future, but have you really planned it out?

◆ Where do you want to be in five years' time? In ten years' time?

◆ Where would you like to be at the peak of your career?

◆ What do you need to do to ensure that you reach these milestones?

◆ What are your personal and intellectual strengths and weaknesses?

◆ Are the weaknesses going to inhibit you from achieving your goals?

◆ If so, how are you going to remedy them and when?

◆ What qualifications, skills and experience will be necessary?

◆ Is your job leading somewhere you want to go?

Turbulent conditions can demand decentralization and devolved responsibility. An evolving or incremental approach is usually best called for with adjustments made within a broad vision of the organization's future. In essence, therefore, companies should avoid over-formal planning processes and instead emphasize learning and flexibility.

Use scenarios

◆ These are alternative views of the future and have been developed by organizations such as Shell to assist prediction in uncertain times.

◆ The best way of understanding scenarios is by comparing them with quantitative forecasts. The table below gives an example of how this can be done.

A scenario	A forecast
A description of the future based on mutually consistent groupings of determinants	A statistical synthesis of probabilities and expert opinions
Says here are *some* of the key factors you have to take into account and this is the way they could affect your business	Accounts relevant factors to yield *the best answer* – what is most likely to happen; this tends *to dictate final decisions*
Designed to be considered with other scenarios – it is valueless on its own	Stands alone
A tool to assist understanding The setting for decision-making, not an integral part of it	Intended to be regarded as an *authoritative statement*
A means of placing responsibility for planning decisions on the managers concerned	Removes much of the responsibility for the final decision – managers rely on the central forecast
Essentially qualitative	Fundamentally quantitative

Forecasts are based on the belief that the *future can be measured and controlled,* scenarios suggest it cannot be. Indeed, planners seek firm answers and optimum solutions, as if uncertainty and change can be assumed away.

Insight: Shell

Shell warns all corporate planners that the forecasts they know, love and rely on are based on the fallacy that the future can be measured and controlled. It likens decisions based on them to pursuing a straight line through a minefield, and views much economic and business theory as a fantasy in which people act as if they had knowledge, where it cannot exist.

Activity 9.7

Key skills – Using information and problem-solving

Identify key variables in the PESTEL environment.

Vary your assumptions about them in order to produce two alternative futures for the year 2009.

Variables might include such factors as the outcome of the next election, the stage of the economic cycle, demographic trends and trade factors.

Environmental audits

Marketer have a toolbox of techniques and approaches to help them understand a turbulent environment including external audits, the environmental set, impact analysis, PESTEL/SWOT analysis, the product life cycle and various forecasting methods.

In this section, we shall discuss how these approaches help us to interpret, evaluate and apply the information derived from forecasting techniques. Other techniques have been described in context, such as competitor analysis, leading indicators and morphological studies.

Knowledge is power. Environmental audits are the means of acquiring this power through the regular identification and collection of relevant information on the current situation.

Exam hint

Have a look at the logo from a CIM marketing conference shown in Figure 9.3. It should sum up your approach to the marketing environment!

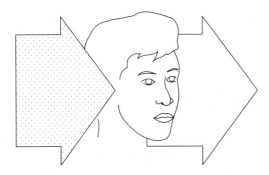

'LISTEN TO THE FUTURE'

Figure 9.3 A marketing logo

Audits are the formalized means of taking stock of the marketing environment. They require the marketer to undertake a detailed examination of external opportunities and threats. As such they include:

◆   Markets, connected stakeholders and competitors

◆   External environments including key macro-economic indicators

Audits help an organization with a variety of functions:

◆   They enable the organization to systematically understand its environment.

◆   They help to provide critical input into the strategic planning process and indicate on what areas an organization should be adapted accordingly.

◆   They also underpin any projected diversification or extension to foreign markets.

- An external audit would normally be complemented by an internal or marketing audit to assess effectiveness in meeting marketing objectives.

- To determine how well the marketing activities and actions matched the opportunities and constraints of the environment requires a sound marketing information system. Some organizations use a consultancy firm for objectivity and to independently verify or challenge any critical assumptions the organization had been making. Stakeholder perceptions could also be investigated regarding future trends.

- Audits are a foundation stone in the process of coping with environmental change.

- They provide the necessary inputs to construct the organization's environmental set.

The environmental set

Every organization faces a set of environmental factors over which it may have some influence but seldom any direct control.

- Small or large, public or private, manufacturer or service organization all operate in the context of a shifting set of what are in fact potential threats or opportunities.

- The set that concerns any specific business will however be individual to its own particular circumstances and situation.

- It will also change over time as the elements in the set shift in relative importance and actual impact upon the business.

- The board of directors, assisted by marketers, must ensure that they monitor changes in their set.

- Elements should be ranked in terms of likely impact on the business. Elements for a manufacturer might include the state of the economy, currency movements, interest rate changes, competitive pressures, wage movements, congestion and even skill shortages.

- The set is the starting point for environmental assessment with SWOT analysis providing the basis for formulating a strategic response. A threat for one organization may be an opportunity for another. For example, private security firms are seizing opportunities provided by Iraqi chaos and the privatization of low-security prison facilities.

Activity 9.8

Key skills – Collecting and using information

Produce a current environmental set for your own organization. Rank the elements to identify and consider their probable significance now and in 12 months' time.

The environmental set concept may be applied to any organization, although those for a voluntary or public sector organization would reflect very different concerns to those of the manufacturer. Since most local government funding derives from the centre, political factors will have more significance than economic ones. If revenues are obtained from local taxation, or payments for services provided, then the state of the local economy will assume greater importance. Clearly, the more buoyant the local economy and the more households and businesses paying local taxes, the better the services that can be provided.

Impact analysis

This is a simple but applied approach to assessing the probable impact of a specific environmental change on an organization or its competitors. In effect, it is measuring the sensitivity of key parameters to changes in environmental variables.

A number of impact grids may be constructed to provide a more informed view of the implications of environmental change. These include:

◆ **Competitor impact grid:**

  ◆ Figure 9.4 shows the effect of potential/probable environmental changes on direct competitors in multiple groceries.

  ◆ The effect is rated on a scale ranging from +++ to – – – with 0 representing a neutral situation.

  ◆ A positive score suggests opportunity and improvement in profits, sales or competitive position.

Environmental future	Sainsbury's	Tesco	Asda	Kwik Save	Aldi
Edge-of-town planning restrictions tighten	– –	– –	– – –	–	– – –
Food Agency set up	–	–	–	–	0
Serious recession	–	–	0	+	+ +
Genetically modified foods backlash	– –	– –	+ +	0	0

Figure 9.4 Competitor impact grid

Activity 9.9

Key skills – using information and problem-solving

Extend the above grid for other potential environmental developments (e.g. takeover of Safeway) or create one for your own industry. Consider the prospective impact of policies or socio-demographic changes.

◆ Competitors vary in their ability to withstand threats or exploit opportunities.

◆ In the above example, most are affected by tightening planning regulations, but some more than others. Aldi is a relatively new entrant to the market and is short of sites for expansion. Wal-Mart/Asda is concentrated in the North of England so the regulations may prevent correction of this imbalance. A serious recession tends to advantage the cost-focused retailers at the expense of Sainsbury's. A boycott on GM foods would advantage those who have publicly declared GM-free zones against those who will merely label ingredients.

◆ This analysis encourages the marketer to assess the effects of environmental change in advance and respond accordingly.

◆ **Environmental impact grid:**

◆ The marketer identifies environmental forces critically impacting on elements of the business and then awards a weighted assessment ranging, say, from 0 (neutral) to 7 (critical impact).

◆ Figure 9.5 provides an outline of the technique using the case of cross-channel ferries.

Environmental factor ⟋ Impact on ferries	Duty free removed	High-speed rail link in place	Exchange rate falls sharply	UK joins Euro	Low-cost airlines win Paris landing slots
Car passenger demand					
Foot passengers					
Lorries					
Ferry prices					
Marketing costs					

Figure 9.5 Environmental impact grid

◆ **Trend impact analysis:**

◆ This is a straightforward development of the environmental impact grid.

◆ Any trend in, say, commodity prices or household composition, is plotted up to date, according to its impact on revenues or costs.

◆ It is then projected forward to highlight any significant change in impact, for example oil or gas prices.

Activity 9.10

Key skills – Problem-solving

Using your own knowledge or common sense to complete Figure 9.5.

◆ **Cross impact analysis:**

　　◆ As the name suggests, this approach recognizes that the impact of a change in one variable may cause consequential impacts on other variables producing either positive (i.e. reinforces initial impact) or negative feedback. For example lower taxes may increase activity levels leading to higher tax payments.

◆ **Influence diagrams:**

　　◆ These are designed to provide the marketer with a clearer perception of the critical environmental influences on the business.

　　◆ These can then be closely monitored in order to provide early warning of threats or opportunities.

　　◆ A response to the contingency can then be planned and executed.

　　◆ A positive relationship in the influence diagram means that a change in any direction by the independent environmental variable will bring about a corresponding movement in the same direction by the dependent variable.

　　◆ A negative relationship applies the pressure in the opposite direction. In Figure 9.6, each environmental factor is designated by a box, a direction arrow and a + or – sign.

　　◆ A firm marketing spas would recognize that sales volumes are influenced by the volume of luxury house building, modernization and refurbishment trends, and the growth in health and fitness facilities. These will, in turn, be influenced by factors such as consumer confidence, house prices and the numbers moving house. Influences on these factors include interest rates, real incomes,

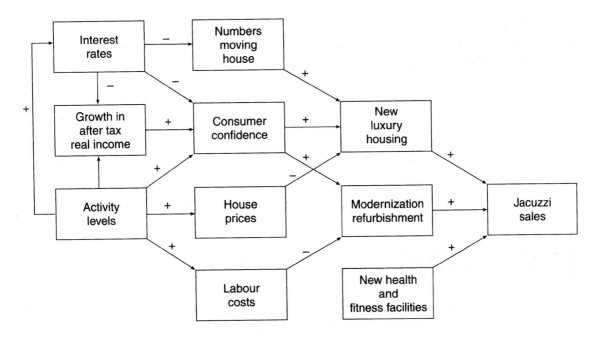

Figure 9.6 Influence diagram for sales of jacuzzis

employment and activity levels and so on. A rise in interest rates would there-fore depress consumer confidence and, in turn, the demand for new luxury houses, causing demand for spas to fall.

Question 9.4

Key skills – Problem-solving

Can you fill in the lower part of the influence diagram relating to environmental influences affecting new health and fitness facilities?

These are currently expanding rapidly in the UK causing spa/jacuzzi sales to rise. There are a number of + and – influence movements to identify.

SWOT analysis

This analysis distils the results of the internal and external audit by providing a framework for the collection and systematic classification of information. It also has several other functions. These are:

◆ When combined with impact analysis, it allows the organization to focus on its critical organizational strengths and weaknesses relative to the threats and opportunities faced in the environment.

◆ The whole purpose of the technique is to encourage the marketer to be outward-looking by anticipating and understanding relevant environmental developments and their impact.

◆ An opportunity represents an area or development that, with appropriate marketing, would enable the organization to achieve a competitive advantage.

◆ Conversely, a threat has been defined as a challenge posed by an unfavourable environmental trend that would lead, in the absence of marketing action, to the erosion of the organization's competitive position.

◆ Every marketer is confronted with a unique array of such forces and these require some means of differentiation because not all threats demand the same degree of concern as the probability of impact and the extent of consequential damage varies.

The marketer naturally wishes to focus on the more threatening or potentially costly ones. Similar thinking applies to the range of emerging opportunities to which the organization's resources could be committed. Resources are scarce and have opportunity costs. The marketer requires some means of ranking opportunities according to:

◆ Potential attractiveness/prospective rate of return

◆ Degree of matching with the organization's critical success factors (i.e. its strengths and weaknesses in key areas for exploiting the opportunity relative to competitors)

◆ Feasibility of alternative courses of action to exploit them

◆ Probability of success – based on risk analysis/assessment

Strengths and weaknesses represent where the organization is now, and opportunities represent where it wishes to be at a given time in the future. Consequently, the role of marketers is to supply the creativity to fill the gap between the two positions.

One classification technique can be seen in Figure 9.7, where opportunities are located in the matrix according to their probability of success and relative attractiveness. The latter is weighed in terms of, for example, potential profitability, projected growth rates and actual/potential competition, while the former is based on assessment of relative strengths. Threats are assessed by judging the likelihood of their happening against the scale of the potential damage, if they do.

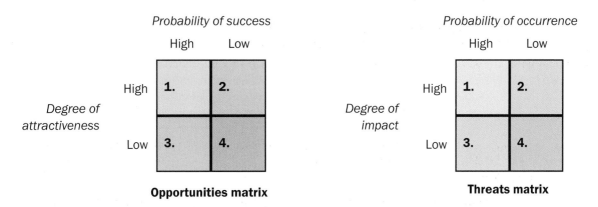

Figure 9.7 Opportunities and threats matrix

Each box in the analysis provides a ranking of significance. Marketers will clearly be more interested in opportunities located in Area 1, since they are both attractive and provide a good fit with organizational strengths. Area 1 threats require more serious consideration than those in Area 4. The analysis can be applied with varying degrees of sophistication through the use of calculated probabilities, weights and so forth. However, at the end of the day, the role of the analysis is to concentrate marketing minds on future plans to exploit the 'right' opportunities and/or defuse serious and imminent threats to the continued success of the business.

Exam hint

Key skills – Improving learning

Make time to apply all of the techniques discussed in this section to 'fix' each one in your mind.

Use them to analyse your organization or college. This activity will help you remember the associated methods.

The Ansoff matrix

The Ansoff matrix is a strategic tool used to aid the strategic thrust, which defines the future direction of the business. The model categorizes the options into four generic alternatives to simplify the process:

◆   Market penetration: existing market/existing product

◆   Product development: existing market/new product

◆   Market development: new market/existing product

◆   Entry into new market: new market/new product

After a marketing audit, a company will be faced with a certain situation. The Ansoff matrix is used with the strategic objective to define the future direction of the business. A company might be faced with declining sales of its products in the domestic market and will use the Ansoff matrix to evaluate the four generic alternatives for the future (e.g. the company would evaluate strategies to penetrate the existing market through pricing or increased brand loyalty). Another option is to develop the product or change design, increase the length of the product life cycle and increase sales. A third option is to export the existing product to other countries or finally stop and completely diversify with new products into new markets.

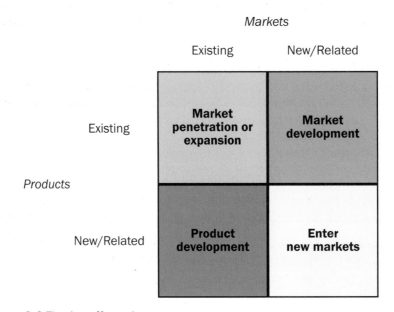

Figure 9.8 The Ansoff matrix

The Ansoff matrix is a simple tool enabling understanding of the fundamental generic options when defining the future direction of a business. The four categories sum up all business options while the model allows a company to go through these options one by one and evaluate their relevance in line with their strategic objectives. The model can save time and resources, as some of the options can be dismissed very early in the strategy development process (e.g. a British water company cannot supply British water to India, as infrastructure for doing so does not exist). By using the Ansoff matrix , the company can clearly identify realistic option and thus spend their time and other resources productively on pertinent options.

Problems with the Ansoff matrix lie in its rigid and rational approach. Markets and customers do not always behave rationally (e.g. the decision to go for a market penetration strategy for a luxury car could lead to the devaluation of the brand and could have the opposite effect).

Management's perception of the future and its vision can be subjective and lead to wrong decisions leading the Ansoff matrix to be based on the wrong assumptions.

The Ansoff matrix assumes that a company can enter new markets and develop new products in a relatively short period of time. In reality the process of product or market development may take years. For a company to remain successful in the long-term, it cannot just diversify into new markets and products without having the competence to do so. Yet, on the surface the Ansoff matrix may suggest otherwise and may lead companies down the wrong strategic path.

Marketing information system (MkIS)

The marketing information system is a crucial tool of analysis to marketers. The following criteria highlight the significance of this tool:

◆ Unless internally and externally generated data are collected, processed, disseminated and promptly acted upon, all other techniques will be of limited benefit to the marketer.

◆ Processing data into meaningful information is the critical activity for marketers.

◆ As we have seen, the knowledge-based society has arrived and the organizations that will succeed in a global information environment will be those that can:

   ◆ Identify opportunities

   ◆ Create value

   ◆ Build their in-house knowledge

◆ A marketing information system is the means by which an innovative business can learn, adapt and change, and is a core competency in the electronic age.

◆ The need is to create repositories of marketing knowledge, improve access and transfer among users and manage the knowledge as an asset.

A marketing information system can be used by organizations for a variety of reasons including:

◆ To generate new knowledge or access it from external sources

◆ To represent knowledge in documents, databases, software, promotions and so on

◆ To embed knowledge in new processes, products and services

◆ To diffuse existing marketing information throughout an organization

◆ To apply accessible knowledge to effective marketing decision-making

◆ To facilitate knowledge growth through market research and competitor intelligence

◆ To measure the value of marketing knowledge assets and their impact

In brief:

◆ It is important that the marketer sets the information agenda, rather than the other way round. Thus, a clear focus is required so that the data gathered fits the intended purpose.

◆ While large amounts of readily accessible information may be economically mined from the public domain, much of the required environmental data is company specific, so resources need careful targeting.

◆ Market research can provide some important specific feedback, but a marketing intelligence gathering system is the main means of identifying emerging trends.

◆ A balance, of course, has to be struck between the benefits of additional information and the costs of collection and of inaccuracy arising from insufficient data.

The continuing impact of new information communication technology (ICT)

Information technology and communication advances are increasingly converging. This has several implications for the marketing environment:

◆ This represents the key drivers of change in a dynamic information-powered environment.

◆ It also offers the ability to create more accurate profiling of customer needs and their buying behaviour. Accordingly precisely-targeted communication and feedback systems to support customer relationship management are enabled.

The explosion in computer, information and communication technologies, demonstrated most dramatically by the global web of computer networks known to all as the Internet, provides the ultimate information source for marketers. It has seen a dramatic expansion both in terms of websites to access and the spiralling number of users. This process was facilitated by Internet Service Providers (ISPs), such as AOL, BT, Tiscali and many others offering discounted services to potential subscribers.

Competition and expansion are set to continue apace with the development of broadband digital services being provided through satellite, cable and aerials to televisions for armchair e-mail, Internet shopping and information searches. Indeed, analogue signals will be phased out completely in the UK over the next few years.

Development is world-wide, but varies in pace with China forging rapid expansion through cable television and the introduction of broadband services. E-mail is becoming a part of everyday life within the government and for increasing numbers of individuals. Internet cafés have been established and most hotels and CIM Training have web access in guest rooms and business centres. Internet connections are still relatively slow in China due to the government control of international gateways and limited numbers of ISPs. Sri Lanka and Malaysia make increasingly heavy use of the Internet for communications, and e-mail is expanding at exponential rates. In Nigeria, by contrast, the use of the Internet is still limited. There are a number of ISPs, but a poor telecommunication infrastructure makes links relatively unreliable and slow.

New websites open daily throughout the world. Important sites for you to access are those of the Chartered Institute of Marketing (www.cim.co.uk) as they offer access to new syllabus information, examiner reports and specimen answers. Most organizations now have a website, and while sensitive information may be withheld, there is much that may be inferred in intelligence terms from what remains. Dot-com fervour has returned in recent months with the 18-month-old video sharing but profitless phenomenon YouTube (and its 35 million viewer base) being bought by Google for $1.65 billion. Other so-called 'web 2.0' start-ups in this second Internet boom include Zubka.com (a recruitment site offering big rewards for referring successful job candidates), Zopa.com (a loan exchange linking borrowers and lenders for a 1 per cent fee) and Crowdstorm.com (a social shopping site using collective wisdom to recommend products).

The interactivity facilitated by the Internet also means that the marketer can readily build information networks and relationships with stakeholders. Information can be both gathered from and distributed to stakeholders, including employees and customers, more quickly and at a fraction of previous cost levels.

As organizations seek to create and fulfil their vision and mission, the only certainty is faster change. As marketers strive to match business delivery to customer demand, converging information communication technologies are opening up an era of connected customers and stakeholders, together with a new age of marketing opportunities.

The world is changing from a physical asset-dominated industrial structure into knowledge and information-based digital societies, with all aspects of doing business being affected:

◆　　Marketing opportunities in gathering data/enhancing relationships arising from two-way interaction with customers and influential external stakeholders.

◆　　Virtual organizations have no boundaries in configuring their structure/relationships.

◆　　Flexibility and competitive advantage can be achieved by creating value-added networks, for example intranets for automating operational decisions and transactions along the value chain.

◆　　B2B electronic commerce is currently the primary driver.

◆　　Emergence of information intermediaries in marketing research/intelligence areas.

Information communication technology is leading to the empowerment not only of buyers but also of stakeholders in general, creating new dilemmas and new challenges for the organization. Fortunately, it is also generating new technologies for dealing with them but marketers must dramatically improve their electronic competencies to emulate best practice.

Summary

In this unit, we have seen that:

◆ It is crucially important for the marketer to monitor change in the marketing environment.

◆ Information is the critical resource and needs to be organized within the framework of an MkIS.

◆ There are problems in making accurate forecasts when the environment is turbulent and unpredictable, but scenarios can provide management with useful alternative views of the future.

◆ Frequent audits provide the necessary inputs for impact and SWOT analysis.

◆ The marketer must be future-orientated and be wary of the patterns of the past.

◆ Issues and environmental challenges should be scanned for continuously with a view to determining the ones that constitute potential threats or opportunities for the organization.

◆ The continuing potential of the Internet and electronic databases in accessing information.

◆ A turbulent environment demands adaptability and flexible strategic planning.

Further study and examination preparation

As the newest element of the syllabus, questions arose more frequently on recent papers, although this will not be so pronounced in the future. Both the December 2004 and June 2005 papers had at least two full or part questions whereas December 2005 had just one and June 2006 one full and one section A. This suggests there will always be a strong probability of a full or at least a part question on this important syllabus area, particularly since it can easily be linked up with other elements. This linkage can also be seen in Question 5a, December 2003, while Question 6, June 2004 is a complete question. Remember that even if you do not prepare a full answer to each question, you should at a minimum prepare an outline plan.

Extending knowledge

Palmer A. and Hartley B. (1999) *The Business and Marketing Environment*, McGraw-Hill.

> Chapter 14: Analysing the Marketing Environment.

> Chapter 5: The Information Environment.

Palmer, A. (2001) *The Business Environment*, McGraw-Hill.

> Chapter 13: The Dynamic Business Environment.

> Chapter 4: The Internet Environment.

Other suggested reading

Lancaster G. and Massingham L. (2001) *Marketing Management*, McGraw-Hill Education.

> Chapter 13: Marketing information systems.

Lancaster G, Massingham L. and Ashford R. (2002) *Essentials of Marketing*, McGraw-Hill Education.

> Chapter 5: Marketing information systems and research

Jobber D. (1998) *Principles of Marketing*, McGraw-Hill, 2nd Ed.

> Chapter 6: Marketing research and information systems.

Kotler P, Armstrong G., Saunders J. and Wong V. (2002) *Principles of Marketing*, 3rd European Edition, Prentice Hall, London.

> Chapter 8: Market information and marketing research.

Bassington F. and Pettitt S. (2003) *Principles of Marketing,* Pearson Education Limited.

> Chapter 6: Marketing information and research.

R.I. Cartwright (2001) *Mastering the Business Environment*, Palgrave.

Websites

www.e-commerce.research.ml.com.

www.pwcglobal.com.

www.ecountries.com/africa.

www.asiansources.com.

Practicising past exam questions

In addition to referring to past exam papers, students should also refer to the specimen paper. This will enable students to familiarize themselves with the new format but also help them understand the way in which exam questions are generally set.

Please see Question 6, June 2004 on the CIM website, www.cim.co.uk.

Please see Question 5a, December 2003 on the CIM website, www.cim.co.uk.

Please see Question 1a, 1b, 6, 7c and 7d, December 2004. For specimen answers go to www.cim.co.uk.

Please see Question 1b(i), 6 and 7, June 2005. For specimen answers go to www.cim.co.uk.

Please see Question 7, December 2005. For specimen answers go to www.cim.co.uk/learn-ingzone.

Please see Question 1c, 1d and 5, June 2006. For specimen answers go to www.cim.co.uk/learningzone.

Answers

Appen

Unit 1

Answers to activities

Activity 1.3

1 – e; 2 – d; 3 – f; 4 – b; 5 – a and 6 – c.

Activity 1.6

You should have considered implications from the employment and marketing fronts.

Women represented 46 per cent of the workforce in 2006 and with immigration contributed the majority of employment growth. This allows flexible staffing using part-time hours but demands changes in personnel policy as a result. Working wives alter the times of peak shopping hours and increase the demand for convenience and frozen foods.

This has also had an effect on society and on the lives of children. As more women join the workforce, much fewer women are at home with their children straight after school hours. Hence, entertainment for children and facilities needed for such children has also had to be re-examined.

Activity 1.10

The vast majority of shareholders will never attend an AGM unless they hold a substantial amount of shares. With a limited number of shares in a given portfolio, the set timing and venue of an AGM, and with little or no real influence over proceedings, the incentive to attend can be very small.

Go through the following questions. After you have attempted to all the questions, review your answers. Attempt to appreciate the impact of all the contentions on the market environment:

◆ The ability to raise considerable amounts of capital is the main attraction of the public company. However, what about does this method really cost the company?

353

♦ What do you think about the degree of scrutiny required by the relevant company legislation?

♦ Does a quotation on the Stock Exchange force the business to think short term rather than long term? Does this imply that the company is at the mercy of market sentiment?

♦ Some public companies, such as The Virgin Group, have decided to buy back their shares. Why do you think that company opted to do so?

♦ Doesn't going public make you vulnerable to a takeover and what if the 'offer' flops? Lastminute.com upset shareholders following their share price collapse

♦ Why do you think a number of companies chose the 'unlimited company' status ever since the law allowed exemption from filing accounts for this status?

♦ The Financial Services Authority reported that in 2004, 29 per cent of takeover announcements were preceded by suspicious share price movements, that is: insider trading. Only 21 per cent of takeover announcements were so in 2000. What do you think about these reports by the Financial Services Authority?

♦ Financial institutions produce pressure to perform. Thus open trading of shares brings the danger of a hostile takeover bid. What do you think?

♦ There is consistent negative publicity surrounding the so-called 'fat-cat' payments. In the early 1990s, Chief Executives in Britain were paid 42 times that of an average worker. A decade later, they were earning 411 times that amount. Directors' pay rose 28 per cent in 2005 following previous annual rises of 13 per cent and 23 per cent. Despite this, there is little evidence that higher pay has led to improved performance. What do you think about this argument?

Activity 1.16

You probably put profit at the top of your business objectives list, but how many others could you think of? What about basic survival in the existing specific market as a motive, or the desire for growth? Did you think about the personal objectives of those who actually decide the strategies and allocate the resources in business? These might diverge from the interests of the shareholders.

Activity 1.18

The need to place the customer at the centre of the whole organization implies being highly sensitive to changes in the environment as well as co-ordinating resources to ensure quick response throughout the organization.

Organizational changes could include:

♦ Marketing representation at main Board/MD level

♦ A flat decentralized structure

♦ Delegation of decision to those closest to the customer

♦ Open communications internally and externally

♦ Profit-centred general manager structure for co-ordination of all functions

◆   Integrated Management Information System (MIS)

◆   Customer service philosophy promoted by the organization

Plausible responses to questions throughout Unit 1

Question 1.1

Your first thoughts were probably about existing and potential markets. The changing tastes and preferences of customers, their disposable incomes, and the price and availability of substitutes will clearly be important, as well as the size, strength and numbers of competitors. Less obvious are the changes in the broader environment which influence these market conditions. These could include legal changes, demographic changes, new cultural trends and technical developments. For example the legal changes revolving around the minimum wage to which businesses have not only implied that labour cost of organizations may have been greatly affected but the purchasing power of the consumers affected by this legal change has by all means also been altered.

Demographic changes alter the population of various market segments. Cultural and technical developments may exert even more powerful influences on the longer-term supply, demand, profitability and life cycle of different goods and services. Rising concerns about global warming and the impact on environments, for example, has caused many businesses to modify their product offerings and methods of production. For instance, in the UK supermarkets such as Sainsbury's are currently reviewing the packaging of their own branded products.

No organization, whether small or large, public or private, profit or non-profit making can afford to ignore its environment. As the strategist H.I. Ansoff poignantly yet simply observed:

> *The firm is a creature of its environment. Its resources, its income, its problems, its opportunities and its very survival are generated and conditioned by the environment.*

Question 1.2

Additional themes could include:

◆   Most organizations tend to exist in an environment riddled with threats and opportunities.

◆   Competitors as well as allies could also operate in the same environment. How then, would an organization relate to these?

◆   Organizations often face the pressure to adapt to changing trends and demands. They must adapt to the unexpected too. Additionally, they are also in competition with other organizations.

◆   In order to keep up to date with their marketing environment, organizations must constantly aware of their surroundings and strive to always understand what is going on in their direct and sometimes even indirect marketing environment.

◆   What are the strengths and weaknesses of an organization relative to its competitors in the environment?

◆ The size and even flexibility of an organization could be the pinnacle of its defensive strategy.

Question 1.3

As a marketing analyst at McDonald's what would you do in practice?

You would certainly collect information about the market environment as well as try to assess the situation of the company. Thus you would assess both the internal environment as well as the external environment within which the company operates:

◆ Criteria that would help assess the market environment:

◆ Has anything changed in the wider environment that is impacting on sales?

◆ Have other fast food operators been similarly affected?

◆ Criteria that would help assess the dynamics of the company:

◆ In which areas was the loss of profit concentrated?

◆ What is happening to market share and volume sales in different markets?

◆ Are franchisees generating the necessary drive and creativity to force sales upward?

You would need to interpret the above information and then present it effectively. Quintessentially, this information would then input into the strategy process so that the best solution(s), strategies and tactics are identified for the company. These of course then will need to be implemented.

Question 1.4

Management may think twice about making as much profit as possible if:

◆ It involves taking high risks, for example, it may lead to an anti-monopoly investigation.

◆ It encourages wage demands and rising dividend expectations.

◆ It is at the expense of sales/market share and attracts new entrants.

◆ It prejudices customers who link the profit to high prices and will turn to alternatives when available.

Unit 2

Answers to activities

Activity 2.1

The information afforded by Market Research or the information generated from loyalty cards should be optimally exploited by companies.

Activity 2.5

A funeral director (Low environmental complexity/Low dynamism), a computer software manufacturer (High environmental complexity/High dynamism), a university (Medium environmental complexity/Medium dynamism), a biscuit manufacturer (Low environmental complexity/Medium dynamism), a pop group (High environmental complexity/Low dynamism), an advertising agency (Medium environmental complexity/Low dynamism).

Activity 2.7

Product availability and promotion would be priorities for distributors while innovation, particularly in product and place, would be the probable means of achieving sustainable advantage.

Activity 2.11

Sectional/interest – Chambers of Commerce, British Medical Association

Cause/promotional – CAMRA and the Mothers' Union

Activity 2.12

Potential benefits include enhanced reputation for companies at the leading edge (e.g. Body Shop or Norsk Hydro – the Norwegian chemicals, paper and energy company which was the first to use independent environmental auditing); attracting a new market segment of environmentally concerned consumers; cost savings through recycling or improved energy efficiency.

Guidelines for implementation might include the following:

◆ Apply from product conception through to final disposal

◆ Responsibility of staff at all levels

◆ Build achievement of environmental objectives into the reward structure of the business

◆ The business should not knowingly do harm to the environment

◆ The business should behave as a custodian of resources for future generations

Plausible responses to questions throughout Unit 2

Question 2.4

Aerosols – CFCs/ozone layer; agriculture – fertilizer runoff; airlines – energy, noise, ozone, global warming; chemicals – effluent, spillage; paper – energy, greenhouse effect; refrigeration – CFCs and disposal; tobacco – health, passive smoking; tourism – areas of natural beauty; toxic waste – leaks, accidents, health.

Other industries coming into the firing line might include biotechnology – genetic implications; transport – congestion, safety and accidents; pharmaceuticals – dependency and ethical considerations.

Question 2.5

Recent examples include McDonald's, Microsoft, Firestone, Equitable Life, KFC, Jarvis, Farepak.

Unit 3

Answers to activities

Activity 3.6

Has low/stable returns

Has low/risky returns – liable to entry in upturns and periods of windfall profit but firms don't exit as conditions deteriorate

Has high/stable returns – very attractive as the unsuccessful leave the industry

Has high/risky returns – unsuccessful stay and fight

Activity 3.10

The Director General of Fair Trading does the following to protect consumers:

1   Receives information on potentially harmful business activities from various sources.

2   Publicizes consumer rights.

3   Actively encourages industry associations to introduce and progressively improve codes of practice.

4   Obtains assurances from or injunctions against persistent offenders or publishers of misleading advertisements.

5   Proposes new laws and makes referrals for investigation.

Plausible responses to questions throughout Unit 3

Question 3.1

Health/fitness, restaurants and large sections of fast food, increasing concentration at top/city end and travel lodges on main routes. Factors include need for close personal attention (restaurants), early growth stage (health/fitness) and easy entry (fast food).

Question 3.2

Examples could include longer opening hours for convenience stores, fast food deliveries and store-interior formats.

Question 3.4

Fragmented is best described by 3, concentrated by 4.

Question 3.5

From London, substitutes include charter and scheduled flights (Ryanair, EasyJet, AirFrance, British Airways), Eurostar, car and ferry or even Hovercraft.

Price performance ratios are relatively close with the exception of charter and some scheduled flights. If opportunity cost, duration and timing are of the essence, the director will justify the latter.

Change is taking place due to the high oil prices, rail disruption and the curtailment of duty-free sales and of more taxes being imposed on flights.

Question 3.6

Aldi – Thompsons – Toyota (cost leadership); Sainsbury's – Thomas Cook – Ford (diff.); Lidl – Wallace Arnold's – Hyundai (cost focus); Iceland/M&S – Kuoni – BMW/Land Rover.

Unit 4

Answers to activities

Activity 4.1

The short answer might be to opt for profits in the short run to recover Research and Development expenditure, but for a more responsible approach is advisable if the pandemic occurs.

Activity 4.2

1 – b; 2 – d; 3 – c; 4 – e; 5 – a

Plausible responses to questions throughout Unit 4

Question 4.1

Few examples exist. These could include: craft industries, personal services (e.g. funerals and nursing homes).

Question 4.2

Sales volume by product, product group, region, channel and market segment. Intelligence reports on competitor prices and promotion, strengths and weaknesses. Assessment of own promotional mix effectiveness. Accounts provide data on cost of sales, debtors, overall sales and analysis of customer variances. Purchasing provides assessment of supplier reliability, stock control and availability and service levels. Operations provide order status, completion dates and production capacity.

Unit 5

Answers to activities

Activity 5.8

Quality, service, value for money and greater durability. Over-60s will be renewing household effects after child rearing and will look for design, not functionality.

As the old become more numerous, better educated and live longer, so their political and economic power will increase. Financially well endowed and with a greater propensity to vote, they will exert more pressure on decision-makers as well as constitute an important but discerning market segment. The marketer should also recognize that the retired will be included among the poorest in society, with nearly two million in Britain qualifying for supplementary benefits and a further one million qualifying but not taking it up. Many of the supposedly affluent 'empty nesters' also have ageing relatives to support, thereby curtailing their ability to consume. On the other hand, nursing homes may be the grateful beneficiaries.

Activity 5.18

Other trends might include health and fitness; novelty and change; energy and environmental friendliness; value for money; supranational or global orientation.

Plausible responses to questions throughout Unit 5

Question 5.1

Those retiring will have state pensions supplemented by private pensions. They will have planned financially for retirement and may have inherited valuable properties in recent years. They will form a market segment with clear ideas regarding their requirements. They will still be fit and active. The mix must reflect this, especially in terms of the product and the financing arrangements. Promotion must therefore address their wants. You may wish to identify what these wants are likely to be.

Question 5.2

◆ New technology can help improve agricultural productivity and industrialization.

◆ A lot therefore rests on development of sustainable technologies and overseas aid.

◆ Population growth does not necessarily mean market opportunities because it tends to correlate with very low or falling income per head.

◆ An optimum population allows full advantage to be taken of resources. A growing population can revitalize and bring larger markets and more mobility. Excessive population as is currently the case in many parts of sub-Saharan Africa and Latin America can unbalance the ecology through overgrazing and deforestation.

◆ Marketers can help governments educate the citizens and distribute the other marketing communications of the governments.

Question 5.3

Apart from logistical considerations, lifestyles will be different. Outlying areas poorly served by public transport will have higher car ownership and infrequent, high-spending trips to retailers.

Question 5.4

The culture, attitudes and buying habits of these groups differ significantly from the indigenous population. The entrepreneurial abilities of some of these minorities are also outstanding: 17 per cent of the Indian community are self-employed against 11 per cent for all groups. However, the traditional 'open all hours' corner shop is under pressure from multiple supermarkets (25 per cent fall in 10 years) and the work ethic of the parents is no longer matched by their aspiring children who are not prepared to put up with this type of long hours of work or even limiting development prospects.

Question 5.5

- For business, the main attraction is flexibility to employ when the labour is required (e.g. retail shopping peaks). Wages tend to be lower and other wage costs are avoided. Exemption from employment legislation and National Insurance also contribute.

- For employees, especially married women, it may fit well with other responsibilities and needs. It also suits the semi-retired.

- For government, it reduces the overall unemployment rate.

- Recent legislation has put part-time workers on equal employment status to full-time.

- A change in work patterns implies changes in buying and shopping patterns. One-stop shopping and convenience purchases are reflections of this trend. It is also more likely that the male is more involved in routine shopping decisions.

Question 5.6

- This classification is based solely on occupation and ignores the fact that changing wage relativities have altered comparative purchasing power:

  - Some C2s are better off than many C1s and Bs, for example, and this is reflected in purchases.

  - Some may not fit the classification (e.g. if living on inherited wealth).

- An alternative classification would be to select specific classes (e.g. upper middle, lower lower) and define the households concerned in terms of source and size of income, place of residence, type of work, core attitudes and so forth.

- Classes tend to have distinct/symbolic/recognizable product and brand preferences.

Unit 6

Answers to activities

Activity 6.3

◆ Downturn:

  ◆ Control stock in line with order slowdown.

  ◆ The psychology is still one of growth with orders up on a year ago.

  ◆ This is the right time to conduct a Pareto analysis to weed out weak products and channel outlets. Recruitment should be halted and no further long-term commitments taken on.

◆ Recession:

  ◆ Companies should sit tight and wait for the upturn.

  ◆ Be aware of brighter times ahead so retain skilled core and upgrade.

  ◆ Order capital equipment for installation, within 18 months, since prices are at the lowest for all resource contracts.

◆ Recovery:

  ◆ Talk is still of recession but the rate of change in orders is upward.

  ◆ Start building stock and encourage distributors to do likewise.

  ◆ Start hiring and prepare new products for launch.

Activity 6.5

Policies fall into six groups:

1 **Stimulate demand for labour directly** (e.g. government spending) – Can this lead to higher prices?

2 **Reduce the number of job seekers** (e.g. more in higher education) – Can this lead to inefficiency?

3 **Improve the matching of unemployed to vacancies** (e.g. better job centres).

4 **Reduce the real wage** (e.g. pay restraint) – Can this lead to strikes or low productivity?

5 **Share out the available work** (e.g. part-time, early retirement) – Can this lead to workers wanting to share work?

6 **Increase domestic activity at the expense of overseas** (e.g. tariff barriers) – Can this lead to inefficiency?

Activity 6.7

Activity, growth and unemployment rates:

◆ Volume of retail sales/comparative per capita output

◆ Industry surveys of investment intentions/confidence

◆ Rates of change in key groups: skilled, young, over-55 and primes, male/female.

Inflation and interest rates:

◆ Cost of living or price index/the underlying rate/main competitor rate

◆ Rate of change in earnings/tax changes in the pipeline

◆ The growth in the money supply.

Trade figures and exchange rates:

◆ Balance on current account (symbol of international 'competitiveness')

◆ Terms of trade reflect relative movement of import/export prices

◆ Share of world trade in manufactures/invisibles reflect longer-term performance.

Activity 6.8

1 – a; 2 – e; 3 – f; 4 – b; 5 – d; and 6 – c

Plausible responses to questions throughout Unit 6

Question 6.1

The only viable solution to this conflict between growth and a pollution-free environment is to pursue *sustainable growth*. Zero growth is not a real option due to concern over rising unemployment in industrial economies and rising populations in less-developed ones. Continued progress towards industrialization is required but by using cleaner technologies, renewable energy and recyclable products.

Question 6.2

◆ The rate of interest:

　◆ As the rate of interest falls, less is saved and more is invested and vice versa. It will not work quickly because other factors also affect the decision to save (e.g. income, expectations and preferences) and invest (e.g. expected returns, competitive pressures).

◆ Where injections are equal to leakages.

Question 6.3

◆ Consumption – This will remain unchanged due to uncertainty and savings as a precaution against unemployment.

◆ Investment – This will be unchanged or falling due to idle capacity and 'wait and see' attitudes.

◆ Exports – These will be unchanged or falling due to depression in overseas markets.

◆ Only *government* spending (*currently 41 per cent of GDP*) can be increased to stimulate activity.

It is not expected that there will be any significant effects in the short-term due to stickiness in the response. In the longer-term however, costs would fall and business would become more competitive leading to higher activity rates.

Note: One should remember that all too often people are seeking immediate or short-term solutions rather than long-term ones.

Question 6.4

China 7.5 per cent to Sri Lanka's 2.5 per cent

An increase in GDP does not automatically mean that this country is better off

(Please refer to the section about the limitations of the data in this unit. That section can offer you reasons why it may not necessarily be better for a country to have an increase in GDP.)

Question 6.5

◆ Recovery:
  - Starts from lower turning point
  - Iincome, output and expenditure rise at an increasing rate
  - Employment rises/unemployment levels off
  - Caution is needed when:
    - a Employing full-timers
    - b New investment planned as confidence recovers
  - Inflation remains low as increased utilization occurs.

◆ Boom:
  - Bottlenecks in faster growth sectors
  - Resource prices bid up and passed on in higher prices
  - Resources are utilized fully
  - Productivity is the only source of higher output
  - Profit, investment and confidence are all high
  - Interest rates rise sharply
  - Imports are sucked in.

◆ Downturn:
  - Starts from upper turning point
  - Momentum through multiplier-accelerator
  - Confidence and spending fall
  - Precautionary savings rise
  - Investment becomes unprofitable
  - Business failures rise and cutbacks multiply.

Question 6.6

High and rising unemployment means downward pressure on wages. Businesses can recruit without raising wages. If many chase each vacancy, managers can pick and choose. Workers are likely to work harder to preserve their jobs and also accept change. The bargaining power of employers strengthens while that of employees weakens.

Question 6.7

Themes included in your answer would ideally revolve around technology transfer, value added (wages + demand for local components + local taxes), balance of payments (initial investment + exports), demonstration effect for positives; competition, remitted profits, power (e.g. avoid taxes) for negatives.

Question 6.8

The answer to this question depends on the rate of inflation involved. If this is slow and predictable then it can be a good thing.

Question 6.9

◆ Small firms who tend to rely on bank credit for cash flow

◆ Small firms who suffer when large customers delay payment

◆ Fast-growing firms

◆ Manufacturing firms with higher working capital requirements

Such firms suffer in three ways – higher interest costs, limited credit and reduced consumer spending power (e.g. small builders).

Unit 7

Answers to activities

Activity 7.3

1 – e; 2 – b; 3 – d; 4 – c and 5 – a

Activity 7.8

1 – a; 2 – d; 3 – c; 4 – b; 5 – f; 6 – e and 7 – g

Plausible responses to questions throughout Unit 7

Question 7.1

You should ideally think about office politics and positioning for promotions and perks. Departmental conflicts arise over resources and priorities. The quality press and periodicals like *The Economist* and *Newsweek*. Trade associations and lobbyists. Also, consider websites, for example lcweb.loc.gov/homepage/lchp.html in the Library of Congress – one of the largest in the world.

Question 7.2

Think in terms of product positioning, 'value for voting' and differentiation of manifestos and policies, that is, clear blue water between the parties.

Question 7.3

This might include the requirement for public liability insurance, laws governing the use of public transport, road traffic laws, health and safety at work, employment protection law including discrimination, unfair dismissal, sexual harassment and equal pay. If you go shopping, then a whole battery of legislation will apply, if you feel unreasonably treated.

Question 7.4

Red tape refers to excessive, unnecessary and often complicated formalities involved in government regulations.

Question 7.5

Many policies were sold to people for whom they were not suitable or really wanted. More and clearer information should be given to potential customers, including the likelihood and cost of early cancellation. Consultation with the industry to ensure workability would probably be advisable. While consumers' awareness of their rights has increased as a result of legislation, considerable ignorance and lethargy still remain. Consumers often have neither the time nor the inclination to exercise fully their existing rights, especially where small-value purchases are concerned.

With payment protection insurance (PPI), a study found that one in six claims are rejected while just 60 per cent of credit card companies let customers see the policy's small print. On the other hand, suppliers are more likely to implement the letter of the law rather than risk their reputation or the wrath of the pressure groups and enforcement agencies. The legislation has successfully removed outright dangerous products from the market and outlawed dubious methods such as pyramid selling and mail-order trading of unsolicited goods

Unit 8

Plausible responses to questions throughout Unit 8

Question 8.1

◆ Examples are numerous, for example IT, pharmaceuticals, chemicals, car design, financial services.

◆ Most have been affected by IT systems. Craft goods and personal services provide possibilities.

Question 8.2

Many of the information technology-based consumer products and services were not available, i.e. PCs, laptops, mobile phones, airbags, cash dispensers, microwaves, camcorders, sophisticated computer games.

Question 8.3

The main threats involve the loss of market share/profitability as a result of technological surprises; when to invest since rapid technological change will make premature investments obsolete. Hi-tech may involve highly specialized plant and inflexibility in the face of changing consumer tastes, high cost of investment (i.e. microchip plants currently cost $1bn), risk and loss of failure (i.e. Sinclair C5 car, Philips videodisc). The main opportunities involve excess profit, competitive advantage, lower costs, faster growth, greater flexibility.

Question 8.4

The motorist would be stranded since microprocessors control ignition, steering, braking and inboard control systems on modern cars. Traffic lights would cease to function, as would petrol pumps.

The marketing department relies on 'information systems' defined as the products, services, methods and people used to collect, store, process, transmit and display information. It also relies on the telephone, now controlled through digital exchanges, not to mention televisions that receive advertisements. Product information derived from bar code scanners would be lost and banking and credit systems would fail.

Question 8.5

An array of marketing strategies is relevant. They could include price skimming and penetration. Licensing and franchising are other possibilities to consider in achieving rapid coverage of the national/international markets.

Question 8.6

The degree of diffusion varies but only the virtual reality holidays (i..e. Second Life) and intelligent motorways appear to be further into the future. According to General Motors, within 50 years, six biofeed sensors in dashboards will detect incipient slumber and vibrate to wake the driver. The motorist could steer into a 'nap lane', set a course using the car's satellite-guided navigation system, engage the autopilot and go to sleep. Computer chips embedded in the tarmac will 'read' the road. Hydrogen-powered fuel cells will replace petrol engines and a joystick will control all movements including braking and accelerating.

Question 8.7

Look for products such as:

◆ Books

◆ Holidays

◆ CDs

◆ Pornography

◆ Clothing and basic foodstuffs

As against:

◆ Fashions (*this is fast increasing;e.g. Next, Hobbs, Debenhams*)

◆ Personal services

◆ Furniture *(this is also increasing; e.g. IKEA)*

◆ Cosmetics and luxuries *(this is also increasing slowly)*

Explanations in terms of these being the subject of leisure or impulse shopping, or requiring personal presence.

Question 8.8

Portable computers are already transforming the capability of the salesforce, giving them the opportunity to access the corporate database to answer customer queries regarding product availability, order status, promotions, and so on. They could also enter orders immediately ensuring that stock is allocated. Intelligence regarding competitors could be input into the system. Together these offer massive potential to the salesforce of the future though legislation and security may limit mobile phone use.

Question 8.9

Factors include lack of competitive pressure, incentive, finance, support from the board, champions, a risk-taking culture, long-term horizons, skills and experience of change, awareness of potential.

Question 8.10

The car: For example, the RAC claimed that the average motorist could be spending up to 14 days per annum stuck in traffic by the end of 2005.

The telephone: For example, the *Daily Mail* claimed the average British spends 45 hours a year waiting on the telephone.

The television: Psychologists have shown that 6-year-olds would rather look at a blank screen than a human face.

The CCTV camera: For example, catches the average person 300 times a day in Britain.

Unit 9

Answers to activities

Activity 9.1

Did you think of scrolling down the index?

Did you scan through Unit 8?

Did you access the glossary on www.marketingonline.co.uk?

Activity 9.3

1 – c; 2 – b; 3 – a; 4 – e; 5 – f and 6 – d

Activity 9.5

1 – d; 2 – b; 3 – c; 4 – e; 5 – f and 6 – a

Activity 9.6

The list could go on, but the important thing is to try to control your own future and not drift along on a hope and a prayer. The environment or your goals will change and the unexpected will occur but a future-orientated plan provides a framework for successful adaptation.

Plausible responses to questions throughout Unit 9

Question 9.1

Classify as key elements in the information process: collection (e.g. EDI); processing (e.g. decision support systems); storage (e.g. servers) and transmission (e.g. broadband).

Question 9.3

Forecasts are necessary whenever resource decisions affecting the future (i.e. investment in plant and equipment, new product research and development, etc.) require a view to be taken of future supply and demand conditions.

Factors affecting supply and demand must be forecasted. This in effect means that all relevant factors in the micro- environment and macro-environment should be considered.

Index